Frontier Indiana

A HISTORY OF THE TRANS-APPALACHIAN FRONTIER

Walter Nugent and Malcolm Rohrbough, general editors

James Davis. *A History of the Illinois Frontier*
R. Douglas Hurt. *The Ohio Frontier: Crucible of the Old Northwest, 1720–1830*
Mark Wyman. *The Wisconsin Frontier*

Frontier
Indiana

ANDREW R. L. CAYTON

INDIANA UNIVERSITY PRESS   BLOOMINGTON & INDIANAPOLIS

This book is a publication of

Indiana University Press
601 North Morton Street
Bloomington, IN 47404-3797 USA

http://www.indiana.edu/~iupress

Telephone orders 800-842-6796
Fax orders 812-855-7931
Orders by email iuporder@indiana.edu

First paperback edition 1998
© 1996 by Andrew R. L. Cayton

The paper used in this publication meets the minimum
requirements of American National Standard for Information
Sciences—Permanence of Paper for Printed Library
Materials, ANSI Z39.48-1984.

Manufactured in the United States of America

Library of Congress Cataloging-in-Publication Data

Cayton, Andrew R. L. (Andrew Robert Lee), date
  Frontier Indiana / Andrew R. L. Cayton.
    p.   cm. — (A history of the Trans-Appalachian frontier)
  Includes index.
  ISBN 0-253-33048-3 (alk. paper). — 0-253-21217-0 (pbk. : alk. paper)
    1. Frontier and pioneer life—Indiana. 2. Indiana—History. I. Title.
II. Series.
F526.c35   1996

997.2—dc20   95-26443

2 3 4 5 6 03 02 01 00 99 98

☙ Contents

Illustrations follow page 126.
Maps follow pages 43 and 300.

Foreword

For most Americans, the phrase "the American West" conjures up the western half of the nation. From the Great Plains across the Rockies and the Intermontane Plateaus to the Pacific Ocean came a flood of popular images, from trappers, cowboys, miners, and homesteading families to the "Marlboro Man" and country-western music. This has been "the West" since the California Gold Rush and the migration of '49ers propelled this region into the national consciousness.

But it was not always so. There was an earlier American West, no less vivid and dramatic. Here the fabled figures were not John Charles Fremont but Daniel Boone, not Geronimo but Tecumseh, not Calamity Jane but Rachel Jackson, not "Buffalo Bill" Cody but Davy Crockett. This earlier West ran, geographically, from the crest of the Appalachian Mountains to the Mississippi River, from the border with Canada to the Gulf of Mexico. It was the West of Euro-American expansion from before the American Revolution until the middle of the nineteenth century, when the line of frontier settlement moved through it toward that next, farther West.

In its initial terms, the story of the First American West involved two basic sets of characters: first, the white people of European origin (and south of the Ohio River, many African American slaves), who spread relentlessly westward; second, the original settlers, the Native Americans, who retreated grudgingly before this flood. These first Europeans, French and Spanish, appeared on this landscape in the 1600s and early 1700s, where their interactions with the original native peoples involved both cooperation and conflict. The English arrived a half-century later. In numbers, the Europeans were almost always a minority, and so both sides sought not conquest or annihilation but mutual accommodation, a joint occupation of the land and joint use of its resources, a system of contact allowing both sides to survive and even to benefit from one another's presence. Trade developed and intermarriage followed; so did misunderstandings and violence. But a delicate balance, supported by mutual interests, often characterized relations among Europeans and native peoples.

When Anglo-Americans began moving through the Cumberland Gap from Virginia into what hunters called the Kentucky country in the 1750s, they soon tilted the balance between the two cultures, occupying large portions of Kentucky and pressing against native groups from Ohio south to Georgia. By 1780, the Anglo-Americans had also occupied the former French settlements of Cahokia in Illinois and Vincennes in Indiana. Despite strong resistance by several native groups, the seemingly unending reinforcements of white families made their gradual occupation of the trans-Appalachian frontier inevitable.

In the 1780s the infant American government issued ordinances spelling out how the land between the Great Lakes and the Ohio River was to be acquired, subdivided, and sold to the citizens of the new republic, and how a form of government organization would lead to statehood and equal membership in the Union. A parallel process was soon set up for Kentucky, Tennessee, and the lands south to the Gulf.

In the 1830s and 1840s, the remaining native groups east of the Mississippi were removed to the West. The expansion of settlement into the trans-Appalachian frontier now continued unchecked into Illinois, Wisconsin, Michigan, and the great cotton lands and hill country of Alabama, Mississippi, and Florida. The frontier period had been completed—as early as the 1820s in Kentucky, and within the next twenty years over much of the Old Northwest and in the Old Southwest.

In brief terms, this is the story of the trans-Appalachian frontier. Over scarcely three generations, the trickle of settler families across the mountains had become more than four million, both white and black. Beginning with Kentucky in 1792 and running through Florida in 1845 and Wisconsin in 1848, a dozen new states had entered the American Union. Each territory/state had its own story, and it is appropriate that each should have a separate volume in this series. The variations are large. Florida's first European arrived in 1513, and this future state had both Spanish and American frontier experiences over 350 years. Missouri had a long French and Spanish history before the arrival of American settlers. Kentucky and Ohio did not, and Americans in large numbers came there quickly through the Cumberland Gap.

The opening and closing of the settlement frontier is the subject of each of these volumes. Each begins with the world that existed when Europeans made contact with native peoples. Each describes and analyzes the themes associated with the special circumstances of the individual territories/states. And each concludes with the closing of the frontier.

The editors have selected these authors because of their reputations as scholars and interpreters of their individual territories/ states. We believe that you will find this history informative and lively, and we are confident that you will enjoy this and other volumes in the Trans-Appalachian Frontier series.

In this volume on Indiana's frontier period, Andrew R. L. Cayton begins in the year 1700 with "The World of the Miami." In the next several chapters, he re-creates a series of "worlds," or worldviews, which contended, accommodated, clashed, disintegrated, or conquered in Indiana over the next century and a half. Cayton defines each "world" through the mind and vision of an outstanding leader—among them the fur-trader George Croghan; the soldier George Rogers Clark; Anna Symmes, the wife of Governor William Henry Harrison; as well as the Miami chief Little Turtle and the Shawnee prophet Tenskwatawa. Through these representative leaders, Cayton brilliantly recreates a succession of fast-passing world views, in a dramatic history of the long-bygone origins of Indiana.

Andrew Cayton is the author of several books on the Old Northwest and the Ohio Valley. Professor of History at Miami University in Ohio, he is an authority on the Northwest Ordinance of 1787, the fundamental document that bound the Great Lakes-Ohio Valley region firmly to the new United States. He is also an acclaimed teacher, and, as you will quickly discover in this book, a captivating writer of history. He will take you on an unforgettable journey from the Indian country of three hundred years ago to the post-frontier, recognizably American Indiana of 1850. You will find him a trustworthy guide and a compelling narrator.

MALCOLM J. ROHRBOUGH
University of Iowa

WALTER NUGENT
University of Notre Dame

Preface

My objective in writing *Frontier Indiana* has been straight-forward: to produce a readable and thorough narrative of the history of the peoples who inhabited the region that became the state of Indiana, one that incorporates as many perspectives as possible but which does not lose sight of the larger question of how and why white immigrant Americans won the struggle for control of the area drained by the Wabash River and its tributaries in an astonishingly short period. In other words, I have tried to write a story that inquires into the nature of the process by which one group of people acquired power over others and then used that power to transform a particular physical and social environment into an idealized image of themselves.

Less grandly, I wanted to write a book about people as human beings. Thus I have organized this history around the experiences of several individuals and families. I make no claim that the people on whom I focus were more significant or representative than others. I chose them because they interested me, because they illustrated points I was trying to make, and because they left records that made reconstructing their lives a reasonable undertaking. My hope is that readers will come to know them as real people making decisions about their lives—and living with the consequences of their actions—within the cultural boundaries of their particular worlds.

Frontier Indiana

I.

THE WORLD OF THE MIAMI,
1700–1754

In the Miami village of Kekionga, near where the St. Marys and St. Joseph rivers conjoin to form the Maumee, toward the end of the second decade of what Europeans termed the eighteenth century, the life of fifty-year-old Jean-Baptiste Bissot, Sieur de Vincennes, came to an end. We do not know what disease or accident killed Bissot. We do not know how long he lingered, whether he died in peace or in pain. We only know that sometime in the winter of 1718–1719, one of the first persons of European ancestry to spend a considerable amount of time in the North American region that less than a century later would become the state of Indiana ceased to exist.

No one can doubt that Jean-Baptiste Bissot—as well as his son and successor, François-Marie—was influential in the Maumee and Wabash river valleys in the early eighteenth century. But neither of these Sieurs de Vincennes was ever as powerful as he pretended to be. Indeed, both of their careers rested on a foundation of illusions about their own importance. However much the Miami and other Native Americans admired, even loved, both of the Vincennes, they were not about to allow anyone to dictate where they lived or with whom they traded and talked.

In other words, while Europeans dreamed in the first half of the eighteenth century of exercising power over Indiana, the Miami actually did. It was their world, and the French enjoyed status and influence within it only so long as they played by the rules of native culture. Unfortunately for Frenchmen such as Jean-Baptiste and François-Marie Bissot, they never fully understood the extent to which they were at the mercy of the people whom they persisted in calling their children.

Vincennes and the Illusion of French Power

Jean-Baptiste Bissot's life began hundreds of miles to the northeast of the place where it ended. Marie Couillard, the wife of François Bissot de la Rivière, gave birth to Jean-Baptiste in Quebec City on January 19, 1668. Declared unfit for "the ecclesiastical state" and finding little profit in farming the estate he inherited from his father, Jean-Baptiste, like many young gentlemen in New France, joined the military. By 1696, he was a subensign in the Troupes de la Marine, earning a reputation as a "good officer." In the same year, Bissot married Marguerite Forestier, the daughter of a surgeon in Montreal, with whom he had seven children over the course of the next decade and a half. Marguerite lived in Montreal until her death in 1748.

Jean-Baptiste, on the other hand, spent much of the first two decades of the eighteenth century in the *pays d'en haut*, the region around the Great Lakes. His principal responsibility was to nurture the attachment to New France of the Miami, who had migrated eastward a few decades earlier from what is now Wisconsin and Illinois to the St. Joseph River in southern Michigan. More specifically, he was to use a combination of rhetorical persuasion and gifts to keep the Miami from exploring the possibilities of trade and other exchanges with British colonists and their Indian allies. Bissot was to make certain that the Miami saw the French as their natural trading partners.

According to Antoine de la Mothe de Cadillac, the French commander at the newly established post of Detroit, Bissot was "very much loved" by the Miami. Clearly he expected to make money from his relationship with them. In 1704, he allegedly planned to sell them 400 jugs of brandy at a price of forty to fifty livres per jug. He had a "cabaret" in Detroit and was accused of using the brandy to "corrupt the savages." The French suspended Bissot from his rank as a subensign for three years over this action. But they needed him too much to discharge him.

In 1704, Jean-Baptiste was dispatched to dissuade the Miami from raiding their ancient enemies the Iroquois, whose war parties had driven the Miami westward and continued to raid their villages. Bissot delivered a speech from Governor-General Phillippe de Rigaud de Vaudreuil, which outlined French assumptions about their relationship with the Indians. The governor-general instructed the Miami to consider themselves Bissot's "brothers" and to think of him as their "father." Vaudreuil then expressed displeasure at the recent behavior of the Miami, whom he regarded as "the most obedient of his children." They had "disobeyed his orders" by attacking the Iroquois. Were they "drunk" or had they "lost [their] mind"? After all, the Indians of the *pays d'en haut* had agreed in the Treaty of Montreal in 1701 to live "peaceably" with the Iroquois. The Miami were to return all prisoners and behave themselves.

This paternalistic language is as complex as it was ubiquitous. Several scholars have explained that Algonquian Indians such as the Miami welcomed the establishment of familial relationships with French agents. The devastating impact of migration and epidemics led them to nurture fictive kinship with strangers. Such relationships could be created through intermarriage or by the ritual offering of a pipe, or calumet, to another person. Ironically, in the words of the historian Richard White, the price for the French of their acceptance as fathers was loss of "the ability to command." Instead they "acquired . . . the obligation to mediate and to give goods to those in need."

If Jean-Baptiste was successful in winning the affection of the Miami, it was undoubtedly because of his skill at integrating himself into the system of obligations which was at the heart of Miami culture. A French agent who failed to fulfill his obligations to protect and honor his fictive kin would be no more successful than one who attempted to use the coercive techniques more familiar to Europeans. According to White, "The French were the strongest when they appeared, at least to themselves, the most weak. . . . They were, conversely, the weakest when they appeared the most dangerous and powerful."

Almost by definition, in short, Bissot's success was illusory. It depended entirely on his appearing to be powerful, both to the Miami and to the French, when he was really relatively powerless. His reputation rested on his ability to manipulate both parts of his world, to position himself as a conduit and mediator between two cultures that wanted to trade with each other. He increased his influence with his French superiors by demonstrating the appearance of control over the Miami; he increased his influence with the Miami by protecting them from their enemies and giving them presents.

In 1712, Vincennes took a leading role in the defense of Detroit from a prolonged attack by the Fox Indians, enemies of the Potawatomi and the Miami. His actions cemented his reputation. In addition to linguistic versatility, he demonstrated both diplomatic and military skills. He negotiated with the allies and fought ably against the Fox. Indeed, he may well have been responsible for convincing some fleeing Foxes to surrender and then encouraging the slaughter of the captured men and the enslavement of the women and children. Charles Regnault, Sieur de Dubuisson, the commander at Detroit, was happy to report to Governor-General Vaudreuil that "M. de Vincennes has faithfully performed his duty and that he labored carefully here, as well as on his journey to the Miamis and Ouyatonons last winter." Such performances endeared him to both the French and the Miami.

The fact remains, however, that Jean-Baptiste exercised influence but little power. The best evidence of the subordinate position of the French was their inability to keep the Miami on the St. Joseph River, where they could be watched over from the relatively close post at Detroit. In the mid-1710s, Jean-Baptiste followed the Miami when they moved to the Maumee River. Vaudreuil reported to his superiors that Bissot had discovered that the Iroquois were trying to tempt the Miami to trade with the British, whose merchandise was "a half cheaper than among the French." Jean-Baptiste kept the Miami from accepting the British offer by reminding them of their loyalty to France and promising them a missionary and a blacksmith to repair their weapons. But he could not convince the Miami to return to the St. Joseph or to forget what the British had to offer. When Jean-Baptiste died, Vaudreuil noted his passing and his failure with the observation that "the Indians have decided not to go to the river St. Joseph, but to stay where they are."

Jean-Baptiste's successor among the Miamis was his son, François-Marie. Born in Montreal in 1700, he had joined his father at Kekionga (present-day Fort Wayne) in 1717. In May 1722, François-Marie was commissioned a half-pay ensign. By that time, the French had established two stockades in what is now northern Indiana. In 1717, Ensign François Picote de Belestre had arrived on the Wabash River with four soldiers, three men, a blacksmith, and a load of goods. They apparently constructed a small stockade at Ouiatanon, about eighteen miles below the mouth of the Tippecanoe River. François-Marie took command of the fort in the early 1720s. The second post, Fort Saint Phillippe des Miamis, was built near the village at Kekionga in 1721. These forts were testaments to the failure of French efforts to convince the Miami and their relatives, the Wea, who lived near Ouiatanon, to migrate back to the north. Like the Miami at Kekionga, the Wea at Ouiatanon were "too close to the English," who "spare neither solicitations nor presents to detach these savages from our interests and to attract them to their side."

Governor-General Vaudreuil's major inducement was trade. In 1714, moths and vermin had ruined many of the beaver pelts in storage in France, eliminating the glut that had kept prices low for two decades. The destruction led to a revival of government interest in the fur trade. Shortly before Jean-Baptiste's death, Vaudreuil had issued four permits for trade with the Indians on the Wabash River. The first ended up in the hands of two traders, or *voyageurs:* Pierre Comme, known as Lajeunesse, and Claude Legris de Lespine. They bought almost 1,200 livres' worth of equipment and goods, most likely items such as powder, lead, and cloth, in Montreal in May 1718 and set out for the Wea. Other men bought two of the three remaining permits. We do not know what happened to their expeditions, beyond the fact that the Miami remained where they were. In the summer of 1720, the governor-general again allowed traders to travel to the Wabash, with the stipulation that they could take their goods beyond Detroit only when it became clear that the Indians would not leave the Wabash Valley.

And, in fact, they did not, and never would, voluntarily depart. The Miami were the masters of Indiana in the first half of the eighteenth century. They were settling and developing the area in ways that suited them. In the drama of early Indiana history, the French may have enjoyed the title of fathers, but they were really little more than peripheral players.

The Miami and Their Ways

By the 1730s, the Miami, the Piankashaw, and the Wea occupied much of the Maumee and Wabash river valleys. They were independent tribes, but they shared the same basic cultural and social characteristics. Their villages lay scattered along the banks of the Wabash and its tributaries, the Eel, the Tippecanoe, and the Vermilion. Snake-Fish, the town of the Eel River Miami, was reportedly three miles long and half-a-mile wide. Typically the villages consisted of one large council house and oval lodges made of poles and rush mats. Later, many lived in one-room cabins. We do not know how many Native Americans there were in Indiana in the early 1700s. But epidemics in 1715, 1733, and 1752 reduced the population to around 2,000 by midcentury. In 1746, the population of Ouiatanon was 600 Indians and twenty French, while Vincennes had forty French, five blacks, and 750 Indians.

The cause of this demographic disaster was European germs. Priests and traders had brought epidemics of smallpox to the Miami long before they came to the Wabash. Now diseases created periodic epidemics that killed large numbers of people. Without the immunities developed by Europeans over centuries, the Native American was susceptible to all kinds of illnesses that the French and other immigrant Americans considered relatively minor.

The devastation wrought by smallpox, measles, and other infectious diseases happened quickly, if sporadically. During one period in 1715, measles killed fifteen to twenty Wea a day, reducing the number of available warriors from 200 to thirty or forty. Nicolas-Marie Renaud Davenne de Desmeloises, Sieur Darnaud, who took command of Fort des Miamis in 1732, witnessed the effects of European contact shortly after his arrival. A party of Miami brought 400 casks of brandy from English traders in Albany. Darnaud claimed drunkenness spread throughout the village. Within a few days, Indians started to die at the rate of four a day. The commander persuaded the Miami to go away for the winter, but not before about 150 people had died. Darnaud was baffled by the deaths. At first he attributed them to excessive drinking. Subsequent investigation convinced him that the culprit was "a poison as subtle as it was shrewd, taking effect only after the passage of a considerable time." It also killed considerable numbers of Wea and Piankashaw who came to visit the Miami at Kekionga.

The Indians nonetheless maintained themselves in the face of such catastrophes. The most important villages were at Kekionga, Ouiatanon, Vermilion, and Vincennes. The French followed the Indians to these locations, erecting forts at three of the four. But it was trade that kept them there. To a post such as Ouiatanon, the Wea and other Indians brought furs and pelts to exchange for manufactured goods such as guns, knives, metallic utensils, cloth, brandy, and jewelry. They also sought out the services of the blacksmith the French usually kept in residence. For the most part, the Indians lacked the technology to repair the goods they obtained. Malfunctioning muskets or pistols were either disposed of or taken to a French artisan for repair.

The French and the Miami maintained a fairly segregated existence at these posts. At Ouiatanon, the French lived in or near their small stockade on the north bank of the Wabash, while the Wea and other Indians congregated in villages on the south side. In the late 1960s, an excavation of the site of the post recovered several items indicating an eighteenth-century French and English presence but virtually none indicating that Indians had lived there. Nevertheless, residential segregation did not prevent relationships from developing between Europeans and Native Americans.

The most important relationships were between French men, whether traders (voyageurs) or officials, and Algonquian women. There were many reasons for these attachments. Foremost was a gender imbalance. Virtually all of the French who ventured west of Montreal were males; disease and war may well have contributed to an excess of females among the Miami and other Indians. To some extent, liaisons between French men and Indian women were simply a response to demographic supply and demand.

These relationships were complicated. Personal liaisons were means of economic and social, as well as physical, intercourse. The marriages, which were generally performed according to the customs of the Indians, were the foundations of relationships that extended far beyond the individuals involved. For the Europeans, an ongoing relationship with a woman, whom they often called a "country" wife, meant a permanent source of entry into a village society. It became the foundation for a social alliance with the woman's kin. The French male had to nurture the relationship with gifts and displays of friendship to his new extended family. More often than not, it was well worth his time. In addition to acquiring a sexual partner and companion, he interested a large number of people in trading with and protecting him.

For Indian women, marriage to a European often brought with it increased influence and privileges for both herself and her kin, among them better access to European goods and technology, some relief from the physical labor of Indian women, and a position of importance among Indians eager to trade with the Europeans. Since the voyageurs lived at the sufferance of the Indians, they generally had to treat them fairly well. It would have been difficult for a voyageur to brutalize a woman when he was living among her relatives. Indian women (or their families) apparently often initiated the relationships. The marriages of individuals cemented larger economic and social ties; they were the most reliable and common links between two cultures with an increasing interest in each other. In short, they were economic and diplomatic alliances.

There were many examples of Indian-European liaisons along the Wabash in the eighteenth century. The French trader Pierre Roy married a Miami woman in 1703 and had at least two sons with her. In 1722, Governor-General Vaudreuil allowed the blacksmith and interpreter Jean Richard to return to the Ouiatanon with his three children because of the sickness of his Indian wife; she had been ill for the two years she had been in Canada. As important as mixed marriages were, their centrality can be exaggerated. For the most part, the Miami reproduced with each other. There were simply not enough French males in Indiana to make a major demographic difference.

Rivers were central to life in eighteenth-century Indiana. They provided water, fish, rich bottomlands for crops, and the avenues on which the birch canoes of French traders brought goods on their semi-annual visits. The Miami used rivers to transport goods, although they preferred dugout to birch canoes. More often than not, the Miami walked. Well-worn trails crisscrossed the region and were frequently used by Miami war parties, as well as trading and hunting groups. They carried Indians to the west to find furs and pelts. They also took them to the south and southeast, toward the fringes of English settlements and the villages of Indians who were migrating ahead of them—the Delaware, who were in eastern Ohio by the 1730s and the Shawnee, who were in southern Indiana in the same period.

Much of the landscape that the Miami dominated in the eighteenth century would look unfamiliar to twentieth-century Americans. Most noticeably different would be the forests, which covered most of Indiana. From the rolling uplands of southeastern Indiana through the flatter countryside of the northeast, beech and maple trees predominated, interspersed with dogwood, redbud, elm, and blue beech. To the west were oak and hickory. But not all of Indiana was woods. Thirteen percent of the state's area, mostly in the northeast, was treeless prairie. There were also plenty of meadows and clearings in the forests. South of Kekionga, Father Joseph Pierre de Bonnecamp found fields whose "herbiage was sometimes of extraordinary height." Even more startling were the wetlands of the northeast—swamps, bogs, and marshes, most of which were drained in the nineteenth century.

At the beginning of the century, Indiana was apparently full of animals. A Frenchman noted in 1718 that along the Maumee "there is at all seasons game without end, especially in autumn and in spring; so that one can not sleep on account of the noise made by the cries of the swans, bustards, geese, ducks, cranes and other birds." At the village of the Ouiatanon, he marveled at the "prairies, stretching farther than the eye can reach, and abounding in buffalo."

Gradually the large herds of buffalo started to thin and disappear. Other animals—beaver, fox, bears, possums, raccoons—also faded in numbers as the Miami trapped and killed them for their pelts and meat. They also depleted the fish of the Wabash and other rivers. The Indians had to turn farther west to get the pelts and furs they needed to trade for European goods. The Miami became middlemen in an international commerce that stretched from Paris and London to the Dakotas.

As important as trade was, the people of the Wabash still depended primarily on agriculture for their sustenance. The glaciers that formed the topography of Indiana some 40,000 years ago and then disappeared had left the earth rich in nutrients. Both the sandy soil of the northeast and the darker clays of the forested region can be cultivated without too much difficulty. The floodplains of the Wabash and its tributaries were especially rich lands.

The most important crop was a white-kerneled corn renowned for its sweetness. Maize had the advantage of growing with little care under a variety of conditions. It was also long-lasting, not spoiling quickly. And it was easily stored. The Miami supplemented their diet of corn and meat with beans, squashes, melons, and pumpkins. They also gathered nuts, berries, and onions. There were bad harvests, of course, but generally people in eighteenth-century Indiana lived relatively well.

The impact of European contact was decidedly mixed. It made life better by providing material comforts. The Miami benefited from the white man's guns, which they could use to fight enemies, from his cooking utensils, and from his higher-quality cloth. But contact also killed them in alarming numbers. And for those who survived, it meant a constant struggle to maintain the integrity of their society in the face of both growing dependence on European goods and the specter of sudden and massive death.

Like many thoughtful people, the Miami did not seek always to control natural events directly. Rather, they saw themselves as parts of a complex world that they could not fully understand, let alone manipulate. Much as English Puritans found strength in a deep faith in an omnipotent God who had ordered the world in a fashion incomprehensible to mortals or French men and women found strength in a deep faith in the rites of the Roman Catholic Church, the Miami found strength in the belief that all parts of the

⚒ 11

THE
WORLD
OF THE
MIAMI,
1700–1754

world had a critical role in the functioning of the whole. They were not superior to the rest; indeed, there were forces far more powerful than they. For them, life depended on successfully interacting with the other parts of the world in a predictable way, that is, by relying heavily on rituals at every important stage of life. Often these were simply actions that confirmed the regularity of relationships.

The rituals of life, the effort to interact with the world and to appease or acquire power, began at birth. According to Charles C. Trowbridge, an Indian agent and territorial official who studied the Miami in the 1820s, infants who survived the first week or two of life were normally given names by an older female friend of their mothers. In return for some goods,

> the old woman goes, and in the presence of the family only, takes the child in her arms and commences a kind of harangue, addressed to the infant, in which she describes the circumstances of some fortunate dream which she has had, & concludes by drawing an inference from each particular fact described, applicable to a point in the character of the infant.

Trowbridge's examples included that of a deer. If the woman saw a deer in her dream, the child would be swift. In no case was a child named after the parents.

The Miami attached remarkable significance to their names. Certain that their names exerted some power over them, or at least described them too well, they sought to reverse bad luck or cure an illness by changing their names, and thus themselves. Far from being trivial, a name was so integrated with the spirit and body of a person that transformation of the person required transformation of the name. To call a person by his or her name was to show a great deal of respect, to acknowledge the person's power.

The Miami told Trowbridge that the harangue they received with their name was not the last. Their parents gave them lectures on the nature of good and evil and the importance of emulating the former and avoiding the latter virtually every day of their childhood. This task was gender segregated: mothers talked to their daughters and fathers to their sons. Like most of the Indians in eastern North America, the Miami were fairly indulgent with their children. Parents normally distributed all gifts and property equally among their children. They expressed their affection for them openly and freely and preferred the art of moral suasion in matters of discipline.

Both male and female children engaged in vision quests, probably about the beginning of puberty. Boys were trained for the duties and responsibilities of men from an early age. They learned how to fast for long periods. The boy would blacken his face and go hunting, fasting until he had a vision of his particular guardian god. The god would then give the young man an indication of his life's calling, being a warrior, for example. Although a boy would not be fully accepted as an adult male until he had accompanied a war party, he was no longer a child. Girls apparently also had visions, although Trowbridge is not specific about when or how. Typically the god they would see would be a woman with a hoe, indicating their future roles as farmers.

This kind of training prepared children for the life they would lead as adults. The Miami taught them to internalize values of discipline and sacrifice, to be responsible for themselves, and to accept their positions as integral members of their community. The visions, like the name changes, exemplified a tendency to study the natural world and humans' places within it as a means of coming to terms with responsibility. They accepted what was necessary without the European tendency to rely on coercion, a process which no doubt reduced the need to rebel or question the way things were. Authority was more internal than external.

Labor was rigidly divided by gender. Women were responsible for the care and distribution of crops in addition to the labors of preparing meals, making clothes, being pregnant, and socializing children. Men's activities were almost all away from the home. They hunted, fished, fought, and traded. Men who did manual labor normally suffered a loss of honor. Women were hardly at the mercy of men. Their control of crops and the fact that men were often gone on long hunting or fighting expeditions gave them room to negotiate their relationships with their husbands.

The rituals of courtship established this pattern. Men ostensibly controlled the process. When a man was attracted to a particular woman, he paid her a visit one night while she was sleeping. Normally the woman would send him away. But if she did so with a smile and a certain reluctance, he would return on another night and they would consummate their relationship physically. On the morning after their first sexual encounter, the man would tarry long enough for her parents to see him and to leave a blanket or some sort of gift behind. Later he would return with meat he had personally hunted for her family.

The man clearly was the most active partner in courtship. But the crucial moment was the woman's response during the first visit. She could terminate the whole business by rejecting her suitor at the outset. No doubt men rarely made the first attempt without some prior indication that it would be welcome.

When a man was uncertain or apprehensive about rejection, he could initiate a courtship by telling his mother about his wishes. She would relay the news to his father and together they would visit the parents of the woman with a load of presents. The woman's parents would then ask their daughter to accept the offer of marriage. If she consented, they would take her to the home of the young man's parents and present her to him. After lecturing her on her duties as a wife, they would depart with the admonition that "there is your bed, see that you do not defile it." Here again, superficially, the woman was at the mercy of both suitors and parents. But one suspects that things only occasionally went as smoothly as Trowbridge describes. There were plenty of opportunities to halt the proceedings. The mother of the man could stop it, and so could the parents of the woman. Most important, she could refuse to accept the offer. No doubt this would cause her much pain in some cases, but her consent was still vital. Without it, nothing happened.

In both cases, an elaborate exchange of gifts sealed the bargain between man and woman and ratified the existence of obligatory ties between their families. Once married, the couple could divorce each other by simple abandonment. Adultery was a criminal offense. Husbands generally had the right to kill either their wives or their wives' lovers, whichever they thought most guilty. Similarly, when a woman killed an abusive husband, she was usually not punished. In this way, the Miami recognized the need for a negotiated relationship between husband and wife. But the bounds of behavior were clearly drawn. A woman belonged to her husband and he could exact revenge when someone else used her. She, on the other hand, had the right to expect decent treatment from him. So did her family, who could come to her aid at any time. For some Miami women, in fact, their relationship with their blood relatives may have been stronger than that with their husbands.

Politically the Miami divided themselves into clans, based on patrilineal kinship ties. Decisions involving the entire group were made by village and war chiefs. Village chiefs were responsible for local administration and negotiation, while war chiefs handled military affairs. These men were not all-powerful, however; rarely did they make decisions without extensive consultations with other people in their villages. In the seventeenth century, the position of chief was usually inherited, although great success in battle could make someone a war chief. On occasion a chief without sons would designate a successor. No doubt these innovations were responses to the demographic disasters caused by epidemics. According to Trowbridge, the Miami also had female chiefs who were in charge of feasts, collecting supplies for war parties, and had the power to bring long-standing feuds to an end.

As in many Native American cultures, reciprocity was a basic principle of justice for the Miami. This was simply the reverse side of the more positive aspects of the profound importance of exchange and obligation epitomized by the exchange of calumets, or pipes, during meetings with strangers. The relatives of a murder victim had the right to demand either property or the life of the murderer in compensation for their loss. If matters got out of hand and a blood feud developed, the women chiefs had the power to end it. Trowbridge contended that they were "more implicitly obeyed than the male chiefs."

War was in many respects an expression of these ideas. Before the introduction of European technology provoked struggles for territory, most conflicts erupted over personal insults and losses. In 1741, a Wea killed a Miami who was returning from business with the British. The Miami's relatives demanded vengeance and talked of war. The French commander averted trouble only by promising to "bring back the murderer" so they could "dispose of him to their liking."

Among the Miami, a council of chiefs determined upon war. Women occasionally could initiate a war through a vision of revenge for a lost family member or of herself in command. When the decision was made, the warriors gathered at the council house in their village and deposited pieces of cloth, which were then tied together into a bundle. They danced around the bundle for most of the night and then ran off in the morning, accompanied by a medicine man carrying the bundle symbolizing their devotion to the group. Miami warriors traveled through the forests of Indiana in single files. When they stopped for the evening, the young men handled food preparation and tended fires. At camp, warriors segregated themselves on the basis of age. A victorious war party returned to its village with great ceremony, while the defeated came back in silence.

Women rarely accompanied the war parties unless they had a vision involving themselves. Trowbridge told of a female Miami who organized a campaign in retribution for an Iroquois attack. She had had a vision in which all prisoners were recovered and all enemies killed. Dressed in a black deerskin, with her body blackened as well, she led the warriors to a fulfillment of her vision. True or not, the story was widely accepted by the Miami in the early nineteenth century.

Prisoners were central to warfare. Native Americans traditionally had fought wars to replace lost relatives or members of their communities. The fate of prisoners was solely at the discretion of the war chief. He could choose persons of the right age and description to take the places of the dead; they were then painted with vermilion and otherwise ritually adopted into the family, literally becoming the deceased person they were supposed to replace. The ceremony of adoption included an elaborate dance and taking possession of clothes and other personal articles belonging to the predecessor. As always, an exchange of gifts marked the whole business. The Miami adopted prisoners of all ages and both sexes. Trowbridge claimed that even war chiefs were replaced in this way, again indicating adaptation to demographic crisis.

Other prisoners suffered the ritual of torture. Warriors painted them black and, upon returning to their village, forced them to run between two rows of women who beat them until they died. As late as the early nineteenth century, the Miami still occasionally burned prisoners. This kind of death was the ultimate test of manhood for Indian warriors. Men who died well, especially when suffering great pain, earned lasting respect. They were truly admirable figures who obviously possessed a great deal of power.

Even when not undergoing torture, the Miami tried to die well. It was, after all, the last ritual of life. They directed the preparations for their burial, took proper leave of relatives and friends, and suggested a dance or some other means by which they could amuse themselves after they were gone. The Miami honored their dead. They washed and elegantly clothed corpses and held emotional wakes about the body. The graves of the deceased were frequently visited, especially by women who prepared food for a friend of the dead to enjoy in his or her stead.

In common with all peoples in eighteenth-century North America, the Miami lived a precarious life. It is not surprising that their culture emphasized rituals and a stoic acceptance of one's fate. The Miami sought solace in a way of life which was predicated upon the importance of individual responsibility and the integration of all people into the larger group. Survival, which understandably occupied their thoughts, came first. And they could survive only by doing what was expected of them within the parameters of their world.

A common speech at burial reflected this belief. Just as an older person greeted an infant with a lecture about life, so the last act of life was a lecture to the corpse from an older Indian.

> My brother (or my sister), the master of life has seen fit to determine that you should die. Your body is laid here by the care of your afflicted relatives in the cold earth, but your soul will not remain. That will go to the regions of the west, to join the vast number of souls which have preceded it. Seek not my brother to take with you any of us, your relatives. We are suffered by the Great Spirit to remain here. We labor only to gain something for the subsistence of ourselves and children and we must, at an appointed time, go to the place where you are now going and where we shall meet. Therefore my brother seek not to take any of us along, as we shall go soon at all events.

It is easy to romanticize the world of the Native Americans, if only because we know the fate that awaited them. But the Miami were sophisticated human beings. They faced a new world in the eighteenth century—new homes, new technologies, new religions,

🐚 17

THE
WORLD
OF THE
MIAMI,
1700–1754

new diseases, new friends, new enemies—and they made sense of it with the tools and traditions that were available to them.

The Defeat of the Younger Vincennes

In the 1720s and 1730s, the European most central to the lives of the Wea, Piankashaw, and Miami was François-Marie Bissot, Sieur de Vincennes. If the French had accepted the fact of Miami settlement in Indiana, they were still anxious to prevent the Miami from trading and allying with the British. Particularly troublesome were the British traders in the Carolinas; they worked with the Chickasaw, who lived in what is now Mississippi. For years, vague French plans called for linking their colonies of New France in the north and Louisiana in the south; the link would be at the Wabash River, creating a barrier to further British penetration of the interior of North America. François-Marie was indispensable to the success of this strategy. Unfortunately, he was no more successful than his father; his tragic fate would only demonstrate the perpetual weakness of the French, who were a presence but never a power in the Wabash Valley. In the 1730s, when the French substituted arms for gifts and the language of coercion for the rhetoric of persuasion, they tacitly recognized the desperate nature of their position.

In the early 1720s, François-Marie Bissot was a rising star among the French. His success in keeping the Wea at peace with their neighbors and his extensive travels in the Ohio Valley made him a valuable commodity. His superiors in Canada and then in Louisiana fought over his services and sought to win him promotions. Governor-General Vaudreuil thought Vincennes had "all the credit imaginable" with the Wea and wanted him to stay among them. The young man was promoted to second ensign in 1726.

Well aware of his importance, Vincennes devoted much of the 1720s to playing officials in Canada and Louisiana off against each other, seeking the best possible deal for himself. The government in Louisiana and the Company of the Indies, which controlled it, had big plans for him. In the mid-1720s, they were moving to fulfill the long-standing French dream of encircling the back of the British settlements with the establishment of a post on the lower Wabash that would connect New France and Louisiana. The company noted that four major rivers (the Wabash, Ohio, Tennessee, and Cumberland) flowed into the Mississippi but only the Wabash provided "the means of communication between Louisiana and Canada."

But could the French control the peoples of the Wabash, or would they find British gifts and goods irresistible? Vincennes's challenge was similar to his father's but on a grander scale: to keep the Indians attached to the interests of the French. Louisiana officials initially wanted to keep him among the Wea at Ouiatanon, hoping "to get from them the service which we desire." They would give him a few more men to hold the Wabash without having to spend money for a fort. By 1730, the eager government of Louisiana had wooed Vincennes away from New France with an annual stipend in addition to a promotion to half-pay lieutenant.

Vincennes quickly earned the money. In 1730, he convinced some Wea to move farther down the Wabash, close to the Piankashaw settlements. Sometime in 1731 or 1732, Vincennes began constructing a post on a level plain on the eastern side of the Wabash about eighty miles above the river's mouth. He received 300 livres to pay for the work and 1,170 livres to pay the ten or so soldiers he had in his service. While Vincennes had little direct contact with the government of Louisiana, officials there considered him brave and active, useful to the colony, and "an officer who serves well, who is in good favor with the Miamis." Moreover, the post at Vincennes would, it was hoped, secure the lower Wabash Valley for the French, less through military might than through the attachment of large numbers of Wea and Piankashaw who would stand in the way of British expansion in return for French protection and trade.

The construction of a post was only the beginning of a concerted effort to consolidate French influence on the lower Wabash. In March 1733, Vincennes reported that there were five tribes in the valley who "could furnish from six to seven hundred men" if necessary. Still, he could not assure anyone of their loyalty. His complaints were the perennial ones of French commanders. He needed "merchandise" to trade and soldiers (at least thirty) to finish the fort and impress the Indians. With them, he could promise "a traffic in skins . . . to the extent of 30,000" per year. Without them, things looked bleak.

≋ 19

THE
WORLD
OF THE
MIAMI,
1700–1754

Indeed, Vincennes never felt safe. He noted that the Indians were "more insolent than they have ever been." He worried about "some evil trick" on the part of the Miami who objected to the fort he was building. He had no money. Meanwhile he had to deal with the raids of Chickasaw warriors from the south, who were attached to British traders in South Carolina. This problem was especially pressing. Six French and two Indians had been killed. Travel was becoming precarious. The Piankashaw expected the French to help with their defense. And, as we have seen, the influence of men such as Vincennes and his father among the Miami depended on their ability to behave in the manner of generous and protective fathers. Failure to do so not only would mean more deaths; it also would essentially destroy his relationship with the Miami. The Indians deferred to the French, but they were not willing to offer unquestioning obedience. What profit was there in obeying an impotent father?

In this crisis, Vincennes left his post in the spring of 1733 to attend to unspecified family matters in Canada. When he returned the next winter, matters had improved somewhat—at least temporarily. The Piankashaw wished to establish a large village near his fort. And Governor Jean-Baptiste Le Moyne de Bienville of Louisiana, recognizing that "the post of Wabash is one of the most important of the colony, being a barrier which is opposed to the progress of the English," had promised to send thirty men as reinforcements. Finally, in 1735, Vincennes persuaded some of the Piankashaw to join in a war on the Chickasaw in Mississippi. The French had virtually no choice but to act against the Chickasaw, whose raids were growing in frequency and deadliness. Thus Vincennes and the Piankashaw departed in the spring of 1736 in the company of over 100 French, 100 Illinois, and some Iroquois. Altogether there were perhaps 400 men, all under the command of Captain Pierre d'Artaguiette, the chief French officer in the Illinois Country.

Governor de Bienville designed a two-pronged campaign against the Chickasaw. He led one prong, attacking from the south through Mobile Bay—but with no success. D'Artaguiette, Vincennes, and their men formed the second prong, approaching from the north and moving into northern Mississippi to await de Bienville. When he failed to arrive, d'Artaguiette led a series of assaults on Chickasaw

villages. On Palm Sunday, March 25, 1736, the Chickasaw drove
back the French and their allies, most of whom escaped in headlong
flight. About twenty Frenchmen, including d'Artaguiette and Vincennes, were not so lucky: they were captured by the Chickasaw.
Stripped and beaten, they were placed on two pyres and burned to
death in a ritual that lasted from midafternoon to midnight. With
them at the end was a priest, the Jesuit Antoine Senat, who heard
their confessions and offered absolution. The French reportedly
sang psalms as they died, causing Chickasaw warriors to remark,
"Truly these Frenchmen are not women, but men."

Vincennes's death destroyed any remaining illusion of French influence in the Wabash Valley, and most of the Piankashaw living
near Fort Vincennes abandoned the village, apparently returning to
a village near the Vermilion River. French officials, complaining of
the cost of maintaining Vincennes and its poor prospects, toyed with
the idea of abandoning it. But fears that the British would occupy
the location kept them from doing so. The fort remained.

The Coming of the British

Among the Piankashaw who received news of the death of
Vincennes was Memeskia (The Dragonfly), whom the French called
"La Demoiselle" and the British "Old Briton." The fact that he
had three names is testimony to the cultural complexity of life in
eighteenth-century Indiana. Like many others, Memeskia drifted
away from the French after the death of Vincennes. In 1745, he
moved to an undetermined location near Kekionga, hoping to persuade the Miami in that area to establish a town farther south. It has
been speculated that he wanted to be closer to the Ohio River because it was the primary avenue on which Iroquois and British
traders carried goods from New York and Pennsylvania to the west.
In other words, he wanted his people to switch their allegiance from
the French to the British. But "allegiance" is not really the right
word. Memeskia was hardly a pawn in a chessboard dominated
by Europeans. He was a clever diplomat and a smart consumer.
He was not trading allegiances; he was seeking the best possible
arrangement for himself and his kin.

🐚 21

THE
WORLD
OF THE
MIAMI,
1700–1754

Memeskia was an odd choice for a powerful Miami leader. He was a Piankashaw who had married a Miami woman and thus had no hereditary right to be a prominent chief. His rise reflected a new pattern of leadership, one based on ability. This innovation was not merely a response to demographic disaster; it also reflected an increasing need for leaders who could actively demonstrate their power by appearing to control the spread of deadly smallpox, for example, or by negotiating better living conditions.

In 1744, after a peace of nearly three decades, France and Great Britain had gone to war with each other. By that time, neither side had much interest in the possibilities of trade with the Miami and other Great Lakes Indians. Merchants in Montreal had long since turned most of their attention to the regions north and northwest of the lakes where the quantity and quality of furs and pelts were much higher. After 1740, the government of New France had insisted upon leasing its posts to merchants involved in the Indian trade. These men then demanded that commanders raise enough money from the sale of goods to cover the cost of the lease as well as that of the goods themselves. The French at Ouiatanon and Vincennes could not afford to sell items at a price that was competitive with what British traders in Pennsylvania and New York offered, usually through Iroquois middlemen. In 1737, Governor de Bienville had complained bitterly that "this policy, added to some presents of brandy, results in the word of the English being listened to in preference to ours." He was also upset that commanders in the service of Quebec would not allow traders from Louisiana to operate within their jurisdictions. Still, his overall point was a valid one. The French were being penny-wise and pound-foolish. They were saving the costs of operating frontier posts and losing the Indian trade to the British and the Iroquois.

The decision of Memeskia to switch to the British as his primary supplier and ally is not surprising in this context. Traders from Pennsylvania were actively enticing him, British goods had been circulating in the Wabash for decades, and French prestige, since the death of Vincennes, had largely dissipated. Time may also have been a factor. It is not coincidental that the Delaware and Shawnee, who had been heavily involved with the British for decades, began to move toward the French at the same time that the Miami began to look to the British. To some extent, the motive for these diplomatic rearrangements may have been little more than the maxim that the grass is always greener elsewhere.

The Miami at Kekionga acted, even though their chief, Coldfoot, was reluctant to abandon the French. Memeskia and many others migrated to the southeast. In the fall of 1747, they established a village on what is now the Great Miami River near present-day Piqua, Ohio. Eventually the town was called Pickawillany. It was a well-chosen site. With a prairie of some size to the west, it was at the center of important rivers and trails. The Great Miami River flowed south to the Ohio. Nearby Loramie's Creek led to a short portage to the St. Marys River, which would take people to Kekionga. Travel up the Great Miami led to a portage to the Scioto River, which flowed south to the Ohio and to a trail to Sandusky Bay. The Wabash River began within a couple of dozen miles. And the village was just north of a major trail that led from Miami settlements on the Wabash to the Ohio River.

Pickawillany attracted a great deal of attention from both the British and the French. But it was Memeskia who initiated diplomatic activity by dispatching his nephew, Assepansa (The Racoon), and the Atchatchakangouen war chief Mishikinakwa (The Turtle) to meet with Pennsylvania officials. On July 23, 1748, they signed the Treaty of Lancaster, which established friendship, trade, and a general alliance between the British colony and the Miami, or at least those at Pickawillany. News of the treaty soon started a stream of people away from the Wabash. The Piankashaw near Vincennes moved to the White River, half the distance to Pickawillany, while others arrived from Ouiatanon and Kekionga.

The French response to these events was tentative at first. Their war with Great Britain ended in 1748 in triumph, but their far-flung North American empire continued to be problematic. Rather than being profitable, it was a drain on French coffers. Policy toward the area between the Great Lakes and the Ohio River, moreover, lacked clarity. Royal officials at the palace in Versailles were wondering whether it was worth the trouble. In this climate of indecision, the new governor-general of New France, the Marquis La Galissoniere, acted.

📯 **23**

THE
WORLD
OF THE
MIAMI,
1700–1754

In the summer of 1749, La Galissoniere dispatched Captain Celoron de Blainville and 213 men on an expedition to lay formal claim to the Ohio Valley. This Celoron accomplished by burying lead plates proclaiming French sovereignty throughout the region and by urging Indians to reject all British overtures. In September, he and his men arrived at Pickawillany. Memeskia refused their gifts of four half-barrels of powder, four bags of bullets, and four bags of paint. Celoron asked him to return to Kekionga, to "the spot where repose the bones of your ancestors, and those of Monsieur de Vincennes, whom you loved so well and who governed you always in such manner that your affairs always went well." Memeskia gave an evasive answer, promising to think it over during the winter. It was a sensible decision.

When Celoron got back to Montreal in November he put the situation succinctly to his superiors. After canoeing and tramping a distance of 3,000 miles, he reported that the fact that the British could sell goods "at one-fourth the price" meant that the Indians "are very badly disposed towards the French, and entirely devoted to the English."

After Celoron's departure, Mishikinakwa oversaw the building of a stockade for the defense of the village. Meanwhile British traders flocked to the Great Miami. Some sixty of them visited between 1747 and 1752. Their goods attracted even more Miami. In 1751, the British trader Christopher Gist found 400 families at Memeskia's settlement, an estimated population of over 2,000. There were reports that only Coldfoot and his family remained at Kekionga.

The French worried a great deal about Memeskia and his thriving village. They tended to see him as an agent of British traders. It seems more likely, however, that the Piankashaw chief was nobody's fool. He knew exactly what he was doing. Still, he was playing a dangerous game in attempting to exercise power in the region by pitting the British colonists against the French. Their interest and cheap goods notwithstanding, the British were in no position to offer the Miami at Pickawillany much assistance in the event of a French attack.

Officials in New France contemplated such an expedition for years. Just when they had decided against military action, Charles Michel Langlade, a zealous and ambitious young man, took matters into his own hands. Born at Mackinac to French and Ottawa parents, Langlade apparently had accompanied an expedition against the Chickasaw when he was ten years old. A twenty-one-year-old cadet in 1750, Langlade was living with an Ottawa woman, with whom he had a son. Exactly what his orders were and who issued them remains unclear. What is indisputable is that he led an expedition of thirty Frenchmen, thirty Ottawa, and 180 Chippewa against Pickawillany in the early summer of 1752.

The Virginia-based trader Captain William Trent met two white American traders in a Shawnee village on the Scioto River on July 6 who gave him an account of the events of June 21 in Pickawillany. It is the only source we have regarding the destruction of the village. Langlade's force struck when most of the warriors were away hunting. In the early morning, they swept into the cornfields beside the village, capturing women who were working there. Quickly the French and Indians trapped some British traders and Miami in their stockade. According to the men Trent encountered, three traders surrendered and betrayed the weak condition of the fort. At a meeting in midafternoon, Langlade promised to leave the Miami in peace if they would give him all the traders. The Indians agreed, and the French surrendered the women they had captured in the fields. They then proceeded to kill at least one trader; two traders escaped, and five others were taken back to Detroit. Fourteen Miami died in the attack. The most important victim was Memeskia. Trent was told that the French "boiled, and eat him all up," believing they could acquire some of his power by consuming his flesh.

In the immediate aftermath, the fall of Pickawillany was beneficial to the French. Trent found the village deserted when he arrived on July 20, and he took away only a few furs. The British estimated their loss at 3,000 pounds sterling. Back on the Scioto River in late July, Trent found Memeskia's widow and son, along with his nephew Assepansa and three men and a dozen women and children, including the Miami war chief Turtle and his family. The two men continued to meet with the Virginians and the Pennsylvanians. In addition, they and their families received £200 from each colony for their suffering. But these measures could not obscure the fact that the British had suffered a severe setback at French hands.

Most of Memeskia's followers returned to their villages on the Maumee and the Wabash, much to the relief of the French. Many died in an epidemic in 1752, which also took the life of the pro-French chief Coldfoot. Meanwhile the French continued to strengthen their position in Indiana by rebuilding the post at Fort des Miamis and increasing their resources in general.

Langlade was well rewarded for his actions. Governor-General Duquesne lauded him for having won "much glory" and asked the French government to grant him a pension of 200 livres per annum. Duquesne would have asked for more had Langlade not been part Indian and involved in a liaison with an Ottawa woman. The victory at Pickawillany turned out to be only the beginning of a distinguished career. Langlade died sometime after 1800, having lived to a ripe old age for an eighteenth-century frontiersman.

Long before his death, however, the ephemeral nature of his victory was obvious, for the destruction of Pickawillany signified the death throes of French imperial policy in Indiana. To resort to force was to acknowledge the failure of personal and commercial relationships, to expose the illusory nature of French power. Within a decade after the death of Memeskia, only fifty years after the arrival of Jean-Baptiste Bissot at Kekionga, the French lost Canada completely. And with the French defeat, the peoples of the Wabash faced another group of Europeans—this one more powerful and more purposeful, determined to remake the Native Americans' world.

2.

THE WORLD OF GEORGE CROGHAN, 1750–1777

In 1763, the Treaty of Paris transferred Indiana from the French to the British Empire, at least as far as Europeans were concerned. In their world, King George III became sovereign of the Wabash. But, of course, the British monarch's claim to authority was as empty as that of his French predecessors, Louis XIV and Louis XV. The French had never really exercised power over Indiana; the Miami had simply allowed them to pretend to do so. Less comfortable with self-deception and cultural accommodation than the French, the British would be more assertive in their imperial ambitions. Indeed, demonstrations of power came easily to them, perhaps too easily. The question was whether they had either the resources or the stomach to make them real.

By the 1760s, thousands of people—Indians, French residents of the villages along the Wabash, British colonists east of the Appalachian Mountains—were vitally interested in Indiana. As diverse as they were, they shared a separate but equal preoccupation with controlling their own destinies. Happy to welcome British officials as cultural mediators and facilitators of trade, they had no intention of submitting to any authority that promised to rearrange the structures of their world in any significant fashion.

Such defiance would be remarkably successful in the 1760s and 1770s. The British blustered about transforming the Ohio Valley, but they actually did little to accomplish this purpose. Their policy amounted to assertion without intimidation. Powerful enough to irritate people into taking up arms against it, the empire was too weak to awe or coerce them into submitting to its authority. Ironically, the British nurtured rebellion rather than stability.

Pontiac's War

The Treaty of Paris confirmed the results of almost a decade of warfare among the French, the British, and Indians in eastern North America. All of the significant battles of what we call the French and Indian War took place hundreds of miles from the Wabash Valley. They were fought for control of the key strategic points—the portals to the interior of North America—at the forks of the Ohio River and the city of Quebec. The triumph of British armies at these places in the late 1750s sealed the fate of the French. In September 1760, the last governor-general of New France surrendered Canada to Great Britain. On November 29, 1760, Major Robert Rogers and his Rangers occupied Detroit. Rogers then dispatched troops to claim Fort des Miamis and Ouiatanon for the British. They arrived at the former within a few days, but they did not get to the latter until 1761.

The finality of the conquest of Canada and the elimination of the French, both as military and commercial rivals of the British, understandably worried Native Americans from the St. Lawrence to the Mississippi. The actions of Sir Jeffrey Amherst, the British commander-in-chief, soon made their sense of unease tangible. Amherst, whose dislike of the Indians was so strong that he advocated giving them blankets infected with smallpox, saw little value in the Indian trade. He ordered western commanders to limit the gifts they gave to Indians, as well as ammunition, and to stop the sale of rum and other liquor. From Amherst's perspective, these were sensible moves designed to encourage economy and to restrain the Indians. But they were little short of disastrous in Indiana, where the exchange of gifts and goods had been at the heart of relationships for decades. Decisions of this sort made by distant officials were wreaking havoc with well-established local economies. The British commander at Detroit continued to give what he could to nearby tribes. Still, the immediate consequence of the British conquest was to disrupt commerce in the Great Lakes, to double prices, and to make the British look ungenerous and inhospitable in comparison with the French. They were behaving like coercive conquerors rather than generous fathers.

By 1763, many frustrated Indians were already talking of reprisals against the British, looking for some way to force them to change their policy. In particular the Ottawa war chief Pontiac urged a fight against the British. On May 9, 1763, he led about 500 Ottawa, Chippewa, Potawatomi, Huron, Shawnee, and Delaware warriors in an attack on Detroit. Failing to take the fort immediately, Pontiac and his warriors settled in for a long siege. Meanwhile, other Indians captured other formerly French posts at places such as Michilimackinac and Sandusky.

In many ways, the war anticipated the actions of British colonists after 1765. The Indians were protesting imperial interference in their local affairs, the disruption of traditional practices, by seizing government posts and officials. Memeskia had not turned to the British in order to have their government stop the trade. Pontiac and his allies sought the restoration of the status quo, the kind of world of mutual obligation they had known with the French, rather than the elimination of the British.

On the Wabash and the Maumee, news of the siege of Detroit led the Miami and other Indians to join in the spreading protest movement. The Miami took Fort des Miamis on May 27. The Miami mistress of Ensign Robert Holmes, the post commander, convinced him to leave the fort, whereupon he was captured. The small garrison then surrendered quickly. At Ouiatanon on June 1, the Wea, Kickapoo, and Mascouten seized the lieutenant in charge and a couple of other men and forced the surrender of the rest. Fortunately for the British, a couple of French traders convinced the Indians to spare their lives and to treat them well during their captivity. Eventually they were sent to the British garrison at Fort Chartres on the Mississippi River.

While Pontiac's War began as a series of dramatic actions, it soon became something of a waiting game. The Indians lifted the siege of Detroit in October and Pontiac went to an island in the Maumee River near Lake Erie. Word of the Treaty of Paris, by which France

🏵 **29**

THE
WORLD
OF
GEORGE
CROGHAN,
1750–1777

gave Louisiana as well as Canada to Great Britain, further stymied the Indians. Pontiac spent much of 1764 in the Wabash Valley, as the British sent military expeditions along the southern coast of Lake Erie and into the Ohio Country. Meanwhile, General Amherst had returned to England and Sir William Johnson, the superintendent of Indian affairs for the Northern District, saw to it that goods for trade and gifts flooded the Great Lakes region, thereby removing the Indians' major grievance.

Croghan on the Wabash, 1765

At dawn on the eighth day of June 1765, some eighty Kickapoo and Mascouten warriors surprised a smaller party of British traders and Shawnee Indians in their camp on the Ohio River a few miles below the mouth of the Wabash. They killed two white men and three Indians and severely wounded many others. Among the injured was the leader of the British and the Shawnee, George Croghan. The British commander in North America, Brigadier-General Thomas Gage, had dispatched Croghan, a long-time trader and deputy of Sir William Johnson, to meet with Indians in the Illinois Country and reconcile them to the consequences of the British conquest of Canada. Now Croghan seemed destined to suffer a fate similar to that of Vincennes and Memeskia.

But the words of a Shawnee chief saved his life and those of his colleagues. According to Croghan, the unidentified man, ignoring a wound in his thigh, "made a very bold speech," informing the Kickapoo and the Mascouten that all the northern Indians "would join in taking revenge for the insult and murder of their people." At this, the attackers backed off and "began excusing themselves, saying their fathers, the French, had spirited them up." They claimed to have thought that Croghan and his party had come from the south to try to enslave them. Their action was thus in the nature of a preemptive strike.

Alarmed by the speech of the Shawnee, the warriors decided to take their prisoners back to their village near Ouiatanon. They left for the north "in a great hurry," but not before they had stolen everything Croghan and his men and allies had brought to use in their negotiations. (He valued the lost equipment at £150 and his money at £421.) The wounded men suffered great pain on their forced march through the "thick woody country" and the "great many swamps, morasses, and beaver ponds" of southern Illinois. For the next week they walked about thirty miles a day, traveling from before daybreak to evening. Croghan and his companions found it hard work, quite aside from their fears about their lives. It was extremely hot and the earth parched. They were thirsty and tired when they arrived at Vincennes on June 15.

There they found "a village of about eighty or ninety French families" situated on the east bank of the Wabash. Croghan took an immediate dislike to the French. They were "an idle, lazy people, a parcel of renegadoes from Canada" who were "much worse than the Indians." He thought them secretly pleased at his predicament. The French traded vermilion and other goods for the gold and silver and supplies they had taken from Croghan and his party.

The Piankashaw who lived in a nearby village were much more helpful. They scolded the Kickapoo and Mascouten for their action, reminding them that they were trying to make peace with the British. Meanwhile they denounced the French for inciting the attack. Croghan had met some of the Piankashaw before and, through their influence, was able to write a letter and buy some horses and equipment, which he promised to pay for in Detroit. Unlike the French, the Piankashaw reacted angrily to Croghan's capture. They accepted some of the plunder from the French but refused to accept presents offered to mollify them. The assistance the British and Shawnee received at Vincennes was virtually all the work of the local Indians.

On the 17th, the warriors and Croghan's party "set out" for Ouiatanon. Traveling again through woods, increasingly interspersed with meadows, the party passed through another Piankashaw village near the mouth of the Vermilion River on the 22nd. The next day they arrived at Ouiatanon. There "several chiefs" of the Kickapoo and Mascouten "reprimanded [their young warriors] severely." Some of the Wea living on the south side of the Wabash, across from the French fort, visited Croghan and "seemed greatly concerned at what happened." They too remonstrated with the warriors and got them to take better care of their prisoners. As always, everyone blamed everything on the French. Croghan was

⟫ 31

THE
WORLD
OF
GEORGE
CROGHAN,
1750–1777

no great admirer of the Indians; he thought them "weak, foolish, and credulous" and "easily imposed on by a designing people, who have led them hitherto as they pleased." Although he spent about a month at Ouiatanon, the British prisoner barely made any mention of the fourteen French families who lived there. Instead he concentrated all his energies on the Indians. He claimed to overcome, "in great measure, their suspicions against the English."

In fact, Croghan the injured prisoner became a powerful negotiator. In a series of meetings with the Wea, Piankashaw, Kickapoo, Mascouten, and Miami, he "was lucky enough to reconcile [them] to his Majesties Interest & obtain their Consent and Approbation to take Possession of any Posts in their country which the French formerly possessed & an offer of their service should any Nation oppose our taking possession of it." In mid-July, he obtained the same agreements from the four Indian nations living in the Illinois Country, including the chief Pontiac. They "desired that their Father the King of England might not look upon his taking possession of the Forts which the French had formerly possest as a title for his subjects to possess their Country, as they never had sold any part of it to the French." That said, "whenever the English came to take possession [of the forts] they would receive them with open arms."

"[A]fter settling all matters happily with the natives," Croghan departed from Ouiatanon on July 25. Heading for Detroit, he took the well-established route. He went up the Eel River and crossed the nine miles of portage to the Maumee. Fort des Miamis was pretty much in ruins. Nearby was the Miami village with "about forty or fifty cabins" and "nine or ten French houses" containing even more "lazy, indolent people, fond of breeding mischief, and spiriting up the Indians against the English, and should by no means be suffered to remain here." Low water made the trip down the Maumee difficult. But on August 17, Croghan and his party finally found refuge within the walls of the fort at Detroit. Two months on the Wabash had transformed his near-death experience into something of a diplomatic triumph. He had won the assent of the Wabash Indians to the British occupation of the posts constructed by the French.

Clearly, given their treatment of him after he was captured, they were more than ready to negotiate. As Croghan noted in writing to Sir William Johnson in July, they did so "More out of fear than

Love." In particular, they feared that the killing of the three Shaw-nee during the capture of Croghan's party would lead to a war with the Iroquois, Shawnee, and Delaware, all of whom had come to terms with the British earlier. "[T]here is Nothing those Na-tions Dread More than a Warr with ye. Six Nations Dallaways & Shannas . . . they Came in A Body to Me yesterday & beggd. in the Most Submissive Maner than I wold give them My Intrest with those Nations to Make up the Affair." It is not surprising that the Delaware and the Shawnee were more threatening than the British, for the latter remained almost exclusively on the eastern side of the Appalachian Mountains while the former had migrated to the east-ern and southern Ohio Country in the 1730s and 1740s.

Still, out of fear of other Indians or the British, all the Indians of the Indiana and Illinois countries agreed that the British could become as the French had been. As powerful fathers, protecting, supplying, and mediating for their independent children, they were welcome to occupy the old posts and continue to trade. But there was absolutely no agreement that they could have any land. For the Indians, the talks with Croghan meant that the status quo would be preserved, albeit with different characters. Indeed, from the perspective of the Miami, the whole situation was rather like a long-running play that experiences a complete change in cast. The actors would be different, but the drama and the production would remain essentially the same.

The Aspirations of British Gentlemen

The British, of course, saw things differently. As interested as they were in trade, they were even more interested in land. They had little interest in simply restoring French ways. Croghan, who understood and admired the French-Algonquin alliance, exemplified their attitude. Wounded, exhausted, and anxious as the Kickapoo and Mascouten led him, his servants, and allies up the Wabash toward Ouiatanon, he still found the energy to evaluate the agricultural possibilities of the terrain through which he passed. Two days after his capture, he noticed "fine rich bottoms . . . which make the finest pasture in the world." The quantity and quality of hemp surprised him. Near Vincennes on June 15, Croghan praised

📯 **33**

THE
WORLD
OF
GEORGE
CROGHAN,
1750–1777

the richness of the "level and clear" country. Wheat and tobacco grown there were "preferable to that of Maryland or Virginia." At Ouiatanon, he admired the soil, water, and "temperate" climate. Croghan was certain that the French had tried to keep the English from learning about the region. "I apprehend that it has been the artifice of the French to keep us ignorant of the country." Now, however, the potential of the rich, well-watered Indiana landscape could no longer be hidden.

These sentiments were not new to Croghan. A native of Ireland, he came to Pennsylvania in 1741, part of the large migration of Scots and Irish to North America in the eighteenth century. Along with many Germans, these British peoples settled predominately in Pennsylvania and along the Great Wagon Road in the Shenandoah Valley of western Virginia and the piedmont of the Carolinas. By 1790, the year of the first census in United States history, over 20 percent of the new nation's population was Scots-Irish, Irish, or Scottish. Only a quarter of Pennsylvania's citizens were English; 15 percent were Scots-Irish, 7 percent Irish, 7 percent Scottish, and 38 percent German. In South Carolina, Scots-Irish, Scots, and Irish made up well over a third of the population. These were the people who led the expansion of the British colonies away from the rivers of the Atlantic seaboard. By 1750, they had settled the foothills of the Appalachians west of Harrisburg, Pennsylvania, and south through Virginia into the Carolinas.

The migration of peoples from the northern borderlands of Great Britain helped to swell a colonial population that was rapidly growing by natural reproduction anyway. From 250,900 in 1700, the number of English colonists reached 1,170,800 in 1750 and 2,460,000 in 1775. In contrast, the population of New France rose from 19,315 in 1714 to 43,382 in 1739. At the end of the French and Indian War in 1763, there were only 125,000 French in all of the Americas. Virginia alone was four times as populous. While the French reproduced as rapidly as the British settlers, they did not have a very large base with which to start; nor was there much immigration in the 1700s. Demographically, George Croghan came to Indiana as the representative of a much more powerful people than the Sieur de Vincennes.

The British advantages went well beyond numbers. Their economies were much more diverse. The fur trade was important, particularly in New York, but it was not dominant. South of Pennsylvania, white settlers and black slaves produced a variety of staple crops, of which tobacco and rice were the most important. In New England, most people were semi-subsistence farmers, growing enough to feed their families plus a bit of surplus to market; in the cities, merchants engaged in overseas trade while artisans and professionals provided essential products and services. But it was the middle colonies of New York and Pennsylvania which were the most economically dynamic. There in "the best poor man's country in the world" people grew wheat and other grains and traded with markets throughout the world, including those along the Wabash.

From Georgia to New Hampshire, British colonists had transformed the landscapes of North America far more thoroughly than the French. While New France remained a long string of towns and outposts situated at key points on the rivers and lakes of the continent, the English-speaking colonies were increasingly consolidated examples of a rearranged ecosystem. Forests had become farms and plantations; outposts had become thriving cities.

By the time Croghan arrived in Pennsylvania, the combination of booming economies and booming populations had turned the attention of many prominent colonists to the west. Like the French, their first thoughts ran to the Indian trade. In New York, merchants in Albany had been engaged in competition with the French for control of the lucrative trade north of the Great Lakes for decades. Men such as Sir William Johnson welcomed the opportunity presented by the conquest of Canada to reap huge profits. Pennsylvania merchants were not far behind. Great mercantile firms in London were eager to advance credit, tens of thousands of pounds over a period of years, to American merchants and traders in order to obtain the finest possible beaver pelts and deer skins for sale in European markets.

The merchants of Philadelphia could not break into the northern Great Lakes, so they concentrated most of their attention on the region between the lakes and the Ohio River. The house of Baynton, Wharton, and Morgan lobbied hard to get exclusive contracts to supply the British garrisons and Indian Department in the Ohio and Illinois countries. When they received them in 1766, they dispatched some sixty-five boats full of manufactured goods down the

✐ 35

THE
WORLD
OF
GEORGE
CROGHAN,
1750–1777

Ohio River from Pittsburgh. With an investment of £75,000 in a period of two years and a work force of over 300 men on the Ohio, the firm overextended itself, went bankrupt, and lost the valuable supply contracts to the Gratz brothers of Philadelphia.

Baynton, Wharton, and Morgan's failure was not simply the result of poor management or unbridled ambition. By the 1760s, the fur and skin trade was seriously declining in the Ohio Valley. It had never been as valuable as that north of the Great Lakes, and now many of the animals had been killed or driven away. French traders, moreover, continued to operate in the region even after the fall of Canada. Their traditional contacts and easier access down the St. Lawrence gave them short-term advantages over their Anglo-American rivals. Still, by the beginning of the American War for Independence in 1775, thirty-seven British traders dominated the trade out of Detroit, even though they were numerically outnumbered by the French.

Not coincidentally, all but two of those men were either Scots or Scots-Irish; the sons of British borderlands were the advance agents of empire in the borderlands of British North America. None was more successful in a dangerous and cutthroat business than George Croghan. The Irishman quickly prospered as an Indian trader. By the late 1740s, he was buying land near Harrisburg, purchasing slaves and contracting with indentured servants to carry and manage his goods, and making valuable acquaintances with merchants in Philadelphia. Within a decade of his arrival, Croghan had become the preeminent Indian trader, with perhaps 100 of the 300 people involved in the business in Pennsylvania connected to him. Colonial officials were calling on Croghan to travel into the Ohio Country to negotiate with Indians. His business collapsed with the French revival in the early 1750s, but he recovered. He worked for Virginia and Pennsylvania as an Indian agent, acquiring a reputation as a fair man among Indians and as a charming manipulator among British colonists.

Here was a very different agent of empire from the Vincennes. Jean-Baptiste and François-Marie Bissot saw profits when they looked at the Wabash. But Croghan saw a wilderness transformed. Not for him the death of a martyr. Not for him devotion to a government or a military hierarchy. Self-interest motivated him—

always. Croghan was a wonderful character, bluff, tough-minded, generous. He did everything to excess. His life knew no bounds, whether he was drinking, taking snuff, rescuing his friends from problems, or speculating in land. While he had a wife, about whom we know virtually nothing, he slept with several Indian women. In the winter of 1757-1758, his mistress was the daughter of a Mohawk chief in western New York. Their daughter, Catherine, later married the Mohawk Joseph Brant. A very popular man, Croghan was a great storyteller. He loved to dress well. Indeed, Croghan reveled in living on a grand scale. His life was an adventure that carried him from Philadelphia to London to Quebec to Detroit. As talented as the Vincennes may have been, it is hard to imagine them finagling their way out of dire predicaments with the dexterity of Croghan. Or anyone ever calling him sieur.

Croghan also differed from the Frenchmen in that his ambitions were not limited to the fur trade and Indian agency. Like other British traders and merchants, he recognized the implications of the decline in the fur trade in the Ohio Valley. And, like them, he was fully aware of the significance of colonial growth. Consequently, Croghan put a great deal of the money he made from the trade into land. At various times, he speculated in land in western Pennsylvania and New York and throughout the Ohio Valley. From time to time, he would lose purchases to his creditors. But he never stopped buying. In 1774, Croghan spent $6,000 to purchase 1,500,000 acres in the Ohio Country from Indians.

Croghan's aspirations differed from those of the Vincennes. They were already gentlemen; their goals were to acquire a fortune through trade and to achieve high rank (both military and social) through service to their government. Croghan, on the other hand, craved the status of gentleman. He wanted to make money. He wanted to use it to acquire position, to emulate the baronial status of his mentor, Sir William Johnson. In the late 1760s, Croghan acquired 250,000 acres on Lake Otsego in New York. There he set about developing Croghan's Forest in the characteristically thorough fashion of British speculators. He made plans for a bridge over the Susquehanna River, a road to the Hudson River, a sawmill, and a grist mill. He employed a couple of dozen servants and laborers in constructing a log home and several others buildings. The house was no frontier shack; indeed, it was supposed to be the home of a gentleman. The laborers put up wallpaper and constructed six fireplaces. Croghan's table had damask cloths and ivory-handled flatware. He imported thirty chairs, six chamber pots, a black slave, tobacco, sugar, raisins, coffee, tea, and chocolate. His windows were made of glass, his locks of brass. And the master of the house had at least two dozen pairs of shoes. This was more than conspicuous consumption. Croghan was trying to retire to the life of an eighteenth-century gentleman, living off of his estate and his herds of cows and sheep rather than working in the brutish and brutal world of trade. He failed miserably. He lost his land in New York and returned to Pittsburgh. Never able to get out of debt, for he manufactured his career on credit, he died in relative poverty outside Philadelphia on August 31, 1782.

Croghan's life was an extreme version of the ambitions many Anglo-Americans had in the mid-1700s. Merchants in Philadelphia and planters in Virginia, not to mention lawyers, soldiers, and farmers everywhere, looked to the west, particularly the Ohio Valley, for the fortune that would become the foundation of their family's social status, their gentility, unto the last generation. They wanted to buy land as cheaply as possible, develop it (which meant survey it, build a small town, and make some transportation improvements), then re-sell it in smaller quantities. If all went well, they could make huge profits. George Washington spent much of his adult life trying to make a fortune through this game. He was hardly alone. Each colony had a group of ambitious men eager to speculate in western lands. So many, in fact, that their interests inevitably brought them into conflict with each other.

The struggles among speculators for control of the Ohio Valley only intensified with the ratification of British victory in 1763. Some members of the Ohio Company, which had been founded by Virginia planters in 1747 to acquire land in western Pennsylvania, formed the Mississippi Company in order to acquire 2,500,000 acres near the confluence of the Ohio and Mississippi rivers. They failed, but their lobbyists worked hard on the project for five years in London. Meanwhile, some Pennsylvania merchants, among them Samuel Wharton and George Croghan, claiming to have suffered great losses at the hands of Pontiac, petitioned for a grant of

1,800,000 acres at a price of £10,000 in what is now West Virginia. The "suffering traders" called themselves the Indiana Company. The British government refused their petition. But, by interesting various London merchants and prominent lobbyists such as Benjamin Franklin in the scheme, they were able to acquire a much larger area, the Vandalia purchase, encompassing the region from the mouth of the Scioto River to the Cumberland Gap to the border of Maryland and Pennsylvania, for the original price of £10,000. The British government, however, delayed the issue of a patent or charter for the colony until the outbreak of the American War for Independence made the issue moot.

American speculators were daunted, but far from defeated, by these setbacks. In 1775, the original "suffering traders" of Pennsylvania attempted to sell land in their proposed Indiana purchase anyway. Both Virginia and Pennsylvania objected strenuously and began an active struggle for control of the Pittsburgh area that would last into the 1780s. Meanwhile, in 1773, William Murray, an agent of Pennsylvania merchants long active in the fur trade, organized a group called the Illinois Company and purchased land on the Mississippi and Illinois rivers from ten chiefs of the Kaskaskia, Peoria, and Cahokia Indians. Two years later, Murray founded the Wabash Company, under whose imprimatur he purchased two tracts totaling 37,497,600 acres from eleven Piankashaw chiefs. Once the United States declared its independence, the Illinois and Wabash companies merged and became the United Illinois and Wabash Land Company. Together they pressed their claims with the new American government.

The Foundations of Empire?

Neither the British Crown nor most members of Parliament were pleased with the activities of colonial speculators, the considerable interest of individual officials in some of the land companies notwithstanding. In the wake of the triumph over the French, British officials sought to bring order and efficiency to their far-flung empire. Under the leadership of a succession of ministers, they sought to standardize and stabilize the diverse political and

☙ 39

THE
WORLD
OF
GEORGE
CROGHAN,
1750–1777

economic structures at least nominally under their control. Their plans raised the hackles of people from Boston to Detroit and beyond. Ultimately they were unable to make their designs for imperial order, for centrally directed development of British North America, work. Still, their efforts were important, both in terms of the reaction they provoked and in the ways that they foreshadowed the actions of the government of the United States in the 1790s.

With regard to the territory between the Ohio and Mississippi rivers, the most important objective was to exercise political power over it. That meant getting both the American Indians who inhabited it and the land speculators and traders such as Croghan who had their eyes on it to recognize the King in Parliament as sovereign, the ultimate arbiter of all disputes, commerce, and land claims. British officials began to work toward this goal with the promulgation of the Proclamation of October 7, 1763. The edict prohibited white settlement beyond the continental divide of the Appalachians until officials in London could purchase land from Indians and establish an orderly system for its occupation. To handle the business of negotiating with the Indians, that is, buying the land, the Crown appointed superintendents for the northern and southern regions. In 1764, in the midst of Pontiac's War, British policy became even more specific. The government required Indian traders to obtain licenses, to obey a set of regulations, and to post bond to ensure their compliance with the rules. They were also limited in their activities to Indian towns and garrisoned posts. British policy thus mimicked French efforts to gain control of the west. But officials never understood the importance of the personal nature of Algonquian-French alliance and the exchange of gifts and respect for power which were at the heart of it.

Failing a wholesale adoption of French methods, the British had to recognize the existence of a new world. That required a strong military presence, a system of government, or a procedure for land transactions. Given the horrendous national debt coming out of the French and Indian War and the refusal of the North American colonists to pay for their own defense, demonstrated so vividly in the Stamp Act Crisis of 1765, the British could not afford any of these things. Without courts of law and bureaucrats, without red-coated soldiers, without some tangible, visible manifestation of imperial authority, edicts from London were pieces of paper—irritating, yes, but nothing more.

The first casualty of the half-formed British policy was the proclamation line, which collapsed. Settlers, encouraged by land speculators in Virginia and Pennsylvania, were moving onto the lands south and west of the Ohio River at a rapid rate. Meanwhile, speculators, including the Ohio Company and the "suffering traders," were lobbying governments both colonial and imperial for the right to purchase even more land. Under this pressure, Superintendent Sir William Johnson, himself a well-known speculator, graciously allowed the Iroquois to cede their claims to the region between the Kanawha and Tennessee rivers as well as western Pennsylvania. This was accomplished in the Treaty of Fort Stanwix in November 1768.

Then there was the problem of maintaining posts in the west. The British had inherited the problems as well as the territory of the French, not the least of which was manning and supplying a line of posts running from Canada to Louisiana. The British, moreover, had two lines, an interior one that cut from New York down to what is now eastern Tennessee and an exterior one consisting of the forts constructed by the French in the Great Lakes and Mississippi regions. The costs of maintenance, what General Gage in 1768 called "the Noise and Complaints of Indian Expences," were high, particularly given the increasing tension between Great Britain and the colonies. With the French threat removed, neither the imperial nor colonial governments had the resources or the fear to garrison the frontier. The Crown depended, therefore, as the French had, on trade. The government made sure there were plenty of goods in the region and allowed French traders to continue to operate. Part of the reason the Miami and others welcomed George Croghan as a mediator in 1765 was that they knew him primarily as a trader. He, after all, had dealt with Memeskia at Pickawillany. And, when captured, he had plenty of goods and money to give and trade. Despite their military cutback, the British intended to maintain and extend their influence through commercial and friendly exchanges at Detroit, Kaskaskia, and other key locations in the west.

The imperial government tried to regulate trade and focus it on a few specific posts. None of the locations along the Maumee or the Wabash was included. The British made no effort to reoccupy Fort Miami or Post Ouiatanon after they were captured by the Miami in 1763. Nor did they send troops to Vincennes after French officials officially surrendered it in the fall of 1765. Worse still, Sir William Johnson failed to designate any post on the Wabash or the Maumee as an official trading center. So, technically, furs and skins had to be carried to Detroit or Fort Chartres on the Mississippi. Neither the French nor the Miami in Indiana liked this situation one bit. British commanders in the west in the late 1760s thus had as much reason to be worried about colonial unrest as their counterparts in New England. In both places, the imperial government was attempting to implement an unpopular policy without the resources to enforce it.

Edward Cole, who had been appointed commissary of Indian affairs at Fort des Chartres on the Mississippi River, traveled south from Detroit along the Maumee-Wabash river system in August 1766. He found the Miami interested in peace with the British. But they also wanted trade and expected gifts from the British. At Fort des Chartres, Cole met with the omnipresent Croghan, who was there to negotiate further with the Indians in the Illinois Country. After talking with Cole, Croghan recommended in a letter of January 1767 to Sir William Johnson that "a Post Should be Erected on the Wabash, from whence *the five Nations*, who are Settled on that River, may be supplied with British Goods[.] And all the French, except those who become English Subjects, be prevented from Trading there."

A Miami chief put the situation directly to some British traders later in the spring of 1767. He and his "People" were upset that their father had interrupted their commerce. His orders "Oblige[d] them to go to Detroit, (they think those Orders very hard)" to get shirts, leggings, and other goods. Just as important, they missed the blacksmith who had been ordered away from them. How, they wondered, did the British "think a person so Necessary amongst them must leave them, How can they Support their Familys and Hunt, if their Guns & Tomhawks are not kept in Repair." The French trader and sometime resident of Ouiatanon and Vincennes, Alexander

Maisonville, repeated these grievances to Croghan. Others told the Irishman of attacks on British traders by frustrated Indians. Meanwhile, traders in Detroit were growing restless. They demanded the rescinding of orders confining them to Detroit and specified posts. In particular, they wanted to trade with the Miami and other Indians along the Wabash.

British officials were making the same mistake in the Great Lakes region in the name of economy and efficiency which they were making in dealing with their colonies as a whole. The American Indians, for the most part, had declared themselves willing to accept the British as long as they protected and maintained the structures of the diplomatic and commercial world they had known for decades. It was not just the fear of the loss of land which disturbed them; it was the disruption of local customs and traditions. British authority was less the problem than British efforts, conscious or not, to change basic economic and social structures. The Indians could deal with Croghan because he was intimately involved in their world. But they could not tolerate faraway British officials making decisions that had severe repercussions in their lives.

No wonder, then, that George Morgan of the Pennsylvania house of Baynton, Wharton, and Morgan complained in December 1767 that British traders were in danger on the Wabash River. Both the French and the Miami were angry with the British, and there was no garrison and very little trade to protect men like him. He and Edward Cole agreed that the cost of a garrison or post on the Wabash would be more than met by the profits from the fur trade. In any case, unless something was done to satisfy the Indians and counteract the influence of Frenchmen operating out of New Orleans and the trans-Mississippi region, Morgan thought the British would have to abandon the entire western country "as it is very evident that not a single Advantage can arrise from it . . . otherways than by a proper Regulation & Encouragement of the Peltry Trade."

Sir William Johnson tended to agree and recommended the establishment of trading posts on the Wabash. Before this policy could be implemented, the British government, faced with severe problems in dealing with its North American colonies, gave up on its efforts to regulate the Indian trade in 1768. Control reverted back to individual colonies, and both French and British traders were free to

📣 **43**

THE
WORLD
OF
GEORGE
CROGHAN,
1750–1777

engage in commerce wherever they saw fit. The British government, in fact, was in a virtual headlong flight from the Indiana and Illinois Country. Rather than establish new posts or garrison abandoned ones, it ordered the evacuation of forts. In 1772, British troops left both Fort des Chartres in the Illinois Country and Fort Pitt. By 1775, west of the Appalachians, the British held only Niagara, Detroit, Michilimackinac, and Kaskaskia. The next year, the last company of fifty men left Kaskaskia. On the eve of the War for Independence, British military and political influence west of the Ohio and south of the Great Lakes was at a nadir.

If, in the 1750s and 1760s, the British had defeated the French and acquired a vast territory, His Majesty's government had been unable to enforce a coherent policy for regulating the relationships of American Indians and European traders as well as the activities of land speculators. The Proclamation of 1763 had contained the seeds of a plan by which the imperial government would direct the orderly development of the lands between the Ohio and the Mississippi rivers. But, in the face of intense opposition and limited resources, the British government failed to sustain its intrusions into local worlds. The Miami and other Indians, French families in Vincennes, British land speculators and traders, and Anglo-American farmers were thus left alone to contend with each other until yet another imperial government could devise more specific and more all-encompassing plans for the development of the lands along the banks of the Wabash and its tributaries.

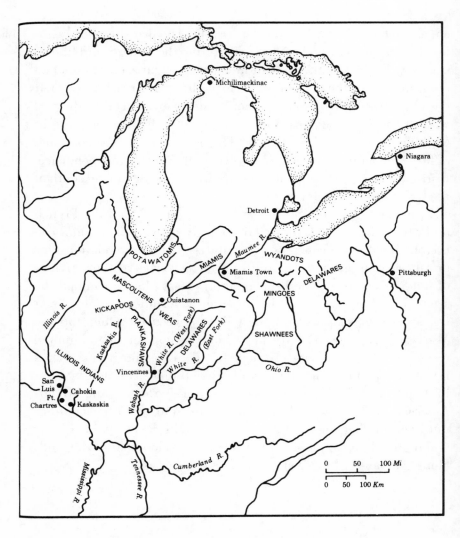

The World of the Wabash in the 1770s. Reprinted with permission from the *Indiana Magazine of History* 83 (1987): 151.

3.

THE VILLAGE OF VINCENNES, 1765–1777

The most striking thing about contemporary descriptions of eighteenth-century Vincennes is their pervasive negativity. Visitors characterized the town's inhabitants as lazy, dirty, and hedonistic and were appalled by what they perceived to be a general indifference to work and morality.

Typical was the reaction of Father Pierre Gibault, a priest living in Kaskaskia on the Mississippi River, who visited Vincennes in the spring of 1770, the first priest to do so in nearly a decade. Gibault found, or so he reported to his bishop in Quebec, a people desperate for civilization. Bereft of organized religion, the residents of Vincennes had given in to "libertinage and irreligion." Gibault reported that his arrival had reawakened their Christian spirit. Crowds of people had greeted him at the riverbank, kneeling, sobbing, and beseeching him as if he were a truly important person. "Father, save us, we are nearly in hell," said some. Others shouted that God had not "utterly abandoned" them, for He had sent Gibault "to make us do penance for our sins." Still others lamented that no priest had been available to perform the sacraments for dead relatives. The fact that Gibault stayed at Vincennes only long enough to direct the rebuilding of the small wooden church did not endear him to his newfound admirers. He almost had to fight his way out of town, so eager were people to keep him around to say mass, perform baptisms and marriages, and offer extreme unction.

Gibault's account was self-serving, of course. It made him and his church look good. No doubt bishops in Canada found it reassuring, this sketch of a wilderness people clamoring for a priest to guide them away from evil habits. But Gibault was hardly alone in his deprecation of the residents of eighteenth-century Vincennes. Indeed, the sense that the French residents there lived a life of sloth and indulgence is so pervasive in the few records we have that it is difficult not to agree with the good priest about their dismal character. But we have to resist the temptation and try to understand these people on their own terms, to place them in their context, not the one created by travelers and officials.

The Notables of Vincennes

In 1763, the year in which the French ceded control of Canada and the west to the British in the Treaty of Paris, Louis Groston de Bellerive de St. Ange commanded the post at Vincennes, as he had for the previous twenty-seven years. St. Ange had arrived at the infant outpost in the fall of 1736 to replace the unfortunate Vincennes *fils*. There he had made remarkable progress in establishing the post as a major center of trade. He had led in the rebuilding of the fort erected by Vincennes, and despite the opposition of the French government in Louisiana, which wanted to move the post to the mouth of the Wabash, he persisted in trying to attract both Indians and French settlers to the settlement.

Neither task was easy. The Piankashaw had virtually abandoned their village near Vincennes after the death of Vincennes in the war with the Chickasaw. Many distrusted St. Ange because he arrived from the French settlements along the Mississippi, where he had been friendly with the Illinois Indians. Meanwhile, few French wanted to settle in a dangerous and deserted place, where land titles were confused and uncertain. Still, St. Ange worked hard, in a less dramatic fashion than Vincennes, and by the 1740s, there were several dozen people in the village. The turning point came in 1742, when the Piankashaw granted over a million and a half acres in the area to the French. By 1750, St. Ange was issuing deeds for small grants of land in and near the settlement. And with the resulting increase in commerce, many Piankashaw soon returned to their former village. While men were fighting for control of Canada and the Ohio Valley in the 1750s, the people of Vincennes built a chapel, which they named St. Francis Xavier, laid out streets away from the fort, which they dubbed Bosseron and Rue de St. Honoré, and developed a profitable trade in furs and deerskins with Indians. Quietly and unspectacularly, St. Ange consolidated the dramatic beginnings of the Vincennes. In thirty years, he oversaw the transformation of his post from a ramshackle fort into a small village of approximately seventy families. St. Ange was perhaps the most important figure in the history of frontier Vincennes, but historians rarely give him much attention, in part because we have few records about him.

The departure of St. Ange on May 18, 1764 (British officials had ordered him to assume command of Fort Chartres on the Mississippi until they could send someone to hold it), was a melancholy occasion. Vincennes was losing one of its oldest and most prominent citizens as well as its commanding officer. St. Ange's brief farewell proclamation tells us a good deal about the ways in which he and a few other men had exercised power in the town. He transferred authority to Monsieur Drouet de Richerville, who would serve as the captain of the local troops, and Sieur de Caindre, a soldier. Their responsibilities were "to maintain good order among the citizens of this post, as also of the voyageurs and the Indians." Most important was the need "to maintain good feelings among the Indians to prevent disorder so long as they are in charge." In addition, they were to make sure "that the citizens keep up their fences" and to "check . . . the disorders which occur too frequently, occasioned by drinking." St. Ange also suggested that in the case of a "complaint . . . made to them against any one they will proceed to call an assembly of the more notable of the citizens of the place, where the matter shall be decided by a plurality of votes."

This brief document gives us some clues, as we shall see, about both the society and the economy of Vincennes in the mid-eighteenth century. But it is most suggestive about the operation of power. St. Ange clearly intended that Richerville and Caindre would act as first among equals. They were to put important issues to a vote, not of everyone but of "notable" local figures. Government in French Vincennes was neither autocratic nor democratic but oligarchic. In the absence of direct French or British authority, the most important citizens would govern themselves in an informal, ad hoc fashion. No doubt, although this is nothing more than an educated guess, St. Ange had been running the place for decades in this way—officially acting as the agent of royal authority while practically acting in consultation with a few key men.

Who were these men, these local notables who exercised authority in Vincennes? The new captain Richerville was a member of one of the most important families in the valley of the Wabash. His real name was Antoine Drouet de Bajolet, although people called him Drouet de Richerville, and he had been born in 1699. His father was Ensign Claude Drouet de Richerville, who had arrived in Canada in the late 1680s and married Marie-Jeanne Desrosiers. Our major interest in their uneventful lives is the fact that together they produced ten children. The sons devoted their careers to commerce and military service in the west, trading as far as Kaskaskia in the Illinois Country. Three of Antoine's brothers died with Vincennes in the 1736 campaign against the Chickasaws, and another escaped only after witnessing the immolation of the others. Yet another brother, Claude Drouet de Carqueville, commanded the French post at Ouiatanon from 1748 through the early 1750s and was killed during the battle against the British troops commanded by General Edward Braddock outside Fort Duquesne in July 1755.

Drouet de Richerville, who married Marie Lamy in 1728, had been an officer at Vincennes since the late 1740s. His major concerns were the fur trade and the accumulation of land. Apparently he did well with both. St. Ange gave him undetermined amounts of acreage in 1754 and at later times and entrusted him with the post in 1764. When Drouet de Richerville died the following spring, he was mourned as "messire" and his wife was called "dame," both titles normally reserved for nobility.

It was the second wife of Richerville who became the key figure in the consolidation of his family's power. In May 1756, after the death of his first wife, Richerville traveled to Kaskaskia and married Françoise Outelas, the daughter of a French officer at that post. Françoise was instrumental in shaping the evolving socioeconomic network in Vincennes. Eight years after the death of Richerville, she married a local merchant named Ambroise Dageny. As important was the fact that her daughters by Richerville married notable men. Françoise (Elisabeth) became the wife of François Rider de Bosseron, perhaps the most important man in Vincennes in the 1770s. The foundation of Bosseron's power was his trading business; at various times he was a militia captain and town official. Another daughter of Richerville and Françoise Outelas, Marguerite, married the influential merchant Paul Gamelin in 1785. Their two sons also did well.

We know virtually nothing else about Françoise Outelas and her children. The findings of historians studying the French settlements along the Mississippi, however, suggest a context in which we can better understand her. In the late 1760s the balance between males and females in Vincennes was virtually even, but that may not have always been the case. It is interesting, for example, that Drouet de Richerville traveled to Kaskaskia to find a wife. There are several possible explanations for this. He may have met Françoise on a trading or social trip. Or he may have wished to marry someone from a particular social background or to cement an alliance with a family in Kaskaskia. It may also reflect a scarcity of eligible women in Vincennes, which was a not uncommon phenomenon in the French settlements. Whatever Drouet de Richerville's motivation, Françoise's is even more obscure. While we do not know her age, this was apparently her first marriage, so she was probably in her late teens. Richerville was fifty-seven. Perhaps his rising position in the French trading and political networks influenced her decision as much as affection. In any case, it was a good marriage for both of them.

This alliance of young woman and older man was far from uncommon, as Susan C. Boyle's study of eighteenth-century Ste. Genevieve (now in Missouri) has shown. More often than not, such marriages worked to the economic advantage of women. French law regarding the protection of family property and the fact that business often took husbands away from home for long periods gave women added experience and power in running their households. In addition, like Drouet de Richerville, older husbands usually died first, leaving their wives in the legally beneficial positions of being widows. Françoise Outelas Richerville was apparently a formidable but not unusual woman in the French settlements. For she lived in a culture in which knowledgeable women took full advantage of demographic and legal circumstances to exercise a fair degree of control over their own lives. Deliberately or not, Françoise delayed remarriage for eight years, negotiated a solid match for herself, and saw her daughters married to the most important men in Vincennes.

Clearly, as the historian Donald Chaput, who has carefully reconstructed the genealogy of the Richervilles, has observed, "the closely-knit Vincennes socioeconomic structure . . . hinged on the Drouet de Richerville family." When St. Ange entrusted power to Richerville in 1765, he was not simply handing it over to another officer or a trusted ally. He was officially confirming the political pattern that was emerging in eighteenth-century Vincennes. The Richervilles were early versions of what historians of nineteenth-century demography refer to as "persisters." They stayed put; they accumulated land, wealth, and important relatives and they became powerful. The alliance of Drouet de Richerville and Françoise Outelas marked the beginning of a family dynasty that would consolidate its position as a local aristocracy over the next few decades.

The Peoples of Vincennes

The Richerville-Outelas family was prominent in a town with a fairly heterogeneous population. In 1767, when the British ordered a census of the French settlements, there were some 232 men, women, and children living permanently at Vincennes (compared with 600 at the biggest settlement, Kaskaskia, on the Mississippi). Two years later, the number had risen slightly to 250. By the 1780s, it was even larger. In 1790, Winthrop Sargent, the secretary of the Northwest Territory, reported the number of heads of French households before 1783 and still resident in Vincennes to be 144, including twenty-four widows; adding wives and children, there were several hundred people in the town. The population was young, with two-thirds of the people classified as children in 1769. Among adults, the gender ratio was neatly balanced. There were fifty women and fifty men "able to bear arms including Servants."

In addition to the permanent inhabitants, Vincennes in 1767 had a transient population of 168 "Strangers." People in this category were no doubt primarily traders involved in the exchange of furs and peltries. They may have spent considerable time in Vincennes, but they were not included in the central core of its citizens. Most assuredly they were not among the notables St. Ange urged Richerville to convene when necessary. Indeed, "Strangers" may well have been the sources of some of the disorders to which St. Ange referred.

Also not among the notables but no doubt closer to them than the strangers were the ten African and seventeen Native American slaves. That was a small number compared with the 303 black slaves in Kaskaskia in 1767 but still an important group of people. We do not know where the black slaves were purchased, but it is virtually certain that they came from either the Illinois French settlements or directly from New Orleans. The Indians were probably captives from tribes west of the Mississippi; local Indians did not object because they practiced slavery, too. But the sheer numbers of Indians encouraged fair treatment of slaves by whites. In the Illinois settlements, Indian slaves worked in homes rather than in the fields and were regarded as status symbols.

The Code Noir, developed by the French to control slaves in their colonies in the West Indies, legally governed the relationships between masters and slaves. The code was a mixed bag for blacks. On the one hand, it gave them the right to due process of law in all criminal proceedings and to appeal death sentences. On the other, it defined them as *meubles*, movable goods, to be treated as commodities in the same manner as domesticated animals. The code also required the French to attempt to Christianize blacks.

According to the historian Winstanley Briggs, the demographic and economic imperatives of life led French settlers in Illinois, and Indiana by extension, to treat their slaves well. Slaves were expensive and scarce investments, and owners wanted to take care of them. They worked side-by-side with whites. Briggs believes that the French therefore emphasized the positive aspects of the Code Noir while essentially ignoring its more punitive provisions. They allowed slaves to use money, keep a few personal possessions, and be sold with the land. Most revealing, perhaps, were efforts to maintain black slave families. The majority of slaves were Catholics. Under the code, it was both illegal and sinful for anyone forcibly to separate members of a recognized family. In the Illinois settlements, the French actively participated in the marriages and baptisms of slaves. Instances of cruelty and excessive punishment were rare. The French could not afford to be inconsiderate. No one could ever describe slavery as a positive experience; still, circumstances ameliorated the kind of treatment slaves received. Simply put, slavery was more flexible in the French settlements along the Mississippi and the Wabash than elsewhere in the Americas.

The little we know about the few slaves in Vincennes confirms the pattern Briggs describes in the Illinois Country. Apparently the first black slaves on the Wabash were named Alexandre and Dorothee. According to the St. Francis Xavier Parish Records, they were "negro slaves belonging to the Jesuit fathers and lawfully married." That fact was noted at the baptism of their daughter, Agatha, on May 30, 1753. Seven years later, on July 12, 1760, a priest baptized a slave named Susanne, who was the property of M. Crepau. Later the same day, Susanne married Joseph, who was also the property of M. Crepau. Crepau sanctioned the alliance by witnessing the marriage. Fourteen months later, Susanne and Joseph brought their daughter, Susanne, to the priest for baptism. There are no records of baptisms and marriages from 1763 to 1785 because there was no priest in residence. But the baptism of slaves resumed when Father Gibault came to live in Vincennes. The larger point is that the slaves (both African and Indian) were integral parts of the households of the notable citizens of the town.

Also important members of the Vincennes community were the Piankashaw Indians. The Piankashaw were Miami who had established a village at the confluence of the Vermilion and Wabash rivers in the 1720s, a village they occupied for decades. In the 1730s, with the arrival of the Sieur de Vincennes, many had migrated to the area near the site of Vincennes. With a few interruptions, the Piankashaw were a permanent presence in the French town and its environs. The Indians hunted in the region drained by the Vermilion and the lower Wabash and traded extensively with the French at Ouiatanon and Vincennes. The exact population is difficult to ascertain, in part because it fluctuated greatly in response to epidemics and war, but one estimate from 1773 puts 110 warriors at Vincennes and another 125 at the mouth of the Vermilion. Adding women, older men, and children makes for a total of over four hundred people.

Relations between the French and the Piankashaw were often ambiguous at best. The main attraction of Vincennes was as a trading post. The French villages along the Mississippi and the British fort at Detroit were, as George Croghan observed in 1765, "too far" for the Indians to go "to fetch their Necessities." Edward Cole, the British official at Fort des Chartres in 1768, informed Sir William Johnson that Vincennes was "the great path throw which all the northward Indians pass, and a Great place of Trade." Indians, particularly the Piankashaw, were virtually omnipresent in the French town. Vincennes was a triracial society, bringing together Europeans, Africans, and Native Americans in a grand emporium on the banks of the Wabash.

Commercial exchange inevitably led to cultural and sexual interaction. Just as the Piankashaw sought the technology of the Europeans in the form of guns and cloth, the French generally aped the Indians in dress, diet, and behavior. They wore sandals and blankets, used canoes, and obviously ate the corn, beans, vegetables, and wild animals which were indigenous to the area. Nearly everyone agrees that there was significant miscegenation, almost always between French men and Indian women. The relative scarcity of European women made casual sexual relationships almost inevitable. But often they were relatively permanent. Several families in late eighteenth-century Vincennes claimed descent from both European and Indian ancestors.

The origins and early life of Jean-Baptiste Richardville illustrate the racial permutations in the Wabash Valley. Richardville was the principal chief of the Miami from 1813, when his uncle Little Turtle died, until his own death in 1841. By adroitly manipulating provisions of various treaties, Richardville became a very wealthy man; he had some $200,000 in cash, owned several trading posts, and held title to thousands of acres of land at the time of his death. One of the most prominent men in Indiana, he lived in a large brick house on the St. Marys River south of Fort Wayne, a house built expressly for him by the government of the United States.

Richardville was the great-nephew of Antoine Drouet de Richerville. His father, Antoine-Joseph Drouet de Richerville, was the son of one of the Richervilles who was killed with Vincennes *fils* in 1736. Antoine-Joseph spent most of the 1750s and 1760s living and trading at Kekionga. There he met Tecumwah, sister of the chief Little Turtle, with whom he had a child, Jean-Baptiste, in or around 1761. Joseph eventually returned permanently to Quebec, and Tecumwah married a local trader named Charles Beaubien. Apparently Jean-Baptiste spent time with both parents, learning to speak Miami, French, and English and working to overcome a pronounced tendency to diffidence. His mother was a strong-willed woman, never shy about expressing her opinions or engaging in trade, and she encouraged her son to assert himself. Eventually he did.

The Richardville family continued the genetic melding of the French and Indians in Indiana. Jean-Baptiste married a Miami woman called Natoequeah around the beginning of the nineteenth century. One of their daughters, Catherine, became the wife of Richardville's successor as chief of the Miamis, Francis La Fontaine. Their daughter LaBlonde married the son of a Miami chief whose name was James Godfrey. The names alone demonstrate the extent of cultural interaction among Europeans and Indians in eighteenth-century Indiana. The larger point is that the story of Indian-white encounters is not one of a series of bloody fights and progress of white over red. There was violence to be sure, as Jean-Baptiste's grandfather discovered to his terror at the hands of the Chickasaw or as his uncle, Little Turtle, would attempt to turn to the advantage of the Miami in the 1780s and 1790s. But much of the relationship between Native Americans and Europeans was mundane, the routine of unexceptional events that makes up the bulk of human history—trading, talking, eating, sleeping with each other, bearing and raising children.

Still, we can exaggerate the ways in which the various peoples of the Wabash Valley complemented each other economically and socially. The Piankashaw and the French, notwithstanding the multitude of almost daily contacts, never fully trusted each other. Witness St. Ange's instructions upon his departure to preserve order with the natives. While they were both part of the larger commercial and social networks of which Vincennes was the hub, they remained separate communities in terms of their perceptions of the impact of the rest of the world on them.

Many of the Piankashaw had supported the efforts of Memeskia to play the British off against the French in the early 1750s. There were scattered attacks on French men in the Wabash and a fairly sizable migration eastward toward Memeskia's village. St. Ange complained in February 1752 that so many of the Piankashaw "that we have near us . . . have become our enemies" that habitants and traders were preparing to leave his post. The murder of Memeskia and the destruction of his town brought the Piankashaw back to their familiar trading patterns at Vincennes. By the 1760s, there were evidently about 240 Indians living near the post, with another 400 near Ouiatanon; in the early 1770s, the number around Vincennes was approximately 400 and trade was brisk.

The Piankashaw continued to operate on their own, however, as the experience of George Croghan, who arrived at Vincennes as a prisoner in 1765, demonstrated. In effect he dealt with two communities who treated him very differently. The French residents "took a secret Pleasure at our Misfortunes and the moment we arrived they came to the Indians exchanging Trifles for their valuable plunder." The Piankashaw, on the other hand, "were very much displeased with the Party that took me telling them our and your Chiefs are gone to peace and you have begun a War for which our Women and Children will have Reason to Cry." The Piankashaw refused to become involved in the business of Croghan's capture.

So close and yet so far away. For decades the French and the Piankashaw lived next to each other, participating as equals in an ever more complex and symbiotic world of trade and friendship. And yet their interests could never be the same. Even with the surrender of French political power to the British in the aftermath of the Treaty of Paris in 1763, which gave the residents of Vincennes and the Piankashaw a common enemy in the form of a new imperial government, they remained unable to act in tandem. In 1772, the French citizens of Vincennes complained that the "savages" gave "themselves over to all sorts of excesses, and . . . act according to their whims." Simply put, there was a foundation of suspicion, the product of different traditions and interests, which could not be overcome as easily in collective as in individual encounters.

The Economy of Vincennes

The decade and a half following the departure of St. Ange constituted what amounted to a kind of golden age for both Indians and French in Vincennes. Despite their complaints about the lack of a priest and formal government, they prospered. In the absence of external control, the market served to link various peoples together in innumerable ways. In fact, the heterogeneous post of Vincennes was thriving in the 1760s and 1770s, an example of localism triumphant.

Like the residents of the Illinois Country, the citizens on the Wabash oriented themselves toward New Orleans. The prosperity of their settlements rested on their ability to supply food to people on the lower Mississippi. In 1796, a visitor noted that the citizens of Vincennes continued to speak of New Orleans "as if it were a walk of half an hour, though it is fifteen hundred miles down the river."

The French seemed lazy to outsiders because they produced far more food than they needed and simply did not have to work as hard. The land along the rivers was extraordinarily fertile. People spent a few weeks planting and harvesting crops, but most of the year, agriculture required little effort. And the French also devoted little time to domestic manufactures, such as spinning, because they relied heavily on consumer goods purchased in New Orleans. The French traveler Constantin François Chasseboeuf Volney complained in the 1790s that the "women neither sow, nor spin, nor make butter, but pass their time in gossiping and tattle, while all at home is dirt and disorder. The men take to nothing but hunting, fishing, roaming in the woods, and loitering in the sun. They do not lay up, as we do, for winter, or provide for a rainy day. They cannot cure pork or venison, make sour crout or spruce beer, or distil spirits from apples or rye, all needful arts to the farmer."

The point, of course, is that the French in Vincennes were not primarily farmers. The most important economic activity in Vincennes was trade. The leading families in the town were merchants. It was, after all, not coincidental that Françoise Outelas and her daughters married merchants. It was the merchants who attracted the "Strangers," the voyageurs who brought furs, peltries, and goods to trade, who dealt with the Miami and other Indians interested in exchanging goods, who communicated with and traveled to Detroit, Kaskaskia, and New Orleans. Vincennes was a long way from the Atlantic Ocean, but in the middle of the eighteenth century its leading citizens were integral and successful participants in the market economy of the North Atlantic world. It may have seem isolated and desultory to visitors, but it was the hub of a great deal of economic activity. One would only rarely find the kind of intensive labor one would expect in a premodern agricultural community, because that was not the primary economic activity. Father Gibault reported in 1770 that while only eighty people devoted themselves to farming, "there are many people of all trades, numbers of young men who are daily establishing themselves here."

The Wabash, the main artery of life in Indiana, dominated the physical environment surrounding Vincennes. It was, according to the American geographer Thomas Hutchins in 1778, a "gentle" river and the contiguous land was "remarkably fertile." Vincennes sat on the east bank of the river at a point that was 200 feet wide, some eighty miles north of where it flowed into the Ohio. From the edge of the Wabash, the land rose to a height of approximately twenty feet, and there some fifty scattered houses stood. Beyond Vincennes was what Volney called "an irregular savannah," somewhat lower than the village, stretching for eight miles along the river and about three miles away from it.

If the French in Vincennes were like the French in Illinois—and there is every reason to believe that they were—the habitants owned lots of at least half an acre as well as strips of land, running two arpents in width by fifty in depth (a legal total of about eighty-four acres), in the common fields along the river. In Vincennes as elsewhere, the French did not live on isolated farms. Because of the importance of access to the river and the need for protection, they congregated in town. There they lived in small whitewashed houses—Volney called it "a cheerful white . . . after the tedious dusk and green of the woods"—made of rows of parallel upright logs interspersed with stone and mortar and topped with steep shingled roofs. Typically the lots also held barns, stables, orchards, and gardens.

In the fields around Vincennes, the French cultivated a wide variety of crops. Volney reported finding corn, tobacco, wheat, barley, squashes, and cotton. Hutchins particularly praised the quality of the tobacco and noted the presence of hemp, grapes, and fruits ranging from apples and peaches to melons and gooseberries. The French also had livestock, including horses and cattle. The 1767 census listed 352 oxen, 588 cows, 260 horses, and 295 hogs in the vicinity.

By the time Volney arrived in 1796, the French seemed indigent and emaciated, reduced to living off the products of their gardens. But between the 1760s and the 1780s, they lived well. The trade with the Illinois settlements and New Orleans was profitable. Apparently they sold foodstuffs and processed grains into flour and beer and fruits and grapes into brandies and wines at the three local mills operating near the village. In 1767, there were an estimated 5,450 bushels of corn and 5,420 bushels of Indian corn "to be reaped," as well as 36,360 pounds of tobacco in the fields.

Still, the bulk of their exports was furs and deerskins. Hutchins estimated the annual value of that trade at about 5,000 pounds sterling. The French acquired the furs and peltries largely from the hundreds of Piankashaw who lived in and around Vincennes. They paid for them with the rum, wine, brandy, salt, and manufactured goods (such as blankets, iron utensils, and knives) that they traded for in Louisiana. The Piankashaw and other Indians got many of the furs and peltries from tribes as far west as the Great Plains. As had long been the case, Vincennes was simply a part of a great international marketplace that stretched from the upper Mississippi Valley and the Great Lakes through Louisiana and into western Europe.

At the center of the European side of the trade was a network of people, several of whom were related to the Richerville-Outelas family. In the 1780s, they included Colonel Francis Vigo, a Spanish soldier whose commerce made him well-known throughout the Mississippi and Wabash valleys; another Spaniard, Laurient Bazadon; and the French house of Lasselle. Also prominent was the son-in-law of Drouet de Richerville and Françoise Outelas, Francis Bosseron.

Bosseron in the late 1770s held what amounted to the position of mayor of Vincennes as well as owning a store and a large trading company. He was the son of Charles Bosseron, one of two brothers who had run a profitable trading business out of Kaskaskia for years. He had been born in 1748, probably in the Mississippi settlement. In 1761, Charles had traveled to New Orleans and then to Vincennes as part of a concerted effort to expand the operations of the fraternal partnership. Francis followed his father and was soon heavily involved in the family business. Since Charles was illiterate, Francis wrote most of the surviving documents from the 1760s.

When the father died in 1774, the twenty-six-year-old son assumed control of a business he knew extremely well. As we have seen, he soon married Françoise Richerville and became guardian of her siblings. With a wife, he also acquired a dowry of some value. Among the things Françoise brought to her new household were a dozen hens, a set of porridge bowls made of blue faience, a full bed, a table, a cloth, and half-interest in a slave. Bosseron's neighbors validated his importance by naming him their chief local official.

His business thrived. As a merchant, he traded with Indians and voyageurs for furs and peltries, which he exchanged in Louisiana for manufactured goods. Bosseron bartered most of these goods to the Piankashaw. He also operated as a general storekeeper. The residents of Vincennes could find all kinds of interesting items at Bosseron's—necessities such as gunpowder, rifles, iron, lead, cloth, shoes, knives; foodstuffs such as beef, flour, and pork; and luxuries, including rum, fine hats, silk stockings, ribbons, handkerchiefs, china, even sugar and Chinese tea. The ready availability of these goods suggests the great degree to which the merchants of Vincennes participated in the larger trading network of the Mississippi valley. It also reveals something about the standard of living among the French notables and their neighbors.

In addition, Bosseron functioned as a source of credit. There were no banks in Vincennes; indeed, apparently there was very little or no money (in the form of specie). Most business was conducted on the basis of barter, not simply goods for goods but sometimes labor for goods. Long-distance transactions frequently involved personal bills of exchange or simple promises to pay from men in Detroit, Kaskaskia, and New Orleans whom Bosseron knew or with whom he traded frequently. In any case, the stores of men such as Bosseron allowed people to buy goods with lines of credit established by depositing furs and crops in them. The economy functioned relatively smoothly without money. Bosseron's account books were as much records of informal loans and deposits as they were of purchases and sales.

In large part, Vincennes prospered in the 1760s and 1770s because its citizens were left to their own devices. Whether French or Piankashaw, they managed their involvement in the world of long-distance market capitalism to their own advantage. Years later, the

French idealized these decades when, "unmolested and sequestered in the heart of the wilderness . . . they passed their lives in hunting, fishing, trading in furs, and raising a few esculents and a little corn for their families." No doubt the harshness of their lives in the 1790s improved their memories of the past. But, like many other peoples in North America, they valued local autonomy and the right to maintain their own households and manage their own destinies.

What upset Britons and Americans about the French was that they violated so many of their assumptions about society. Gender relationships seemed out of kilter. Men did not work industriously in fields; many pursued gentlemanly pursuits such as hunting and fishing. Women also seemed to have stepped out of normal roles: they did not spend much time spinning and sewing; they directly managed the economic affairs of their households in the absence of their spouses. The French seemed promiscuous, in more ways than one, in their intercourse with the Indians. They did not value individual property correctly, in the eyes of the British; they demonstrated little interest in transforming the landscape of the Wabash Valley into supposedly higher stages of agricultural development.

When petitioning the government of the United States to confirm their land holdings in 1787, the French at Vincennes ritually confessed what others saw as their sins: "[B]eing chiefly addicted to the Indian trade, [we], in great measure, overlooked the advantages that can be derived from the cultivation of lands, and consequently neglected" to secure title to them. "Contented to raise bread for our families, we neither extended our culture for the purpose of exportation, nor formed an idea of dividing among ourselves our fruitful." In fact, they declared in a sentence that can be taken several ways, it was only "when we were connected with the United States, [that] we began to be sensible of the real value of lands." Thus the French did more than admit their failings; they pointed out the differences between the attitudes of the Americans and themselves toward the development of the Wabash. As residents of a key outpost in the long-distance fur trade, they had had no need to worry about land until the arrival of the Americans.

The Origins of Rebellion

For decades the French and the Piankashaw had maneuvered, each in their own ways, to preserve and protect their way of life from outside interference. They looked upon imperial governments, whether in France or Great Britain, as potential benefactors. In return for maintaining the valuable fur trade and holding the land, they expected protection and occasional assistance. They wanted outside authorities to confirm and defend their culture, not to disrupt it or to attempt to transform it.

Such was clearly the case in their dealings with the Roman Catholic Church. The French wanted a priest to perform the sacraments, not to bring civilization and order. They needed someone to baptize their children, to grant extreme unction to the dying, to marry them. For several decades they had a priest in residence with them. The records of the church of St. Francis Xavier date from April 21, 1749. Officiating at the first wedding was Father Sebastian Louis Meurin, a member of the Society of Jesus. Three other priests followed Meurin, until the Jesuits were expelled from the Louisiana colony and ordered back to France in the fall of 1763. Meurin expressed deep regret at the abandonment of Vincennes by the Roman church. "Disorder," he wrote to the bishop of Quebec, "has always been great there," but it had increased greatly in recent years.

For Meurin, disorder seems to have meant ignoring the rites of the church. Lamenting that the "majority" of people "do not wish nor can they" go to Kaskaskia, the people of Vincennes were improvising. When they wanted to be married, the bans were published for three Sundays. A few then traveled to the Mississippi to seek a priest. The rest declared "in a loud voice their mutual consent." Meurin had serious reservations about the regularity of such a ritual and sought the advice of his superior. Still, his letter demonstrates the commitment of the French in Vincennes to maintaining the forms of the culture, even if they were not sanctioned by legitimate authority. The disorder lay less in the failings of the citizens of Vincennes than in the inability of the Roman church to provide them with a priest.

When Father Pierre Gibault paid Vincennes his visit in 1770, one of the most frequent complaints was "Ah, Sir, why did you not come a month ago, then my poor wife, my dear father, my loved mother, my poor child would not have died without the sacraments." Gibault returned to perform such duties in 1771 and 1773 and finally took up residence in 1785. He concentrated on the young people, teaching them catechism and showing boys how to serve mass. Despite the endless complaints of the priests about the lack of religion and libertine behavior, the people of Vincennes always welcomed them to their town and tried to convince them to stay by rebuilding churches and offering them hospitality. In short, what was lacking in Vincennes was sanctioned religious authority, not the desire for it. Most of the French were practicing Catholics and they needed a priest to ensure the salvation of their children, not to mention themselves.

Similarly, the core community in Vincennes demonstrated no great desire to evade the authority of the British government in the 1760s and 1770s. What the people wanted was the same thing they had required of the French but never received—a much greater financial and military commitment to their village. After the departure of St. Ange in 1764, the British essentially left the people of Vincennes alone. They stationed no officials or soldiers there; that would have been too expensive and troublesome. Lieutenant-General Thomas Gage, the British commander in chief in North America, explained in August 1770 that there was no advantage to encouraging settlements in the Wabash and Mississippi valleys, "for the Country can produce Nothing that will enable the Inhabitants to Make Returns for the Manufactures carried to them, except Skins and Furrs; And they will naturaly decrease as the People increase." At the moment, the French seemed disposed to accept British authority, so there was nothing to be engaged by forcing the issue. Besides, Gage and other officials of the Crown were somewhat preoccupied with disorder in their seaboard colonies.

Gage, moreover, had a profound understanding of the history of the French in North America. In an extraordinary letter to Hillsborough, dated November 10, 1770, the general gave a cogent overview of the British dilemma. The French, he wrote, had established forts and settlements in the interior to secure "a Communication" between Canada and Louisiana and had labored to win "the Affections of the Savages." Their goals were to monopolize the Indian trade and "when convenient, [to] excite the Indians to make Incursions on the British Provinces." Because the French sent few men into the region and assimilated much of their culture, they "became almost one People with them. By these means the French Succeeded, and at a small Expence."

Gage followed this succinct and generally accurate history with the observation that the British required "other Systems." Their interests were not the same as those of the French. They needed to protect their trade, awe the Indians and keep them away from the French, "and where Settlements are made," to hold "the Settlers in Subordination to Government." Gage thought forts might have some value in exerting authority over the French. But he seriously doubted they would accomplish anything else. The general, writing in line with overall British thinking on the subject, preferred to see settlers confined to the east of the Appalachians, leaving "the Savages [to] enjoy their Desarts in quiet." Only in this way could the British government effectively control its subjects and develop the interior of the North American continent in an orderly fashion.

In the early 1770s, the British finally moved against the French on the Wabash. Disturbed by reports that the French were encouraging violence against British traders in the Wabash and Mississippi valleys and eager to assert Crown authority somewhere in North America, Gage took action against what he called a "Nest of Villains" at Vincennes. The French town was experiencing "Surprizing" growth and loomed as a threat to British interests in the region.

In the summer of 1772, Captain Hugh Lord, commander at Kaskaskia, arrived in Vincennes with a proclamation dated April 8, 1772, and signed by Gage ordering the town's residents to get out. It stated that because "a great number of persons have established themselves, particularly on the river Ouabache, where they lead a wandering life, without government, and without laws, interrupting the free course of trade, destroying the game, and causing infinite disturbance in the country, which occasions a considerable injury to the affairs of the King, as well as to those of the Indians," King George III was "pleased to order . . . all who have established themselves on the lands upon the Ouabache . . . to quit those countries instantly and without delay, and to retire, at their choice, into some one of the colonies of His Majesty, where they will be received and treated as the other subjects of His Majesty."

Gage explicitly recognized the importance of the Piankashaw by sending a separate letter to them explaining the reasons for this sudden action. They did not receive it, however, because the principal chiefs were away on a hunt. Still, Old Tobacco and his son, the leaders of the Piankashaw near Vincennes, could not have been pleased at the news. For the departure of the French would entail a substantial reorganization of their lives.

The proclamation predictably incensed the citizens of Vincennes. Its reception was similar to that given by the residents of Boston to the Stamp Act. In both cases, relatively prosperous and free peoples responded angrily to the efforts of the imperial government to re-structure their lives. The French had nothing to gain by moving to another British colony. They were not the same as the king's other subjects. Their circumstances were very different. Why should they abandon a growing and relatively prosperous settlement in response to what appeared to be the whimsical orders of an ignorant imperial officer? The French replied respectfully that they were willing to give "proof of our fidelity and of our obedience" to the king; still, they thought him "not acquainted with the titles of concession which we have to these lands." In September, they addressed an-other memorial to Gage. Again they expressed a desire to obey legal authority, but they devoted the bulk of the letter to insisting that they were not "vagabonds." Rather, they were "settlers" with wives and children. To leave Vincennes "would indeed cause us to deserve the title of vagabonds." They suggested firmly that the king be in-formed of their situation, with the assurance that they "shall always be ready to sacrifice our lives and our property whenever his service shall in reality require it." The key words in the sentence are "in re-ality." Clearly the residents of Vincennes were determined to decide for themselves when their king needed their obedience.

A longer memorial, dated September 18, 1772, was even more de-fiant. In language that echoed the rhetoric of British Americans on the Atlantic coast, the French appealed to basic principles of justice. Arguing that they owned land granted to them by St. Ange, acting as the agent of the king of France, they suggested that Gage's proclamation threatened the sanctity of property. The French also angrily rejected the charge that they lived without laws or government. To the contrary, they wanted government to protect their trade and to "restrain" and "guide" the Indians. "Let troops be sent to us. You will see everything returning to order—trade reviving, and ourselves becoming useful men." For years they had "fruitlessly desired" a military garrison at their town. In other words, if there was no legitimate government at Vincennes, exactly whose fault was it? Who was responsible for "the state of neglect"? The French blamed it on His Majesty's government. After all, "it is a father who makes them [laws and government] to children incapable of taking care of themselves; it is duty to provide for them."

Gage responded to these protests by asking for verification of their land claims. St. Ange and other officials wrote in support of the settlers and they prepared a list of landholders. But by the time it was completed, Gage's attention was focused squarely on disorder in the colony of Massachusetts. So too was that of the British government. On June 2, 1774, rather than forcing the issue in the midst of widespread disobedience, Parliament passed the Quebec Act, which assimilated the French settlements along the Wabash and Mississippi into the province of Canada and assured the people of Vincennes of their rights to practice the Catholic religion and to exercise their customs.

For three years the British left the French in the west alone while they attempted to deal with violent resistance and then overt rebellion from Georgia to New Hampshire. The Quebec Act had smoothed some of the ruffled feathers in the Wabash Valley. But neither the French nor the Piankashaw had much to gain from their connection with the British. His Majesty's government had demonstrated only a desire to control them, not a commitment to nurture them. And when the British finally sent an official to take up residence in Vincennes, his mission was to protect their interests in the region from possible attacks by Anglo-Americans. Shortly the British failure to see the Wabash as anything more than a nuisance or a very minor part of a very large puzzle would cost them their tenuous hold over the region.

The Englishman who arrived in Vincennes on May 19, 1777, was Lieutenant Governor Edward Abbott. Trained in the late 1750s at the Royal Military Academy in Woolwich, Abbott had served extensively in the Great Lakes region between 1762 and 1773. There he had married Angelica Desrivieres; together they had two sons. In 1773, Abbott and his family went to London, where he successfully lobbied for the lieutenant-governorship at Vincennes created by the Quebec Act of 1774.

After returning to Detroit, Abbott, his wife, and sons traveled in time-honored fashion down the Maumee-Wabash waterway, escorted by several Indians, including three Piankashaw chiefs. At Miamitown he encountered twenty-five residents of Vincennes and thirty-six Indians who had come to take him to the town on the lower Wabash.

There was little overt hostility, but there was an abundance of tension. British officials sent no troops with him, so the lieutenant-governor spent a small fortune in gifts designed to win the loyalty of the Indians. He had help from Jean-Baptiste Celeron and Charles Beaubien, the British agents at Ouiatanon and Miamitown.

Abbott's arrival in Vincennes was clearly a major event. The greetings were more than signs of hospitality; they were demonstrations of respect and good will. The reservoir of good will was not particularly deep, however. Abbott acted as a representative of a government that had committed itself to encouraging the Indians of the Wabash region to attack Anglo-American settlements in the Ohio Valley. But the Miami, the Piankashaw, and others were not inclined to go along with such a policy. They gained little from a British connection except disruption of their existing world—their economic exchanges with the French and their intermittent wars with the Chickasaw and Cherokee south of the Ohio River.

Once at Vincennes, Abbott set about organizing three companies of militia (fifty men each) among the apparently accommodating French. But the lieutenant-governor never felt secure in the village. Frightened by the hundreds of Indians who moved through the town, Abbott constantly sought troops and cannon to enhance his position. He got nothing from his superiors in return for his efforts. He and his family abandoned Vincennes in February 1778, and upon arriving in Detroit, he resigned his position. Obviously unsuited for his job, lacking both the zeal and the courage of the Sieur de Vincennes, Abbott essentially deserted his post because he feared that he would not have enough supplies to keep the Indians happy. He was also under fire from his superiors for spending too much money.

Abbott criticized British policy for being so cheap and for depending upon inciting the Indians against the Americans. The practice of economy on one hand and the encouragement of violence on the other may have seemed reasonable in London or Detroit, but it left the people of Vincennes thinking themselves "cast off from His Majesty's protection." In fact, Abbott recommended that the British encourage the Indians of the Wabash Valley to be neutral in the spreading conflict with the United States. They would then avoid alienating Europeans in the region and save money.

Abbott's advice had no impact on British policy, which continued to depend heavily on Indians as surrogate warriors. The nervous lieutenant-governor did leave one substantial legacy in the Wabash village, however—a fort on the banks of the river, named Fort Sackville after Lord George Sackville (later Lord George Germain), approximately two hundred feet square. But Fort Sackville was the sum total of the British contribution to the worlds of the French and Piankashaw in and around Vincennes.

A decade and a half of Crown control had given these peoples every reason to be disgusted with the British. His Majesty's government had attempted to take their land, remove them from the Wabash, and reorganize the fur trade; his officials had insulted and denounced the habitants of the Wabash and appeared to be inciting the Indians against them. To be sure, the Quebec Act was a positive act from the French perspective. But it did not have the immediate, direct impact of Gage's 1772 proclamation. Some of the French and the Indians, of course, remained loyal to the British Crown, particularly those on the upper Wabash, at Miamis Town and Ouiatanon, who depended on trade with Detroit. The majority of the French and Piankashaw on the lower Wabash, where the orientation was more toward the Mississippi settlements and New Orleans than Detroit and Canada, found little reason to prize their connection with the French.

Thus we should not be surprised to learn that most Vincennes residents were very pleased when news arrived in July 1778, via Father Gibault and others, of the fall of Kaskaskia and Cahokia on the Mississippi River to fewer than 200 men under the command of

George Rogers Clark, an officer in the service of the commonwealth of Virginia. Indeed, they were eager to cooperate with the Americans. Historians have argued about whether Father Gibault was responsible for the easy conquest of Vincennes by the Virginians later that summer. Gibault always denied it. Given the experiences of the French with the British in the 1770s, however, there is little reason to suggest that they had to be coaxed into abandoning His Majesty's government and swearing fidelity to Virginia. For, cultural differences notwithstanding, the people of Vincennes had much in common with rebels in eastern North America. What most of them wanted, at least initially, was to be left alone to pursue their lives in their own ways and on their own terms; all resented the intrusions of an inconsistent and unsympathetic imperial government. As in the east, those people with direct ties to the British often remained loyal. But the people of Vincennes had no reason to continue their connection with the Crown. Why not ally themselves with the Anglo-Americans, who seemed less of an immediate threat and who also despised the efforts of imperial officials to control and regulate their lives?

So, as Randolph Downes pointed out decades ago, George Rogers Clark did not take Vincennes from the British (although he did have to capture Fort Sackville with the assistance of the townspeople and the Indians in 1779). Rather, the French and the Piankashaw chose to join with the Americans. Neither the town nor the peoples were pawns in a larger strategic contest. The core of traders and their households, people who lived comfortably and who participated in extensive economic and social networks, decided their own fates. Had the French and the Piankashaw thrown their support to the British, Clark would have had a much more difficult time of it in the Old Northwest. But they did not, for reasons that grew out of a defense of their interests and their world, reasons that had less to do with fear of the Americans than a sophisticated and rational assessment of their peculiar situation. When the British tried to retake Vincennes, the French helped the Virginians defeat them.

The world the French and Piankashaw had known before 1777 faded into nostalgia as they adjusted to the new world of the Americans. As we have seen, the citizens of Vincennes noted in a 1787 memorial to the Congress of the United States that they had only become "sensible of the real value of lands" with the arrival of the Americans. They were right in more ways than they fully understood in 1787 and certainly more than they knew in 1777. For the Virginians and the government of the United States would destroy the world of the French and the Piankashaw far more effectively than the British government contemplated in the early 1770s. To a significant degree, the 1760s would seem so good in retrospect because the 1780s were so bad.

4.

THE WORLD OF GEORGE ROGERS CLARK, 1778–1787

Late in the evening of the 23rd of February, 1779, Lieutenant-Governor Henry Hamilton, commander of His Majesty's troops at Vincennes, was playing cards with his prisoner, Captain Leonard Helm of the commonwealth of Virginia, within the walls of the recently reoccupied Fort Sackville. The time was nearing midnight and the moon was about to set over the Wabash. Occasionally Hamilton and Helm heard what sounded like sporadic gunfire in the distance. The noise did not alarm them, for the French and Piankashaw often fired weapons at odd hours.

Suddenly the unmistakable sound of a coordinated volley rang out; a bullet shot through a portal and wounded a British soldier. Startled by the noise, Hamilton rushed from the game and called his few dozen men to arms. Looking out into the night beyond the walls of the fort, the anxious officer sought the identity of his opponents. Soon enough he would learn what he had assumed was impossible. Under the command of Lieutenant-Colonel George Rogers Clark, who had conquered the French settlements on the Mississippi for Virginia in 1778, 130 men had marched some 180 miles overland in the dead of winter, slogging through cold rains and marshy prairies, from Kaskaskia on the Mississippi River to claim Vincennes for Virginia.

🪓 71

THE
WORLD
OF
GEORGE
ROGERS
CLARK,
1778–1787

Colonel Clark's army was a coalition of allies united by the common goal of evicting the tyrannical and inconstant British. About half of the 130 men were Virginians and Pennsylvanians; the other half consisted of French volunteers, who had been blessed by Father Pierre Gibault in Kaskaskia. Clark would soon receive more help from both the French and the Algonquian residents of the Wabash. When the colonel approached Vincennes on the morning of February 23, he wrote a letter to the French habitants warning them of his attack. Clark "request[ed] of such of you as are true citizens and willing to enjoy the liberty I bring you to remain in your houses." Loyalists were to seek refuge in the fort. None did.

Then, recorded Major Joseph Bowman, at dusk Clark's little army "all in order with colors flying and drums brased . . . mounted the rising ground" on which sat Vincennes and Fort Sackville. Believing himself outnumbered, the colonel was determined "to appear as Darring as possible." The Virginians and the French surrounded Fort Sackville and commenced the firing that eventually got Hamilton's attention. Young Tobacco, a chief of the Piankashaw, offered Clark the services of the 100 warriors in Vincennes. Clark refused, pleading the dangers of confusion in the dark. The chief agreed and "sent off his Troops," although he remained with Clark "giving all the Information he could." In the morning, many of the habitants of Vincennes joined "the Troops & Behaved exceedingly well in General." Together the French, the Virginians, and the noncombatant but approving Piankashaw forced the British to surrender. Since the allies suffered no wounded, compared with seven for their enemy, the bombardment was, in the words of Bowman, "fine Sport for the sons of Liberty."

Bowman was not exaggerating. They were all sons of liberty in the sense that they believed themselves to have been abused by their fathers, the British. The grievances of the Piankashaw, the French, and the Virginians differed in their particulars, but they had in common a desire to protect and extend their way of life from what they perceived as British treachery. During the day of the 24th, Clark seized an opportunity to demonstrate graphically the failure of the British to behave paternally in terms that no Algonquian or habitant could mistake.

A small party of pro-British Indians, returning from a raid on Virginia settlements south of the Ohio River, blundered unawares into Vincennes in the middle of the battle for Fort Sackville. Clark's men captured six of them, "two of them Scalped and the rest so wounded as we afterwards learnt, but one Lived." The colonel granted them no mercy; in his own words, he "Ordered the Prisoners to be Tomahawked in the face of the Garrison." His men obeyed. All but one of the prisoners, who was saved by the defiance of his father, a French lieutenant from Kaskaskia, were brutally and mercilessly killed. The British officers, particularly Hamilton, later offered this incident as proof of Clark's lack of control. None witnessed the events, but they claimed that he had killed the Indians himself. One wrote that "in cold blood [Clark] knocked their brains out, dipping his hands in their blood, rubbing it several times on his cheeks, yelping as a Savage. . . ."

Certainly George Rogers Clark was capable of such behavior. He was always a passionate man. But there was method to his madness. For, in essence, his actions ritually announced to the Indians and the French the transfer of power in the Wabash Valley. Clark explained in a letter to George Mason in November 1779 that he saw the capture of the Indians as "a fair oppertunity of making an impression on the Indians that I could have wished for; that of convincing them that Governour Hamilton could not give them the protection that he had made them to believe he could. in some measure to insence the Indians against him for not exerting himself to save their Friends." The tactic worked: "insted of making their friends inviterate against us, they upbraided the English Parties in not trying to save their friends and gave them to understand that they believed them to be liers and no Warriors."

The key to European influence in the Wabash Valley had always been the ability to maintain the illusion of power, whether as manitous, embodying some supernatural force, or as mediators, suppliers, and protectors. Now Clark shattered the illusion, completely humiliating Hamilton and, by extension, His Majesty's government. Not only did the Virginian force the lieutenant-governor to surrender his post; he demonstrated the British officer's impotency, his stark inability to protect his children, his lack of power. No doubt the witnesses to the murders of the prisoners were appalled by their

73

THE
WORLD
OF
GEORGE
ROGERS
CLARK,
1778–1787

suddenness and their brutality. But where we can see only savagery and murder, they, who grew up in the culture of the Great Lakes, also saw a ritual castration of an inconstant father.

Such a fate was particularly tough for Henry Hamilton. The scion of minor Irish gentry, the officer was about forty-four years old in 1779. He had been in the military for over twenty years, progressing through a series of administrative assignments in Canada, Bermuda, and the West Indies before attaining the post of lieutenant-governor at Detroit in 1775. There Hamilton was the principal British officer in charge of dealing with the Indians of the Old Northwest. As Bernard Sheehan has shown, Hamilton was exceedingly interested in the American Indian; he painted them and romanticized their history and cultures. But his assignment from 1775 was to encourage the Indians to attack and harass American settlements in the Ohio Valley.

Hamilton quickly mastered the role of patriarch. He showered gifts on important Indians and participated in ceremonial exchanges of friendship as well as dances and songs. While he believed that Indians had a "natural propensity . . . for blood," he followed his orders by rewarding them for attacks on American settlements. The worst blow to his historical reputation came from the fact that he accepted dozens of scalps from returning Indians—so many that he was nicknamed the "Hair-Buyer." Horrible as this sounds, Hamilton could not very well have refused the gifts of the scalps and expected to maintain a decent relationship with his allies. Similarly, on his trip from Detroit to Vincennes in the fall of 1778, the reluctant British officer acted the expected role of father by accepting and smoking pipes, exchanging war belts, feasting, and participating in songs and dances. When Hamilton arrived in Vincennes in December 1778, he had acquired a powerful reputation. Apparently this was a man with whom to contend, a man of power and influence, this "Hair-Buyer"; he was very different from his predecessor, Abbott.

In the end, however, Hamilton lost everything to Clark. Like the Virginian, the British officer depended on French militia (from Detroit) and Indian allies for the bulk of his troops. He commanded three officers and thirty British regulars. But most of his 100 French militiamen and seventy Indians deserted him shortly after their arrival in Vincennes. Despite Hamilton's observance of the rituals of exchange, his efforts to act as a father, he could not command more than the temporary allegiance of most of the French and Indians. He could not, alone, reverse the current of a decade of British negligence and incompetence in the Wabash Valley. The Wea, the Piankashaw, the Kickapoo, and the French villagers had no reason to welcome him, given recent experience with the British, and they tolerated him only until the arrival of Clark's army consolidated opposition to him. Within twenty-four hours after hearing the first shots, Hamilton, bereft of allies and power, surrendered his command. The Virginians took him, his officers, and a couple of prominent French allies to Williamsburg, where they were thrown into the common jail and kept in heavy irons—a punishment endorsed by the new governor, Thomas Jefferson—until the last of them were paroled in October 1780.

Clark's victory and ritual exposure of Hamilton did not do many of the things historians have claimed for them. They did not change the course of the American War for Independence or secure Indiana for Virginia or, most important, achieve their primary goal of stopping Indian raids below the Ohio River. If the surrender of Fort Sackville was not a decisive event militarily or diplomatically, however, it is also true that things were never quite the same along the Wabash after the Union Jack came down the flagstaff on the 24th of February, 1779.

Europeans and Indians had been living together in Indiana for at least three generations. They had fashioned a world of their own, negotiating relationships within the borders of their own particular cultural imperatives. Their relationships with governments and peoples beyond the Wabash had long been ambiguous at best. The French and the Miami, Wea, and Piankashaw looked to European governments and those of their colonies for protection, mediation, and access to distant markets. Before the 1760s, they had been able to maintain a high degree of local autonomy by playing rival Europeans and their governments off against each other. Just as important, they had made the Wabash Valley their territory. While there was plenty of violence in the area, some of it brought by distant peoples such as the Chickasaws, it had never been a full-fledged battleground. Vincennes had died in what is now Missis-

☙ 75

THE
WORLD
OF
GEORGE
ROGERS
CLARK,
1778–1787

sippi, Memeskia in Ohio, and the British had barely bothered to occupy the region drained by the Wabash and its tributaries.

The arrival of Clark and his men changed all of that. It inaugurated a period of intermittent but systematic war among the Algonquians, the British, and various Americans in the Wabash Valley which would last for almost half a century. At issue were fundamental questions about the nature of economic structures and the control of trade and territory. Also at stake was the very nature of human relationships, how people should deal with each other, with the land, and with the world in which they lived. The Virginians consciously disrupted the commercial nature of economic structures, the patriarchal nature of political culture, and the multicultural societies along the Wabash; in their place, they advocated agricultural development, a brotherhood of citizens, men who were no longer dependent on fathers for anything, and a strong confidence in the righteousness of Anglo-American ways of doing things. In so doing, they brought a revolution to Indiana. Eventually people like them would decisively transform the natural and human landscape of the region. That would take time as well as greater patience and planning than George Rogers Clark could muster. Clark and his men were an advance guard; they could breach a gap, they could take a fort with little more than bluff and bravado. But they were ill-equipped by temperament to hold, let alone consolidate, their position once they had achieved their immediate goal.

George Rogers Clark and the Virginians

Born on November 19, 1752, about two miles east of Charlottesville in Albemarle County, Virginia, George Rogers Clark was the product of a society as distinctive as those which had produced Vincennes, Memeskia, and Croghan. Six feet tall, with red hair, a strong build, and dancing black eyes, he swaggered through his life like a rebellious adolescent—proud, passionate, energetic, temperamental. His virtues—courage, decisiveness, charm—were also his flaws. Like many other young white males in eighteenth-century Virginia, Clark was accustomed to getting what he wanted or knowing the reason why. He sought immediate gratification in virtually everything; not for him a life of patience and accommodation. Confident and self-assured, he had a natural instinct for command and a desire to control everyone and everything around him. What interested him were personal independence and mastery of his universe—now. The famed march across the Illinois Country in the dead of winter was exactly what we should expect from Clark; it was rash, risky, impetuous, and defiant. The man played his life like a game of chance, with victory going to the boldest. When he won, he was strong and decisive. When he failed, he was silly and pathetic.

Such a man was clearly an eighteenth-century Virginian. A quarter-century before Clark's arrival in Vincennes, the Anglican minister Andrew Burnaby characterized Virginians as "indolent, easy, and good natured" men whose "authority over their slaves renders them vain and imperious. . . . They are haughty and jealous of their liberties, impatient of restraint, and can scarcely bear the thought of being controuled by any superior power. . . ." No less an authority than Thomas Jefferson agreed. As he wrote to the Marquis de Chastellux in September 1785, southerners were "fiery, voluptuary, indolent, unsteady, independant, zealous for their liberties, but trampling on those of others," habits he ascribed to the influence of a warm climate.

Perhaps weather played a role in producing impulsive men like Clark, but there were other reasons as well, reasons that lay in the foundations of Virginia society. The Chesapeake region had attracted mainly young and unattached immigrants in the seventeenth century. Working as indentured servants or small farmers, they focused their attention on the production of the dominant crop, tobacco. They lived in a deadly world, where disease killed large numbers of people at a young age. Consequently the structures of family and community were never quite as strong in Virginia as they were in New England. In the 1600s, life for Virginians was generally short and brutish, and they compensated by demanding satisfaction from it at every possible point. There were few incentives to restrain oneself, to practice discipline, or to delay gratification. The introduction of black slavery on a large scale in the last third of the seventeenth century did little to improve matters in this regard. The role of master, or would-be master, only reinforced the tendency to self-indulgence. By the mid-1700s, gentry parents were deeply con-

77

THE
WORLD
OF
GEORGE
ROGERS
CLARK,
1778–1787

cerned about the perpetuation of such traits in their sons. They worried that the obsession with immediate gratification, the lack of mastery over emotions and impulses, would destroy the delicate social and political structures of the colony.

For those depended upon the leadership of a few disinterested men. Virginia was an aristocratic and patriarchal society, largely ignored by the British Crown in the first half of the eighteenth century. Its governors were men of property and influence. A small group of planters and lawyers held and exercised power through the central institutions of life. On the local level, they dominated the county court, serving as powerful justices of the peace and adjudicating much of the business of their neighbors. These men, in turn, served in the House of Burgesses or on the Governor's Council and managed the affairs of the colony as a whole. Other people, whether white or black, looked upon these gentlemen as "great men" to whom they owed obedience and deference. The tangible symbols of their power were their homes, their carriages, their land, their dress and wigs.

But above all was their style, their way of behaving and carrying themselves. A gentleman acted the part. He rode his horse well. He demonstrated his prowess as a farmer in the quality of his tobacco. He attempted to master himself and his emotions. For what earned the "great men" of Virginia deference was their reputation, meaning the public appraisal of their behavior. Truly great men mastered themselves; that is, they controlled their emotions, they masked their feelings, they participated in life as a series of dancelike rituals. More than this, they had to appear to be disinterested, to be above petty interests and conflicts. The most famous eighteenth-century Virginian, George Washington, achieved social eminence less because of specific achievements than because of the way he handled himself. Not only did he ride a horse better than any man alive, he was the very model of decorum.

Washington achieved fame precisely because his accomplishment was so great, the obstacles so difficult. Virginia's political culture required white males who mastered themselves, but its society nurtured men who thrived on demonstrating their importance to others. They took risks, they gambled, they fought; they were impetuous and headstrong. They were accustomed to leading and to bending other people and other things to their wills. They needed to behave like wise fathers when, by inclination, they acted like defiant sons.

George Rogers Clark was the son of lesser gentry. When he was five, his father sold the farm on which he was born and moved to a small plantation in southwest Caroline County. There they became part of a network of relatives and friends, at least one of whom, George Mason, would play an influential role in George's career. John and Ann Rogers Clark were devout Episcopalians who instilled a profound respect for God in their children. Their son's education was minimal, although he apparently liked to study history and geography and was fascinated by natural phenomena. Undoubtedly more important were the social and physical aspects of his life. Judging by the diary entries of his older brother, Jonathan, the Clark children spent a great deal of time in the rituals of planter society. Visiting was a major pastime. They partied, danced, attended barbecues, weddings, funerals, court proceedings, and participated in cockfights, deerhunts, and other competitions. As a teenager, George Rogers Clark became adept at managing crops and picked up the skills of a surveyor from his grandfather.

In many ways, Clark's youth was typical of the lives of Virginia's rough gentlemen. He learned how to be gregarious and charming, but he learned very little about self-control and dealing with disappointment. He had neither Jefferson's mastery of ideas nor Washington's mastery of style. Like many other young white men in late eighteenth-century Virginia, Clark remained impetuous and bold. If he lacked the polish of a true aristocrat, he possessed in abundance the confidence of a Virginia gentleman.

Many members of the gentry would find discipline and restraint in the demands of political life or evangelical religion. But others did not, abandoning what they perceived to be the increasingly crowded and clotted world of the Virginia piedmont for the land and promises of the Ohio Valley. The Ohio Company and other speculative ventures of the 1740s and 1750s pointed the way to the west. There was a place in which the restless energies of men such as Clark could find meaning and reward. In June 1772, he and some companions traveled to Pittsburgh and then down the Ohio River to the mouth of Kanawha River, where they located land claims.

🐚 79

THE
WORLD
OF
GEORGE
ROGERS
CLARK,
1778–1787

This was not an isolated enterprise. Hundreds of other men were doing the same thing. Their approach to the Ohio Valley was very different from the approaches of the other people we have followed into the region. Clark was not interested primarily in the fur trade or in speculating on lands at a distance. What occupied Clark and his companions in the early 1770s was the acquisition and preparation of land for cultivation. The Virginians were after the land itself. And they were only tangentially interested in it as it was. They admired its natural beauty, but what fascinated them, always intrigued them, was its possibilities.

They wanted to change it, to transform it into farmland. They wanted to grow tobacco, wheat, and other cash crops. They girdled trees, they burned and cleared away brush, they laid out boundaries and began to think about fences. Meanwhile, men like George Washington were already imagining ways to link the Ohio River with the Potomac, to facilitate travel and commerce. And everyone thought in terms of rapid settlement of the west by thousands of people, for only by creating a demand for their land could speculators ever see a rise in the price of lands and thus a profit.

The key word is *improvement.* They wanted to alter the landscape and make it over in their own image. Unlike the French and the Indians and the British traders such as Croghan, they wanted to rearrange the world to suit their interests. To be sure, these other peoples had had an impact on the landscape. Still, they depended on trade in furs and skins rather than a wholesale transformation of forests and rivers. The difference was that the Virginians saw themselves as the masters of the environment; it existed to serve them. When they looked at the land, they saw it not as it was, but as it could be. It was an attitude that generations of scholars celebrated and that more recent writers have lamented.

For men such as Clark, the land of the Ohio Valley not only promised riches; it also held the lure of financial independence. Property, after all, was the securest foundation of freedom. With enough property, a man could thumb his nose at the rest of the world; he required no patrons and thus was dependent on no one. He could live his life as he saw fit. A man without property, however, was a man who depended on others, a man who had to worry about what others thought and wanted. In large part, it was this desire for the absolute independence they thought property offered them that motivated many Virginians to take up arms against the British and to migrate to the west, to the Ohio Valley, to Kentucky, Tennessee, Ohio, and eventually Indiana.

Making it all the more tempting was the apparent degree to which acquisition of land in the west rested on personal attributes, on precisely those qualities which defined the unrefined Virginia gentleman. In the absence of clear legal authority, in the midst of suspicious Indians, what seemed to matter most were strength, courage, endurance, and decisiveness. He who could clear a parcel of land, establish boundaries, and protect it from all enemies, Indian or American, was very often its owner. "As soon as a man's back is turned another is on his land," wrote the Virginian and speculator William Crawford in 1772. "The man that is strong and able to make others afraid of him seems to have the best chance as times go now." It was a situation made to order for young Virginians. Their personal characteristics made them ideal pioneers, while the acquisition of land served to reinforce those characteristics.

The greatest impediment to settlement of the west in the minds of men such as Clark was the Indian. While Indians were useful for trade and as models for fighting and hunting, they were more generally seen as nuisances. For the Virginians and Pennsylvanians, the Indians who had been the economic, social, and political allies of the French were simply obstacles to the transformation of the west. The goal was not to negotiate with them but to conquer them. Eventually some Virginians, most notably Jefferson, would take a great deal of interest in revising Indians into settled farm families. Like the land itself, people were to be rearranged to the benefit of the Virginians. In the meantime, they had to be dealt with in more direct ways. The transformation of the west had to be complete.

By 1774, Clark and others like him had their eyes on the land in what would eventually be called Kentucky. Their preparations for descending the Ohio and the activities of surveyors in the region aroused the anger of the Shawnee, among others, and precipitated what is known as Dunmore's War (after the royal governor of Virginia). To a large extent, this brief struggle was the result of the failure of the British to develop a workable policy for the west. It also reflected a split among the Indians, many of whom continued to

✇ 81

THE
WORLD
OF
GEORGE
ROGERS
CLARK,
1778–1787

work for peace. But the Shawnee, who had the most to lose in Kentucky, reacted to the belligerence of the Virginia and Pennsylvania surveyors' incursions into the Ohio Valley with anger. Increasingly there were violent raids along the upper Ohio. One of the most notorious involved the murder of several members of the family of Logan, a Mingo (formerly Iroquois) chief, by settlers. Still, such massacres did not deter the Virginians. Lord Dunmore recruited men in preparation for war. Seeking to gain a quick, preemptive strike, 300 Indians, with the chiefs Cornstalk and Logan, attacked an army of Virginians in October 1774. The Indians fought well and nearly won what became known as the Battle of Point Pleasant. But, exhausted and short of ammunition, they withdrew across the Ohio at the end of the day. Their failure to defeat the Virginians resulted in an agreement by the Shawnee to stay north of the Ohio River.

In the wake of this arrangement, Clark and others like him wasted no time in occupying the bluegrass region of central Kentucky. By the summer of 1775, there were some 150 settlers in the area; that number rose to some 5,000 by 1777 and 50,000 by 1787. Virginia officially recognized the settlements in the bluegrass region and along the Ohio River by organizing them into a county in the fall of 1776. People rushed in to take advantage of the new paradise. "A richer and more Beautifull Cuntry than this I believe has never been seen in America yet," wrote George Rogers Clark to his brother Jonathan in July 1775. Once he had seen it, their father would never "rest until he gets in it to live." Meanwhile, George was "engrossing all the land" he could.

Kentucky in the 1770s was far from utopia, of course. In addition to incredible confusion in land claims, the tensions with the Indians to the north of the Ohio River remained unresolved. Dunmore's War was more of a beginning than an end to conflict over the Ohio Valley. Raids on the stations, as settlements in Kentucky were called, continued. Difficult as this situation was, it was tailor-made for someone with the talents and temperament of George Rogers Clark. Settlers elected him to lobby with the government in Williamsburg for greater protection. Clark did so, with the pithy point that "a country . . . not worth protecting . . . was not worth claiming." Commissioned a major in the Virginia militia, George was entrusted with organizing the defense of Kentucky.

Still in his mid-twenties, Clark possessed a physical courage and a decisiveness that made him a natural leader. But his talents were not more than a product of personality; he simply happened to be good at what came naturally to a great many Virginians. He was an engaging and imposing person who easily commanded respect. Another Kentuckian noted that Clark's "appearance, well calculated to attract attention, was rendered particularly agreeable by the manliness of his deportment and the intelligence of his conversation."

As important as his bearing, however, was his family. Through his father, Clark was well-connected with important men in Virginia, such as George Mason. He was the perfect man for missions to Williamsburg because he knew a great many people personally; he was at ease both there and in the bluegrass. Clark's power, to a significant degree, rested on the interplay of his reputation in the two places. The notion that he could be influential in the Tidewater increased his influence in the bluegrass. When Clark traveled to Williamsburg, in turn, the imprimatur of settlers added to his reputation there. Like many politically astute men, Clark enhanced his power in one place by appearing to be powerful in another.

Still, connections notwithstanding, the situation in the Ohio Valley favored men whose talents were immediately apparent, who were decisive and quick. It was in flux; the lines of authority and the parameters of power were confused. In such a world, physical and temperamental men were at an advantage. This was no place for ambivalence or ambiguity. Here a man mastered others less by ritually mastering himself than by repeatedly demonstrating mastery of both other men and his natural environment.

It was also a world in which men attained positions of power through elections by their peers. The men of the bluegrass chose Clark as their representative to Williamsburg. Repeatedly, moreover, Kentuckians voted about when, where, and how to launch an attack on the British and the Indians north of the Ohio River. On his campaigns, Clark's legitimacy came both from his appointment as an officer of the commonwealth of Virginia and the acquiescence of his men. Clark and his officers depended on both. They used their titles, but they lived and dressed like their men. Clark was not

☙ 83

THE
WORLD
OF
GEORGE
ROGERS
CLARK,
1778–1787

an illusory patriarch in the style of Vincennes or a would-be father in the manner of Hamilton. Rather, he was the first among equals, the chosen head of a band of brothers, a group of ambitious and passionate young men who would brook no restraints from anyone.

The Conquest of the Old Northwest

The greatest success of Gorge Rogers Clark and his men was their 1778–1779 campaign in the Illinois and Wabash countries. Operating under the assumption that the best defense is a good offense, Clark believed that the key to ending Indian attacks on the Kentucky settlements was to destroy their alliance with the British. Like most American frontiersmen, Clark held the British at Detroit, particularly Henry Hamilton, primarily responsible for the raids on Kentucky. The scheme, then, was to conquer the British posts along the Mississippi and on the Wabash, thereby relieving pressure on the Americans living south of the Ohio. The fundamental flaw in the plan was the Virginians' inability to take the Indians seriously and their almost exclusive focus on the British. Still, Clark convinced Virginia's governor, Patrick Henry, of the strategic value of his scheme. With secret instructions from Henry ordering him to take Kaskaskia and a promotion to the rank of lieutenant-colonel, Clark proceeded to raise a force of 175 men.

He did so in time-honored fashion. Clark appointed friends with some social status in Virginia and good reputations in Kentucky—in other words, men who could command confidence in both places— to raise companies. Working east of the Appalachians, captains Leonard Helm and Joseph Bowman recruited men to serve with them in what amounted to their personal companies. Clark only told them that he was raising troops for the defense of Kentucky. By the time he reached an island near the Falls of the Ohio at what is now Louisville, he had far fewer men than he had expected.

Undeterred, Clark told Helm and Bowman and their men of his intention to attack Kaskaskia and asked them to accompany him. Most agreed to do so, despite their fears about being outnumbered and abandoning the settlements in the bluegrass. The expedition was a bold gamble, for Clark and his men were leaving Kentucky exposed to attack. But this kind of aggressive behavior was completely in keeping with his personality and the culture that had nourished it.

The men who elected to go with Clark were Virginians and Pennsylvanians acting with both a collective and a personal purpose. The public motive was the defense of the new republic of Virginia from all enemies and the extension of what they saw as the blessings of liberty to the French in the Old Northwest. Governor Henry's orders included an admonition, which Clark observed, to treat the French "as fellow Citizens" if they behaved. Privately the soldiers expected to obtain land. In January 1778, George Wythe, George Mason, and Thomas Jefferson assured Clark that his "Volunteers" should receive "some further Reward in Lands in the Country . . . in addition to the usual pay if they are so fortunate to Succeed." There would be at least 300 acres for each soldier, with more for the officers, in the territory they conquered. Eventually Clark and the men got 149,000 acres in southern Indiana.

These men, then, came to the Wabash in February 1779 with very different attitudes from the French and British traders. Their goal was to secure the Ohio Valley for settlement and agricultural development by removing the British presence north of the river. They had accomplished the first part of Clark's plan with relative ease, forcing the surrender of Kaskaskia on July 4, 1778, and of Cahokia soon thereafter. Now they achieved the second stage by defeating the surprised Hamilton and taking Vincennes. As had been true for three-quarters of a century, the combatants were less interested in Indiana as a homeland than as a crossroads. The Wabash was the best route to Detroit—or to Kentucky. They met in the middle, and the brave and impetuous Clark won.

The next summer he wanted to proceed on to conquer Detroit. It, after all, was the center of British activity in the region. But Clark did not have enough men willing to mount an assault on a fort far more powerful than those on the Mississippi or the Wabash. His victories had had the unintended consequence of reassuring people about their safety in Kentucky to the point that they were not interested in further prosecuting the campaign. News of his success won him gratitude but little support in mounting a campaign against distant Detroit. Despite his return to the Falls of the Ohio in 1779, Clark

☙ 85

THE
WORLD
OF
GEORGE
ROGERS
CLARK,
1778–1787

continued to harbor designs on the British post. But he was unable to bring them to fruition. Virginia's troops were withdrawn from Vincennes in the spring of 1780. Fort Patrick Henry (the new name of Fort Sackville) was left in the hands of Major Francis Bosseron and the French citizens of the town.

So the significance of the victory at Vincennes from the point of view of the Virginians and Kentuckians was that it appeared to secure the Ohio River as a barrier against attack. Settlers poured into the bluegrass in the aftermath of Clark's campaign. But Indiana was still too far away; the Wabash was still only a route between the Ohio and the Great Lakes. By defeating Hamilton at Vincennes, Clark had won Kentucky, not Indiana. That was not the way the Americans worked. They moved slowly and methodically across the countryside, with only the vaguest interest in the establishment of outposts in the manner of the French. The Wabash could not be of importance to the Virginians until they looked to the lands along its banks as their next area of settlement.

Virginians versus Indians

Obviously the American Indians who already lived in the region saw matters from a different perspective. They fully realized that Virginians such as George Rogers Clark were not the same as the Europeans with whom they and their ancestors had been dealing for over a century. They knew, too, that there was a certain inevitability about the movement of the Virginians and Pennsylvanians across the continent, in large part because many had migrated with them. These included the Shawnee and the Delaware.

In the seventeenth century, the Shawnee had lived in villages in the western Ohio Valley. Under pressure from the Iroquois in the 1680s, they had dispersed to the Illinois and Cumberland river valleys. Most of them eventually followed the lure of British trade to the Savannah River in South Carolina and Georgia. Others migrated to eastern Pennsylvania, where they lived among the Delaware. But the expansion of Anglo-American settlements gradually pushed the Indians farther and farther to the west. By the mid-1700s, the Shawnee and Delaware were living back in the Ohio Valley. The latter concentrated in what is now eastern Ohio while the former located their villages along the Scioto, Great Miami, and Mad rivers. Eventually they would move into Indiana.

In Indiana in the 1770s and the 1780s, the Miami were still dominant. Large numbers of Piankashaw lived near Vincennes; their primary chiefs were Old Tobacco and his son. The Wea, the Kickapoo, and the Mascouten remained around Ouiatanon. And the main villages of the Miami continued to be at the juncture of the St. Joseph and St. Marys River, the present-day site of Fort Wayne. The older and larger village, Kekionga or Miamistown, dated from the time of the elder Vincennes. Located about a quarter of a mile above the confluence of the St. Joseph and the St. Marys on the west bank of the former, Kekionga was often called Pacan's Village after the principal chief. The other settlement, Le Gris's Village, nestled between the Maumee and the St. Joseph, was about two decades old in the 1770s. Both Pacan and Le Gris were middle-aged men who had earned the respect of their peers no doubt in ways similar to those of Clark.

Abandoned by the French and mistreated by the British, the Indians of the Old Northwest in the 1770s were in a difficult position. Clearly the greatest threat to them came from the Virginians and Pennsylvanians, who not only coveted their land but had little interest in the traditional fur trade or in maintaining ongoing relationships with them. For the first time, the arrival of Europeans entailed the complete destruction of their world. The Indians were unable to develop an alliance to resist the Americans during the War for Independence. Rather, they conducted war much like the Virginians. It consisted of a series of raids across the Ohio River by young men with the implicit sanction of their elders. Where the government of the commonwealth of Virginia aided Clark with supplies and promises of land, British officers in Detroit encouraged Indian attacks on the Americans with supplies and the exchange of gifts.

The war in the Old Northwest was never that clear-cut, of course. The sands were always shifting. The Piankashaw, particularly the chief Old Tobacco, were inclined at the beginning of the War for Independence to encourage ties with the Americans, sharing the disaffection of their French neighbors from the British. The Delaware and the Shawnee, on the other hand, who were bearing the brunt of the Anglo-American incursions, were more directly allied with the

☙ 87

THE
WORLD
OF
GEORGE
ROGERS
CLARK,
1778–1787

British. Most managed to play a waiting game with a patience and perspicacity foreign to Virginians like Clark.

Both Le Gris and Pacan welcomed Henry Hamilton on his expedition to relieve Vincennes in the fall of 1778 and accompanied him down the Wabash to Fort Sackville. This made perfect sense, for the British were still the dominant European military force in the region. Moreover, the Miami traded primarily with French and British traders out of Detroit. Geography and trade routes as much as anything else determined the respective allegiances of the Indians.

Once Hamilton was at Vincennes, most of the Indians returned home. But numbers of Piankashaw, Wea, and Miami, with Ottawa, Wyandot, Delaware, gathered at Fort Sackville on February 21, 1779. There, on the day before the arrival of Clark, they heard Young Tobacco renounce his loyalty to the Americans and pledge allegiance to the British. But when Clark's troops arrived, the Piankashaw, as we have seen, quickly offered to join the Americans. The other Indians, including Le Gris, simply waited outside of Vincennes for the outcome of the battle between the Europeans. The American victory confirmed the preference of the Piankashaw for the Virginians; Young Tobacco even sold them land in southern Indiana across the Ohio from Louisville. The Miami, meanwhile, returned to their villages and reaffirmed their loyalty to Great Britain. From the perspective of the Indians, then, Clark's victory humiliated the British and revealed their weakness. But his subsequent failure to consolidate his position on the Wabash demonstrated the weakness of the Virginians.

Besides which, the Virginians and the Pennsylvanians from Pittsburgh through Louisville constantly demonstrated their lack of interest in reaching a true accommodation with the Indians. At Kaskaskia, Clark had chosen to deal with the Indians in the "French and Spanish mode which must be preferable [to] ours, otherwise they could not possibley have such great influence among them." He tried to make common cause with them, as with the French: a struggle of local peoples against the tyrannical and inconstant British. But Clark's habit of directness, his lack of patience, his quick temper, all worked against him. Like other Virginians, he had no interest in a stable long-term alliance with the Indians. His approach to them, while respectful, was instrumental. How best to manage them, to get them out of his way in order to conquer his real enemy, the British? The charming swagger that worked so well with the settlers in Kentucky only alienated Indians in the Old Northwest, accustomed as they were to the patriarchal style of the French and, to a lesser extent, of the British. The hot temper that brilliantly displayed Hamilton's impotence in the streets of Vincennes did not work so well at the council fire. The Indians feared Clark, but those who allied with the Virginians did so largely out of economic and strategic interests, not genuine respect for him. Clark could humiliate fathers, but he could not be one.

The conquest of Vincennes thus laid out the parameters of conflict in the Wabash Country in the 1780s. Supported by the British, whose influence revived with the failure of the Virginians to consolidate their position north of the Ohio, the Miami, the Delaware, and the Shawnee struggled against the settlers in Kentucky and Pennsylvania with raids in the early 1780s. The Anglo-Americans reciprocated in kind. In the late summer of 1785, Clark led yet another expedition of several hundred Kentuckians, gathered at the mouth of the Licking River, across the Ohio. They destroyed Shawnee villages and fields at Chillicothe on the Scioto and at Piqua on the Great Miami. Still, his repeated and elaborate efforts to mount an expedition against Detroit, preferably via the Wabash, came to naught.

The 1783 Treaty of Paris brought the War for Independence to an end and marked British recognition of the sovereignty of the United States of America, but it did little to resolve the conflict in the Ohio Valley. Indeed, it is best to think of the war in the west as a series of episodes only tangentially related to the War for Independence. In the treaty, the British gave up their legal claim to the Old Northwest. On the other hand, they refused to surrender their posts at Detroit and throughout the Great Lakes. Meanwhile, British officers and agents encouraged the Indians to resist the advances of the Americans.

This they did with great success. For all practical purposes the Ohio River remained the boundary between the Virginians and the Indians throughout the 1770s and the 1780s, perpetuating the agreement reached at the end of Lord Dunmore's War in 1774. Neither side attained a great advantage over the other, despite temporary

☙ 89

THE
WORLD
OF
GEORGE
ROGERS
CLARK,
1778–1787

appearances to the contrary. Rather, the raids continued. And hundreds of people, Indian and white, male and female, old and young, continued to die violent and gruesome deaths. The situation was stable in its murderous instability.

In the mid-1780s, the Indians of the Old Northwest—the Iroquois, Huron, Miami, Delaware, Shawnee, Ottawa, Chippewa, Potawatomi—managed to form a kind of confederation to deal with the Americans. Several older chiefs signed a series of treaties with the new government of the United States. But they meant little. For the chiefs could no more control their angry young warriors than the American government could control angry young Kentuckians and Virginians. The war had become a stalemate of murderous revenge. On both sides were young warriors, often blinded by rage, exceedingly local in their perspective, interested in little more than settling scores. This was the Age of Clark in the Old Northwest.

The Americans, who were the heralds of a new society based on a brotherhood of independent citizen-farmers, were also the disrupters of an established world of patriarchy and interdependence. The frontier, in the European sense of a place in which there is no dominant power structure, was largely their creation. Nowhere was their legacy more clearly revealed than in Vincennes, the most obvious initial beneficiary of the Virginians.

The French and the Virginians

The French and the Piankashaw had welcomed Clark's army as freedom fighters, ushering in a new world of prosperity and independence. Virginia had appointed John Todd in 1779 to govern its territory north of the Ohio River and he had commissioned several leading French men, including Jean Marie Philippe Le Gras, Pierre Gamelin, and N. Perrot, to serve as magistrates of a court. Essentially they acted like Virginia justices of the peace; they had political as well as judicial responsibilities. Todd stayed only a brief time, so that in the 1780s, the court acted virtually on its own in governing the town of Vincennes.

A decade of life in the midst of war had had a devastating impact on the French residents of the village. Those who had welcomed the Americans as liberators from the British had come to regret their enthusiasm. For citizenship in the commonwealth of Virginia had brought them disaster. Not only did the state fail to offer adequate protection or to establish much more than the outlines of official authority; the incursions of its troops also had disrupted the trade on which the men and women of Vincennes had depended for their livelihood. War upset the delicate nature of European-Indian relationships in the Wabash Valley. Most directly, the Virginians had demonstrated nothing but bad faith with the French who had fought along side them in the conquest of Fort Sackville.

By Clark's own account, he had depended on the French for supplies. Among others, Le Gras and François Bosseron had buried ammunition to hide it from the British and then had given it to the Virginians upon their arrival. The merchant Bosseron continued to supply his new fellow citizens with food and other necessities, accepting promises of payment in return. In effect he loaned the commonwealth of Virginia the money necessary to support its troops at Vincennes. In February 1780, Clark directly described the relationship when asking for Bosseron to supply the troops there with food: "Sensible that you have always done whatever lay within your power to support the Troops even to your own disadvantage, and would continue the same Service, had you the funds to support you, yet I must solicit you to exert yourself once more in behalf of the State." Bosseron complied. But Clark's promise that Virginia would reimburse him was not fulfilled. The paper money he and others in Vincennes were given was largely worthless. By the end of the War for Independence, Virginia owed the merchant some $26,000. In 1783, the Assembly authorized payment of only $300. The next year, the merchant sold half of Virginia's debt for one-third of its value. When Bosseron died in 1791, he was bankrupt.

No wonder the people of Vincennes looked back upon the 1760s and 1770s as a kind of golden age. With their trade disrupted, surrounded by warring Indians and Virginians, the people of Vincennes reported a rapid decline in their standard of living in the 1780s. The leading citizens, including Bosseron, summarized their complaints in a 1781 petition to the governor of Virginia. They protested "the very serious grievances to which they ha[d] been exposed, since the arrival of the Virginia troops in this country." They had "zealously furnished provisions and goods" but had been

📯 91

THE
WORLD
OF
GEORGE
ROGERS
CLARK,
1778–1787

offered worthless continental money in return. The Virginians had insisted that the paper be accepted "as of equal value with specie." Worse, the troops had killed their cattle and hogs, "with arms in their hands threatening all who should resist them." When they left, they took all the ammunition, "thereby depriving us of the only means of defending ourselves against the fury of the savages whom they have excited against us. This, then, is the manner in which the Virginians have acted in this country."

Others joined in the chorus of complaints, even Father Gibault, the priest who served Vincennes but lived in Kaskaskia in the 1770s. Despite the evidence of his "love for the cause of liberty" in helping Clark, he told commissioners from Virginia in 1783, he had not received "a sou of indemnity." To be sure, this kind of pleading was somewhat disingenuous. Gibault was essentially trying to recover his expenses. But the French were not simply whining. They had suffered, and with good reason they held the Virginians responsible. "Never should I have made these representations if the necessity and poverty into which the Americans have plunged us, myself and my people, had not made it impossible for me to keep silent," wrote Gibault. "I pass in silence an almost infinite number of grievances, molestations, wrongs, and acts of violence of every kind which have almost completely ruined the country. . . . it is for you, sirs, to inquire why and by whom we have been so inhumanly treated." No compensation was forthcoming.

As problematic were the conflicts that erupted in Vincennes in the 1780s between the French and the Virginians over virtually everything. In the 1780s several dozen American families (totaling perhaps sixty) took up residence in Vincennes. According to John Filson, an American who visited the town in 1786, the immigrants supported themselves by selling liquor to the Indians. Alcohol had always been a prized commodity on the Wabash. But with the breakdown of traditional lines of commerce and authority in the 1780s, it became even more valuable. The French judges tried to restrict the trade by levying fines on the retailers, but they had little impact. Indeed, the French merchants seemed to have been as guilty as the Americans.

The political and social ramifications of the growth of the liquor trade were many. It contributed to an increase in incidents of personal violence between the Europeans and the Indians. Filson reported "frequent murders" and he, like Gibault, lamented the lack of order in the town. The people seemed occupied with parties and nightly "reveling." Profanity and "Vice" were ubiquitous. Filson attributed this situation in part to the absence of authority beyond the local court. Later historians would blame "frontier conditions." But the drinking and fighting and partying in Vincennes in the 1780s had less to do with a frontier—after all, the town was half-a-century old—than with the cultural confusion brought about by the disruption of a well-established and well-integrated economic, social, and political system.

For years the French and Indians in Vincennes had prospered in a world of long-distance commerce. Now the introduction of the widespread sale of alcohol by the Americans was equivalent to the introduction of cocaine in the twentieth century. It not only perverted the behavior of consumers; it also affected the behavior of suppliers. There was money to be made and men grabbed at the chance to do so. Life in Vincennes became more tense; there was an edge to social interaction that had not existed before. More important, there was a growing conflict over what was economically profitable and what was socially useful.

By 1786, the liquor trade had contributed to what Filson called "a Spirit of Jelousy and aspersion between the french and americans" in Vincennes. The Americans believed that the French magistrates were also selling liquor to the Indians even as they punished others for the practice. No doubt that was true, although we can wonder about differences in scale and intention. The French, in turn, took offense at these charges. Occasionally there was physical fighting between the two groups. Matters were getting out of hand.

These quarrels went beyond the liquor trade. Tension was inevitable, for the Americans were essentially demanding that the French reorganize the world they had carefully constructed in the mid-1700s. Like the British, the Americans thought the French lazy. They ridiculed the local court, according to Filson, because they prostituted "their Characters to Gambling & Luxury" and revolted against their authority. In the summer of 1787, in a petition to the Congress of the United States, they noted that they had endeavored to change the French: "Our industry became a spur to their's; from

☙ 93

THE
WORLD
OF
GEORGE
ROGERS
CLARK,
1778–1787

us they learnt the usefulness of husbandry; and, if there be any merit in promoting a love of rural employments, we flatter ourselves we have deserved well of mankind by disseminating the arts beneficial to human societies." Apparently the French reliance on long-distance commerce appalled the Americans.

Even more upsetting was their casual attitude toward land, which was the highest priority for the Americans. The immigrants purchased land from the French and received deeds from the local court. But the government of the United States, which assumed control of the territory from Virginia in 1784, refused to recognize the French claims to the soil. In response, the French voluntarily surrendered their claim to Congress in the summer of 1786. Throwing themselves on the mercy of that body, they asked for a grant of about 520,000 acres. They admitted that they had "overlooked the advantages that can be derived from the cultivation of lands" and never "formed an idea of dividing among ourselves our fruitful country." But "the moment we were connected with the United States, we began to be sensible of the real value of lands."

No doubt their new neighbors, who were exceedingly angry at both the worthlessness of their titles and the weakness of the French in conceding everything to Congress, had excited their interest. If the French had sought the mercy of yet another benevolent father, the Virginians were by nature simply more defiant. They were upset that they might "be totally deprived of [their] improvements." After all, they had come to Vincennes "searching for a fertile soil on the banks of the Wabash river" and, "invited by the bounties of nature," had settled there. Now everything, meaning their land titles, was in doubt. To correct this situation, they petitioned Congress for a permanent land office, "for the purpose of obtaining valid rights to lands, under the conduct of proper gentlemen." More than that, they wanted "a regular government in this place and territory" to restore "order, law or government."

The tensions between Americans and French in Vincennes also grew out of different attitudes toward the Indians. The French complained that the aggressive behavior of Virginians had earned them "the enmity of those Indians who had, time immemorial, called us their fathers and friends." Now they had to give "large presents" in order to protect their town. The Americans suspected the French of being pro-British and were certain that they were far too friendly with the Indians. In March 1786, the Americans wrote to George Rogers Clark seeking his "Patronage and direction." They complained that Vincennes, which "once trembled at your victorious arms, and these savages overawed by your superior power is now entirely anarchical." They shuddered "at the daily expectation of horrid murthers and probably total depopulation of the americans by imperious savages." They lived under what John Filson called "a hovering Cloud pregnant with innumerable evil."

While the stream of requests from the Wabash for a government were understandable, the Virginians were blaming the French for the derangement of society along the Wabash when they themselves were largely responsible for it. There had been no anarchy in Vincennes in the 1760s or 1770s; the confusion in the 1780s came about not because the Americans were nasty but because they introduced a competing culture into the region. Neither side could control the other. The frontier was not the absence of order but a situation in which no one could get the upper hand. There was a government in Vincennes—the court appointed by John Todd. The Americans simply chose to disobey it. In other words, the Americans wanted not government but a particular kind of government which would support, protect, and defend their interests.

In the summer of 1786, soon after Filson's visit, matters reached a crisis point along the lower Wabash. On June 21, Indians attacked a party of Americans working in a cornfield outside Vincennes. They wounded two men, one of whom they scalped. The angry Americans, led by Daniel Sullivan, whom Judge Le Gras called "very dangerous and pernicious to the public peace," returned to the town and killed and scalped a sick Indian. They then dragged his body around "like a pig on the tail of a horse." No incident more graphically demonstrated the difference between the Americans and the French when it came to dealing with the Indians. Judge Le Gras, outraged by this insult both to the Indian and to his own authority, ordered all Americans who could not produce a legitimate passport, in the words of American settler John Small, "to leave this place Bagg and Baggage Immediately." The Americans refused. According to Small, "Danger and Distruction stears every american in the face."

📜 **95**

THE
WORLD
OF
GEORGE
ROGERS
CLARK,
1778–1787

The Virginians feared not only for their lives but also for their crops. Afraid to work in their fields, they remained cooped up in Vincennes. There they fretted and brooded and grew even testier with their French neighbors. John Small could not understand why the French would allow Indians in Vincennes, "which Indians we are shuer are our Enemys the French has repeatedly told us that they would keep the Indians at this place." Le Gras, on the other hand, could not comprehend "through what motive the Americans seek only to surprise and even betray those who are peaceful and their allies, which affords a pretext to all nations to band together and form numerous parties to attack entire villages." The Virginians and the French were not speaking the same language, not operating under the same assumptions. Their attitudes toward the Indians belied more fundamental disagreements about nearly everything. Of course, these people did not understand that they were suffering from cultural confusion; they simply distrusted each other.

Daniel Sullivan even charged that the French would soon allow the Indians "to Sacrifice us in the bounds of the Town." He was wrong. When, in July, several hundred Indians appeared outside Vincennes with the expressed intention of eliminating the Americans who were the source of so much trouble, Judge Le Gras and François Bosseron saved the Virginians. Refusing a request to join the Indians against the Americans, they were able to talk them out of violence, using a multitude of gifts and calumets, what John Small described as "presents to a very considerable amount." The Indians then left for their villages on the upper Wabash. Firing some shots into the house of Daniel Sullivan and burning crops, they promised to return in the fall when they "would know how to make gates for entering without asking."

News of these events created a stir in Kentucky and Virginia. When the government of the United States refused to act, Governor Henry did. He and his council authorized the Kentucky militia to defend the region. In August, the officers in Kentucky voted to interpret that instruction as authorizing an offensive expedition against the Wabash Indians. Under the command of George Rogers Clark, several hundred men set out in September. Clark was well aware of the recent events on the Wabash, for most of the letters written by Small and Sullivan were addressed to him.

The expedition was a disaster. It was poorly organized and supplied; most of Clark's food was delayed and spoiled by the time it reached Vincennes. More troublesome was the apprehension of the men Clark commanded. As they ascended the Wabash from Vincennes, their nervousness about fighting large numbers of Indians increased. By the time they reached the mouth of Big Vermilion River, many had had enough. The cry rang out, "Who's for home?" With over half of his men joining in what amounted to a mutiny, Clark had to retreat. Returning to Vincennes, he remained there with 250 men while the rest of his troops straggled home to Kentucky. Working with Le Gras, he attempted to negotiate a peace with the Indians without success.

A frustrated Clark, desperate for supplies, turned his attention to Spanish traders in Vincennes. In October, acting with his usual bravado, he convened a military court and confiscated their property on the grounds that they were trading on American soil without permission. This preemptory action outraged pro-Spanish merchants in Kentucky, notably James Wilkinson, who demanded that Clark be punished and replaced. Virginia flirted with filing criminal charges against the general but settled for civil suits. They continued for years. Meanwhile the United States, concerned about war with Spain, ordered troops under the command of Colonel Josiah Harmar to disperse Clark's men. In the spring of 1787, the general at last gave up the town he had conquered so boldly and brazenly eight years earlier.

In the end, then, the Virginian George Rogers Clark could not bring order to the frontier he had helped to create. The very characteristics that allowed him to capture Vincennes in 1779, his boldness, his bluster, and his impatience, made him a very poor governor of that which he had conquered. He could defy, but he could not hold. He could be an angry son, a loyal brother, but he did not understand the role of disinterested patriarch. His humiliation of Hamilton and the British had created a vacuum that he could not fill.

Clark's 1786 expedition was similar in many respects to that of 1779. To some extent, it demonstrated how little matters had changed in the 1780s. The Kentuckians still came to the Wabash to fight Indians and, by extension, their British allies. They would still

97

THE
WORLD
OF
GEORGE
ROGERS
CLARK,
1778–1787

only go as far as their commander's bluster and their personal interests would carry them. Clark himself had not changed much in a decade, except perhaps to become more persuaded of his own infallibility. But the world along the Wabash was not the same. Patterns of commerce were upset; the notion of patriarchal authority was in disrepute; young men exchanged blows rather than gifts. The French in Vincennes, alienated from their comrades of 1779, had seen their standard of living fall. American settlers were uncertain of legal titles in the region. Divided and worried, the Indians were reforming relationships among themselves and with Europeans. After the events around Vincennes in the summer of 1786, the Piankashaw apparently abandoned their village there and moved up the Wabash toward the present-day site of Terre Haute. The Sons of Liberty who had attacked Fort Sackville in 1779 were no longer making common cause.

Clark and his men were harbingers of a new economic and social order. But they had neither the character nor the power to make it work. They were too few, too bound by the imperatives of personal honor and collective white male democracy, too limited in both their objectives and their visions. They wanted land and they wanted glory—as quickly as possible. They had no explicit long-range vision of the ways in which they could conquer and develop the Old Northwest. In essence they were very parochial, relying on ad hoc measures that worked well one year and failed the next. The only strong impression they made in the region was a destructive one. They intruded, laid waste to what they encountered, and created tensions and confusion. But they did not conquer or remake the Old Northwest. That worthy endeavor would be the work of men who, while perhaps less brave and charismatic than George Rogers Clark, had the patience and the power to define, implement, and enforce a far more elaborate vision of the region's future than anything he had ever imagined.

5·

THE WORLD OF JOSIAH HARMAR AND JOHN FRANCIS HAMTRAMCK, 1787–1790

Of the several governments that attempted to take control of the Wabash Valley in the eighteenth century, none initially seemed less likely to succeed than the United States of America. Just over a decade old in 1787, the new nation was hardly an intimidating presence in world politics. True, it had won its independence from arguably the strongest national power in Europe in 1783. But that achievement was less an organized, systematic defeat of Great Britain than the result of patience, perseverance, and more than a smattering of good fortune. With victory in hand, most of the citizens of the United States had little interest in giving their national government the stature and coercive powers of the empire whose alleged tyranny they had struggled for so long to escape. Under the Articles of Confederation, the first constitution of the United States, the national government could do very little. It lacked the essential power to tax its citizens to pay for its efforts. From the mountains of western Massachusetts, where Shays' Rebellion was still fresh in people's memories, to the mountains of the western Carolinas, where some proposed the creation of the separate nation of Franklin, most Americans were decidedly more comfortable with local rather than national governments.

Certainly the Indians of the Wabash Valley, the French habitants of Vincennes, and the English-speaking peoples of the Ohio Valley

99

THE
WORLD
OF
JOSIAH
HARMAR &
JOHN
FRANCIS
HAMTRAMCK,
1787–1790

had no reason to welcome the intrusion of the United States into their world. After all, they had rejected the British in the 1770s for precisely the same reasons the artisans and farmers on the Atlantic coast had proclaimed: the defense of local autonomy and privileges against an ambitious, arbitrary, and inconstant foreign power. Where was the profit in accepting the sovereignty of a young and weak government seemingly determined to repeat the history of Great Britain in the Ohio Valley?

While virtually no one recognized it at the time, the answer lay in the breakdown of the political structures of the region during the 1770s and 1780s. The Ohio Valley, and particularly the Wabash Valley, had *become* a frontier in the sense that there was no longer a dominant group or even a clear-cut conflict between different groups. One definition of a frontier is a borderland, a contested area in which the rules of behavior are at issue. While there were raids and counterraids throughout the Ohio Valley and Great Lakes, the territory between Lake Erie and the Ohio River more than met that definition at the end of the eighteenth century. Virginians held sway in Kentucky, British officials and their Indian allies dominated in the north. In between, everything, as the history of Vincennes in the 1780s demonstrated, was in flux.

The eventual success of the United States in conquering the Old Northwest had a lot to do with the timing of its appearance in the region. Twenty years earlier, the great plans of the national ordinances of the 1780s would have met with the same fate as their British predecessors; twenty years later, the Virginians would have been impossible to control. Precisely because the Old Northwest was a frontier, precisely because there was a fairly balanced contest among the peoples of the region, the small efforts of the United States had an impact well beyond their intrinsic importance or strength. The vacuum of power left an opening that officials of the United States seized and then exploited to the last full measure available to them in the closing decades of the 1700s.

The Creation of the Northwest Territory

The American nation was not the weak nonentity that it appeared to be at first glance. Despite sectional rivalries and rampant suspicions of institutions and authority, the nation had enormous demographic and economic potential. Its population increased at a staggering rate, doubling every twenty years. The 1780s, in fact, saw one of the greatest proportional increases in American history. Economically the United States was diverse and powerful, producing an abundance of grains and valuable staples and offering the beginnings of domestic manufacturing.

Most important, perhaps, was the tremendous confidence of many Americans in the possibilities of their future. Victory in a long and difficult war with a powerful enemy had reinforced a pronounced tendency to identify themselves as a chosen people. Apparently providence smiled upon Americans, or so they repeatedly said. Freed from Britain, they also saw themselves as freed from tradition. They were ready to embrace the future with an enthusiasm that seems foolish to some in the late twentieth century. Projects for improvements, for canals and balloons and cities, popped up; speculations in frontier and urban lands skyrocketed; internal migration grew dramatically. There was a widespread belief that the United States had been released from the restrictions of the past and was ready to take advantage of the new order its Revolution had set in motion. The rhetorical celebration of common people, the exaltation of liberty over power, the belief that human beings could take charge of their world and transform it as they saw fit, were all evidence of the potential inherent in this rapidly growing and diversifying nation. Youth was on the side of the United States. Its citizens were eager and untroubled by the prospect of failure.

But some men—a shifting coalition of politicians and developers—worried that the nation could not realize the full extent of its potential greatness without a strong national government directing and guiding its development. These nationalists, or federalists as they were called in the late 1780s, supported efforts to strengthen the United States that culminated in the replacement of the Articles of Confederation with the present Constitution in 1788. By this document the national government obtained the crucial power to tax, as well as complete control over diplomacy with foreign nations and the regulation of economic and legal disputes between the states and among their citizens.

The nationalist movement had its origins in disillusionment with the slow and piecemeal nature of the War for Independence. But it focused during the 1780s on, among other things, the development of the trans-Appalachian West. Nationalists saw the vast acreage of the region as a source of dependable income for the beleaguered government of the Confederation. Divided into small plots, it would bring in revenue for years to come. In May 1785, Virginian Richard Henry Lee called the lands north of the Ohio River an "amazing resource" that promised to relieve the new American states from the "distress" of indebtedness.

THE
WORLD
OF
JOSIAH
HARMAR &
JOHN
FRANCIS
HAMTRAMCK,
1787–1790

Land speculation was a matter of political economy as much as anything else. Undeveloped, unsecured acreage was worth little. Without reliable modes of transportation, urban centers, predictable courts, and physical protection, settlers would not migrate to the region to buy the available lots. In fact, failed land speculations were widespread in late eighteenth-century North America, in part because promoters could not develop their holdings fast enough to make them attractive to purchasers. Since Americans, unlike the French or the British, wanted to transform the west into a paradise of commercial agriculture, the national government had a potential bonanza on its hands. Or so many people thought.

The problem was that the United States lacked clear title to the Ohio Valley. Most difficult, from the American perspective, was the fact that thousands of Indians not only lived there but had repeatedly demonstrated their determination to hold on to the land by any means necessary. Slightly less troublesome was the state of Virginia's claim to the land north of the Ohio River, a claim rooted in the conquests of George Rogers Clark as much as anything else. Its citizens in Kentucky had long since revealed their hunger for the fertile lands of the Wabash. In addition, there was the continuing presence of European governments. By the 1783 Treaty of Paris, Great Britain had legally ceded its claims to the region south of the Great Lakes, but His Majesty's government made no effort to evacuate its posts in Detroit and elsewhere. Spanish officials stood by in the Louisiana territory west of the Mississippi, eager to exploit all opportunities that might prove beneficial to them.

The goals of the American Confederation with regard to the Old Northwest in the 1780s were simple. To take advantage of the economic possibilities of the region, the government would have to secure it, both legally and physically. The United States was trapped in a conundrum. The prerequisite for power was money.

Before ratification of the Constitution, the greatest potential source of money was land in the West. But that land could not be profitably sold until the government had exerted its power over it. The United States had to demonstrate power in order to obtain power.

Congressmen and promoters in the East in the 1780s had great plans for the Northwest. Once secured, they intended to develop it into the very model of a republican society. They envisioned the region as an orderly world, buttressed by such essential social institutions as churches, schools, and governments and supported by the widespread practice of commercial agriculture. Men such as George Washington had dreams of linking the Potomac and Ohio rivers through a series of canals and improvements. Others thought in terms of gaining the right to navigate on the Mississippi. Either way or both, the United States would expand in a systematic fashion across the continent; its well-planned territories would bring revenue to the government and glory to the nation as a whole.

These were grandiose ideas. Given the state of the Confederation in the mid-1780s, they were almost laughable. With far more experience and greater resources, Great Britain had failed to obtain control of the Northwest in the 1760s. Neither the Proclamation of 1763 nor the Quebec Act of 1774 had brought order to the region. To the contrary, the British had only provoked some Indians into armed resistance and alienated the French at Vincennes and other Indians. By the 1780s, moreover, land company schemes to develop the Ohio Valley had a history of almost half-a-century of failure. Why suppose that the Confederation could achieve what the strongest government in Europe and powerful coalitions of speculators such as the Ohio Company could not?

Sometimes, however, foolhardiness is its own best asset. Idealism encourages boldness when realism demands caution. The Confederation achieved what it did in the West because its agents and officials acted as if they could achieve something. They refused to be daunted. To say that they were idealistic does not mean that they were innocent or naive. Far from it. The congressmen and promoters who laid the foundations for the American conquest of the Old Northwest were tough men with an often pessimistic view of human nature. In fact, they succeeded in large part because they were stubborn enough to persevere in the face of reality.

THE
WORLD
OF
JOSIAH
HARMAR &
JOHN
FRANCIS
HAMTRAMCK,
1787–1790

After three years of negotiation, Virginia ceded its claim to the land on the north side of the Ohio River to the United States in 1784. It did not do so, however, without some recognition of the service of its citizens in the Northwest during the War for Independence. Virginia received about half of the close to one million dollars the commonwealth demanded as reimbursement for the costs of George Rogers Clark's activities in the Northwest. Congress agreed to confirm the property holdings of the French Canadians who had professed loyalty to the United States. Virginia also asked that the grant of up to 150,000 acres it had promised to the officers and men who had accompanied Clark in 1778 and 1779 be honored. Congress accepted the provision with the stipulation that all the land be in one place to be selected by the majority of the officers. They chose a tract directly across the Ohio River from Louisville, establishing the town of Clarksville in 1784.

With the transfer of sovereignty completed, Congress appointed a committee headed by Thomas Jefferson of Virginia to devise a system of government for what came to be known as the Northwest Territory (today, the states of Ohio, Indiana, Illinois, Michigan, Wisconsin, and part of Minnesota). On April 23, 1785, Congress adopted a revised version of the committee report as the Ordinance of 1784. It provided for the creation of some ten states. Congress would authorize "free" adult males to govern their district "by adopting the constitution and laws of any one of the original States" until such time as it had 20,000 "free inhabitants." Then they could draft their own constitution and be accepted into the Union when their population matched that of the smallest existing state. In other words, the ordinance was no more than a vague guideline for the government of the region ceded by Virginia.

Congress did insist, however, that the new states adhere to certain basic principles. Among them were permanent allegiance to the United States, subordination to the Articles of Confederation and the Congress, respect for the sanctity of federal lands, willingness to assume a proportional share of the national debt, exclusion of federal lands from state taxes, commitment to republican forms of government, and promises that nonresident landowners would not be taxed at a higher rate than those residing in the state. Nebulous though the details of the 1784 ordinance were, Congress made it abundantly clear that recognition of the supremacy of the United States of America, its agents and interests, were the *sine qua non* of western development. The ordinance was as much a declaration of American authority in the region north of the Ohio as it was a plan for government.

Congress asserted its economic and political interests in the Ohio Valley more concretely in May 1785, when it adopted a Land Ordinance to prepare the lands ceded by Virginia for sale. Arguments over the details notwithstanding, Congressmen agreed on a land policy of what historian Peter Onuf has called "prior survey, controlled development, and compact settlement." The goal was to entice people to buy land; the means was to make land into easily traded commodities. Congress authorized the appointment of a surveyor from each state to work under the direction of the geographer of the United States. Together they were to "proceed to divide the said territory into townships of six miles square, by lines running due north and south, and others crossing at right angles, as near as may be, unless where the boundaries of the late Indian purchases may render the same impracticable." Starting at the western border of Pennsylvania, the surveyors would work to the west. They would create square townships divided into thirty-six square lots of 640 acres.

The Confederation Congress completed its plans for the assumption of the region with the passage of "An Ordinance for the government of the territory of the United States North West of the river Ohio" in July 1787. The famous Northwest Ordinance superseded the Ordinance of 1784. It created the specific status of territory as a preliminary state before statehood and was much more precise about how the territory, or sections of it, could become parts of the Union. Like the previous ordinances, the 1787 legislation clearly delineated the authority of the United States in the region. But it was far more specific and detailed about the establishment of American power. Congress would appoint a governor and three judges to administer the territory. The governor in particular had extraordinary powers. With the judges, he could adopt laws from the original states. He was commander-in-chief of the militia, appointed all officers below the rank of general, appointed all magistrates and civil officers, and created counties and towns. When the governor accepted evidence that there were 5,000 free adult males living in the territory, he could authorize the meeting of an elected general assembly and a legislative council elected by the assembly. But he retained "the power to convene, prorogue and dissolve the General Assembly, when in his opinion it shall be expedient." At least three but no more than five states were to be formed from the Northwest Territory. When a region had 60,000 free inhabitants, Congress could authorize its admission to the Union as a state. It would be equal to the existing states, "in all respects whatever." And its citizens could form their own government, so long as it was "republican, and in conformity to the principles contained in these Articles."

The principles of the Northwest Ordinance were relatively specific. They included acceptance of partible inheritance, the notion that each child should receive an equal part of his or her father's estate; freedom of religion, as long as people behaved "in a peaceable and orderly manner"; the rights of trial by jury, the writ of habeas corpus, and reasonable punishments; encouragement of public schools; "good faith" toward the Indians with regard to their "property, rights, and liberty"; and a prohibition of slavery and "involuntary servitude" except for criminal punishment. Throughout all the provisions ran the theme of the sovereignty of the United States. Territorial and state residents would have to obey the laws and customs of the national government, pay their share of federal debts and taxes, and treat the lands and customers of the national government fairly. In short, the United States demanded that all peoples in the Northwest Territory, present and future, recognize its political authority and accede to the rules of its culture. The only exception to this general rule was made in the case of the French peoples "who have heretofore professed themselves citizens of Virginia" and "their laws and customs now in force among them relative to the descent and conveyance of property."

Taken together, the ordinances of the 1780s offered a remarkably specific blueprint for the economic, social, and political development of the Northwest Territory. Like the French and British governments before it, the Congress of the Confederation proposed to take over the Wabash Valley. But from the beginning, its efforts involved more than political regulations and institutions. Indeed, they entailed nothing less than the complete transformation of the region. Congress had established procedures by which the territory would become part of the United States. Its ordinances did not call for the adaptation of American interests to the peoples and landscape of the Northwest Territory. To the contrary, they assumed the adaptation of the Indians, the French, and the natural landscape to the economic and political imperatives of the United States. Congressmen would remake the Northwest in their image of the best of all possible worlds.

Mixing economic interests, political cunning, and enlightened optimism, the American government approached western development with an emotional detachment and a sense of power that bordered on the fantastic. Before it had any real control over the Northwest, while thousands of people continued to live there in social and economic ways that had functioned well for decades, while thousands of young men in Kentucky and western Pennsylvania hungrily eyed the land north of the Ohio River, the government of the infant American Confederation announced to the world elaborate plans for its future. The burden of proof then fell on the handful of men chosen to enact its policies.

The United States Army in the Old Northwest

Over and over again in appointing commissioners, suveyors, and officials, Congress called upon former officers in the Continental Army. Many of these men believed themselves wronged by the American people; they felt underpaid and unappreciated by the nation whose independence they had won. They believed that they had earned national appointments and the salaries and status that came with them. The government, on the other hand, wisely sought to take advantage of the military experience of these men in extending its authority to its frontiers. However aggrieved, the officers were generally loyal to the United States, or at least to the person of their former commander-in-chief, George Washington. On some level they were the most trustworthy men the government could find for the difficult assignment of carrying the flag of the United States into the interior. The problem, by and large, was that while generally competent and professional, they were neither imaginative nor bold.

The first group of soldiers recruited by Congress in the summer of 1784 were the 250 members of the First American Regiment. Most

☙ 107

THE
WORLD
OF
JOSIAH
HARMAR &
JOHN
FRANCIS
HAMTRAMCK,
1787–1790

of them were Pennsylvanians; they were for all practical purposes the United States Army. Their commander was Lieutenant-Colonel Josiah Harmar. A native of Philadelphia whose mother had died when he was only three months old, Harmar had spent his childhood with a distant father, an aunt, and his friends at a Quaker school. In October 1776, when he was twenty-three, he enlisted as a major in the Third Pennsylvania Regiment. Harmar served throughout the War for Independence; he was at Montreal, Fort Ticonderoga, Valley Forge, and Yorktown. He distinguished himself more for his organizational skills than his personal bravery and rose to the rank of lieutenant-colonel. Harmar emerged from his service in the Continental Army as a young man with aristocratic pretensions and a passion for order. Well-connected, he carried the ratified treaty to Paris in 1784 and spent some time there and in London before returning to Philadelphia and an October wedding to Sarah Jenkins.

Like others of his type, Harmar saw himself as a gentleman and had virtually no respect for the men who served under him. To the contrary, his letters are full of disparaging comments about his soldiers and about frontiersmen in general. Harmar was a confirmed member of that unofficial brotherhood of Continental officers who spent much of their lives nursing slights and insults, some real, some imagined, and planning the inevitable moment when they would demonstrate to the world why they deserved the respect few seemed willing to accord them. Accordingly, Harmar went about the business of commanding the unrepentant "banditti," both in and out of his army, with great gusto. Securing the power of the United States was inextricably tied up with securing the reputation of Josiah Harmar.

The First Regiment's initial assignment was to protect other agents of the United States in their efforts to secure the Northwest. Foremost among these agents were commissioners appointed by Congress to negotiate with the Indians. The attitude of the United States in this area was as naive and as cocky as in everything else regarding the West. Congress acted on the assumption that the Indians had forfeited their lands by their "defeat," along with the British, during the War for Independence. The victorious government, however, had generously decided to allow them to keep their territory west of the Great Miami River in return for a cessation of hostilities. At Fort McIntosh in western Pennsylvania on January 21, 1785, commissioners, bearing no gifts and offering no compensation, signed a treaty with some Delawares, Wyandots, Chippewas, and Ottawas arbitrarily drawing a boundary through what is now central Ohio. Congressional commissioners and the Shawnee reached a similar agreement at Fort Finney at the mouth of the Great Miami River on January 31, 1786. In the long run, these treaties meant very little. But they revealed the depth of American bravado.

The most important thing Harmar did was to establish the presence of the Confederation in the Ohio Valley. He did so against great odds. Harmar was chronically short of men. In April 1785, Congress had authorized the recruitment of 700 troops for three-year terms. There were few incentives for men to respond; who would want to work for a government that had virtually no visible means of support? With the several hundred men Harmar was intermittently able to muster, he proceeded to establish a military presence along the Ohio. Following the Treaty of Fort McIntosh, Captain John Doughty and Captain Jonathan Heart led several dozen men in the construction of Fort Harmar at the mouth of the Muskingum River, some 140 miles southeast of Fort McIntosh, in October 1785. Meanwhile a company under Captain Walter Finney put up a temporary fort (named for himself) at the mouth of the Miami. Captain John F. Hamtramck and his men built Fort Steuben in eastern Ohio during the winter of 1785–1786, largely to protect the nationally appointed surveyors who were busy laying out townships in the seven ranges of eastern Ohio. At the end of the following summer, Captain Finney abandoned his post and reestablished Fort Finney on the north side of the Ohio River just above the falls at Louisville. Nearby was Clarksville, the home of George Rogers Clark and several dozen families of the veterans of his campaigns.

All of this activity came under the supervision of General Henry Knox, whom Congress had appointed secretary at war in March 1785. A former bookseller and a beneficiary of a good marriage, Knox had served with General Washington during the Revolution. The general was himself a great land speculator, with ambitious dreams of manorial glory that would reach partial fruition on the Maine frontier in the 1790s. He was also an ardent supporter of a strong national government. Knox proved himself to be an adept

🏴 109

THE
WORLD
OF
JOSIAH
HARMAR &
JOHN
FRANCIS
HAMTRAMCK,
1787–1790

manager of meager military forces. Working with few resources (including a staff of three), he efficiently carried out the orders of Congress while offering the members thorough and astute reports on the situation in the West. The secretary's successful tenure in the 1780s was a major reason for his appointment as secretary of war when George Washington assumed the presidency under the Constitution in 1789.

The construction of military outposts announced the arrival of the United States in the Ohio Valley. There was nothing more likely to impress people with the authority of the new government than stockades with flags flying above them or uniformed soldiers acting in the name of the Confederation. But the forts were not simply there for display. They were there for the specific purpose of disabusing all peoples—British, French, Indians, Kentuckians—of any notions they might have about resisting or ignoring the grand plans outlined in the legislation of the 1780s. In fact, the troops spent a considerable amount of their time warning away the hundreds of Virginians and Pennsylvanians who were attempting to settle on the north side of the Ohio River.

While Harmar's forts were the American analogues to the French posts at Detroit, Ouiatanon, and Vincennes, they existed not to integrate the Americans into existing economic, social, and political structures but to prepare the way for the establishment of entirely new customs and institutions. On the surface, they seem like minor achievements. Harmar was constantly complaining about the quantity and quality of his men. And he could hardly stop the unending raids between whites and Indians which had become part of the rhythm of Ohio Valley life any more than he could prevent squatting on federal lands, which Congress had forbidden as early as 1783. At Fort Harmar in 1786 and 1787, the soldiers occupied their time by counting the hundreds of flatboats floating by them on the way to settlements in Kentucky. Still, it would be exceedingly rash to underestimate the importance of the military presence. Feeble as the United States appeared, it quickly became an important player in regional conflicts, if only because they seemed so unresolvable.

American officials in the late 1780s prided themselves on their treatment of the Indians, which is why they called for the equity and responsibility in Indian relations in the Northwest Ordinance.

In fact, they disparaged the behavior of white frontiersmen as much as they did the Shawnee, Delaware, and Miami. "The deep rooted prejudices, and malignity of heart, and conduct, reciprocally entertained and practised on all occasions by the Whites and Savages will ever prevent their being good neighbours," Secretary Knox informed Congress in July 1787. "The innocent and helpless" were trapped in "the flames of a merciless war" of revenge. The Confederation could not afford a long war against Indians and its own citizens in the West, however. It needed a quick resolution of the situation in the Ohio Valley in order to establish its authority, bring federal lands into the market, and attract settlers who would begin to build towns, plant crops, and trade with the rest of the world. Somehow the United States, in the words of Knox, had to "keep them [Indians and settlers] in awe by a strong hand, and compel them to be moderate and just" in dealing with each other.

The balance of power between Indians and Kentuckians in the Wabash Valley and the rest of the Northwest worked to the advantage of the Americans. George Rogers Clark's inability to conquer the region, French disillusionment with both Virginia and Great Britain, British hesitancy about abandoning their northwestern posts, and lack of unity among the Indians—all contributed to the growth of American power in the region. While the government was obviously going to side with the whites in a showdown, it had the illusion of being an arbiter of disputes, a power broker in a region without a dominant power.

Colonel Harmar in Vincennes

Such was the role it assumed in the spring of 1787. On April 24, Congress, having heard reports of Clark's dismal campaign in the Wabash Valley and eager to extend its authority into the heart of the Northwest Territory, ordered Knox to "direct" Harmar to dispossess "a body of men who have in a lawless and unauthorized manner taken possession of post St. Vincents in defiance of the proclamation and authority of the United States." The secretary did as he was told.

In June, Colonel Harmar gathered men and supplies at Fort Finney in preparation for his movement on Vincennes. On the 19th he wrote to Colonel Le Gras and Major Bosseron, men he had heard

III

THE
WORLD
OF
JOSIAH
HARMAR &
JOHN
FRANCIS
HAMTRAMCK,
1787–1790

were "good friends to the United States," to inform them of his intentions. Harmar assured the French that they would "be protected in their rights" and asked Le Gras and Bosseron to tell the Indians that they should not be alarmed by his activities: Congress simply wanted to punish the "set of lawless banditti" (that is, Clark and his Kentuckians) who had been harassing the peoples of the Wabash. There was no cause for alarm. After all, Harmar and his men were "not a set of villains but regulars, and sent by the authority of the Grand Council of the Empire."

Le Gras responded quickly to this grandiloquent announcement. He told Harmar, in a letter written on June 26, that the French citizens of Vincennes welcomed an end to their sufferings as the "prey of vagabonds." They wanted a resolution to the confusion about whose "authority" they lived under. Apparently not everyone in Vincennes thought the United States was the answer to their prayers. Bosseron did not respond to Harmar. Perhaps Bosseron had had enough of distant governments—whether British, Virginian, or American—promising peace and prosperity. Le Gras, on the other hand, flattered and cultivated Harmar. He and a few others would come to the mouth of the Wabash to escort the American troops up the river to Vincennes. "It is in the name of all the people who desire you that we have the honor of being sincerely and frankly your very humble and very obedient servant and faithful subject of the United States of America," concluded Le Gras.

The colonel was no fool, as he had amply demonstrated in his dealings with Clark. His eagerness to greet Harmar seems excessive in retrospect. But it is important to remember the context, the history of Vincennes. For decades the citizens of the town had been greeting representatives of the British government on the upper Wabash and accompanying them to their town. This was not mere courtesy or simply a means of ingratiating oneself. It was a ritual, part of the custom of life along the Wabash in the eighteenth century. Among both Indians and Europeans, men greeted each other with gifts and expressions of mutual respect. They also took the opportunity to assess each other and to try to set the tone and terms of ensuing negotiations.

Despite Le Gras's promise, no one met Colonel Harmar at the mouth of the Wabash. The 300 troops floated down the Ohio on Kentucky boats. Some poled their way upriver on boats, although the low level of the water made that a slow and arduous process. Others drove cattle and horses along the banks. It was early July and hot. The men on land were carrying two weeks' worth of flour on their backs and they tired easily. Lieutenant John Armstrong complained about both the heat and a lack of water. Sometimes they went as many as ten miles "without a drink." He thought the whole place "a desert." After a march of six-and-a-half days through heavy thickets, the army dispatched by the Grand Council of the American empire arrived, with some relief, at Vincennes at noon on July 17. They camped outside Fort Sackville that night and then moved about a quarter of a mile upriver (at the foot of Buntin Street) where they would soon construct Fort Knox.

Harmar and his men were, of course, instant celebrities in what the American commander described as "a very considerable village" of 400 buildings, home to close to 900 French "souls" and some 400 Americans. The peoples of the Wabash came to greet them but did so warily after two decades of experience with inconstant British and Virginians. Colonel Le Gras and leading French citizens were "most respectfully submissive" when they welcomed the Americans on the 19th. But Harmar had to call upon the Frenchman the next day to demand the official records of land transactions and town business. Since they were in French, he delayed examination of them. Meanwhile he reinstated the French magistrates and laws.

Harmar blustered about Vincennes with all the delicacy one would expect from a self-important agent of a self-important government among peoples he considered ignorant and backward. His job, as he saw it, was "to prevent illegal encroachments on the public lands, to secure happiness to the inhabitants, and to protect private property from arbitrary invasion, and to remove if possible diffidence, fear and jealousy from the minds of the Indians." Accordingly, Harmar posted copies, in both French and English, of the 1783 congressional proclamation against intruders in the Northwest Territory, "which amazed the inhabitants exceedingly, particularly those who stile themselves Americans." He thought his actions would have the proper effect on Kentuckians, especially veterans of Clark's campaign, who eyed the lands of the Wabash that by law, if nothing else, were the property of the United States. On July 29, Harmar met with eight Piankashaw Indians who had come from

🪶 113

The
World
of
Josiah
Harmar &
John
Francis
Hamtramck,
1787–1790

Terre Haute to speak with him. They exchanged small gifts while Harmar "assured them of the friendly disposition of the United States." But when some Indians killed one of his men working on the Wabash on August 5 and captured another, Harmar warned everyone of the dangers inherent in bringing down upon themselves "the vengeance of the United States."

Most of his time was spent trying to sort out the records of land holdings and transactions he had gotten from Le Gras. In this business, of immense importance to a government committed to the development and sale of the Northwest Territory, Harmar relied heavily on the advice and translations of Barthelemi Tardiveau. Thirty-seven years old in 1787, Tardiveau had been born in Nantes, France, and migrated to Philadelphia in 1777. In the early 1780s, he was in Kentucky working as a supplier for George Rogers Clark. By the time Harmar arrived on the Wabash, Tardiveau had established himself as a trader and the principal liaison between the French settlers in the Old Northwest, particularly at Kaskaskia, and the government of Virginia.

In a remarkable letter dated August 6, 1787, Tardiveau offered Harmar some savvy advice on how to achieve his goal of protecting the lands of the United States from intruders and Indians. Foremost was the necessity of drawing a distinction in the minds of the French in Vincennes between the United States and the Virginians, between "the legal acts of a respectable nation, and the unwarranted proceedings of an unprincipled multitude." Harmar should appoint an attorney to prosecute criminals. He should recognize land grants before Clark's 1778 conquest as valid and disallow those made since. Even more challenging was the problem of the Indians.

Tardiveau believed that the Indians were more loyal to some Europeans than others because of differences in their "modes of government." Weak governments that could not control their own citizens should not expect peaceful relations with Indians. Rather, they would find repeated acts of violence. "[H]ow much soever we may despise the Indians," wrote the French trader, "they have very noble notions of order and subordination; and they can hardly be persuaded that the subjects wou'd dare to treat them in a manner that they conceive to be injurious, if government did not countenance them." This must particularly have been the case, given

Harmar's repeated assertions of the pretensions of the United States government. Either it had power or it did not. There was no middle ground here. Indeed, Tardiveau wanted "a more absolute government" where "the hand of power holds every where with equal steadiness." Trade would be "reduced to a system," and regulated in such a way that mistreatment of an Indian would be more of "a public offence" than "a private injury." Treaties would be worthless unless Harmar was "invested with power energetick enough to keep the whites under subjection." Tardiveau was sensitive to American respect for individual liberty. But he wanted a "military" government in the Northwest until more "respectable and well disposed men" should settle in the region. Otherwise, "adventurers" would "soon swarm" into Vincennes and other places, bringing "the disturbing operations of their jumbled elections, mob-made magistrates, pack'd juries, and partial laws."

Tardiveau recommended that the United States extend its authority farther up the Wabash. Flattering Harmar as "an officer of . . . distinguished military talents," he nonetheless pointed out that a few hundred men were not enough "to inspire respect" among the Indians. The colonel needed "at least a thousand more men, two hundred of whom are cavalry," in order to intimidate the Miami, Wea, and other Indians on the upper Wabash. In other words, Congress should invest the center of Indian society in the region, "without which the Indians can never be awed or gained over." To stay at Vincennes or engage in expeditions from that post would be counterproductive at best.

Tardiveau effectively summarized the major problems confronting Harmar. He had to impress Indians, the French, and Virginians/Kentuckians with the majesty of the United States at the lowest possible cost in both men and money. And he had to act under difficult circumstances: his army was dangerously overextended in the heart of a territory where it could trust no one; his men and officers were increasingly unhappy with their situation; and his authority was not entirely clear. Historians have generally assumed that Harmar failed to achieve many of his objectives because of these problems and the general weakness of the Confederation. But the colonel and his officers, in conjuction with other officials, actually managed to accomplish quite a lot.

📯 II5

THE
WORLD
OF
JOSIAH
HARMAR &
JOHN
FRANCIS
HAMTRAMCK,
1787–1790

Major Hamtramck and Fort Knox

Harmar, whom Congress had promoted to brevet brigadier-general in July, departed Vincennes on October 1 to travel to the French settlements on the Mississippi, then return to Fort Harmar for the winter. He left the Wabash in the hands of Major John Francis Hamtramck. A thirty-one-year-old native of Quebec, Hamtramck had a French Canadian and Roman Catholic background that ideally qualified him for command at Vincennes. He also had the requisite military credentials. Hamtramck had been a brevet major in the New York line of the Continental Army during the Revolution. In 1785, he became a captain of a New York company in the Confederation Army and was promoted to major in October 1786. Since then, Hamtramck had operated mainly in the upper Ohio Valley, protecting surveyors and evicting squatters. Now the five-foot, five-inch major had responsibility for the most exposed and socially complex outpost of the United States in the Northwest.

In general, Hamtramck was up to the task, although one can be misled by his correspondence. Any reader of his many letters to Harmar will be struck by the predictability of his complaints. His men did not like Vincennes, in large part because they found it too expensive. Many of them, including Hamtramck, were frequently ill with a variety of fevers and complaints. The major constantly worried that he did not have enough men or supplies to meet his objectives of maintaining peace and protecting the property of the United States. Hamtramck's anxiety reinforced the nervousness of Tardiveau about the small size of American forces. He expressed concern that Congress act quickly to take control of the region and relieve him from his exposed position. To a significant extent, Hamtramck's nervousness was understandable. He and his men had a great deal to do. But they were hardly inactive. Harmar and Hamtramck may have lacked imagination, but they were persistent.

The most tangible achievement was the construction of Fort Knox, which was completed during the winter and spring of 1788. Major Hamtramck worried incessantly about it. There was not enough timber, and what there was cost far too much. In addition, his soldiers were frequently ill with fever and unable to work. Worst of all, he had no flag—a symbol Indians in particular wished to see displayed. But Hamtramck persevered. By April, the fort had fences and two-story block houses. By August, he was sending Harmar "a ground plan of the garrison" and begging him to provide a name for it. Harmar not unwisely chose the name of his superior—Knox.

Fort Knox was more impressive than its predecessors. A rectangular affair, some seventy yards long by fifty-five yards wide, it sat just above the eastern bank of the Wabash. At each corner stood a two-story blockhouse equipped with a platform to hold cannon. The palisades were eleven feet high. The main gate was on the side away from the Wabash with a sally port near the river. Inside Fort Knox there were five one-story barracks for enlisted men and two two-story quarters for officers. There was also a blacksmith's workplace and a magazine. The solidly constructed fort housed members of the United States Army for at least a decade. More important, it was a tangible expression of the commitment of the United States to the Wabash Valley. Fort Knox demonstrated the existence and power of the new republic to everyone who traveled along the river.

The completion of the fort in the summer of 1788 did not end Hamtramck's headaches. Major sources of tension were his officers and men. Many disliked Vincennes. They found it an "extravagant" place to live. In addition, the army and its contractors did not get food or medical supplies to the fort on a regular basis. Captain William Ferguson complained to Harmar in August 1788 that many of his men were "so disgusted with this place" that they would not reenlist; they were subsisting on bread and beef, which was often very bad, and "whiskey, soap, candles, and vinegar are seldom or ever issued." The men were frequently ill, but their doctor had nothing with which to treat them. Hamtramck worried at the end of August that the fort "will inevitably fall unless another mode of supply takes place."

Part of the problem was having to bring goods up the Wabash, especially since the water level fluctuated wildly in the eighteenth century. But the problem was complicated by poor planning and the usual confusion and corruption of the contractors. Like François Bosseron with George Rogers Clark, François Vigo and others in Vincennes supplied the troops with corn and other necessities. Hamtramck claimed that they got nearly a third of their rations of

117

THE
WORLD
OF
JOSIAH
HARMAR &
JOHN
FRANCIS
HAMTRAMCK,
1787–1790

flour from the French on a regular basis. The major and Harmar attempted to get the United States to reimburse Vigo, but the government's accountants refused to do so, claiming that the contractor should assume responsibility for the debts. Caught in the middle, Hamtramck did the best he could. The American troops survived; many even reenlisted.

In fact, the longer they were in Vincennes, the more they liked it. The difficulties both the French and the American troops faced may have served to bring them together. Hamtramck is the best example of the growing friendliness. As early as May 1788, the major requested a leave to return to New York, which Harmar denied. In January 1790, he finally gave Hamtramck permission to take some time off. But the major rejected the offer, citing "an unforeseen event"—most likely his relationship with Marie Josepte Edeline Perrot, the widow of Nicholas Perrot of Vincennes. The two were married sometime in the summer of 1790. They had three daughters. The first died of a fever in the spring of 1793; the other two, Julienne and Henriette, survived. Hamtramck had more than accommodated himself to life in Vincennes. The town was his wife's home and the birthplace of his children. He was, in fact, replicating the experience of French settlers throughout the eighteenth century.

The major's personal happiness accompanied a general improvement in relations between the troops and the townspeople. Shortly after his arrival, in November 1787, Hamtramck had complained of the "great confusion" in local politics. "Many people," both French and American apparently, were "displeased with the magistrates." Le Gras and his allies had been in power for a long time, after all, and it had not been a particularly happy period at that. The major wrung his hands about the situation. What should he do? What were the limits of his authority? Congress had to do something quickly; the citizens of Vincennes were demanding action. A pathetic Hamtramck confessed to Harmar that he had "been very much at lost how to act on many occassion."

Whether because of the news of the Northwest Ordinance or the appointment of territorial officers in the winter of 1787–1788, or simply because of growing self-confidence, Hamtramck eventually found a way to act. In April 1788, he responded to a petition against the government of the Le Gras and Gamelin families by dissolving the court, calling for new elections, and establishing regular procedures and lower fees for the magistrates' court. The death of Le Gras in February undoubtedly paved the way for Hamtramck. The election of five new magistrates—Jean Baptiste Miliet, Moses Henry, Nicholas Baillardjon, James Johnson, and Thomas Dalton—marked a revolution in the local power structure. The old French "ottoman families" would now have to share offices with Virginians and other newer settlers. Henry had been in Vincennes for years and had sought the aid of Virginia in the mid-1780s; Dalton had served with Clark and had been one of the lawless banditti investing Vincennes in the summer of 1787 (Harmar expressed surprise at his election). The Gamelins and the Richervilles—families who had dominated the town for decades—remained influential. But the French had had to accommodate themselves to their American neighbors.

Hamtramck thus demonstrated the key to the success of the United States in the region. Had the French and Virginians in Vincennes been united, had there been some kind of consensus about how local government should operate, the major would never have been able to interfere successfully in their affairs. But they were not united and they invited Hamtramck to break the tie, to fill the vacuum, as an arbiter. In this way, the authority of the United States increased because the pretensions of its officials intersected with the political situation in the Wabash. Among Europeans, the government gained credibility as the ultimate umpire in old disputes.

The Government of the Northwest Territory

Hamtramck's intervention in Vincennes occurred at the same time as the arrival of the first "official" American settlers in the Northwest Territory, at the mouth of the Muskingum River (across from Fort Harmar) in eastern Ohio in April 1788. In July 1787, at the same time as the passage of the Northwest Ordinance, Congress had sold hundreds of thousands of acres to a joint-stock company of Continental officers and soldiers called the Ohio Company of Associates. This was a bargain for both sides. The speculators got lots of land inexpensively while the government got men committed to its success in positions of some authority in the Northwest. The leaders of the Ohio Company were fervent exponents of national

THE
WORLD
OF
JOSIAH
HARMAR &
JOHN
FRANCIS
HAMTRAMCK,
1787–1790

authority; they strongly supported both the federal government created by the Constitution of the United States and the territorial government created by the Northwest Ordinance. Congress also sold a huge tract of land in the valley of the Great Miami River to John Cleves Symmes of New Jersey, a man who would prove to be less devoted to national interests.

There was a serious overlap between these speculators and the government of the Northwest Territory. Congress appointed Symmes and two directors of the Ohio Company, Samuel Holden Parsons of Connecticut and James Mitchell Varnum of Rhode Island, as the three territorial judges. Later, Ohio Company Superintendent Rufus Putnam, a diligent but unimaginative officer from Massachusetts, would serve as a territorial judge. Winthrop Sargent of Massachusetts, the secretary of the Ohio Company, was also the territorial secretary (and acting governor from time to time). The governorship went to Major-General Arthur St. Clair, a Scotsman who had begun his public career as a local magistrate in western Pennsylvania, had moved on to an undistinguished career as a Continental officer, and had become a member of Congress from Pennsylvania. The pompous St. Clair, who was better known for his drinking than his legislating, sought the position as a stepping-stone to higher office under the new Constitution.

Governor St. Clair arrived in Marietta in the summer of 1788 and proceeded to establish the apparatus of local government under the Northwest Ordinance. He created Washington County and appointed local officials and militia officers, relying again on the military veterans in the Ohio Company. These offices were far from inconsequential. The justices of the peace, some of whom heard civil cases as members of the court of common pleas and others who dealt with petty criminal cases as members of the court of quarter sessions, exercised a great deal of local power. In January 1790, St. Clair created Hamilton County in the Symmes purchase. Later in the year, he appointed George Rogers Clark's cousin, William, captain of militia and justice of the peace for the Clarksville settlement.

Because of pressing business at Fort Washington, which was rapidly becoming the central headquarters of the American army in the Ohio Valley, St. Clair left the business of organizing local government along the Wabash to Secretary Sargent. The Americans, of course, did not organize government; they reorganized it. The arrogant and difficult Sargent, an even more self-important person than Harmar, arrived at Vincennes in June 1790, and created the county of Knox. To fill local offices, Sargent turned to both the old French families (Gamelins, Vigo, Richerville, Bosseron) and the American settlers of the 1780s (blacksmith John Small became sheriff, James Johnson and Luke Decker were named justices of the peace). In other words, the United States simply ratified the emerging political structure in Vincennes. And the new leaders were appropriately grateful. In July 1790, they went out of their way to acknowledge to Sargent "the just and humane attention paid by Major Hamtramck during his whole command, to the rights and feelings of every individual craving his interposition demands. . . ." It was a welcome relief "from the frequent change of masters" they had experienced in the 1770s and 1780s.

Hamtramck had established the authority of the United States in large part by exploiting the intersection between the interests of the nation and those of the French in Vincennes. Sargent, like General Harmar, was not so subtle. The secretary of the Northwest Territory was happy to receive the respect of its "respectable citizens." But that ranked below the "Happiness" he experienced in "merit[ing] the approbation of the soverign Authority of the United States by a faithful discharge of the important Trusts committed to me." Most important was their "Fidelity and Attachment to the General Government of the United States" and its "August President." Certainly that government was "the best Possible Palladium for the Lives and Property of Mankind."

Nothing would stand in the way of Sargent's determination to assert American authority. His stubborn insistence upon putting the reputation of the government above local interests later led him into a series of scrapes with the citizens of Cincinnati and the Mississippi Territory. In Vincennes in June 1790, Sargent and judges Symmes and George Turner (who had replaced the deceased Varnum) drew up specific regulations for the Wabash region. Forbidding the sale of liquor to Indians, they restricted the trade to licensed merchants. They also outlawed liquor and gun trading between soldiers in Fort Knox and the citizens of the town. They prohibited gambling and the spontaneous firing of guns. Acting alone, Secretary Sargent or-

121

THE
WORLD
OF
JOSIAH
HARMAR &
JOHN
FRANCIS
HAMTRAMCK,
1787–1790

dered all men between sixteen and fifty to serve in the militia. More dramatically, he "strictly" prohibited anyone who was not an American citizen from "hunting or killing any kind of Game . . . either for the Skins or Flesh." Sargent also wanted all persons, "whether Whites, Indians or Negroes," who arrived in Vincennes to report within two hours to Fort Knox. Sargent and St. Clair refused to make Article Six of the Northwest Ordinance retroactive, thereby allowing the French to continue to hold as slaves those human beings they owned in the territory before 1787. The territorial officers were willing to temper their restrictions with occasional concessions to secure the loyalty of the French.

In any case, the regulations were virtually impossible to enforce completely. They simply embodied Sargent's desire to go beyond Hamtramck's actions and make the United States more than an arbiter and protector in the Wabash Valley. Like the British in the 1760s, the secretary wanted to regulate both the economic and social structures of the region. More than that, he sought to make the new national government of the republican empire the supreme director of the development of the Old Northwest.

Whether the people of Vincennes obeyed the specific laws and proclamations is beside the point. Harmar, Sargent, and especially Hamtramck succeeded in establishing the authority of the United States more securely than that of any previous foreign power. The people of Vincennes increasingly looked to the republic to solve their problems. In 1787, a Spanish officer seized $1,980 worth of goods and peltries from Joseph St. Marie, a Vincennes trader traveling on the Mississippi River to New Orleans. The French-born American citizen saw as his "only and last Resource . . . the honorable the Congress of the United States of America." St. Marie was not reimbursed, but the way he ritually invoked the majesty of the United States suggested the degree to which European-Americans along the Wabash had accepted its authority. At last there was a government worthy of their respect.

Sargent devoted most of his six weeks in Vincennes in the summer of 1790 to dealing with the much-disputed question of land holdings. Here again a successful resolution of a long-standing crisis only served to affirm the authority of the United States. Neither Great Britain nor Virginia had straightened out the often vague and conflicting claims of the French and later of the American settlers. But the United States saw the questions of private property and legal procedures as central to their interests in the Northwest. In fact, the American claim to the region had less to do with conquest or possession than with a carefully constructed assertion of legal rights. Congress had acquired its power through cessions and ordinances. It could have ignored the claims of the Vincennes settlers. But both the fact that it took them seriously and dealt with them through federal political structures demonstrated the American commitment to a predictable and reliable system in the holding and transfer of property. The United States took the Old Northwest, but it did so in ways that laid the foundations for challenges to its power. In other words, as important as getting the land itself was, the process by which the French and Americans petitioned Congress and obtained redress for their grievances was fundamental to the eventual acceptance of American authority.

On August 29, 1788, in response to several petitions from the people of Vincennes, Congress passed a resolution ordering "that measures be taken for confirming in their possessions and titles the french and Canadian inhabitants and other settlers at post St. Vincents who on or before the year 1783 had settled there and had professed themselves citizens of the United States or any of them . . . the several tracts which they rightfully claim and which may have been allotted to them according to the laws and Usages of the Governments under which they had respectively settled." Each "head of a family" was to receive 400 acres in a square tract laid out by the territorial governor "in whatever direction the settlers shall prefer."

Sargent devoted much of July to determining who qualified under this resolution. Few people had regular titles or much in the way of concrete evidence. This was one time, however, when the secretary's stubborn persistence paid off. Sargent conducted interviews with residents and pieced together what information he could obtain. Eventually he concluded that some 158 people (including twenty-three widows or deserted women, one of whom was the wife of Major John Hamtramck) met the description detailed in the congressional resolution. Sixty people clearly owned seventy-two small farms (perhaps 66 to 136 acres in size) and 128 had 162 town lots. The Americans who had settled in Vincennes after 1783 were not

123

THE
WORLD
OF
JOSIAH
HARMAR &
JOHN
FRANCIS
HAMTRAMCK,
1787–1790

happy with their exclusion from the resolution and asked Sargent to do something about it. In March 1791, Congress included virtually everyone in an act confirming the work of the officious Sargent. Indeed, every person enrolled in the militia on August 1, 1791, was entitled to at least 100 acres.

It took two decades of litigation to bring the conflict over property holdings in and around Vincennes to an end. Still, the relatively decisive action of Secretary Sargent and the Congress contributed immeasurably to the growth of federal power in the Northwest. While the United States gave away some of its domain, it gained a great deal in return. As in other areas, the young and untested republic secured its position in the Northwest by resolving long-standing disputes in what most people apparently accepted as a fair process. What the United States lost in land, it more than regained in respect.

Territorial Officials and American Indians

The agents of the national government won the loyalty of the Europeans of Vincennes with laws and sympathy. They had far less success with both Kentuckians and Indians, neither of whom believed they stood to gain much from the establishment of a strong American presence in the region.

In the 1780s, the Confederation used both carrots and sticks to win over or at least neutralize Indians and American settlers. For the latter, Congress authorized negotiations with Spain in order to secure the navigation of the Mississippi River, which was crucial to the economic development of the Ohio Valley. It also offered its soldiers and forts as protection for legal settlers in both Kentucky and the Northwest Territory and as a signal to the British in Canada that the United States, under the terms of the 1783 Treaty of Paris, expected them to evacuate their posts south of the Great Lakes. Negatively, Congress attempted to stop the occupation of the Northwest by illegal settlers. Indeed, the soldiers of the United States Army were in the region more to coerce Kentuckians and Pennsylvanians into respecting congressional authority than to evict the Indians or the French.

With regard to the Indians, by the late 1780s, the United States was moving away from its hard-line position that the lands of the

Northwest belonged to it by virtue of military conquest. The 1787 Ordinance promised "the utmost good faith" in dealing with Indians; more specifically, that meant respecting their "property, rights and liberty," getting their "consent" to give up "lands and property," and engaging only "in just and lawful wars." Historians often see this as hypocritical, since Virginians and Pennsylvanians engaged in a series of raids with the Indians of the Northwest. They forget the distinction men such as Knox and Harmar made between the national government and the banditti of the frontier. The clause in the Northwest Ordinance was not empty rhetoric; it was directed at both Indians and white frontiersmen.

Governor St. Clair extended the policy of negotiation with Indians in Marietta in January 1789. The Treaty of Fort Harmar, signed by St. Clair and representatives of the Iroquois and a few other nations, offered some small compensation for the lands ceded earlier at Forts Stanwix and McIntosh. The significance here was not the amount but the shift in American policy back to the traditional practice of paying the Indians. In fact, Congress had begun to deal with the Indians, both north and south, in a fashion similar to the ways in which they dealt with foreign nations, thus recognizing their autonomy and sovereignty. After his election as president under the Constitution of 1787, George Washington insisted that the Senate ratify the Treaty of Fort Harmar just as it would a treaty with France or Spain.

As part of its larger scheme for securing the Northwest Territory, the national government intended to regulate Indian-white relations and reduce them to a system. As Secretary Knox advised Congress in July 1787, "Government must keep them both in awe by a strong hand, and compel them to be moderate and just." These were bold words, as Knox well knew. Accordingly, he and his officers devoted much of their time to lobbying for more troops and more money and complaining about how difficult their jobs were. How were they to enforce the will of Congress when their actual power was so "feeble"? The sheer bulk of words about weakness and problems naturally leads readers to accept the officers' assessment of their predicaments. But we have an advantage they lacked—the ability to see their activities from a longer perspective,

📪 125

THE
WORLD
OF
JOSIAH
HARMAR &
JOHN
FRANCIS
HAMTRAMCK,
1787–1790

to evaluate their work from the arc of their careers rather than specific incidents.

When about sixty men from Nelson County, Kentucky, led by twenty-eight-year-old Patrick Brown, "who calls himself a major," arrived in Vincennes in August 1788, Major Hamtramck was beside himself. Brown was a veteran of one of Clark's expeditions and many frontier scrapes. He and his men were "after Indians"; in fact, they claimed to have killed nine on the same day Hamtramck encountered them. Brown and Hamtramck argued about who was in charge. Hamtramck demanded by what authority Brown acted. That of the governor of Virginia, he replied. But he had no orders or legal papers. An outraged Hamtramck pointed out that "there was a great differance between following Indians who had forfeited their lives, or looking out for other that were in a pasific state and under the protection of the United States." Since only Congress could authorize a war with the Indians, Hamtramck "ordered [Brown] in the name of *the United States* to depart immediately, and told him I should report him." The Indians he had killed were under the protection of the American government. He also demanded that the Kentuckians return six horses they had stolen from the French.

Brown agreed, but failed to comply. One can only wonder what he made of the short French-American commander's angry orders. Hamtramck, for his part, was profoundly humiliated by Brown's defiance. "Never was my feeling so much wonded before," he told Harmar. "But what could I do?" he asked in the whiny tone so dear to American government agents when writing to their superiors. "I had but nine men fit for duty, the American militia would not have fought them if I had been able to have marched 50 men, what French there was in town at that time would have joined me cheerfully and would have perhaps persuaded Mr. Brown to accept of my propositions."

Hamtramck tried to assuage the Indians, with only limited success. Within two weeks of Brown's raid, he reported the murders of two women and an infant on the western side of the Wabash. The American officer and the French in Vincennes stood together against the Kentuckians, but they were unable to maintain peace. They could not stop the escalating cycle of revenge, the angry defense of family and honor—what Henry Knox called in 1787 "the right that each party assumes of being judges and prompt executioners in their own cause."

By 1790, President Washington and Generals Knox, St Clair, and Harmar had concluded that it would take stronger measures to establish the authority of the United States in the Northwest Territory. They had to act. They had to intimidate both Indians and settlers, awe them with the power and majesty of the American government, demonstrate that the United States could accomplish what no other power—not France, not Great Britain, not Virginia—had done. The resulting military strategy would take half a decade and would involve immense problems and some of the worst defeats in American history. But in the end, the torrent of complaints about the lack of men and the insults of Kentuckians notwithstanding and in the face of powerful opposition, the agents of the United States did establish it as the supreme power north of the Ohio River. The same John Francis Hamtramck who despaired of his position in Vincennes in the late summer of 1788 would command the left wing of the victorious American army at Fallen Timbers in 1794, oversee the construction of Fort Wayne at the confluence of the St. Joseph and St. Marys rivers later that year, and assume command of Detroit when the British finally evacuated it in 1796. In other words, Patrick Brown's wounding of the pride of Hamtramck and the United States was hardly fatal. To the contrary, time made it far less severe than it first appeared to be.

The Old French House, built for fur
trader Michel Brouillet, is an example
of an early nineteenth-century
Vincennes dwelling. COURTESY OF THE
BYRON R. LEWIS HISTORICAL LIBRARY,
VINCENNES UNIVERSITY, VINCENNES, INDIANA.

George Rogers Clark. His life and
reputation peaked in his "conquest"
of the French settlements in the late
1770s. COURTESY OF THE INDIANA HISTORICAL
SOCIETY LIBRARY, INDIANAPOLIS, INDIANA.

Jean Baptiste Richerville, chief of the Miami and a nephew of Little Turtle, from an 1827 painting by J. O. Lewis. COURTESY OF THE INDIANA HISTORICAL SOCIETY LIBRARY, INDIANAPOLIS, INDIANA.

Josiah Harmar, commander of the American forces in the Ohio Valley in the late 1780s, from an original painting by Raphael Peale. COURTESY OF THE INDIANA HISTORICAL SOCIETY LIBRARY, INDIANAPOLIS, INDIANA.

This likeness of Little Turtle, supposedly from a 1797 portrait painted by Gilbert Stuart and lost when the British burned Washington in 1814, shows him during a period of transition. With the resistance of the early 1790s behind him, he was learning the ways of accommodation. COURTESY OF THE INDIANA HISTORICAL SOCIETY LIBRARY, INDIANAPOLIS, INDIANA.

We have no portrait of the young Anna Symmes Harrison. But hidden under the huge bonnet, the eyes of the elderly woman still shine bright and confident. COURTESY OF THE CINCINNATI HISTORICAL SOCIETY, CINCINNATI, OHIO.

Governor William Henry
Harrison of the Indiana Territory,
from a portrait attributed to
Rembrandt Peale. COURTESY OF THE
INDIANA HISTORICAL SOCIETY LIBRARY,
INDIANAPOLIS, INDIANA.

Grouseland, the Harrison home in
Vincennes, reflects the ambitions
and achievements of the family.
COURTESY OF THE BYRON R. LEWIS
HISTORICAL LIBRARY, VINCENNES
UNIVERSITY, VINCENNES, INDIANA.

A likeness of Tenskwatawa, the Prophet. COURTESY OF THE INDIANA HISTORICAL SOCIETY LIBRARY, INDIANAPOLIS, INDIANA.

In this portrait, Jonathan Jennings, one of the leaders of the opposition to Governor Harrison, seems young, smooth, and a bit of a dandy. COURTESY OF THE INDIANA HISTORICAL SOCIETY LIBRARY, INDIANAPOLIS, INDIANA.

1816

The State Capitol in Corydon. COURTESY OF
THE INDIANA HISTORICAL SOCIETY LIBRARY,
INDIANAPOLIS, INDIANA.

William Conner became an important regional entrepreneur after making a fortune as a trader with the Delaware Indians. COURTESY OF THE INDIANA STATE LIBRARY, INDIANAPOLIS, INDIANA.

William Conner's choice of a second wife, Elizabeth Chapman Conner, represented the transformation of frontier Indiana. He married her after he had helped to arrange for the removal of his first wife, a Delaware woman, and their children from Indiana.
COURTESY OF THE INDIANA STATE LIBRARY, INDIANAPOLIS, INDIANA.

"Stump Speaking in Early Bloomington," from a painting by Theophilus Adam Wylie. COURTESY OF THE INDIANA UNIVERSITY ARCHIVES, BLOOMINGTON, INDIANA.

"A Family in Early Bloomington," from a painting by Theophilus Adam Wylie. COURTESY OF THE INDIANA UNIVERSITY ARCHIVES, BLOOMINGTON, INDIANA.

"Sin-Is-Qua" and her children, from a sketch by George Winter in Kee-Waw-Nay village in Indiana on July 20, 1837. Sinisqua was converted to Catholicism by Father Benjamin Marie Petit. She and her daughter (her son had died) participated in the Potawatomi migration of 1838. She later settled in Michigan. COURTESY OF THE TIPPECANOE COUNTY HISTORICAL ASSOCIATION, LAFAYETTE, INDIANA. GIFT OF MRS. CABLE G. BALL.

"Line of Mounted Figures," a sketch drawn by George Winter, depicts the forced emigration of the Potawatomi from Indiana in 1838. COURTESY OF THE TIPPECANOE COUNTY HISTORICAL ASSOCIATION, LAFAYETTE, INDIANA. GIFT OF MRS. CABLE G. BALL.

Calvin and Sarah Hill Fletcher. COURTESY OF THE INDIANA
HISTORICAL SOCIETY LIBRARY, INDIANAPOLIS, INDIANA.

Opposite top: "Fifth Street" in Richmond, Indiana, from
a sketch by Lefevre Cranstone done in 1859-1860.
Cranstone's series of drawings convey an idealized sense
of urban life in mid-nineteenth-century Indiana. This
one strikingly emphasizes the order and gentility
wealthy and middle-class people hoped would become
synonymous with life in the American Middle West.
COURTESY OF THE LILLY LIBRARY, INDIANA UNIVERSITY, BLOOMINGTON,
INDIANA.

Opposite bottom: "Main Street" in Richmond, Indiana,
from a sketch by Lefevre Cranstone done in 1859-1860.
This drawing depicts the commercial center of the town
as prosperous, solid, and virtually indistinguishable from
the business districts of dozens of communities in
Indiana and the Middle West. COURTESY OF THE LILLY LIBRARY,
INDIANA UNIVERSITY, BLOOMINGTON, INDIANA.

Richmond Indiana
Fifth Street

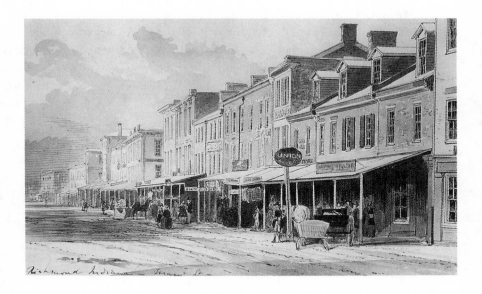

Richmond Indiana   Main St

The incursion of the United States into the Wabash Valley provoked differing reactions among the Native Americans living along
its banks. To some degree, proximity to the Americans determined
whether the Indians were willing to negotiate or resist their actions.
The Piankashaw tended to tolerate their new neighbors more than
the Wea, while the Miami, Shawnee, and Delaware, many of whom
were living in and around Kekionga (Fort Wayne) in 1790, were
actively hostile. British agents encouraged the resistance of the
latter groups with promises of material support. The United States
failed to exploit these differences, however, and managed to alien-
ate almost all Indians living in the region. So intent were the
stubborn soldiers of the republic on establishing its authority that
they remained largely oblivious to the decades-old political structures and customs of the Wabash.

Above all, the Americans were cheap. Federal agents rarely
handed out the gifts that signaled the acceptance of Indians as equal
partners or gave much credence to the ceremonies of the calumet. In
part, this was because the government did not have much money.
More important was the fact that the Americans had little interest in
establishing ongoing relationships with Indians, in becoming fictive brothers or fathers. Since the United States intended to transform the lands of the Northwest into commodities and sell them to
households that would rearrange the landscape into a paradise of

🏴 **139**

THE
WORLD
OF
LITTLE
TURTLE,
1790–1795

commercial agriculture, the new republic had a difficult time seeing a role for Indians. Either they would become like Americans or they would be removed. It was as simple as that. What differentiated the Americans and the Virginians from the French and the British in the region was not inherent racism or a refusal to see the Indians as anything but uncivilized savages, but a completely different sense of purpose about the place itself. They acted on their notions of the Wabash as they intended it to become, not as it was.

The republican ideology of the Americans also made it culturally difficult for them to participate in rituals emphasizing dependence and mediation. For most Americans, the point of their Revolution had been the destruction of personal ties of dependency, whether to kings, priests, aristocrats, or fathers. Liberty was not being a slave, or a wife, or a child. It meant being autonomous, independent, free. Finding the proper way to behave in this new world obsessed and confounded men such as Sargent, Harmar, and Hamtramck. They valued order and obedience, especially as officers and admirers of George Washington, but they railed against any perception that they had not voluntarily submitted themselves to legally established authority. In general, they felt more comfortable, or more confident, dealing with people through laws and in uniforms than they did in personal relationships.

But behavior that was largely a product of a profound change in Anglo-American society appeared to be little more than arrogance, bluster, or cruelty to the peoples of the Wabash. Americans might accept the title of father, but they were unwilling to behave like one. They were demanding obedience rather than earning respect. And their pretensions and rhetoric clearly demonstrated that the future they imagined held little room for Indians. If the United States could accommodate the French and fight with the Kentuckians, it could offer Indians only the total destruction of their world. They responded accordingly.

The Mission of Antoine Gamelin

On October 6, 1789, an uncertain President George Washington requested Governor Arthur St. Clair to determine the mood of the Indians living along the Wabash. How would the United States secure the Northwest Territory? Was it to be by treaty? Or by force of arms? In January 1790, St. Clair forwarded the request to Major Hamtramck at Vincennes. The governor enclosed a speech to the Indians which demanded that they offer assurances of their peaceful intentions. If they refused, the United States would have to "chastise them."

Hamtramck already knew the answer. The Piankashaw and others along the lower Wabash were inclined toward peace, but the Miami were not. The obedient major nonetheless dispatched a messenger up the Wabash River to warn Indians to gather in their villages to hear the words of the territorial governor. He then appointed the magistrate Pierre Gamelin to deliver the speech. Pierre got as far as the Vermilion River, where he ran into an old enemy, and decided to return to Vincennes. Fortunately, his brother, Antoine Gamelin, the clerk of the court, agreed to assume his responsibilities. He departed from the town on April 5, 1790, traveled to Kekionga at the forks of the Maumee, and returned in May.

As a member of a prominent French family, Gamelin was ideally suited for his task. The Indians apparently considered him friendly and fair. But it was also clear that they did not trust the government of the United States. As Gamelin ascended the Wabash, hostility toward his mission intensified. The Piankashaw at the mouth of the Vermilion asked the Frenchman to consult with the Miami, "their eldest brethren," at Miamitown (Fort Wayne), before they could give him "a proper answer." They would let him know what they thought when they had heard "what reception" Gamelin got from the Miami.

The Piankashaw were clearly stalling, as people caught in the middle between more powerful communities usually do. For decades, they had lived in relative peace with the French at Vincennes; they had offered to help Clark when he appeared to offer them and the French relief from British oppression. Things had changed in the 1780s, however. Raids from Kentucky, including those led by Clark and Patrick Brown and the hostility of the American settlers in and around Vincennes, had taught them a powerful lesson. The Americans were not the same as the French; in fact, they were worse than the British because they were far more numerous.

The Piankashaw had responded with actions more than words. In 1786, they sold land in the Vincennes area to the French in the town

🐚 **141**

THE
WORLD
OF
LITTLE
TURTLE,
1790–1795

and moved away. Winthrop Sargent reported the transfer of 150 acres in 1786, "when the last of them [Piankashaw] moved off." By 1788, there were approximately 120 Piankashaws at Terre Haute (about sixty miles north of Vincennes) and about 800 Indians (most of whom were Piankashaw) sixty miles further upriver at the mouth of the Vermilion.

With the arrival of American troops in Vincennes in the summer of 1787, many Indians frequently visited the town. Major Hamtramck and General Harmar when he was at Fort Knox occasionally offered gifts and smoked pipes with small groups of Indians. Numerous Indians apparently were discriminating between the Virginians in and from Kentucky and the agents of the national government. They were exploring the tantalizing possibility that the new army might restore the *status quo ante*. In January 1788, Hamtramck reported some 400 Indians were trading in Vincennes; among them were Piankashaw, Wea, and Miami under the leadership of Pacan.

These comings and goings did not herald a restoration of old ways, however. Tensions remained high. Wea and some Piankashaw participated in raids on Kentucky. There were also attacks on troops and traders on the Ohio and Wabash rivers. Sometimes people were killed, sometimes horses were stolen, sometimes both. Patrick Brown's expedition in August 1788 was probably in retribution for the attack on some Americans at the mouth of the Wabash by a Piankashaw war party led by La Grosse Tete. Hamtramck briefly imprisoned the chief next summer. Meanwhile the depredations of Brown and his men shattered the attempts to bring peace to the Wabash, alienating those Indians who had made friendly overtures to the Americans. Pacan's people migrated to Terre Haute and then he led them back to Miamitown. The Piankashaw in Vincennes abandoned the town in the fall of 1788; some went to Terre Haute or the Vermilion, but many headed west for the French settlements along the Mississippi River. None of the Wabash Indians attended the conference that led to the Treaty of Fort Harmar in January 1789.

No wonder, then, that Gamelin got such an indifferent response from the Piankashaw. The Kickapoo he encountered on April 11 were even less accommodating. They strenuously objected to a clause in St. Clair's speech which said, "I do now make you the offer of peace; accept it or reject it, as you please." Gamelin hastily withdrew these "menacing" words. The Kickapoo allowed him to proceed, but they could not give him an answer at the present. Besides, where were the presents, the ammunition, the food, that they expected from such an ambassador? Gamelin knew better: "[A] bearer of speeches should never be with empty hands."

The Wea joined the chorus at Ouiatanon on April 14. They, too, deferred a decision about how to answer St. Clair's speech until they knew what the Miami thought. While lamenting British influence over their young men, the Wea complained of the niggardliness of the Americans. Their chiefs "always" returned "all naked" from meetings with them; "and you, Gamelin, you come with a speech, with empty hands." Why could not Governor St. Clair himself come to Ouiatanon, "the sepulcher of all our ancestors"? Like the Piankashaw and the Kickapoo, the Wea were uneasy and uncertain. The Americans were not only a threat, they did not seem to behave in predictable ways. They had no sense of the rituals of mutual obligation, of personal reciprocity, that had so defined the political world of the Wabash. The Americans were foreign radicals who promised to do far more than take their lands.

Antoine Gamelin's increasingly difficult mission reached its climax on April 23 when he arrived at Miamitown. There he spoke to an assemblage of Miami, Shawnee, Delaware, and French and English traders and showed them a copy of the Treaty of Fort Harmar. They listened respectfully, but they were "displeased" until Gamelin assured them he was there to offer them peace, not coerce them to accept it. During the next week, the Frenchman met with several chiefs, including Blue Jacket of the Shawnee, and Le Gris of the Miami. They blamed the tensions on each other and on the Americans. Clearly they did not believe a word of what the Americans had to say. "From all quarters," Blue Jacket complained, "we receive speeches from the Americans, and not one is alike."

In the end, the Indians at Miamitown gave Gamelin no formal answer to his speech. They delayed, claiming a need to consult with the British at Detroit. Then they suggested Gamelin go on to Detroit. He refused. On the 29th, they promised to send a written message to Vincennes within a month. Blue Jacket, however, made

143

THE
WORLD
OF
LITTLE
TURTLE,
1790–1795

it emphatically clear that he did not trust the Americans, who were insincere and deceptive. They had killed young men and stolen women. A defiant Blue Jacket assured Gamelin that he had no intention of allowing the Americans "to take away, by degrees, their lands." There was too much "pain," too many "affronts." Gamelin thus left Miamitown without a definitive answer.

All along the Wabash, as he floated back to Vincennes, Indians expressed their approval of this lack of resolution. President Washington, Secretary Knox, Governor St. Clair, and General Harmar had the opposite reaction. The failure of Gamelin's mission confirmed their decision to send, in the words of Knox, an "expedition" against the "bad people" among the Wabash Indians. St. Clair concluded in August that "there was not the smallest probability of an accommodation" with them. The governor and Harmar devised a plan to strike at what they considered to be the heart of the problem—Miamitown. In October, Major Hamtramck was to lead several hundred men up the Wabash while Harmar brought over a thousand cross country from Fort Washington. According to Knox, the purposes of the expedition were "to exhibit to the Wabash Indians our power to punish them for their positive depredations, for their coniving at the depredations of others, and for their refusing to treat with the United States when invited thereto. This power will be demonstrated by a sudden stroke, by which their towns and crops may be destroyed." Knox rejected St. Clair's recommendation to establish a fort at Miamitown as too expensive. The campaign was to be little more than a legal punitive raid on the grand scale. As much as anything else, it would demonstrate once and for all the power of the United States of America to the Indians, peaceful or not; the British (who were informed of the expedition in advance); and the Kentuckians. For decades there had been battles all around the Wabash; now full-scale war was coming to Indiana.

Miamitown

Miamitown, the object of the fall campaign, the place to which the Indians along the Wabash deferred, was a logical choice. It had grown considerably since the Sieur de Vincennes followed the Miami there in the early eighteenth century. By 1790, the area around the forks of the Maumee had become home to several communities of Indians, most of whom were ill-disposed toward the United States. There were the older Miami villages of Pacan (Kekionga), Le Gris, Turtletown, and more recently, two Shawnee communities (including that of Blue Jacket), and two or three Delaware villages. Le Gris's sat between the Maumee and the St. Joseph, with Kekionga across the St. Joseph and a little to the north; the Shawnee were a few miles down the Maumee; and the Delaware were to the south on the St. Marys.

Indian populations were relatively stable in the 1780s and early 1790s and the formidable concentration of human beings at the forks of the Maumee numbered well over a thousand. They lived in some 300 bark cabins and fed themselves on the acres of corn growing along the banks of the rivers. There were vegetable gardens as well as cattle and horses. Le Gris's village was also home to a few dozen French and British traders. In fact, the British in Detroit were a major presence in the lives of the people in the Miami towns. Detroit was relatively close and accessible via the Maumee, and trade and travel between the two places was brisk.

Historians have amply exploited the journal of Henry Hay, a trader from Detroit, who spent the winter of 1789–1790 at the forks of the Maumee. It is the most complete source we have on life there before the arrival of the American army in the fall, although it deals mostly with the Europeans, since many Indians were away on hunting trips.

As in Vincennes, the French families had been around for decades, making their living as middlemen in the fur trade. By and large, they lived well. Hay attended teas and late-afternoon parties where his hostesses served European liquors. Several of the women were able to sport imported ostrich feathers and ribbons. One woman, Madame Adahmer, depended on the labor of a slave whom Hay called "a ponnie [Pawnee] wench." The French and English devoted a great deal of time to entertaining themselves. They played cards, sang, danced, ice skated, courted, and played jokes on each other. Elaborate balls were held on special occasions, such as the queen's birthday and Mardi Gras. Despite the exceedingly cold weather, Hay seems to have thoroughly enjoyed himself. He played the flute he brought with him in an impromptu trio with

📖 145

THE
WORLD
OF
LITTLE
TURTLE,
1790–1795

the silversmith and violinist John Kinzie and the trader-violinist LaChambre. All told, this sounds like a variation on French life in Vincennes in the eighteenth century.

But, as Richard White has pointed out, Miamitown differed significantly from Vincennes and the French settlements on the Mississippi in that the lines separating the worlds of the Europeans and the Indians were not as sharply drawn. They lived side-by-side in Le Gris's village, not in distinct communities. Indeed, Miamitown was an Indian community with French and English residents; Vincennes was a European town with a Piankashaw village nearby. John Hay, himself the son of an English father and a French mother (his first name was Pierre), was an intimate of Le Gris and a "very great friend" of his deceased daughter. French boys obeyed the orders of Le Gris, who behaved "quite like a general or a commandant," and French families quartered Indian warriors in their homes. Across the St. Joseph, Jean-Baptiste Richardville, son of a French trader and the sister of Pacan, governed in the latter's absence. Since Jean-Baptiste was too "bashful" to speak in council, his "very clever" mother, Marie Louisas (Tecumwah), did it for him. The world at the confluence of the Maumee, as White has written, was a multiracial society in which people defined the rules and parameters of social relationships on a daily basis. Here was a place in which Europeans and Indians not only traded and slept together but also talked, ate, and interacted with each other regularly. Quite often, several Indian warriors would have breakfast with Hay.

It would be wrong to romanticize life in "this very pretty place," however. In addition to the normal cycle of illnesses and deaths, the difficulties of surviving hard winters, and the burdens of those who were slaves, concern about the ever-approaching Americans was omnipresent. People knew that there were troops building "redoubts & block Houses" at what became Cincinnati. A middle-aged prisoner of the Delawares provided this information. Irish-born, he had lived in Fauquier County, Virginia, for two decades before coming to the Northwest. The Delaware did not harm him and gave him the freedom of the place; all they wanted was "to learn intelligence of what those People were about."

Other prisoners were not so fortunate. On the 19th of December, the Miami chief Little Turtle, who lived at Turtletown on the Eel

River some eighteen miles northwest of Miamitown, arrived with fifteen or sixteen men from a raid on the Americans on the Ohio. They had captured two men. One, a black man, they left with some whites on the Little Miami River. The other, a "very tall," elderly white man, was killed almost immediately. One of the warriors, in a rage about the deaths of some relatives, "struck him twice or thrice in the back an[d] side." So great was the passion aroused by the raids and counterraids of the 1770s and 1780s that people lashed out in bitter frustration whenever they were given the opportunity. Even the merry Hay, who spent much of his time drinking and flirting, paused for a moment when he saw the dead man's "Rifle Horn & Pouche Bagg." But that was not the end of it. The next morning the warriors showed him the man's heart. "[I]t was quite drye," Hay reported calmly, "like a piece of dryed venison, with a small stick run from one end of it to the other & fastened behind the fellows bundle that killed him, with also his Scalp." Soon afterward, another war party arrived, with men dancing over the river, "one with a stick in his hand & scalp flying."

In this world of revenge and retribution, there were clearcut rules. The violence was not mindless. Directed at specific people in specific contexts, it was a powerful, cathartic response to severe emotional trauma. Americans and Indians increasingly saw each other as less than human. They were behaving in ways that literally did not make sense. What do people do in the midst of such a crisis? They can dither, as many Indians did; they can bluster, like federal officials; they can dance and drink in the face of brutality, as Hay did; or they can act. They can do something.

Little Turtle

The last option was the course chosen by the Miami war chief Mishikinakwa, or Little Turtle, with whom Hay frequently ate in the winter of 1789–1790. At the time, Little Turtle was about forty-two years old. The son of Mishikinakwa, The Turtle, and a Mohican woman whose name we do not know, he was born in 1747 in a Miami village on Blue Lake, about eighteen miles from Miamitown. Since his father was a close associate of Memeskia, Little Turtle spent much of his first five years in the cosmopolitan trading village of

🐚 147

THE
WORLD
OF
LITTLE
TURTLE,
1790–1795

Pickawillany. We know virtually nothing about his life thereafter, except that he lived in Turtletown, until 1780.

In that year, a forty-year-old ambitious Frenchman named Augustin Mottin de La Balme traveled across the Atlantic with the young Marquis de Lafayette to offer his services to the new American republic. Congress granted him a commission as a colonel. But that was not enough for La Balme. He was in a hurry to achieve fame and fortune. He resigned his commission almost immediately and embarked on an ambitious scheme to take Detroit from the British, probably in the name of France. In the late summer of 1780, La Balme appeared in Kaskaskia and then in Vincennes, raising men and supplies. His call to arms attracted about 100 men who accompanied him up the Wabash to Ouiatanon in October. But his appeal quickly began to fade, and as he approached Miamitown, he had only sixty men still with him.

Rather than attempting to negotiate a relationship with the people at the forks of the Maumee in preparation for an attack on Detroit, La Balme let his men loose on Kekionga and Le Gris's village. For twelve long days, they plundered the stores of French and British traders, including those of Charles Beaubien, a British agent and second husband of Tecumwah, sister of Pacan and mother of Jean Baptiste Richardville, and François La Fontaine, who later married Richardville's daughter. They met with a great deal of resentment, if not resistance, as they got drunk and harassed local residents. With the stores exhausted, La Balme, who had belatedly come to the conclusion that discretion was indeed the better part of valor, abandoned the villages and moved to a position on the Eel River about twelve miles west of Miamitown. Unfortunately for him and his men, most of whom had been to their last party, their camp was only three miles from Turtletown.

On the morning of November 5, 1780, Little Turtle responded to La Balme's destructive and blundering expedition with the decisiveness that made him such an extraordinary leader. The Miami chief knew how to read a situation; he was a master of the art of the possible, and he understood when to wait and when to jump. He had left La Balme alone while he was at Miamitown; now he had him on his territory. Little Turtle and his warriors sprang on the French just before dawn. The Europeans fired one volley before they were completely overrun. Within a few minutes, La Balme's life, as well as his dreams of glory, was over. Little Turtle had his first major victory over invaders on the lands of his people. The Miami lost five men in the short battle. The French casualties numbered thirty dead plus several taken prisoner; others escaped to return to Vincennes and Kaskaskia.

In the 1780s, Little Turtle added to his reputation by leading several successful raids against American settlements in Kentucky and along the Ohio River. Convinced that the Miami had to hold the Americans at the Ohio, the chief was determined to protect the lives and interests of his network of relatives and friends. Little Turtle was doing little more than defending the local world in which he lived from an outside force that was apparently determined to remake it. Like the citizens of Massachusetts in April 1775 or the people of Vincennes in February 1779, the Miami were willing to take up arms to preserve and protect not only their lands but also their customs and practices. Brutal indeed were the fights between Americans and Indians. But there was too much at stake to be calm. To hesitate was to lose everything.

The Indians who gathered in 1789 at the forks of the Maumee, "the headquarters of iniquity," as St. Clair termed it, were committed to the Ohio River as a boundary between the United States and themselves. Whether Shawnee, Delaware, or Miami, they rejected the treaties of the 1780s, particularly that of Fort Harmar, and refused to acquiesce in the orders of the American government. Historians sometimes call the Indians in and around Miamitown the Miami Confederacy. But they were not formally united. And there were significant differences among them. The Delaware, who had migrated from eastern Ohio, wanted the Miami to assure them that they could live in peace in the region south of Miamitown. The Shawnee, especially Blue Jacket, expected to assume leadership of the tenuous alliance and relied heavily on the favors of British agents Alexander McKee and Matthew Elliott, who had married women of their tribe.

Harmar's Expedition

Generals St. Clair and Harmar were not particularly concerned with the nature of Indian resistance as they planned the fall 1790

☙ **149**

THE
WORLD
OF
LITTLE
TURTLE,
1790–1795

campaign. The possibility of defeat was there, but it was never directly confronted. Indeed, once they decided to go ahead with a raid on Miamitown, they devoted their energies to organization and preparation. These were the kinds of tasks Harmar, who was to command the expedition from Fort Washington, liked best. Despite his years of service in the Continental Army, he had had little experience in combat command. His duties in the Ohio Valley had largely involved overseeing the construction of posts and the warning away of squatters. Harmar's achievement in establishing an American military presence in the Ohio Valley had not required tactical skill or decisive leadership. There was no reason to believe that he would handle his army well in battle.

The general enjoyed the life of a gentleman on the frontier; like all officers, he was attended to by a servant. Harmar and his wife lived well and entertained lavishly. His officers were constantly sending Mrs. Harmar pecans and other goods. They were very convivial people. Rumor had it that General Harmar was inordinately fond of the bottle. Even President Washington believed that he was a drunk.

The United States, not able to afford enough regular troops, recruited 1,133 of the 1,453 man army from the Kentucky and Pennsylvania backcountry. The regular officers dismissed them as a group of poorly trained, poorly armed men who were either too young or too old to be much good; many, they claimed, were simply substitutes. What disturbed Harmar the most was their insubordination, their lack of respect for the hierarchy of military command that he valued so highly. Within the American army in 1790, then, there was as much division as among the Indians at Miamitown. The methodical, disciplined regulars were at odds with the impulsive militia units.

As soon as the Kentuckians arrived at Fort Washington in September, they began behaving in a highly personal, democratic fashion, subverting the forms of regular military procedure. There was a contest for command of the militia between Colonel John Hardin and Lieutenant-Colonel James Trotter. Neither was popular with the regulars. Hardin, a forty-year-old veteran of Indian warfare, had led a force of over 200 Kentuckians into the Wabash Country in the summer of 1789. Trotter had served in similar raids. Apparently, Trotter enjoyed greater popularity with the Kentuckians, for many declared they would go home if he were not preferred over Hardin. The partisans of these two men disputed their importance for several days. Then Harmar was able to resolve matters, at least superficially. He appointed Trotter to command the three Kentucky battalions and Hardin the chief officer of the militia as a whole.

This was not an idle controversy. Indeed, it exemplified the cultural differences between the Kentuckians and the regulars. The direct, personal, emotional style perfected, at least temporarily, by George Rogers Clark contradicted the American officers' emphasis on regular procedures. Looking back at the campaign, Harmar's officers remembered how well the general observed the forms; in the vernacular, he went by the book. Harmar strictly adhered to an elaborate order of march with the regulars at the front center of the column. At night, he diligently put his force into a square order of encampment. The general wanted every man to know his place and his assignment. The militia may not have been capable or disciplined, but Harmar's expedition was meticulously organized.

The troops left Fort Washington at the end of September and proceeded north up the valley of the Great Miami River to the Auglaize and Wabash rivers and then northwest to Miamitown. When Harmar reached his destination at about noon on Sunday, October 17, he recorded the distance from Fort Washington as 170 miles. The general also noted that it was a "clear" day and a beautiful situation. But it was in keeping with his character that the specific number of miles interested him. Captain John Armstrong also punctuated his daily diary entries with the number of miles covered (typically nine or ten). The officers commented on the weather and the terrain, but there is a methodical quality to their writing that understates the anxiety they must have felt as they pushed farther and farther away from the Ohio.

If the American army was divided and nervous, the Indians at Miamitown were the same. By October, they had heard from various sources, including the British, that thousands of troops, some said six to eight, were on their way. Indian leaders called for help from other villages; many came, but by mid-October, they could muster only about 600 warriors. Reluctantly but firmly, the Indians began to evacuate Miamitown on October 14. The Delaware went south

151

THE
WORLD
OF
LITTLE
TURTLE,
1790–1795

toward the White River; the Shawnee, with most of the European traders, went down the Maumee toward Lake Erie and Detroit; and the Miami headed to the northwest in the direction of the Eel River. With women, children, and infirm dispersed, warriors quickly slaughtered cattle and hid as much corn as they could. Shortly after dawn on the 15th, they set fire to Kekionga to keep it out of the hands of the Americans and went into hiding in the countryside.

Thus Colonel Hardin and the militia found no opposition when they rode across the Maumee into Miamitown later that afternoon. Two days later, Harmar recorded that "the traders and savages" had left "in great consternation." The apparent victory emboldened the Americans. The general and his officers began to contemplate a movement on Ouiatanon and a possible rendezvous with Hamtramck, whom they assumed was moving up the Wabash. But to their disgust, they could barely keep control of the militia; plunder was the order of the day as Kentuckians began foraging about the forks of the Maumee looking for what one of them called "hidden treasure."

Outnumbered, Little Turtle and his Miami warriors waited for the Americans to make a mistake. Sunny Sunday turned into a cloudy Monday while the militia partied in and about the deserted Miamitown. During the night, some Indians drove away dozens of packhorses and cavalry mounts. An anxious Harmar sent the popular Lieutenant-Colonel Trotter with 300 men on an expedition to the northwest to look for Indians. Trotter's men killed and scalped two warriors but spent most of the day noisily dawdling about, planning an ambush that the Miami warriors could have heard for miles. When Trotter returned on Monday evening, Colonel Hardin, no doubt still angry with his rival, demanded that Harmar allow him to lead a contingent the next day. He would restore the honor of the militia lost by the grandstanding Trotter. Harmar agreed to the request and Hardin led about 180 men, including Captain Armstrong and thirty regulars, out of camp at about 9 A.M. on Tuesday. The militia went with Hardin reluctantly, and some began straggling back almost immediately.

The bold Kentuckian led the rest of them into a trap. Hardin's foray took him in the direction of Turtletown. Little Turtle, knowing his enemy far better than they knew him, had planned well.

The Americans were marching in single file through the woods when Captain Armstrong, hearing a gunshot and seeing horse tracks, became alarmed. Hardin ignored the warnings, disdainful as ever of the capabilities of the Indians, and proceeded toward a small meadow surrounded by timber and a swamp on one side. At the far end of the opening were scattered Indian goods and a spreading fire. The possibility of booty broke American discipline entirely as the troops rushed to get their share of the treasure. Many ran to their deaths. For behind the fire crouched Little Turtle and close to 150 Miami warriors with loaded muskets.

They fired first from the Americans' right, driving the troops to the left and another blast of relatively coordinated gunfire. Immediately Hardin and the Kentuckians headed for the rear. One can hardly blame them. They were in unknown terrain with an unknown enemy. Still, it was Hardin who had been so anxious to restore what one of Harmar's officers described as "the character of his countrymen." So the headlong flight through the woods has a certain sense of justice to it. In the confusion, Little Turtle ordered a charge. Captain Armstrong and his regulars stood and fought. But they were fighting under impossible circumstances. Twenty-two men sacrificed their lives that day upholding the honor of the government of the United States. Armstrong and eight others escaped and returned to camp, although the officer had to hide in the swamp to avoid capture. For three hours, he endured the sights and sounds of the Indian victory. It was gruesome. His men, he recalled, "fought and died hard." All told, well over half of Hardin's command failed to report back to Miamitown.

Little Turtle and his warriors put the American army into a panic. Harmar did not know what to do. Should he let Hardin have another go at the Indians? How could he maintain control of troops gripped with fear? The general chose the tried and true, falling back on what was familiar. He followed his orders strictly. On October 20, the Americans burned all the villages near the forks of the Maumee. With them went stacks of corn, beans, vegetables, hay, and fences. Harmar reported that his men destroyed some 300 houses and around 20,000 bushels of corn. Meanwhile he made preparations for a return to Fort Washington. The general who was

153

THE
WORLD
OF
LITTLE
TURTLE,
1790–1795

so good at organization was a disaster in a crisis. As much as the militia were at fault, the fact is that he was no leader. He could not inspire his men; he could not make quick decisions; he allowed his officers to coerce him into decisions; he refused to concentrate his forces on the enemy but divided them into smaller groups. On October 21, Harmar led his army eight miles away from Miamitown, having declared his mission accomplished.

Throughout the day, Hardin lobbied the general to allow him to go back to the forks and punish the Indians who would be coming back to the villages. Harmar was worried about an ambush on the way to Fort Washington, and Hardin found his opening. By evening, the general had relented. He ordered Major John Wyllys, a stern regular officer and veteran of the War of Independence who had once ordered the summary execution of three deserters, to lead 100 regulars and 300 militia under Hardin back to Miamitown. They marched at 2:00 A.M. on October 22. Within a couple of miles of the forks, Wyllys divided his men into three columns designed to trap unsuspecting Indians in a noose of American troops.

Little Turtle, along with Jean-Baptiste Richardville and other Indian leaders, however, knew about Wyllys's expedition almost as soon as it began. By dawn they had warriors lying in wait along the banks of the Maumee. These men shattered the American ranks, but the Kentuckians did not run this time. Regrouping, the infantry stormed across the Maumee and, sensing victory, began running north toward the St. Joseph, followed quickly by Major Wyllys and the regulars. It was here that Little Turtle again surprised the cocky Americans. From a supposedly desolate cornfield arose dozens of armed warriors. They fired into Wyllys's ranks and within a few minutes were upon them. The fighting was hand-to-hand, an exchange of bayonet thrusts and tomahawk chops. A group of warriors surrounded Wyllys and killed him as he sat on the ground grasping at his chest. The regulars again fought well, but their casualty rate was an astonishing 82 percent. Soon, equally intense fighting led to a loss of 27 percent of the militia. The Americans tried to regroup and then fled back toward Harmar, groups of frightened, chastened men, harassed occasionally by Indian snipers. The last many of them saw of the forks of the Maumee was the figure of

Ebenezer Frothingham, lieutenant in the United States Army, sitting pale and bleeding by the river, too exhausted to escape what he most assuredly knew was coming.

What was horror for the Americans was triumph for the Miami, the Shawnee, and their allies. The cautious and uncertain Harmar was no match for the decisive Little Turtle. No doubt in shock, the general congratulated his men on a job well done and methodically herded them back to Fort Washington. For Harmar there was disgrace, court-martial, and resignation; whether he liked it or not, he had failed. True, he had followed his orders to destroy Miamitown. But his army had lost two engagements. If the Indians could not save their homes or their corn, Little Turtle and his warriors had exacted a terrible price for their losses. They had outled and outfought the Americans at every turn. They had humiliated the United States, and they ritually took their revenge on the bodies of their enemies and the three unfortunate soldiers they captured.

Scott's Expedition

Harmar's Defeat did not deter the Americans. An angry and embarrassed President Washington was now more determined than ever to display the power of the United States in the Northwest. In March, the government replaced Harmar with St. Clair while Congress authorized the expenditure of over $312,000 to pay for another federal regiment and more militia. St. Clair began making preparations for leading a 3,000-man army against Miamitown, this time with orders from Secretary Knox to "establish a strong and permanent military post at that place," for "awing and curbing the Indians in that quarter, and as the only preventive of future hostilities. It ought, therefore, to be rendered secure against all attempts and insults of the Indians."

Virginia and the United States worked together in the winter and spring of 1791 to forestall possible attacks from the Wabash Indians. The previous October, the supremely prudent Major Hamtramck had advanced only as far as the Vermilion River, where he had burned the Piankashaw village, before returning to Vincennes. That was not nearly enough as far as the Kentuckians were concerned. Whites in the Ohio Valley were afraid that the Indians,

🐚 **155**

THE
WORLD
OF
LITTLE
TURTLE,
1790–1795

"being flushed with victory," would "invade our settlements, and exercise all their horrid murder upon the inhabitants thereof."

In response to such pleas, Governor Beverly Randolph of Virginia appointed Charles Scott, a man with over three decades of experience fighting Indians, brigadier-general of the militia of the district of Kentucky and authorized the raising of troops. In March, Secretary Knox informed Scott of the president's desire "to impress the Indians with a strong conviction of the power of the United States" and ordered him to lead a force of 500 mounted men on the villages of the Wea. In particular the secretary wanted the Kentuckians to capture women and children as a way of demonstrating to the Indians "that they are with our reach, and lying at our mercy." The prisoners were to be delivered to a federal officer at a convenient post. With authorization from both his state and his nation, Scott led 800 men across the Ohio River on May 23 and set a course for Ouiatanon. Among his troops were Colonel John Hardin and other veterans of Harmar's expedition, men who were more interested in restoring their personal honor than in rectifying the insults to the United States.

Contrary to the fears of the Kentuckians and the national government, Little Turtle and other Indian leaders were not contemplating an attack on the Americans. An unusually cold and snowy winter killed many of the buffalo in the Illinois Country on which the Wabash Indians depended for food. That natural disaster, along with the impact of the destruction of the harvest at Miamitown by Harmar, meant that the Indians were more concerned with survival than with conquest. In addition, while they could continue to defeat relatively small groups of Americans through surprise attacks and defensive ambushes, they did not have either the organization or the equipment to mount serious challenges to the American posts on the Wabash or the Ohio.

Under such circumstances, the Miami, Shawnee, and Delaware became increasingly dependent upon the material and advice of the British. It was no coincidence that took Little Turtle and Le Gris to Detroit shortly after the defeat of Harmar. They wanted to ascertain British intentions. While Little Turtle was in Detroit, the Miami and others rebuilt their homes at Miamitown. But many began to migrate up the Maumee and settle in and around the mouth of the

Auglaize. There lived Alexander McKee and Matthew Elliott, two British agents who had married Indians. Great Britain wanted to harass the United States, but it had no desire to get involved in a full-scale war in the Northwest. If anything, His Majesty's government hoped to act as a mediator while drawing as many Indians as possible back within its sphere of influence. Like the superpowers of the late twentieth century, the British sought to influence and take advantage of a local controversy without themselves being ensnared in it.

There were hundreds of warriors in the Glaize when word arrived of Scott's expedition. But the Indians misunderstood his purpose. Warriors rushed to Miamitown. By late May, a force of perhaps 2,000 men stood ready to defend the forks of the Maumee yet again. Five hundred of them came from the Wabash villages that were Scott's true objectives. Had the Kentuckian marched to Miamitown his fate might have been similar to, or worse than, Harmar's. But he never had any intention of attacking the Indian stronghold. His was what federal officers called a "desultory" raid, designed to soften the Indians up for St. Clair's expedition later in the year.

Scott's men rode through the forested countryside of southern Illinois and Indiana in the midst of driving rains and thunderstorms. They traveled 155 miles in about a week. Suddenly, on June 1, they emerged from the woods along the Wabash to see two small villages at the edge of "an extensive prairie." Scott split his forces, sending Hardin and 200 men to subdue the Kickapoo village while he advanced on Ouiatanon. The Indians were clearly surprised, and while there was fighting, it was not prolonged. In fact, a considerable part of the battle involved Kentuckians shooting at warriors who were trying to escape in canoes. Scott accomplished his purposes. Only five of his men were wounded in an action that killed thirty-two warriors and captured fifty-eight women and children. The next day, the little army burned Ouiatanon, the Kickapoo village, and the cornfields and gardens. In the evening, Scott sent Colonel James Wilkinson and 360 men to Kithtippecanuck, eighteen miles to the northeast on the Tippecanoe River. Within twenty-four hours, they had destroyed it as well.

As in Miamitown, the sacking of the Wea and Miami villages was an attack on the Indian-European culture that had developed along

🐚 157

THE
WORLD
OF
LITTLE
TURTLE,
1790–1795

the Wabash throughout the eighteenth century. Scott noted in his report that they burned seventy houses, "many of them well finished," along with corn, peltries, and other goods. A veteran of Wilkinson's brief raid on Kithtippecanuck found it even more impressive. With 120 houses, eighty of them with shingle roofs, and gardens and "truly delightful improvements," the place was "every thing considered, not a little wonderful; there was a tavern, with cellars, bar, public, and private rooms; and the whole marked a considerable share of order, and no small degree of civilization." The Americans marveled at this world, but they had no desire to engage it; they simply wanted to get it out of their way.

Scott and his men rested for two days. Then, on June 4, the general released sixteen of his prisoners, who were sick or old, and departed. Before leaving, Scott gave the Indians a speech emphasizing the patience and mercy of the United States; he told them that the captives would be treated humanely by Governor St. Clair at Fort Washington until they were ready to live in peace. If they refused, "Your warriors will be slaughtered; your town and villages ransacked and destroyed; your wives and children will be carried into captivity; and you may be assured that those who escape the fury of our mighty chiefs, shall find no resting-place on this side the great lakes. . . . the hatchet will never be buried until your country is desolated, and your people humbled to the dust." Scott's only regret, he told Knox, was that he had not been able "to carry terror and desolation to the head of the Wabash."

Twice within a year, Americans had set out to destroy the eighteenth-century world along the Wabash. Whatever their losses, both expeditions had had some impact. The warriors at Miamitown went back down the Maumee to meet in council early in July. There Alexander McKee convinced the reluctant Miami to accept the Muskingum River as a border with the United States, abandoning their insistence on the Ohio River. They agreed, since they had little to lose with such a concession.

St. Clair's Expedition

The Americans, however, were relentless in their determination to terrorize the Indians of the Wabash and the Maumee into accepting their wishes. The United States was in no mood to negotiate. Instead the Americans put their financial and emotional energies into the planning of St. Clair's expedition against Miamitown.

Delays and confusion dogged the campaign from the start. Again, most of the troops were poorly trained, poorly equipped, and reluctant to accept military hierarchy. Exacerbating matters were gross inefficiency and corruption in the handling of supplies and equipment for the army. St. Clair, unfortunately, shared Harmar's lack of imagination and boldness. In addition, he was not nearly as attentive to detail and organization. Harmar commanded his expedition, although he was not always sure what to do with it. St. Clair was little more than a tired, gouty old man who wanted to accomplish as much as possible with as little effort as possible.

Originally the governor intended to begin his movement toward Miamitown in July. When that proved impossible, he made September his target date. Meanwhile he detached now Brigadier-General James Wilkinson with about 500 Kentucky mounted militia on another "desultory" raid against the Wabash. They attacked and burned Kenapakomoko, a large village stretching for two or three miles along the Eel River about six miles above present-day Logansport, killed several men, and captured between thirty and forty women and children. One participant recalled surprising the inhabitants so completely that just before the attack he saw "several children playing on the tops of the houses" and heard "the hilarity and merriment that seemed to crown the festivity of the villagers, for it was the season of the green corn dance." The women and children taken prisoner during Scott's and Wilkinson's raids were taken to Fort Washington, where they remained incommunicado even to the pleading parents who came to claim them.

Wilkinson's expedition added to the misery of the Wabash Indians. But it had little strategic impact. Most of the warriors were already in the Maumee Valley, where perhaps 1,400 men from all over the Great Lakes region had gathered to resist the Americans' second campaign against Miamitown. In September, they learned that St. Clair had left Fort Washington and was proceeding slowly to the north, his men carving parallel paths through the forests. Reports soon followed that his army was building Fort Hamilton on

📖 **159**

THE
WORLD
OF
LITTLE
TURTLE,
1790–1795

the Great Miami and then Fort Jefferson, six miles south of present-day Greenville, Ohio.

In late October, the united warriors met in council at the forks of the Maumee and decided to entrust leadership to Little Turtle. He immediately organized the warriors into messes of twenty (with four to serve as hunters), then proceeded to the southeast in dispersed groups, traveling as lightly and as quietly as possible. Within a few days, they were on three sides of St. Clair's army, which was near the Wabash River. The general spent much of his time battling gout, which forced him to be carried on a litter, and handing out "pains and penalties" to his often surly and poorly organized troops. There were so many deserters that on October 31 St. Clair sent a regiment under Major John Francis Hamtramck to retrieve them. The governor was not even sure where he was, suspecting he must be near Miamitown. But Little Turtle knew all about St. Clair's army, including its diminishing size (about 1,400) and its declining morale. In the words of the veteran Indian trader Simon Girty, "The Indians were never in greater heart to meet their enemy, nor more sure of success—they are determined to drive them to the Ohio."

During the cold night of November 3, 1791, Little Turtle and his fellow war chiefs made their final plans for an early morning attack on St. Clair's army. Exhausted, the Americans had camped for the evening on about six to seven acres of high ground, surrounded on two sides by what the governor assumed was the St. Marys River. In fact, this wet woodland, crisscrossed by creeks, was near the head of the Wabash. Little Turtle massed his 1,000 warriors, Wyandots on the right, Ottawas, Chippewas, and Potawatomis on the left, and the Indians most directly threatened by St. Clair, the Shawnees, Delawares, and Miamis, in the center.

At daybreak on November 4, hundreds of screaming Indians rushed out of the woods and quickly overran the American pickets. Advancing in irregular lines, they were warriors with clearly defined tactics. Little Turtle had appointed his son-in-law, William Wells, and a handpicked group of Miamis to kill the gunners in charge of St. Clair's four cannons. They were more than effective; all but one artillery officer fell in the battle. In general, the Indians tried to kill officers in an effort to destroy American discipline and coordination; Major-General Richard Butler, the second-in-command, was soon mortally wounded, all but three of the officers of the Second United States Regiment were killed, and St. Clair himself felt a bullet graze his cheek and saw two of his horses and a servant killed. The governor later remarked that his brush with a bullet cured his gout; at least temporarily, he could walk without pain. In short, the Indians' tactics worked. The cannons were not brought to bear on the Indians, and soldiers panicked at the sight of wounded and dead officers. Closing in from three sides, the Indians pinned the Americans down in the northeast corner of their camp, their backs against the Wabash. At about 9 A.M., St. Clair called for a retreat, but repeated efforts to break out failed. Finally, around 9:30, some men rushed forward and gained the road they had been carving out of the woods; others followed, with the Indians giving chase for about three miles. The survivors reached Fort Jefferson after sunset, still more scared than humiliated. Dishonor would follow soon enough.

Little Turtle and his men had defied the conventions of war by attacking an army with artillery. This was no ambush. Indeed, they had inflicted one of the worst defeats in the history of the United States, killing 634 of their enemies and wounding another 279. St. Clair lost $33,000 worth of equipment and supplies in a complete and utter rout. Indians spent most of the day rummaging through their captured booty, which included 1,200 muskets and bayonets, eight cannons, and the personal possessions and uniforms of the officers. In their triumph, they tortured and burned the wounded and prisoners and mutilated and dismembered bodies. It was an anger born of frustration, fear, and pain. Generals Scott and Wilkinson had brought terror to the lower Wabash; now Little Turtle brought it to the heart of the American army. Sitting against a tree, Major-General Butler, who as a commissioner in the 1780s had often explained to Indians how Americans owned the Old Northwest by right of conquest, received death in the form of a tomahawk to his skull. His scalp was dried and sent to the Iroquois; his heart was cut out and divided into portions for each tribe participating in the battle to eat; and his corpse was left to the animals. "We plainly tell you that this country belongs to the United States—their blood hath defended it, and will forever protect it," Butler had

🦃 **161**

THE
WORLD
OF
LITTLE
TURTLE,
1790–1795

announced in 1787. Now his blood flowed freely into the soil he and others coveted.

Little Turtle's victory was an awesome event. The Indians thoroughly humiliated the Americans. Still, its significance in the long run can be exaggerated. No one knew this better than Little Turtle himself. Time and numbers, if not competent generals and well-trained warriors, were on the side of the Americans. Increasingly, the key to Indian resistance was the British. How far were they willing to go in support of their Indian allies? With them, Little Turtle and other warriors could counter the Americans for some time; without them, the task was nearly impossible.

The Battle of Fallen Timbers

The United States responded to St. Clair's defeat in two ways. First, it began preparing for another assault on the Indian villages along the Maumee. At an annual cost of $350,000, Congress created the Legion of the United States, a regular army of 291 officers and 4,272 men. In April 1792, President Washington appointed Anthony Wayne of Pennsylvania, another veteran of the War of Independence to command the legion. Unlike Harmar and St. Clair, Wayne had a flair for military command. His men respected him, if they did not like him. And he proved adept at mixing caution and boldness. Wayne began drilling troops in the fall of 1792, arrived at Fort Washington on May 5, 1793, and marched his army to Fort Jefferson in the fall of that year. His men constructed Fort Recovery at the site of St. Clair's defeat and prepared for a summer campaign to avenge the bespattered honor of the United States.

Meanwhile the national government made efforts at negotiating a settlement with the Indians. In the spring of 1792, Secretary Knox and General Wilkinson dispatched Captain Alexander Trueman and Colonel John Hardin on separate missions to the Indians on the Maumee. Both were killed en route, along with their companions. More important was the appointment of General Rufus Putnam, a judge of the Northwest Territory, as a commissioner to the Wabash Indians. Preceded by sixty soldiers and the women and children captured by Scott and Wilkinson in 1791, Putnam left Fort Washington with the Moravian missionary John Heckewelder for Vincennes on August 18, 1792. Some of Major Hamtramck's troops met them at the mouth of the Wabash and escorted them to Fort Knox. Heckewelder reported that the sight of the Wabash made the Indian captives "quite cheerful." Putnam opened a conference with the Eel River Miami, the Wea, the Piankashaw, and the Kickapoo on September 24. The Indians welcomed the offer of peace but demanded that the Americans stay south of the Ohio River. According to Heckewelder, they wished for as much of a return to the world before the arrival of the Virginians as possible. They wanted to undo the changes that were transforming their lives. The Indians "expressed the wish that they & the white people might never live too close to each other because they were very bad people on both sides. They wanted and begged for trade with us, and requested that Congress might not take away from the French who lived here the land their fathers had given them in former times."

Still, thirty-one chiefs signed peace accords on September 27. Their primary motivation was to secure the return of the hostages seized by the Americans. Putnam released the women and children to the Indians and presented them with gifts of food and brandy. The Senate refused to ratify this treaty in January 1792 because the Indians would not recognize the right of Americans to settle north of the Ohio River. But the treaty was important in winning the neutrality of the Wabash Indians, many of whom had migrated, or were migrating, to the Illinois Country anyway.

Meanwhile the Miami, Delaware, and Shawnee on the Maumee continued to strive for some way to prevent further American intrusion into their lives. Most of the residents of the villages around Kekionga moved down the Maumee to Au Glaize in the spring of 1792 to be closer to the British. Little Turtle and others adopted a military strategy of attacking the American supply lines in order to disrupt their movements and discourage them. In November 1792, Turtle and 200 warriors attacked Columbia, near Cincinnati.

These actions aside, the Miami, the Delaware, and, to a lesser extent, the Shawnee were becoming uncomfortable with their dependence on the British. His Majesty's government's influence rose in 1792 and 1793 as it provided the Indians at Au Glaize and elsewhere with food, guns, and ammunition and defied the Americans by continuing to hold on to Detroit and other posts. British officials

163

THE
WORLD
OF
LITTLE
TURTLE,
1790–1795

and agents, moreover, encouraged the Indians to believe that they recognized no boundary with the United States in the Northwest and were willing to fight against American invaders. But it became painfully obvious in 1794 as Wayne's legion slowly moved toward Au Glaize—what the general called "the Grand Emporium of the hostile Indians of the West"—that the British were all talk and no action. When Little Turtle went to Detroit in the summer of 1794 to request two cannons and twenty British troops for an attack on Fort Recovery and was refused, the proverbial handwriting was on the wall. Or so it seemed to Little Turtle, a man the British officer at Detroit called the "most decent, modest sensible Indian" with whom he had ever spoken.

Under these circumstances, the Miami chief concluded that it made more sense to talk with the Americans than fight them. As Wayne's army captured Au Glaize in August 1794, Little Turtle reportedly warned in council that the Indians could not expect always to be lucky. Besides, Wayne was a better leader than Harmar or St. Clair; he would not be surprised. "Think well of it," he said. "There is something whispers to me, it would be prudent to listen to his offers of peace." With these words, Little Turtle withdrew.

On August 20, the Legion of the United States encountered about 900 warriors in an intense battle that lasted only about an hour. Given the name Fallen Timbers, this minor conflict was more significant than either Harmar's or St. Clair's defeat. The most important moment came later in the day when the British troops in the recently constructed Fort Miami on the Maumee refused to aid, or even open their doors to, the needy warriors. Once again the British proved themselves to be unreliable fathers. In a few hours, the strategic advantages, if not the honor, gained by Little Turtle and other warriors against Harmar and St. Clair were lost.

On September 14, Wayne's army began a difficult march up the Maumee, fighting the thickness of the woods and the frequent creeks. The legion arrived at the forks of the Maumee on the 20th. This time, some three years and eleven months after Harmar's troops had fled the place in terror, the Americans came to stay. In the middle of a long period of cold and violent rainstorms, 250 men began to build a fort on the morning of the 22nd. They cleared 500 acres on an elevation in the angle between the Maumee and the

St. Marys and erected two two-story blockhouses connected by a 250-foot-square palisade.

A month later, on October 22, they were finished. Colonel Hamtramck, to whose hands it was entrusted, dubbed the stockade Fort Wayne. The soldiers fired off fifteen rounds and gave three cheers in a kind of christening ceremony, then marched into the new post. Now the old Maumee-Wabash waterway that had attracted both the Indians and the French to Indiana nearly a century earlier was for all practical purposes in the hands of the United States. Wayne informed Secretary Knox that the posts at Au Glaize (Fort Defiance), Miamitown (Fort Wayne), and Vincennes (Fort Knox), with perhaps a blockhouse on the Wabash near Fort Wayne, ensured for the United States "the possession of all the portages between the heads of the Navigable waters of the Gulfs of Mexico & St Laurence & serve as a barrier between the different tribes of Indians settled along the margins of the Rivers emptying into each."

The Treaty of Greenville

Little Turtle was right to be philosophical about this turn of events. Despite the great victories over Harmar's men and St. Clair, there was an inevitability about the advance of the Americans. Indeed, one need only plot the appearance of posts in the Northwest to see what was happening. The United States had come down the Ohio, up the Wabash, up the Great Miami, both up and down the Maumee. Military defeats could stem but not stop this surge.

On July 4, 1795, American officers throughout the Northwest celebrated the nineteenth birthday of the United States with great merriment. At Fort Wayne, Colonel Hamtramck, who had already begun complaining about a dearth of men and supplies at his new post, invited all gentlemen to his quarters for dinner. There they drank what one guest called "15 sentimental toasts" and watched the firing of 150 artillery rounds. At Greenville, near Fort Recovery, General Wayne was meeting with delegations of Indians from all over the region. He had warned them on July 3 that the Americans would mark the anniversary of their independence "with shouts of joy, and peals of artillery." They were not to worry at such noise, especially now that they were meeting in "brotherly union." Tomorrow, said Wayne,

🏳 165

THE
WORLD
OF
LITTLE
TURTLE,
1790–1795

the flag of the United States, and the colors of this legion, shall be given to the wind, to be fanned by its breeze, in honor of the birth-day of American freedom. I will now shew you our colors, that you may know them to-morrow; formerly, they were displayed as ensigns of war and battle; now, they will be exhibited as emblems of peace and happiness. This Eagle, which you now see, holds close his bunch of arrows, whilst he seems to stretch forth, as a more valuable offering, the estimable branch of peace; the Great Spirit seems disposed to incline us all, to repose, for the future, under its grateful shade, and wisely enjoy the blessings which attend it.

Little Turtle and over 1,000 other Indians, including Le Gris and Blue Jacket, had come to Greenville to make peace with the Americans. General Wayne was the perfect host, providing them with food, drink, and shelter as the negotiations continued through July and into August. Little Turtle, speaking through his interpreter and son-in-law, William Wells, was among the most outspoken of the Indian chiefs. At first he rejected the proposed cession of most of what is now south-central Ohio. He expected that "the lands on the Wabash" and in Ohio "belong to me and my people" and that they had been "disposed of without our consent or knowledge"; "the prints of [his] ancestors' houses are every where." Wayne countered by demonstrating respect for the secret burial of dead warriors and promising peace. Little Turtle sought time, proposed an alternative boundary, offered documents signed by President Washington guaranteeing certain lands, made specific demands about trading posts and traders. Although the general found Turtle a stubborn and litigious character, he remained patient. Wayne refused to change the border, but he did make concessions with regard to trade.

After a few days of celebration, representatives of the 1,130 Indians, including 381 Delawares, 143 Shawnees, 72 Miamis, and twelve Weas and Piankashaws, officially agreed to the Treaty of Greenville on August 3, 1795, which President Washington approved and the Senate ratified. By its ten articles, the Indians gave up their claim to south-central Ohio and a slice of Indiana and allowed the Americans to take land for posts in the Wabash-Maumee region; in return, they got peace, $20,000 in goods, an exchange of prisoners, protection from white intruders, licensed traders, and annuities ranging from $500 to $1,000. No words were more significant than those of the last sentence, which proclaimed that the treaty was "Done at

Greenville, in the territory of the United States northwest of the river Ohio." The following July, as a result of the Jay Treaty, Great Britain finally turned over Detroit to the United States.

Little Turtle eventually responded to the American victory by urging his people to adapt to their world, to take up farming and lead a more sedentary life. In the winter of 1797–1798, the middle-aged chief was in Philadelphia to meet with President John Adams. The government treated him as an important curiosity, giving him medical care for his gout and rheumatism. This was the chief's second visit to the capital of the United States; he had met with President Washington in November 1796. Little Turtle learned to wear the clothes of the Americans and to adopt some of their customs and manners. Later he and his son-in-law, Wells, tried to sell small parcels of land, albeit slowly, in order to benefit themselves and their people.

When Little Turtle took leave of General Wayne in a private conference on August 12, 1795, he seemed to hope that the Americans would be like the French and the British—generous fathers whose primary interest was trade. He thanked the general for his hospitality and sincerity and attributed his initial resistance to the treaty to a sense of duty. Now Little Turtle was "fully convinced" that it was "wisely and benevolently calculated to promote the mutual interest, and insure the permanent happiness of the Indians, and their Father, the Americans." He pledged to "adhere religiously to its stipulations." He hoped that the United States would soon send traders, including some particular favorites of his, to their villages and build a fort at Ouiatanon to help restore the trade there. Meanwhile Little Turtle would live "near fort Wayne, where daily experience should convince his Father of his sincere friendship." The great war chief of the Miami may have resigned himself to the inevitability of the Americans, but he obviously had only a glimmering of the kind of changes these new people would bring to the Wabash and the Maumee. His farewell speech described a world in which the United States would simply take the place of Great Britain, which had so inconsistently taken the place of France. But it was not to be.

7.

THE WORLD OF ANNA TUTHILL SYMMES HARRISON, 1795–1810

We do not know what Anna Tuthill Symmes was thinking when she married William Henry Harrison on November 25, 1795. But we can safely assume that she was very much in love with her husband, for she married him in defiance of her father's wishes. John Cleves Symmes, a judge of the Northwest Territory and owner of a large tract of land between the Miami rivers, was hardly adamant on the subject. He simply was not sure what to make of his daughter's suitor. Nancy, as Judge Symmes called his second daughter and youngest child, had known Lieutenant Harrison for about a year. They had met in Lexington, Kentucky, at the home of her sister, Maria Short. Now, waiting until Symmes had ridden away from his home at North Bend into Cincinnati on business, Doctor Stephen Wood, a Symmes tenant and a justice of the peace, officiated at what the judge later called "rather a run away match." Soon thereafter the newlyweds departed North Bend to take up residence at Fort Washington in Cincinnati.

Whatever Anna Harrison had expected on her wedding day, the pattern of her life quickly took shape. On September 29, 1796, ten months after her marriage, she gave birth to a daughter, named Betsey Bassett in honor of her husband's mother. Over the next eighteen years, she would bear nine more children, at regular two-year intervals. Unlike many of her contemporaries, Anna survived all of her confinements. In fact, she lived until February 25, 1864, long enough to bury her husband, all four of her daughters, and five of her six sons. Under this barrage of death, it is hardly surprising that she increasingly found consolation in religion.

When Anna was in her sixties, she wrote a brief letter to a nephew consoling him on the death of a baby. She remembered the loss of her last child, the only one to die in infancy, causing a pain "like tearing my heart assunder." While God provided a means of persisting for ever restless and imperfect human beings, the most difficult challenge of this world was accepting that He knew best. Yet that was also the most important thing to do. "To mourn we must," Anna wrote, "but we must try to keep from mourning, very dark are the ways of Providence to us, short sighted Mortals—but we know one thing, that watever God does is right altho we cannot often feel it so to be. You have left you, two s[w]eet Children—Oh how many parents have lost their all—I remember to have read in some Books, that we must hold all of our blessings with a tremling Hand, but hold fast to the giver, of all of our blessings." There was, after all, so little to be sure of.

Anna had learned that lesson at a young age. Her mother, Anna Tuthill Symmes, had died in 1776, when her second daughter was less than a year old. John Cleves Symmes, busy with the political and military affairs of the state of New Jersey in the first flush of revolution, was ill-equipped to handle an infant daughter. Consequently, Anna had grown up with her maternal grandparents in Southold, New Jersey, enjoying a comfortable existence. When she joined her father in the Northwest Territory in 1794, she was a relatively well-educated and poised young woman of nineteen. The experience of being something of an orphan may have inspired two of Anna's lifelong characteristics: her ability to adapt easily to new environments and her devotion to members of her family. No matter the situation, Anna was patient, forgiving, and affectionate. She never accepted the estrangement from her father, named her first son after him, and was playful and teasing when dealing with him. In 1811, she urged him to visit her family in Vincennes by invoking the memory of his indulgence with her before she was married and accusing him of treating her "unkindly" when he refused her "many requests." "This Papa is but a renewal of the same old story." Anna instructed Judge Symmes to make up his mind and come to her. "I

⏚ 169

THE
WORLD
OF
ANNA
TUTHILL
SYMMES
HARRISON,
1795–1810

remain," she concluded, "your affectionate Daughter. Mr Harrison and all the Children send a great deal of love[.]"

For all this talk of affection, however, Anna was also stubborn and direct when she knew what she wanted. It was no coincidence that she defied her father in making the one great choice of her life: to marry William Henry Harrison. The judge had good reason to worry about the twenty-three-year-old officer. Symmes conceded that the lieutenant had "understanding, prudence, education, & resource in conversation" as well as "about £3,000 property" and the judge wanted "the assistance of some young man in my own arrangements." The problem was that Harrison had "no profession but that of arms." "[A]bilities he has, what his application may be I have yet to discover." This was all perfectly reasonable. Indeed, the judge intended to "consult" with his daughters about the whole business while Nancy considered Harrison's offer. In the end, it seems, Symmes objected less to Harrison than to the timing of the match. But fathers in late eighteenth-century North America had increasingly less influence over their children's marriages. Romance and passion were the order of the day. Nancy made her own choice and she made it primarily for love.

John Cleves Symmes was a temperamental man, in part because of his nature and in part because he could not control the world as much as he would have liked. He handled his huge land speculations badly, incurring the permanent enmity of a great many people and years of law suits. Meanwhile, his younger daughter married without his permission and his third wife, Susan Livingston, whom he married in 1794, refused to grant him power over her extensive fortune. In 1808, the couple separated permanently and Susan Livingston Symmes returned to her family in New York. The 1788 marriage of his elder daughter, Maria, to Peyton Short, a Virginian who lived in Kentucky, was also a source of sorrow. Symmes had approved of this son-in-law, but Peyton proved to be an inveterate speculator and poor financial manager. By the end of the first decade of the nineteenth century, he was ruined. Maria Symmes had died in 1801, leaving two sons and a daughter in the hands of an impetuous father.

The confusion in the Symmes household was of a piece with a general rearrangement of family relationships in the United States at the end of the eighteenth century. The judge's status as a beleaguered patriarch was hardly uncommon. In colonial America, the household had been the basic unit of social organization. Households were not simply nuclear families; rather, they included everyone—such as indentured servants and slaves—who worked to satisfy the needs of the household. And people worked hard, if erratically. Unlike late twentieth-century families, members of households spent the bulk of their waking hours producing rather than consuming goods.

The normal household was a patriarchy in which men and women had different but complementary roles. Legally, the father exercised near absolute authority over everyone else, and other social institutions—churches, governments, schools—reinforced his power. In fact, the organization of the household replicated that of the kingdom as a whole. Children, women, slaves were dependents of the father and husband; they had virtually no public role other than to attest to the importance of the male. Women, children, and servants were not so much different from men as they were inferior, a status that they were taught from the beginning of their lives. Dependents were, by definition, weak, malleable creatures who relied on men to give direction to their lives.

The economic and political transformation of American society in the late eighteenth century, however, empowered people traditionally classed as dependents. Challenges to traditional ways were rampant in republican America. Not just kings were under attack; so were fathers. Indeed, Anna's decision to ignore Judge Symmes's wishes and to treat him, at least in her letters, in the manner of an affectionate schoolmarm, were part of a larger cultural pattern. The United States was a very young nation, demographically as well as chronologically, and its white population felt very much disposed to doing as they saw fit with their lives. Why pay attention to a father such as Symmes, a man who had some degree of political eminence and economic influence but who had chosen alternately to ignore and indulge his daughters? Many women came to the Northwest Territory reluctantly; they resented leaving behind familial and social circles. Anna Symmes Harrison's feelings may have been no different. But she was, in some sense, on her own; without a mother, with an often-absent father, she quickly made a life of her own in the Ohio Valley. She fell in love and she got married. Fathers fre-

🐚 **171**

THE
WORLD
OF
ANNA
TUTHILL
SYMMES
HARRISON,
1795–1810

quently have doubts about their daughters' love affairs; John Cleves Symmes was not unique in that respect. But what is instructive is the degree to which the couple and the community, including one of Symmes's own tenants, conspired to deceive him, apparently with little fear of retribution. This then was the republican patriarch of the frontier, with power aplenty in the public world, unable to control the decisions of his daughter or his wife.

Beyond bewailing his fate, Judge Symmes reacted to the problems of his private life by maintaining as close as possible relationships with his daughters and their families. He also became obsessed with preserving the memory of his ancestors. During an August 1802 visit to New Jersey, Symmes went to see the grave of his first wife, the mother of his children. There, he reported to Anna, "Melancholy overwhelmed me, and tears ran plentifully from my eyes while I leaned on the marble stone at the head of her grave." He described the setting at length and then launched into a brief history of his family and their grave sites. Tracing the Cleves and Symmes families back to seventeenth-century New England, he urged his daughter to "preserve this small sketch for your children—even this may afford them some satisfaction when I am no more." Seven years later, Symmes enthusiastically imagined a tour of New Jersey and Long Island for his grandson, Charles Short, in which he would show him where he had been born and point out "the site, the time, the occasion, the exploit, and the result, of some of the most remarkable transactions of [his] ancestors."

In addition to genealogical reveries, the judge took it upon himself to write frequently to his grandchildren, both in Kentucky and in Vincennes. He encouraged them to reciprocate, to correspond with each other, and arranged for them to visit him as often as possible. In 1805, he informed the Short children that he hoped to come see them during the summer on his way to visiting their "dear aunt Harrison & your little Cousins . . . for I long to see you all exceedingly." By the end of the decade, Symmes was acting as a surrogate father for the Short children; he arranged for one boy to return from Princeton and helped to establish his two grandsons in professions in Cincinnati.

The world did not work as Symmes would have liked. He found himself guiding the affairs of his family less by patriarchal authority than by paternal affection. He did not direct; he advised and consulted. His daughters and his grandsons listened, if only because Symmes so obviously loved them all so well. Beneath the temperamental exterior of the public judge was a patient and accommodating father who forgave nearly everything and labored to keep his family together.

William Henry Harrison

The Symmes family remained within a few days' travel of each other. Not so fortunate were the Harrisons, the family into which Anna married. Indeed, it was the waning of that venerable household that had brought the young lieutenant to the Ohio River in the first place. William Henry was the sixth child of Elizabeth Bassett and Benjamin Harrison and the descendant of several prominent Virginia families. While assiduously accumulating wealth, principally in the form of land and slaves, Harrisons had taken leading roles in governing Virginia since the middle of the seventeenth century. Elizabeth Bassett had given birth to William Henry on February 9, 1773, in a bedroom of Berkeley, a two-and-a-half-story red brick mansion fronting on the James River near Westover, which was both the center and symbol of the Harrison family's power. Behind the house ran fields of tobacco tended by dozens of African American slaves; nearby were mills and a small shipyard; in front was a wharf, connecting the Harrisons, via the James, with merchants in Great Britain and their friends and allies in the largest and wealthiest of British mainland colonies. Presiding over all was William Henry's father, Colonel Benjamin Harrison, a patriarch with immense local influence, member of the House of Burgesses from 1748 to 1775, delegate to the Continental Congress in 1774–1777, signer of the Declaration of Independence, governor of Virginia from 1781 to 1784, and member of the Virginia Constitutional Convention in 1788. At his death in 1791, Benjamin Harrison was worth £4,286 and owned 110 slaves and forty head of cattle.

When considering William Henry as a son-in-law, John Cleves Symmes knew that all of that was to William Henry's credit. But he also knew, or at least sensed, that this world of landed gentlemen was crumbling. Benjamin's political success could not hide long-

📖 **173**

THE
WORLD
OF
ANNA
TUTHILL
SYMMES
HARRISON,
1795–1810

term economic distress, made worse by British soldiers under General Benedict Arnold who ravaged Berkeley in 1781. As the third son of a distinguished but land-poor family, William Henry's prospects as he approached his maturity were not good. Few of his Virginia-born contemporaries would achieve the political or economic stature of their fathers and grandfathers, at least in the region of the Chesapeake. Indeed, his older brother Benjamin had already joined a mercantile firm in Philadelphia.

Despite a passion for military history, William Henry decided upon a career in medicine, like the law a professional refuge for the younger sons of declining gentry. At the age of fourteen, he attended Hampden Sydney College but left soon after his arrival in the wake of a Methodist revival. The religious upheaval was no doubt a socially as well as theologically troubling experience for the son of an Episcopalian gentleman accustomed to the deference of both slaves and local whites. Four years later, Benjamin dispatched William Henry to Philadelphia to study at the Medical School of the University of Pennsylvania under the guidance of his good friend Robert Morris.

In the City of Brotherly Love, Harrison's fortunes reached a nadir. News of his father's death soon arrived. In his will, Benjamin left his youngest son 3,000 acres, which he would sell in 1793. More immediately, however, there was no money left to pay for his education. What to do? The eighteen-year-old failed to obtain a position in the new federal government. Despairing, he sought the advice of a family friend, Richard Henry Lee, who recommended the army. Without consulting his guardian, Robert Morris, Harrison went to the War Department and received a commission as an ensign in the First United States Regiment of Infantry. The young Virginian left Philadelphia on September 20, 1791, for his assigned post with a company of eighty men. They arrived at Fort Washington in November, just in time to witness the men and women fleeing for their lives from the debacle of St. Clair's Defeat.

Tall and thin, William Henry Harrison had the bearing of an aristocrat. He carried himself well, perhaps too aloofly for some of his new comrades. Harrison disdained the dueling and drinking that occupied many of his fellow officers. He devoted himself instead to reading military history and to enforcing discipline. Somewhat above the crowd, Harrison acted with confidence and self-control. Not for him the necessity to prove his mettle in spontaneous displays of courage. To the contrary, the young man won promotion to the rank of lieutenant by catching the eyes of his superiors with his devotion to duty and his willingness to follow orders. Harrison was reliable, compassionate, and, above all, sure of himself. But his was not a cocky arrogance born of insecurity and a need to prove himself worthy of command. Rather, William Henry Harrison knew who he was, knew his own value, and acted as he had learned at Berkeley. He commanded respect, even as a junior officer. At Fallen Timbers, his fellow officers admired the cool courage of a man who carried General Wayne's orders into the heat of the battle. William Henry Harrison was not showing off or drawing attention to himself; he stayed within the rules; he was just following orders.

None of this, however, made him a likely son-in-law for John Cleves Symmes. The judge respected Harrison's family and admired his character. But what could he offer Anna besides a name and sword? The lieutenant owned some land, which he had purchased from Symmes, and was a partner in a distillery. Perhaps he could farm? Still, the judge could not get around the fact that William Henry "was bred to no business, & therefore I can set him at none." So he said no to the marriage, a decision that only brought him the humiliation of public deception.

The product of mutual choice, the marriage of Anna Tuthill Symmes and William Henry Harrison united two individuals who had chosen to put their own immediate happiness first. Like Anna, William Henry was on his own, bereft of father and fortune. Both came from disordered households that, while offering them sustenance and nurturing them, offered them little incentive to subordinate their interests. In setting out on their own, William Henry and Anna were only doing what thousands of other young men and women in the early republic were doing. The young lieutenant had described his independence and his determination succinctly when he planned the courtship of a Miss M. of Philadelphia, some time before he met Anna. Should he fail, he informed his brother, he would suffer no loss of honor. "I have been long enough a Soldier to have learned that there is no Disgrace in a *Well Meant* & *Well Conducted* enterprise," he wrote from Greenville in November 1794.

📖 **175**

THE
WORLD
OF
ANNA
TUTHILL
SYMMES
HARRISON,
1795–1810

William Henry promised to concede the field to anyone who loved Miss M. more and could make her happier than he. After all, his "Sword [was] almost [his] only patrimony." Still, "while I wear that Sword & the livery of my Country, I will not disgrace them by owning myself inferior to any person."

The Structures of the Harrison Household

Anna and William Henry, then, came together voluntarily, married because they chose to be together. On some level, their union exemplified the extraordinary stretching of the bonds of traditional patriarchal households in the early American republic. But on another level, their subsequent lives demonstrated less change in their upstart marriage than first appeared. For, following a pattern set by many of their contemporaries, what the married couple did in the aftermath of the defiant moment of their marriage was carefully set about the business of reconstructing a relatively traditional household. Bluntly put, Anna began bearing and raising children and William Henry began looking for a stable and permanent source of income. Together they worked to solidify and improve the position of their household.

To a surprising degree, the end of the Indian war in 1795 filled Lieutenant Harrison with some dismay, because it meant an end to opportunities for advancement and the status of a gentleman guaranteed by his commission as an officer in the United States Army. Judge Symmes tried to give his son-in-law some business in 1796, but the young man's heart was not in it. Instead, Harrison pursued a career in public service; it was, after all, the line of work to which the men of his family were bred. Commanding Fort Washington, he won not only promotion to the rank of captain but also the respect of several influential men in the Northwest Territory. Harrison's integrity and talents impressed men with widely disparate personalities and politics and he began to win appointments to minor public offices. In 1798, he finally resigned from the army to become register of the Land Office in Cincinnati. Upon the recommendation of the outgoing Winthrop Sargent, President John Adams commissioned Harrison as secretary of the Northwest Territory in June, a post with few responsibilities and an annual salary of $1,200. Within a year, Harrison had allied himself with his father-in-law and other critics of the territorial governor, Arthur St. Clair. In the fall of 1799, he won election as the territory's delegate to Congress by a margin of eleven to ten. In Washington, the young man continued to attract attention. He was the principal author of a revised land law and a measure to divide the Northwest Territory in two.

In 1800, the Congress of the United States, responding to the growth in the population of whites living north of the Ohio River in the years after the signing of the Treaty of Greenville, divided the Northwest Territory into two parts. On July 4, people living west of a line drawn from the mouth of the Kentucky River to Fort Recovery and then north to the Canadian border became residents of the new Indiana Territory. To govern them under the provisions of the Ordinance of 1787, President Adams appointed as chief executive William Henry Harrison. Harrison accepted the office, but only after receiving assurances from friends that Thomas Jefferson would retain him in office if the Virginian won the presidency. The new governor was clearly a very adept political animal, with a talent that would provide his future critics with a great deal of ammunition.

And what of Anna in these years? We know very little about her, but in some ways we know everything. She was pregnant. In the same letter, dated July 13, 1800, that Harrison explained to his friend Thomas Worthington of Chillicothe why he had reluctantly accepted appointment as governor, he reported that "Mrs. H. expects daily to be confined." It was her third pregnancy in five years. Within a year of her arrival at the territorial capital at Vincennes, she would have yet another. Not surprisingly, Anna was often ill. "Mrs Harrison is not in good health," Harrison coyly told Worthington in June 1802, "but I am in hopes she will be much better in a *few Months*." Three years later, the governor ended a letter full of political news to Worthington with the usual "Mrs Harrison is not very well but desires her respects may be presented to you—she presented me in October with the 3rd son & the 5th child." By 1811, William Henry jovially bragged to Worthington about his wife's pregnancies. He was proud to announce that "whilst [he] was upon the late expedition [Tippecanoe] Mrs Harrison added to our family

🗝 **177**

THE
WORLD
OF
ANNA
TUTHILL
SYMMES
HARRISON,
1795–1810

a son which brings up my number of children to eight of whom five are sons. I hope that you have been equally successful."

Since such male posturing tends to offend modern sensibilities, it is easy to overlook the fact that the governor was not simply bragging about his own potency. He was also proud of his wife and the growth of his household. Anna's eight pregnancies had all produced living children. Professional men in similar circumstances later in the nineteenth century or the twentieth century might react less happily to the birth of an eighth child. But Harrison saw his children as assets, not liabilities. And he cultivated the size of his family with the same persistence with which he watched over the size of his salary and his official perquisites.

Anna seems to have been an unusually gracious but otherwise fairly typical white upper middle-class woman. Her very few surviving letters suggest that she was relatively contented, her frequent pregnancies and illnesses notwithstanding. Clearly she delighted in spending time with other women. Sometimes these were the wives of her husband's friends, such as Mary Worthington. Most important were her relatives, particularly her sister, Maria Short. After an 1801 visit by Anna and her children, Maria wrote her sister that "our house appeared so lonesome for some days that I hated to go ought of my Room—I think I feel much worse about our being so far apart then I ever did[.] pray write me a long letter by Mr. Short and tell me what kind of a time you had and how the Children is." The affection between the two sisters was very strong; their conversation centered on the problems that confront all parents, such as cutting teeth and unruly behavior. When Maria died in 1801, Anna must have been devastated. But she quickly and warmly welcomed Jane Short, when Maria's husband remarried in 1803, to her circle of friends. Judge Symmes's letters to the Short family suggest a regular round of visits and correspondence among the households in Kentucky, Ohio, and Indiana. In fact, they were so close that first cousins Betsey Bassett Harrison and John Cleves Short were later married. Pregnancy and child rearing defined the world of Anna Harrison, and she immersed herself in them with the same ardor that her husband brought to public affairs. Their worlds were like intersecting planes. They came together to perpetuate the household; otherwise their lives were relatively separate, despite their genuine affection for each other and Anna's unhappiness when William Henry was absent for long periods.

The burgeoning Harrison household arrived in Vincennes in May 1801. The governor had spent a few weeks on the Wabash in January before traveling to the Short house near Lexington to collect his family. They came to Vincennes with much hope, although their fondest desire was less to change the world than to reconstruct their household in new circumstances. The Harrisons were the first couple of the new territory, but in their youth, their fertility, their division of responsibilities, and their desire to transform the landscape of Indiana into something familiar and useful, they were thoroughly typical immigrants.

The Peoples and the Landscape of the Indiana Territory

One of the most important tasks of the new territorial secretary, John Gibson, after his July 22 arrival at Vincennes was to complete a census of "the Whole number of persons in the Territory of Indiana." After a year of investigation, the secretary duly reported that the population amounted to 4,875 free whites and 135 slaves, of whom 2,517 and twenty-eight respectively lived in what is now the state of Indiana. Nine hundred twenty-nine whites resided in the Illinois or Clark's Grant, the 150,000 acres across the Ohio River from Louisville which Virginia had reserved for veterans of George Rogers Clark's 1777–1778 expedition when it ceded its claim to the Northwest Territory in 1784. The principal settlement was Clarksville, described by the Scottish doctor George Hunter in 1796 as consisting of "a few scattered Cabbins, with one indifferent farm." It had grown by 1800 but still remained very much what the 1806 traveler Thomas Ashe called "a village of no importance" lying in the shadow of Louisville. Gibson also recorded fifty whites and two slaves living on the upper Wabash River. By far the largest number of people were residents of Vincennes and its environs. The town itself had a population of 714 (including eight slaves), with 804 whites and fifteen slaves in the immediate vicinity.

The most striking fact in the census was the preponderance of youth. Almost half of the whites (1,232) were under the age of six-

🐚 **179**

THE
WORLD
OF
ANNA
TUTHILL
SYMMES
HARRISON,
1795–1810

teen; 874 were not yet ten years old. Only 187 were forty-five or older. Governor Harrison, after all, was just twenty-seven when he first arrived in Vincennes, and Anna but twenty-five. There was a relatively close gender balance. Men outnumbered women by 1,289 to 1,113, but when the French traders on the Wabash were excluded, the totals were much closer. These numbers suggest the importance of families in Indiana at the close of the eighteenth century. By and large, the residents of the Indiana Territory in 1800 were members of households consisting of two parents and many children. Among the fur traders, there were forty-eight males (only four of whom were under age twenty-six) and two females (one of whom was under four). Many of these men undoubtedly had Indian wives or partners who were not recorded. Still, their world was clearly on the decline.

Not only were most people living in households; they were also moving into the countryside. Throughout the eighteenth century, Europeans had concentrated in small settlements along the Wabash, relying on trade with Indians for their livelihood. Now the Americans were living beyond urban areas. They were spreading out. Gibson found more people living near Vincennes than in it, while the vast majority of the settlers in the Clark Grant had rural homes. Ignoring the boundaries established by the Treaty of Greenville and persistent Indian resistance, white Americans were moving into the woods and onto the prairies and beginning to remake the landscape of the Wabash and its tributaries.

The United States government encouraged this activity in at least two ways. First, Governor Harrison devoted considerable time to securing further land cessions from the Delaware, Miami, and other Indians. By 1809, he had secured, at least from the American point of view, title to the southern third of Indiana, with a boundary running from just north of Terre Haute southeast to Jackson County and then northeast to a place above where the Wabash River crosses into Ohio. Congress had established a system for sale and distribution of the public lands. The Land Act of 1800, passed in part because of the lobbying of William Henry Harrison, then delegate to Congress from the Northwest Territory, allowed for the purchase of federal lands in units as small as 320 acres at a price of two dollars per acre. The legislation also created an installment payment plan, requiring one-fourth of the price as down payment with the balance to be paid over the next four years. In 1804, the United States dispatched John Badollet, a Swiss-born friend of Secretary of the Treasury Albert Gallatin, to Vincennes to open a land office and to supervise the sale of the lands ceded by the Indians at public auctions. Within a decade, Americans were buying over 50,000 acres a year in the Indiana Territory; by 1814, the total was 166,312. Ballodet, who was an astute observer, worked in the land office until 1836, the year before his death.

Many of the early white settlers of Indiana do not appear in the official territorial census or the records of the land office. As early as the 1780s, Virginians and Pennsylvanians had squatted on lands along the Ohio River and in the Whitewater Valley of eastern Indiana. After the Treaty of Greenville, their numbers swelled. Two Moravian missionaries traveling up the Whitewater Valley with some Christian Indians were surprised when they found so many white settlers. For the first hundred miles they came upon a farm about every mile laid out by enterprising Kentuckians. The settlers were very hospitable, providing them with food, selling them flour from a mill, and telling them about the Indians who frequently came to buy their cattle. By 1804, there were small outposts around the present-day site of Brookville. Two years later, a group of North Carolina Quakers established a community that became Richmond.

Legal or not, the settlers were virtually unanimous in choosing agriculture as their chief means of livelihood. Immigrants and travelers continued to praise the terrain that had diverted the attention of George Croghan from his captors half-a-century earlier. The Scotsman George Hunter reported spending entire days in 1796 passing "good Land for farms, altho but indifferently watered; The soil kindly, well timbered, good mold on a sandy bottom which absorbs the water as it falls." In January 1797, the visitor Moses Austin claimed that people had abandoned a quarter of the 200 houses in Vincennes in order to move to the country and take up farming.

William Henry Harrison, to be sure, intended to ground the stability of his household on land largely devoted to commercial agriculture. If his farm was to be like others in the region, it would produce corn, wheat, tobacco, and hemp and nurture hogs and cattle for sale at markets as distant as New Orleans. Nearby mills

⬧ 181

THE
WORLD
OF
ANNA
TUTHILL
SYMMES
HARRISON,
1795–1810

and distilleries would process some of these goods, and flat and keel boats would carry them down the Wabash and the Ohio. By 1807, the Indiana Territory was contributing its share to the flood of over 1,200 flatboats that arrived in New Orleans that year. Men and women divided the labor of processing raw materials. The latter most likely were the principal users of the 1,350 spinning wheels and 1,256 looms in the Indiana Territory in 1810. Men, on the other hand, operated the thirty-three grist mills, fourteen sawmills, eighteen tanneries, twenty-eight distilleries, and one cotton factory. Together they produced $159,052 worth of cloth, $16,230 in distilled liquors, $9,300 in tanned leather, $6,000 in wine, $4,000 in nails, and $1,800 in gunpowder, not to mention 50,000 pounds of maple sugar.

Like his friend Worthington, who had an elaborate home called Adena on a small hill outside Chillicothe, Ohio, Harrison spent a great deal of money on a Vincennes mansion that reminded many of the house of his childhood in the Virginia Tidewater. The work of a man who meant to demonstrate both his importance and his permanence, Grouseland was by far the most imposing residence in the Wabash Valley when it was completed in 1804. The family created by the runaway match of 1795 now moved into a two-and-a-half-story brick home, complete with chimneys. Of its thirteen rooms, the two largest were on the first floor. Harrison intended to use them primarily for receiving people, whether for political meetings or for balls and receptions. No visitor to Grouseland, seeing its black walnut wainscotings, hand-carved mantels and doors, English window glass, semicircular staircase, admiring its shrubbery and gardens through six-foot windows, could help but be impressed. The governor spent so much money on this embodiment of comfort and display that he never made much profit from land speculation. It cost him some 400 acres of land (valued at $1,000) to pay for the bricks alone.

Around his home and out into the country, Harrison wanted to establish a plantation. Grouseland would be to Vincennes what Berkeley was to Williamsburg, and the governor its public and private patriarch. Within months of his arrival, Harrison excitedly informed Worthington that the Wabash was "the most beautiful [country] in the world." His government would bring stability and attract "respectable citizens." These immigrants would not leave the landscape alone. It would not be long until "we shall as far excell in the arts of cultivation as we certainly now do in Natural beauties." In October, the confident Harrison told his friend James Findlay of Cincinnati that he had bought a 300-acre farm, which was being cleared. Could Findlay sell the 419 acres Harrison owned near Cincinnati?

Harrison was doing on a grand scale what virtually all other white men in the territory were also doing: trying to accumulate land and start a farm. That is, everyone except the French. John Badollet, the superintendent of the Vincennes Land Office, told his friend Secretary Albert Gallatin that the "ancient french inhabitants" were "an ignorant, harmless & indolent race" who viewed the prospect of living on a farm with "as much abhorrence as if they were dropped here from the middle of Paris." They preferred to "live cooped up in this village (the only place in America to which that name applies with the meaning it has in Europe)," generally in great poverty, having sold the lands granted them by the United States. Thus "the farmers" were "all american." Living away from the exorbitant costs and sicknesses of Vincennes was very attractive to Badollet: "In a country where land is cheap, where the soil is fertile, and the produce of the earth is high, there is no room for dispondency." But there was room for aggravation with the French. Their profligate expropriation of the trees around Vincennes for firewood and bark roofs made the location of a farm close to the city impossible. Badollet lamented frequently the death of trees. "If you stand on an eminence in the neighbourhood of this place or in the commons," he told Gallatin in June 1807, "you perceive the trees strewed over & covering the ground, just as if a west indian hurricane had exerted its destructive fury on the land, & the whole appearing like a barren waste."

This was not the complaint of a pioneer environmentalist. To the contrary, trees were essential to American plans for transforming the Indiana landscape. Settlers had no intention of relying on urban amenities and erratic commerce. On isolated farms, trees were critical for survival. They provided shelter, materials for buildings and tools, and especially fuel. Without trees, families would face the same fate as two young lawyers, Jacob Burnet and Arthur St. Clair, Jr., in Vincennes one night in December 1799. The French had so

📖 183

THE
WORLD
OF
ANNA
TUTHILL
SYMMES
HARRISON,
1795–1810

exhausted the supply of small trees that the two men could find only a few pieces of timber on the ground with which to boil coffee and thaw a roast chicken; the rest of the night they huddled in the snow under blankets and coats in the middle of a cold rain. Burnet recalled that in the morning they felt as if "they had slept in the bed of the river."

The importance of trees notwithstanding, the Americans brought many of them down as they began to lay out farms in the 1790s and early 1800s. Typically they built a small lean-to first, with a fireplace at the south end, while they turned to the more important business of clearing land and planting crops. This business was time-consuming and back-breaking labor. The French traveler André Michaux complained that his four-day trip from Louisville to Vincennes in August 1795 was "one of the most difficult" he had undertaken in North America, "owing to the quantity of Trees overturned by storms, to the thick underbrush through which one is obliged to pass; to the number of Flies by which one is devoured." Still, farmers persisted, felling some trees with axes and girdling others so that they would eventually die. The burning of excess timber and brush created a kind of permanent smoky haze over the territory in the early nineteenth century.

With the trees dead or dying, farmers broke and turned the soil with a plow, usually a jumping plow that cut only small roots or, if they were from the Northeast, a stronger iron instrument. All over the river and creek valleys of southern Indiana, American farmers then planted corn and gardens of beans and vegetables in the broken soil still dotted with stumps and decaying trees. Corn was ubiquitous. It thrived even in the crudely rearranged landscape of the Old Northwest while providing perhaps twice the amount of food per acre of any other grain. Once harvested, women pounded the corn into meal or transformed it into hominy. Much of the corn went to livestock, particularly hogs, who otherwise roamed the woods foraging for foods. Like corn, hogs were everywhere, in large part because they required little care. Still another use for corn was to make whiskey.

With crops planted, American families turned their attention to improving their shelter. The lean-tos gave way to crude but efficient cabins built of notched logs; the spaces between the logs were filled with clay and mud. The roofs were clapboard. Inside there was usually a dirt floor with a few pieces of essential furniture, including homemade bedframes, tables, and stools, and some cooking utensils made of gourds and wood; most families would bring with them a couple of iron skillets in which women would prepare the bulk of the food they would consume. Outside there would be a few lean-tos for storage and livestock.

The American impress on the Indiana landscape was not limited to these small farms, however. Growing numbers of hunting fathers and sons reduced the populations of buffalo, deer, bear, wild turkeys, and pigeons in the first decades of the nineteenth century. Children and women gathered wild fruits (such as the crab apple) and berries. The Americans also brought new phenomena to the forests. The honey bee, for example, migrated just ahead of humans and provided sweetening. In an amazingly short time, American farm families rearranged the flora and fauna of the region, making more of an impression on the landscape than the French and the Indians had in three-quarters of a century.

While the new immigrants continued to rely heavily on waterways for transportation and communication (most people settled in the valley of a river or creek), they also began to think about laying out roads and improving river navigation. In 1802, Governor Harrison recommended that the old Buffalo Trace from New Albany on the Ohio to Vincennes be improved into a wagon road with inns situated about every thirty to forty miles for the convenience of travelers. These improvements, argued Jared Mansfield in 1804, "would invite immigration, & raise the value of these lands, as well as those of the interior in its vicinity." By that time, the trace had been a post road for four years, with a rider carrying the mail from Louisville to Vincennes and back every four weeks, at least in theory. Regular mail delivery encouraged Elihu Stout to establish a newspaper in Vincennes in the summer of 1804, although the editor of the *Western Sun* frequently lamented the failure of the post system when he had little or no news to print. Indeed, travel by road had become so regular that John Cleves Symmes even contemplated traveling through the woods to Vincennes in May 1804. The General Assembly tried to legislate transportation improvements in 1807 by requiring all men between twenty-one and fifty

⧩ 185

THE
WORLD
OF
ANNA
TUTHILL
SYMMES
HARRISON,
1795–1810

who had lived in a county for more than thirty days to devote up to twelve days a year to opening and repairing local roads and bridging smaller streams.

Labor and Households

By far the greatest impact of the American migration into the Indiana Territory in the decades after the Treaty of Greenville resulted from the sheer number of people who took up residence in the region. In fact, the demographic characteristics of the Indiana Territory—the youth, the high fertility rate, mobility, the rural character—intensified in the first two decades of the nineteenth century. By 1810, the white and black population, now within the familiar boundaries of the modern state, reached 24,520. Since 1800, some 16,458 people had migrated into the region, while 2,421 had been born there. Residents were also far more dispersed than in 1800. Now, 7,945 people lived in Knox County, 7,310 in Dearborn, 5,670 in Clark, and 3,595 in Harrison. The population boom, moreover, was just beginning. In the next decade, 111,681 people came to Indiana and women gave birth to 10,977 children, raising the total population to 147,178 in 1820.

John Modell's detailed study of the census completed in that year found the median size of a household to range from five to seven persons. Anna Harrison was not the only woman often pregnant in the territory. Families were overwhelmingly nuclear in structure. In only four of thirty-three counties did the proportion of households with just one member exceed 4 percent of the whole. In only three counties were 5 percent or greater of the households without a male eighteen years or older. And in only three counties did the number of households with more than two adults over the age of twenty-five exceed 15 percent. According to Modell's statistics, the fertility ratio, that is, the ratio of the number of children nine or younger to the number of women of childbearing age (sixteen to forty-four), was over two in all but three counties. In each case, one of the exceptional counties was Knox, which contained Vincennes. Within the city in 1820, 44 percent of households had only one member and the median size was 3.33. That demonstrates a clear relationship among households, fertility, and farming in the Indiana Territory.

In large part, it was the need for cheap labor that lay behind the large families and high fertility rate in the Indiana Territory. Children were not yet the economic liabilities that they would become in the twentieth century. They began to work at a very early age. They were laborers, another pair of hands to assist in the tasks of maintaining the household.

Within the family, gender roles were not as rigidly separated as they would become in the towns and cities of the nineteenth-century Middle West. Still, men and women had different responsibilities. The latter were primarily mothers; their major task was reproduction. American women of childbearing age were almost always pregnant, carrying, bearing, and nursing the infants whose labor was so sorely needed. They also supervised the socialization of young children, teaching them what was expected of them and how to behave. Once the young person needed less direct supervision, sex-specific training began.

Girls learned that women worked very hard. As the historian Laurel Thatcher Ulrich has suggested, while women had few social or economic opportunities in the early American republic, they had a multitude of social and economic responsibilities. In addition to the burdens of regular pregnancies and child care, mothers also shouldered responsibilities as cooks, gardeners, clothmakers, barnyard tenders, and housekeepers. Imagine the amount of time and labor which went into preparing food. Women typically grew as well as cooked the vegetables they fed to their families; they raised chickens, wrung their necks, plucked their feathers, cleaned, cooked, and served them; they fed and tended a cow, milked it, and made butter. Cooking involved keeping a fire going, banking it at night, getting it going in the morning, hauling firewood and water. When a woman was not preparing food, she would spend considerable amounts of time making or repairing clothing. Later, with an increase in traffic and people, women would be able to sell or barter butter, cloth, and other goods. While mothers and daughters had no legal or public political role, then, they were indispensable to the survival of the rural households that were occupying the river valleys of southern Indiana at the turn of the nineteenth century. No male could have transformed acres of woods into a rudimentary farm without the skills and labor of a female.

187

THE
WORLD
OF
ANNA
TUTHILL
SYMMES
HARRISON,
1795–1810

Men were hardly shirkers, of course. To them fell the physically demanding work of clearing, plowing, and harvesting corn, as well as maintaining the physical structures that the household occupied. They also hunted and fished for food. Men, moreover, had important public responsibilities. It was through them that households most frequently dealt with the rest of the world. The land was in their names; they went to court when boundaries or debts were in dispute; they had the right to vote when the opportunity presented itself. The father bore public responsibility for the activities of all members of the household. He made the decisions about where the family lived and when it moved. Landed gentleman John Cleves Symmes complained in 1807 that "I have great cares on my mind & labors on my hands, in the line of husbandry; many hands at work, and no body in door nor out that I can fully confide in. I must be first up and the last to bed every day of my life, or all is motionless, and nothing done as it ought to be." But, in the vast majority of cases, the business of the household as a whole was a shared affair: although women and children had little formal power, their contributions were crucial.

The Demand for Slaves

The contributions of enslaved African Americans also were crucial. For white men, there was plenty of opportunity in Indiana. There was lots of land, with waterways that would carry produce away to markets. But there was not enough labor, never enough people to work. Thus there was not only a high fertility rate; there was a growing clamor in the early nineteenth century to legalize slavery, or at least to allow indentured servitude, in order to clear the forests of the Wabash and its tributaries into an agricultural showplace dominated by independent white males and their dependents.

Governor William Henry Harrison was at the forefront of the pro-slavery forces. While he spoke about farming as an occupation, he had no intention of taking up the plow and breaking the soil of Indiana himself. Farming meant developing land into a secure source of income. A gentleman like Harrison would leave the backbreaking work to other members of his household. His role was to govern his household and his territory free from the necessity of working in the fields. This was hardly an uncommon attitude. Harrison's Ohio friend Thomas Worthington called himself a farmer, but the man never stood behind a plow until the economic depression of 1819 forced him to do so.

The Harrison household, like many others, thus required labor, which was in very short supply in the Wabash Valley in the early nineteenth century. White men stood to gain little by hiring themselves out to would-be nabobs when they could buy land relatively cheaply and on credit or simply squat on a piece of soil and start to clear it themselves. The dearth of free labor was not a problem for men such as Harrison who had grown up in slave societies. The governor, after all, had arrived in Vincennes in January 1801 accompanied by a black manservant who had traveled with him from Berkeley. Technically, Article VI of the Ordinance of 1787, forbidding the introduction of servants or slaves northwest of the Ohio River, was still in force. But in practice, the French and some Americans had held slaves in and around Vincennes for decades. Governor St. Clair refused to enforce the article.

With an acute labor shortage, it did not take Harrison and other like-minded men long to try to circumvent the ordinance entirely. Slaves were the obvious answer to their problem. Within two years of his arrival on the Wabash, Harrison presided over a convention of territorial citizens who voted to petition Congress for a ten-year suspension in the operation of Article VI. The petition, signed by Harrison, stated that the article had "been extremely prejudicial to the Interest and welfare" of 90 percent of the men attending the convention. More specifically, "it has prevented the Country from populating and been the reason of driving many valuable Citizens possessing Slaves to the Spanish side of the Mississippi, most of whom would have settled in this Territory, and the consequences of keeping that prohibition inforce will be that of obliging the numerous Class of Citizens disposed to emigrate, to seek an Asylum in that country where they can be permitted to enjoy their property." In other words, white immigrants, unwilling to work for each other, needed slaves to clear forests and break prairies, and if they could not have them in Indiana, they would go elsewhere.

🕮 189

THE
WORLD
OF
ANNA
TUTHILL
SYMMES
HARRISON,
1795–1810

The petitioners, most of whom seem to have been residents of the Vincennes area, were not interested in a permanent migration of African Americans. They wanted to limit the suspension of Article VI to ten years, with the proviso that all slaves "and their progeny" brought into Indiana during that decade would "be considered, and continued in the same state of Servitude, as if they had remained in those parts of the United States where Slavery is permitted and from whence they may have been removed." Governor Harrison and his allies were seeking the immediate benefits of slave labor. It is important to note, moreover, that the call for a suspension of Article VI was only one of several demands. They also called for the opening of more lands, a recognition of squatter rights, grants of lands to support schools and seminaries in several settlements, the encouragement of "good waggon roads" with "houses of Entertainment," territorial acquisition of salt springs, the expansion of the suffrage to include all free males over twenty-one, and an adequate salary for the territory's attorney-general. While slavery was first on the list and quickly attracts the eye of the historian, the petitioners apparently saw its prohibition as only one of many obstacles to the development of Indiana.

Like all early settlers and land speculators, Governor Harrison and his allies wanted to attract people to the Wabash. They coveted a population rise. More settlers meant more farmers, higher taxes, more consumers. By increasing demand for land and services, population growth raised prices and allowed those who had engrossed large tracts of undeveloped land to clear substantial profits—at least in theory. Leading citizens in the Indiana Territory well knew that immigrants were coming primarily from Virginia and the Carolinas via Kentucky. Why discourage those who owned slaves from settling on the Wabash? Why outlaw the most likely source of labor when the need to clear land and plant crops was so high?

Congress referred the petition to committees. Harrison particularly lamented the inability of his friend Worthington, who, while a Quaker, had employed many indentured servants, to support the cause. But perhaps encouraged by a favorable committee report in 1804, the territorial legislature renewed its appeal in December 1805. In Indiana, the argument went, slaves would be spread out on farms, not "herded together," and thus more "comfortably provided for." In addition, "dispersing them though the Western Territories is the only means by which a gradual emancipation can ever be effected."

While Congress sat on this petition, Governor Harrison and his pro-slavery allies acted on their own. In September 1803, the territorial government adopted a Virginia law requiring "all negroes and mulattoes . . . who shall come into this territory under contract to serve another . . . to perform such contract specifically during the term thereof." Masters could whip or otherwise punish those who refused and add time to those who were deemed lazy. These contracts, moreover, could be sold or inherited. All of this was legal. The Indiana Territory was simply recognizing bona fide agreements into which all parties had ostensibly entered voluntarily for a fixed number of years. Masters were supposed to provide food, shelter, and clothing for their servants and present them with a blanket and clothing at the end of the contract. In practice, of course, the servants in these contracts were African American slaves who had little other recourse than to sign them. They could complain to public officials, but Governor Harrison and the territorial judges made it illegal for blacks to testify against whites two days after enacting the law covering indentured servants.

When the Indiana Territory acquired a legislature in 1804, Harrison and his largely southern-born allies in the council quickly tightened the restrictions on blacks. An 1805 "Act concerning the introduction of Negroes and Mulattoes into this Territory" allowed masters to bring slaves into Indiana for up to sixty days. In the first month, they had to agree on a contractual arrangement or the white could sell the black to someone in a slave state. African Americans could not refuse to accept indentures, which averaged forty years in Knox County and included periods of up to ninety years. Their children were also affected. Sons had to work for the holder of the indenture until they were thirty, daughters until they were twenty-eight. The following year, the legislature further restricted "Slaves and Servants"; those traveling without passes could be whipped with the approval of a justice of the peace, as could those charged with trespass, riot, unlawful assembly, or "seditious speeches." Stiff penalties also awaited those who sheltered or in any way aided runaways or servants. Nothing could be clearer than the intention of

191

THE
WORLD
OF
ANNA
TUTHILL
SYMMES
HARRISON,
1795–1810

Governor Harrison and others in the Vincennes and Illinois areas to circumvent Article VI.

Not everyone agreed that allowing slavery was an important prerequisite for the development of the Indiana Territory. John Badollet of the land office was outspoken on the subject. In early 1806, he argued privately that since only the northern and middle states could "spare population for settling new countries," the legalization of slavery would harm the territory in the long run by checking immigration from such places. After all, "the rapid population and prosperity of the State of Ohio, sufficiently evinces which of the two slavery or no slavery most effectually invite new settlers." In the spring of 1809, Badollet went public with his opposition in a series of letters to the Vincennes *Western Sun*, earning the enmity of Governor Harrison.

Still, Badollet was hardly alone. Some citizens of Clark County met in October 1807 to dissent from the pro-slavery position of the territorial government. They claimed their representatives to the 1802 convention had been "decidedly opposed" to the suspension of Article VI and that a majority of the legislature had voted against the 1805 petition. In any case, they were sure that anti-slavery forces were on the ascendancy and that Congress would respect their wishes. These men were certain that slavery was "repugnant to the inestimable principles of a republican Government." In fact, many had migrated to Indiana "to get free from a government which does tolerate slavery." Whether or not slavery impeded or encouraged migration, however, was not the question, for the institution was "either right or wrong." There were no shades of gray.

Clearly there was opposition to slavery in the territorial assembly. In 1807, a recently elected delegate from Knox County, General Washington Johnston, chaired a committee that called for repeal of the 1805 law regarding servants. He angrily pointed out the "most flagitous abuse of that law," with blacks forced to agree to serve for the balance of their lives. For Johnston it was a question of moral justice: "what is morally wrong can never by expediencey be made right." Still, the bulk of his report attacked the notion that slavery would encourage migration. Like Badollet, he claimed that many migrants would be coming from the northern and middle states. More than that, Johnston argued that the northern states were more prosperous than the southern ones. Since "the hand of freedom can best lay the foundation to raise the fabric of public prosperity," their roads, canals, manufactures, etc., were naturally "superior." Again, the example of Ohio cinched the argument that "the exertions of the free man who labors for himself and family must be more effectual than the faint efforts of a meek and dispirited slave whose condition is never to be bettered by his incessant toil." Johnston worried, as many before and after him did, that slavery would have a deleterious effect on whites, making them cruel, unfeeling, uncontrolled, proud, and arrogant: "[M]ust the Territory of Indiana take a retrograde step into barbarism and assimilate itself with Algiers and Morocco?" The assembly apparently thought so, for it refused to rescind the legislation.

While leading white citizens of the territory argued about the economic value of slavery and anti-slavery, African Americans lived as de facto slaves. Emma Lou Thornbrough's careful study of early court records revealed that between 1805 and 1810, whites in Clark County filed thirty-two indentures involving thirty-six people; those in Knox County registered forty-six indentures involving fifty people. Sixty of the blacks were originally from Kentucky, eleven from South Carolina, five from Tennessee, three from Virginia, and one each from North Carolina, Georgia, and Maryland. Like the white population, black people were overwhelmingly young; only two were over fifty and seventeen were under fifteen. The majority was under twenty-five. By 1810, there were 630 blacks in Indiana. Of those, 393 were supposedly free, but most of them were undoubtedly indentured servants. By far the greatest number of African Americans (384) lived in Knox County, with 92 (all listed as free) in Dearborn, 121 in Clark, and 33 in Harrison.

We know very little about their lives. But it is reasonable to assume that most of them lived as members of households. Women would have labored as domestic servants, cooking, cleaning, child-caring, tending animals and gardens, making clothes and butter while men were at work bringing down trees, plowing, and harvesting crops. Certainly their labor had expanded beyond the demands placed on them by the French, who kept so closely to towns and the fur trade.

📯 **193**

THE
WORLD
OF
ANNA
TUTHILL
SYMMES
HARRISON,
1795–1810

Slaves completed the Harrison household, helping to secure the comfort and independence of their master and his family. We do not know how many lived at Grouseland, but we do know that the governor was frequently dealing in slaves. In May 1806, Harrison informed a correspondent in New Jersey that in return for a parcel of land he owned he "would freely take one or two negroes either male or female & get the favor of you to keep them til an oppurtunity of sending them occured—it would make no difference whether they are slaves for life or only serve a term of years." No difference to Harrison, at least.

Playing by the Rules

In the last decade of his life, John Cleves Symmes wrote several letters to his grandsons, John and Charles Short, advising them about life. He urged them to read, particularly about the history of Rome, to study geography, "to observe Oeconomy in every thing," to exercise, and, most of all, to cultivate good manners. The judge's primary lesson was that success and happiness in life depended on being civil. Never mind that Symmes himself had never learned it. Or perhaps that was the reason he insisted on it so strongly? If young men were well-educated "in books and science," they could more easily learn about "men and the world," and then they would "be [great] as well as good men. Your state will make you [judges] or members of Congress, and it may be something higher. [B]ut in order to be beloved" by others "you must never be proud and scornful, [never] quarelsome and fight, nor hard to please [nor] [find]ing fault with every thing that falls in your way. On the contrary you must always be in a pleasant humer, seemingly well pleased with every thing." More specifically, as the judge said in another letter, "there are many words in the English language that boys ought never to learn, such as I will, I won't, you shall, you shan't, You lie, you dog, you scoundrel & &. . . . [T]he manner of your expressions has a wonderful effect, let it be neither blunt nor affected, too low nor too loud, be graceful, not speaking with your eyes another way, and appear all attention while others speak to you, over your inferiors never seem to triumph, & to your superiors be submissive but not abashed. [N]ature is the best preceptor in such cases, custom is often a tyrant."

These were common enough observations from someone like Symmes. They were also a recipe for encouraging submission and discouraging autonomy. In essence, the judge was advising his grandsons to be passive, to seek happiness not by taking chances or defying authority but by making peace with the world. Given the history of his life, his own unhappiness, the difficulties he had experienced with defiant family members, Symmes's advice is far from surprising. Both boys, overcoming the financial reverses suffered by their father, became upstanding citizens of the Ohio Valley, John Cleves Short as a lawyer in Cincinnati and Charles Wilkins Short as a physician and professor in Louisville. This was a long way, however, from the world of the ambitious and aggressive young men who accompanied George Rogers Clark into the Wabash Valley in the 1770s and 1780s. And, to a significant extent, both Judge Symmes's advice and the eagerness with which his grandsons accepted it reflected a decline in the pervasive challenges to estab-lished authority and the restless ambition of the revolutionary era.

No matter their class or cultural backgrounds, white males moved to the Ohio Valley in large part to acquire the land that would ensure them competency and independence. William Henry Harrison was no different in this regard from George Rogers Clark. But Harrison and growing numbers like him were not the same as Clark; Harrison was less interested in asserting his independence from families and governments than in establishing his interdepen-dence with them. If he was as ambitious as any white male in the region, he was more methodical and systematic in his attempt to achieve his goals. Harrison worked within the system: he cultivated patrons and depended on government jobs. As in the army, he played by the rules. In the end, his defiance of his father-in-law in marrying Anna was less characteristic of him than the fact that he wed the daughter of an important and influential man. William Henry Harrison came to the Indiana Territory not as an angry young man but as a young man in a hurry to rise within the exist-ing political structure. It is hardly surprising that he made it to the very top, serving as president of his country for one month in the

THE
WORLD
OF
ANNA
TUTHILL
SYMMES
HARRISON,
1795–1810

winter of 1841, without anybody being exactly sure of what his principles were.

Anna fit her father's prescriptions for male behavior well. She was simply a nice person. The most interesting thing about her letters is her constant struggle to accept the will of God without complaining. The more independent of the two Symmes daughters, she made the less problematic and far happier match. Whether because she was shrewd or lucky or both, her ardor led her to a comfortable life, even as she suffered the pain of so many deaths. While her husband worked in the first decade of the nineteenth century to clear the Indiana Territory of the remaining obstacles to its development, Anna concentrated on keeping alive the bonds of affection that knit her family together. Judge Symmes helped in this task, offering to teach her eldest son "the art and business of farming" and to entertain her daughters in his home. More important, he regularly told his dear Nancy until his death in 1814 that he hoped "that all possible blessings and peace in life may be your portion and everlasting happiness hereafter." This was a foolish sentence from a sixty-seven-year-old man who had experienced more than enough travail to know the improbability of such hopes. But love, as any fool knows, is only intermittently sensible. It was, moreover, the one constant in the lives of the Symmeses, Harrisons, and Shorts.

8.

THE WORLD OF TENSKWATAWA, 1795–1811

On March 13, 1806, seven Delaware Indians, "with painted faces," burst into a tiny settlement of Moravian missionaries on the White River about twenty miles southwest of Munsee Town. They seized a Christian Indian, Josua, Jr., and took him away, promising to return him when he had told Chief Tedpachsit "to his face that he had no poison stored in his house." The Mohican son of an influential Moravian convert, Josua had lived with the German Christians for his entire life. He had grown up in eastern Pennsylvania, married his wife, Sophia, in Philadelphia in 1764, then accompanied David Zeisberger to western Pennsylvania in the late 1760s and the Ohio Country in the early 1770s. Like Anna Harrison, Sophia had ten children, producing one about every other year for two decades; unlike Anna, Sophia saw half of them die in childbirth. Americans killed the two oldest daughters during the 1782 massacre of Christian Indians at Gnadenhutten. Sophia survived until February 1801, when she died after "an extended sickness."

Almost two months later, on March 24, Josua left eastern Ohio as a member of a party intending to establish a new mission on the White River. He went in the company of the missionaries John Peter and Anna Marie Kluge and Abraham Luckenbach and the Christian Indians John and Catherine Thomas, their children Marcus, Juliana, and Bethia, another couple named Jacob and Mary, a widow named Abigael, her daughter Anna Salome and two grandchildren, his son Christian, and two other helpers. The three Europeans were volunteers. John Peter was a thirty-year-old veteran of six years' service among the natives in Surinam, Dutch Guiana. Abraham was a twenty-three-year-old novice. Anna Marie had only just met and married Kluge. He had asked for a wife in Pennsylvania, but no woman would agree to a marriage until Anna Marie at Lititz. The trio had arrived in the Ohio Country late in 1800 and had spent the winter learning the language and customs of the Delaware in preparation for their journey to the White River in the spring.

The Moravians were essentially following the Delaware, many of whom had moved to what is now east-central Indiana in the aftermath of the Treaty of Greenville. More specifically, they were living in a string of nine villages along the White River north and east of the site of present-day Muncie. In early 1800, Tedpachsit sent a large wampum belt to the Moravians inviting them to establish a mission near the new villages. They accepted the invitation and sent the Kluges and Luckenbach to bring Christianity to the Indiana Delaware. The missionaries and the Delaware families arrived on the White River in late May 1801.

The closer they got to their destination, the more they became disturbed by the behavior of the "heathen" Indians they encountered. According to the Kluges and Luckenbach, most of them were very drunk. This was especially true of the part during the trip that occurred on land, between the sites of present-day Richmond and Muncie. On the night of May 15, a family came into their camp "with two barrels of whiskey and remained overnight." Another Indian arrived and "the drinking began at once." The latest arrival painted himself black and yelled "like a wild animal in the woods." The Kluges spent the night in terror, although the Indian lost consciousness. The next morning, the departing Indians left him a pint of whiskey so that he could start again. But Kluge poured it out before he awoke.

The next day, May 16, two Delawares who were serving as the missionaries' boatmen and another Indian "began drinking to such excess that they did not know what they were doing. They poured this horrid drink, by the pint, down their throats." When the missionaries asked them to stop, "they got angry and told us to leave them alone." The Kluges went ahead and ran into two more "drunken heathen." Matters improved only briefly the following day. By nightfall, they had encountered another Indian with two barrels of whiskey and several men, including a couple of Christians, got drunk. "No one who has not seen an Indian drunk can possibly have any conception of it," lamented the missionaries in their diary. "It is as if they had all been changed into evil spirits." The Kluges and Luckenbach prayed for strength and perseverance, but they "slept little during the night." The next morning, the Indians were contrite, looking ashamed and acting as if they had been sick. The missionaries, meanwhile, could only reflect on how Indians "who, when sober, looked like innocent lambs and were at all times friendly to us" could become "like wild animals." They did not drink during the day. But at nightfall the bottle came out again. Despite their promises and excuses, the Indians were simply "perfect slaves to drink."

With the kind of determination that provokes both admiration and consternation from less brave souls, the Moravians pushed on, crossing the terrain from the Whitewater Valley to that of the White in a few days and establishing their post a few miles from Delaware villages. They built huts, planted and tended corn, and attempted to convert the heathen. Chief Tedpachsit welcomed them and urged "his young people" to go and hear the "great word" of God. But all was not well on the White River. The heathen continued to behave in what the missionaries thought of as inexcusable ways. Even Josua, upon whom they relied for translations, was not always faithful. Once he took his sick son to "a witch doctor," an act of betrayal that the Moravians thought undermined the credibility of their mission. Similarly, the Kluges and Luckenbach had to resist the desires of their Christian Indians to go to Fort Wayne to get presents with the heathen Delaware.

The Europeans worked hard, spending their days tending their crops and relentlessly preaching to a few Indians and themselves. But the fact remains that they made little progress in attracting converts. At the end of 1801 only four "heathen" had joined them. Two years later, there were but thirteen people in the village, six of whom were children; the population fell to nine by the end of 1805. The Indians could not overcome their fear of the European intentions (especially given the fresh memory of the Gnadenhutten massacre), their own frequent illnesses, and their large appetite for liquor. The Moravians and their religion were simply not a plausible answer to their problems. How could Christianity, preached by invaders, overcome the obvious disintegration of the Indians' world in the presence of the relentless European intrusion? What did it have to offer to a people seeking solace from defeat, death, and division?

Indians, Alcohol, and Cultural Crisis

The decade following the Treaty of Greenville was simply disastrous for the Indians on the Wabash and its tributaries. In addition to the ongoing problems of recurring flu and smallpox epidemics, they had lost the ability to deal with the Americans on relatively equal terms. The British, preoccupied with the wars of the French Revolution, had little interest in stopping the expansion of the United States. European conflicts also adversely affected the fur trade by sharply cutting demand and limiting the amount and quality of goods English merchants had to exchange. The supply side of the equation was similarly in bad shape. At the end of the eighteenth century, the rapid American advance decimated the animal populations in Indiana. The American settlers, unlike the French and the British, reduced the size of forests, making the landscape increasingly hostile to deer and beavers. While American officials suggested that Indians turn to agriculture, few did. Indian males were simply not willing to till the earth, a role traditionally filled by women. To farm was to emasculate themselves. Some males exacerbated the situation by excessive hunting and trapping for the sole purpose of selling skins and furs. American hunters were even worse in this respect. Complaining about the disappearance of deer, bear, and buffalo in 1801, William Henry Harrison expressed the widespread opinion that one white hunter killed "more game than five of the common Indians." The governor ordered whites to stop settling and hunting on Indian land, even as he continued to negotiate to get legal title to it. The end result of this crisis in the hunting economy was increasing dependency on annuities paid by agents of the United States at Fort Wayne and other posts. Indians had dealt with Europeans for a century in the Wabash area, but never before as supplicants.

Within the Indian villages on the Wabash, White, Eel, and Maumee, there was also a high degree of social and political tension. The migration of Delaware and Shawnee into the region, which intensified after Greenville, brought a demographic rearrangement. Indian villages were now heterogeneous communities, with a mixture of tribal loyalties and cultural origins. There was little sense of coherent political action. Local chiefs often engendered as much hostility as respect. Governor Harrison was able to negotiate several treaties in the first few years of the nineteenth century by exploiting these divisions.

In sum, Miami, Shawnee, and Delaware villages were home to peoples feeling the full effects of spatial, ecological, and cultural dislocation. Virtually everything in Indian society was at issue, from gender roles to the power of shamans to the role of hunting. In this world, Christian missionaries such as the Kluges and Luckenbach, however well-intentioned, were simply another source of pressure to give up old ways. Many Indians told the Moravians that their preaching made sense, but that they could not resist the taste of whiskey. They were always embarrassed by their behavior when sober. But whiskey was readily available from both American settlers and British traders, and it offered an escape from the psychological effects of life in a disintegrating culture.

The efforts of American officials to stop the liquor trade failed. One of Governor Harrison's first proclamations, issued July 20, 1801, forbade the "selling or giving any Spirituous Liquors" to Indians within Vincennes; such transactions had to take place across the Wabash or "at least one mile from the village." He further ordered local magistrates to punish drunken and riotous persons and admonished local citizens to help "apprehend the disorderly and rioutous persons, who constantly infest the streets of Vincennes and to inform against all those who violate the Sabbath by selling or Bartering Spirituous Liquors or who pursue any other unlawful business on the day set apart for the service of God."

The governor was responding to the behavior of Piankashaw, Wea, and Eel River Indians in Vincennes. Sometimes thirty to forty gathered in the village, thoroughly intoxicated. They accosted people with knives, broke into homes, tore down fences, and killed hogs and cattle. Mostly, however, they injured themselves, killing each other "without mercy." Harrison estimated that 6,000 gallons of whiskey arrived on the Wabash every year. "This poisonous liquor," the governor told Secretary of War Henry Dearborn, "not only incapasitates them from obtaining a living by Hunting but it leads to the most attrocious crimes—killing each other has become so customary amongst them that it is no longer a crime to murder those whom they have been most accumstomeed to estem and regard. Their Chiefs and their nearest relations fall under the strokes of their Tomhawks and Knives."

Not surprisingly, Indian leaders were even more anxious. In January 1802, Little Turtle asked President Thomas Jefferson to prohibit liquor sales. Governor Harrison then issued another proclamation outlawing all sales to Indians within Indian territory. This was unenforceable, in no small part because the trade continued in areas that Indians had ceded to the whites by treaty. But men such as Little Turtle remained deeply concerned about the disintegration of all social cohesion in the wake of massive consumption of rye whiskey from western Pennsylvania and corn whiskey from the bluegrass region of central Kentucky.

Little Turtle was interested in more than self-restraint. In the aftermath of Greenville, he had decided that the Indians' future lay in accommodation to American ways. Under Thomas Jefferson, the United States government was committed to a policy of cultural assimilation of the Indians. Enlightened notions about human development led to a belief that the Indians could be transformed from hunters to farmers. Christianity and civilization would complete the great remaking of the landscape of the Wabash by leading the Indians away from their supposedly barbaric and heathen customs. Jefferson thus applauded efforts like those of the Moravians on the Wabash. As he wrote in a famous letter to Governor Harrison in February 1803,

> The decrease of game rendering their subsistence by hunting insufficient, we wish to draw them to agriculture, to spinning and weaving. The latter branches they take up with great readiness, because they fall to the women, who gain by quitting the labours of the field [for] these

which are exercised within doors. When they withdraw themselves to the culture of a small piece of land, they will perceive how useless to them are their extensive forests, and will be willing to pare them off from time to time in exchange for necessaries for their farms & families. . . . In this way our settlements will gradually circumscribe and approach the Indians, and they will in time either incorporate with us as citizens of the United States or remove beyond the Mississippi.

The president informed the Miami directly in 1808 of their foolishness in continuing to hunt. Instead, he argued, "temperance, peace, and agriculture, will raise you up to what your forefathers were, will prepare you to possess property, to wish to live under regular laws, to join us in our government, to mix with us in society, and your blood and ours united, will spread again over the great island."

Governor Harrison had long since developed this theme. The Virginian told a council of Indians in Vincennes in August 1802 of the divine purposes of agriculture. President Jefferson wanted them situated in towns where they could farm and raise animals under the guidance of American agents. This was not a secular plan. No, it was God who wanted people to farm. "It is necessary that the grain should be deposited in the earth, and the intruding beasts kept off and noxious weeds destroyed; the munificent Deity performs the rest" by providing the nurturing rain and sunlight. If shifting from hunting to farming was too hard, then the Indians should allow their children to make the change while they were still young and malleable. But change they must. For hunting would only ruin their lives; it exhausted the forests and offended both secular and sacred authority. "There is nothing so pleasing to God," concluded Harrison, "as to see his children employed in the cultivation of the earth. He gave command to our ancestors to increase and multiply until the whole earth should be filled with inhabitants. But you must be sensible my Children that this command could not be obeyed if we were all to depend upon the chase for our subsistence."

In practice, however, the American government offered little assistance to Indians interested in change. The activities of its agents at Fort Wayne seemed intent upon trapping Indians in a cycle of dependency on federal annuities and trade goods. In 1800, the United States built a new and larger fort near the site of the one constructed under the direction of Hamtramck. The various commandants who followed supervised an area of about one square mile. Its residents ranged from the fifty to eighty soldiers in residence at any given moment to several traders and settlers, Indian agents, their families and slaves, and the French who continued to live at the forks of the Maumee despite wars and multiple disasters. There were also French people in a village across the river. Most numerous, of course, were the Indians who moved in and out of the post to receive annuities and to trade and visit.

In 1802, the United States established the Fort Wayne Indian Factory to control trade with the local Indians. The factor, or head of the trading post, was John Johnston. Irish by birth, Johnston had served as a wagoner in the 1794 campaign and was a failed merchant and struggling law clerk. His compensation as factor was $1,000 per year plus three meals a day. Johnston supervised the construction of buildings and the arrival of goods. In 1803, $1,677.02 worth of tea, indigo, saltpeter, spices, rice, vinegar, coffee, soap, sugar, tomahawks, traps, buttons, coats, nails, needles, tobacco, locks, china, rifles, cloth, and other items arrived in twenty-five large packages. Apparently trade was not limited to Indians. Officers, white traders, and Johnston himself ran accounts at the Indian factory. Still, the primary exchange was with local Indians, who brought in skins and furs to trade. Fort Wayne was the most successful American Indian factory in the Old Northwest in the first decade of the nineteenth century. Johnston shipped furs to Detroit every fall and spring; primarily deer and raccoon, they also included bears, wolves, otters, beaver, and mink, and sometimes were valued at over $10,000. There was little incentive at Fort Wayne to switch to agriculture even when, after a few years, the trade declined from a total of $7,766.31 in 1808 to $1,265.05 in 1810.

The Indian agent at Fort Wayne was William Wells, the American-born son-in-law of Little Turtle who had lived much of his life among the Miami. His primary function was to distribute the annuities promised by the government of the United States in the Treaty of Greenville. Each year he gave away over $5,000, including $1,000 each in cash and goods to the Miami (raised to $1,600 in 1805), the Delaware, and the Potawatomi, and $500 each ($750 after 1805) to the Wea and Eel River Miami. Wells also supervised the construction of a large council house for meetings. But it was the control of money and goods which made him and Little Turtle so powerful.

Neither Governor Harrison nor factor Johnston ever trusted Wells; indeed, Johnston detested him. Both accused Wells of self-interest and fraud; they charged him with trying to make money for himself and with manipulating the Indians for his own purposes. Little Turtle's most recent biographer believes that this hostility prevented Little Turtle and Wells from fully implementing their strategy of accommodation with the Americans. Be that as it may, the annuities and goods made the agents in Fort Wayne and those who cooperated with them powerful men.

Little Turtle traveled to Washington during the winter of 1801–1802 and spoke with the president. He complained about the sale of "this fatal poison," alcohol, and asked for a blacksmith at Fort Wayne and plows and agricultural instruments. The *sine qua non* was the prohibition of alcohol. The Indians "have not the command over themselves that you have, therefore before anything can be done to advantage this evil must be remedied." The chief made a final trip to Washington in 1808–1809, winning the admiration of Americans for his dress, dignity, and demeanor, but little else. Over the course of the decade and a half that followed Greenville, he had moved from hostility to resistance to objection to accommodation with the Americans and their insatiable desire for land. In no way, however, had he improved the situation of the Indians. While he exercised power by virtue of his reputation and his ties with federal agents, he offered little comfort to a people in crisis.

Little Turtle was hardly the only Indian leader to move toward an acceptance of the Americans' victory in the 1790s, to talk of the necessity of shifting, albeit slowly, from an economy based on hunting and trading to one resting on plow agriculture. The Delaware Tedpachsit invited the Moravians to the White River, and the Shawnee Black Hoof did, too; but they were unable to sway the mass of their peoples, who remained ambivalent about the Americans and frequently lost in drunken states. Alcohol was simply assuming greater importance in Indian culture, becoming an integral part of the rituals and ceremonies central to the daily lives of the Miami, Shawnee, and Delaware.

Tenskwatawa

One of the most dramatic phenomena of this period was the increasing number of visions reported by Indian residents of the villages along the Wabash, the White, and the Eel. The Moravians noted an increase in festivals and ceremonies among the Delaware in late 1804 and early 1805. People streamed by their small settlement going to hear about the visions experienced, more often than not, by women. The content of the visions typically laid the blame for the disintegration of Indian cultures less on the whites than on the spiritual failure of the Indians themselves. They were not observing properly the rituals that kept them in harmony with the rest of their world. "Never, in all the time that we are here," reported the Moravians in March 1805, "have the Indians been in such a state of revolution as they are at present." They would not listen to talk about Christianity; they expressed indifference: "For the present they do not want to hear anything at all except what they learn through the extravagant visions."

Among the several people living along the White River who experienced visions was a Shawnee who called himself Tenskwatawa ("Open Door"). While he was only one among many at the beginning, he soon attracted a great many followers. Tenskwatawa, also known as the Prophet, quickly became the most powerful Indian in the region. He preached a curious mixture of Indian and European beliefs and customs and successfully convinced many Delaware, Shawnee, and Miami to renounce their evil habits and undergo a spiritual and cultural rebirth. The essence of his message was that while the Americans were devils who were not to be trusted or even dealt with, the major reason for the decline of Indian power lay within Indian societies themselves. People had neglected the rituals that gave them power and demonstrated their ability to handle it and use it effectively. The Indians were failing primarily because they deserved to fail. To reverse matters, they would have to undergo a reformation, a spiritual renewal that would revive the old ways but with distinctly different twists necessitated by lengthy exposure to the onrushing Americans. Tenskwatawa's power, then, came from traditional sources. He observed the proper rituals and he showed Indians not only how they could resist Americans but also how they could *earn* successful resistance. Hundreds of Indians embraced the teachings of Tenskwatawa. Many followed him when he relocated first to eastern Ohio and then, in May 1808, to a new village on the Wabash, just north of the site of present-day Lafayette, which they called Prophetstown.

Born Lalawethika in early 1775, Tenskwatawa was an unlikely candidate for a position of spiritual leadership. Though he was a brother of the great Tecumseh, he was a well-known drunk and braggart who had proved ineffective at most everything in his life. Not that his life had been easy. To the contrary, he experienced all of the evils visited upon the Indians of Trans-Appalachia (that is, the Ohio Valley) in the late eighteenth century. His father died at the Battle of Point Pleasant, a few months before his birth; he developed little competence as a hunter or warrior (in fact, he wounded himself and disfigured his right eye with an arrow); he fought at Fallen Timbers but never distinguished himself in the manner of Tecumseh; and he was an indifferent medicine man, a vocation he took up in his late twenties. Mostly Tenskwatawa drank, developing a notorious reputation among the Indians with whom he lived on the White River in the first few years of the nineteenth century.

Then, following a winter of disease and death, he had his vision. He fell into a trance, becoming so still that preparations were made for his funeral before he revived. Some villagers were skeptical, but most of the nearby Delaware and Shawnee believed what he told them when he was able. News of the event spread quickly, and he soon became a figure of some renown in the area. This was less because of personal charisma than the content of his vision, which obviously bore directly on the fate of the Indians. One man assured the Moravians "that this new Indian teacher had been a very bad person, but that now he spoke only good things, for which reason the Indians believed what he said." Tenskwatawa reported that he had seen a paradiselike heaven—a fertile land with plenty of animals and fish and cornfields where Indians could live as they once had. Only the virtuous could enter, however; those who sinned in this life would be given a tantalizing glimpse of paradise before being taken to a great hut where they would experience all kinds of fiery torture. They might one day enter heaven, but they would never enjoy its pleasures.

Other visions followed. With them, Tenskwatawa quickly developed a coherent prescription for a social and spiritual rebirth among the depressed and despondent Indians. His mission, he said, was to save them from "bad habits" and lead them to a peaceful life. First and foremost, they must give up alcohol or suffer hideous torture. In addition, they had to deal with each other affectionately and refrain from violence within households and communities. Tenskwatawa also talked of the great value of monogamous marriages and the dangers of promiscuity and polygamy. The Master of Life wanted the Indians to perform rituals: starting new fires in their lodges without using flint and steel, praying to Him twice a day, and demonstrating their fidelity. He also demanded that they reject as false prophets those men who scorned Tenskwatawa or refused to give up their medicine bundles.

Tenskwatawa was initiating among the Delaware and the Shawnee what the anthropologist Anthony F. C. Wallace called a "revitalization movement" in his study of the Iroquois prophet Handsome Lake. His mixture of a rejection of new customs (such as drinking) with an elevation of old ones was a rebirth of individual discipline and social cohesiveness. The Prophet told the Indians to return to the old ways: to eat, dress, and work in the manner of their ancestors. They were to avoid the food (bread and hogs, for example) and the technology (guns, metal, clothes) of the Europeans. More specifically, they were to stay away from Americans. The British, French, and the Spanish were their friends. But of the Americans the Master of Life said: "The Americans I did not make. They are not my children, but the children of the Evil Spirit." In fact, they had grown "from the scum of the great Water when it was troubled by the Evil Spirit. And the froth was driven into the Woods by a strong east wind. They are numerous, but I hate them. They are unjust. They have taken away your lands, which were not made for them." The only reasonable course for an Indian was to avoid all contact with Americans.

Tenskwatawa warned strongly against the activities of Indian witches, the agents of the Evil Spirit who were allegedly responsible for much of the disorder in the villages. Anyone who opposed the Prophet was, ipso facto, a witch and had to be eliminated. Those who believed, however, would ritually confess their sins and ceremonially shake Tenskwatawa's hand, whereupon they would be instructed in the word of the Prophet. But those who refused, especially those who were closely identified with Americans, were to be executed as witches. Indeed, it was the intense search for such people that brought the seven painted Delaware to the Moravian village on March 13, 1806, in search of the unfortunate Christian, Josua.

The Indians took Josua to their village at Woapikamunk, where he joined a group of about one dozen alleged witches, including Chief Tedpachsit. Almost all denied having poisoned the community with evil power. Tenskwatawa arrived on March 15 and, while examining each prisoner in a circle, decided who would be condemned to death and who would survive. He, after all, claimed, according to the Moravians, "that he can look into a man's heart as well as into his face, and knows all that is going on in it." One of first to go was Tedpachsit. The chief had admitted to using poison, which was in a ceremonial bundle hidden in Josua's hut at the Moravian mission. This confession had implicated Josua, although his lifelong connection with the Moravians might have doomed him in any case. The Kluges and Luckenbach could do nothing to save him except pray.

On March 17, two days after Josua's kidnapping, ten Indians, their faces painted black, suddenly escorted Tedpachsit into the Moravian village. When the chief could not produce his bundle, they struck his head with a tomahawk and "threw him half-alive into the fire. Meanwhile they stood near and rejoiced over the pitiful cries and movements of the unfortunate one." The Indians then demanded food and tobacco, which the terrified missionaries provided. An inquiry about the fate of Josua brought a quick response. Josua was a prisoner because "he was familiar with the black art and could destroy the lives of Indians or cause them to become lame." The same day the followers of Tenskwatawa tomahawked Josua twice and burned him. News of his death put the Moravians into a panic. They would have left the White River immediately but for the cold weather. Kluge wrote and asked to be sent elsewhere.

The Moravians agreed, and the Kluges and Luckenbach abandoned their settlement in September 1806. The missionaries were "ready and willing to be used further in the service of the dear Saviour, *only not here.*"

Other Indians soon followed Tedpachsit and Josua to the stake. By mid-April, the frenzy of accusation and recrimination had passed, but Tenskwatawa was established as a powerful spiritual leader. He secured his position in Greenville on June 16 when he accurately predicted a solar eclipse. Governor Harrison had demanded the Prophet show his power. Tenskwatawa knew of the coming eclipse and called for both the disappearance and reappearance of the sun to demonstrate his power. Few any longer doubted it. It was not just magic, however, that made the Prophet; it was a sense of purpose, of energy, of meaning that he brought to many Indians throughout the southern Great Lakes Region. Hundreds flocked to him at Greenville, where he lived in 1806–1807, to see and share in the power of his medicine. Tenskwatawa brought terror to whites and Indians allied with whites. But he also brought self-respect to the despondent Indian villages of the Wabash and the Maumee. Drinking did not cease, but it became less pervasive.

Tenskwatawa and Harrison

The growing numbers and assertiveness of the Prophet's followers alarmed officials in the state of Ohio. By the end of 1807, they were openly hostile and planning action against Greenville. Tenskwatawa was also finding it difficult to feed all the people flocking to see him. Brushing aside the angry opposition of Little Turtle, he decided in January 1808 to move to the west and establish a new, larger town, more remote from the white settlements. According to his biographer, R. David Edmunds, the Prophet was turning to more secular solutions to the problems faced by the Indians. He began insisting on a boundary between whites and Indians. More important, he started to look to the British in Canada as potential allies in his struggle to keep the whites at bay. Tenskwatawa's brother, Tecumseh, informed the British in June 1808 that the Prophet was "endeavoring to collect the different nations to form one settlement on the Wabash . . . in order to preserve their country from all encroachments." The Indians would not attack the whites, but they would fight if the Americans came to them and would welcome the aid of His Majesty's troops.

Prophetstown took shape. Located just below the mouth of the Tippecanoe River on the northwestern bank of the Wabash, the village consisted of a series of rows of bark wigwams running from the river onto the prairie. There were at least three major buildings. The first was the "House of the Stranger," built near the Wabash for the comfort of visitors. On the other side of the village were a council house and a medicine lodge for the Prophet. Dozens of warriors and other Indians came to the new town. Intertribal rivalries, food shortages, and a serious epidemic during the first winter offered serious challenges to Tenskwatawa, for his power rested on his ability to demonstrate through ritual some mastery over the world. When he could not cure illnesses or prevent catastrophes, he suffered a loss of faith that hurt his reputation. Still, he persisted in the first decade of the nineteenth century in offering the most persuasive answer to the problems of the Indians on the Wabash. Tenskwatawa's emphasis on the separateness of Indians and whites, his frequent denunciations of Americans and all those who had contact with them, laid out a clear-cut path of resistance to the encroaching white culture.

Harrison's reactions to Tenskwatawa varied with the kind of information he was receiving. From the beginning of his service as territorial governor and superintendent of Indian affairs, he had pursued an aggressive policy of purchasing tracts of land at every possible opportunity. On June 7, 1803, the Delaware, Shawnee, Potawatomi, Miami, Eel River Miami, Wea, Kickapoo, Piankashaw, and Kaskaskia had agreed at Fort Wayne to sell thousands of acres around Vincennes. A little more than a year later (August 18 and 27, 1804) at Vincennes, the Delaware and Piankashaw gave up the region southwest of Clark's Grant along the Ohio to the Wabash. The August 1805 Treaty of Grouseland transferred land from the Delaware, Potawatomi, Miami, Eel River and Wea to the United States covering the area north and east of Clark's Grant to the Treaty of Greenville line. In December, the Piankashaw ceded the southeastern corner of what would become the state of Illinois.

There were serious rumblings about these transactions, especially among the Delaware and Miami. But, like a good Anglo-American republican, Harrison attributed opposition to two major causes: vanity and corruption. In other words, those Indians who were unwilling to recognize what was best for everyone and who insisted on asserting themselves were the ones who opposed him. When Little Turtle opposed the 1803 cession, the governor "easily accounted for" his behavior: "Conscious of the superiority of his Talents over the rest of his race and colour he sighs for a more conspicuous theatre to display them." Little Turtle wanted to be at the center of everything; he needed to gratify his "vanity" and his "ambition." Harrison refused to believe that opposition was widespread and criticized William Wells for relying too heavily on Little Turtle.

The governor, like Jefferson and other federal officials, always believed that the British lay behind Indian behavior and rhetoric of which they did not approve. His Majesty's government, they were certain, would go to great lengths to stir up the Indians against the Americans. It was doing so through corruption, buying the Indians off with goods, gifts, and promises of support. Here Harrison was both blind and disingenuous. He refused to consider the legitimacy of Indian opposition to land cessions. He railed against British efforts to gain the loyalty of the Indians, which were exceedingly modest before 1807, at the same time that his government employed annuities and gifts to "attach" the Indians to American "interests." The governor of the Indiana Territory was shocked to find that other human beings, whether Indian or British, might behave as he did.

Following the orders of President Jefferson, Harrison in 1805 dutifully promised Little Turtle "fifty dollars, per annum, in addition to his pension" and "directed Captain Wells to purchase a negro man for him, in Kentucky." The conference that produced the Treaty of Grouseland cost the United States thousands of dollars in annuities. Harrison complained about the expense being "greater than usual" because of the need to treat all the chiefs with the same "indulgence" he showed to Little Turtle. For the Indians, the gifts were a necessary part of the diplomatic structures that had taken shape with the French in the eighteenth century; not only were they a sign of respect and friendship, but they also established a relationship between the parties involved. For the Americans, steeped as they were in the ideas of classical republicanism, the Indians' acceptance of annuities was a sign of weakness, a willingness to exchange the manly independence that Harrison and others so valued for the position of dependent. In short, cultural misinterpretations worked both ways. The Americans granted what the Indians considered symbols of a respectful relationship but scorned those who would accept permanent corruption as unworthy of respect. Indian males lost their honor in the eyes of the Americans; they became like women, children, and slaves.

It was in this context that Harrison dealt with the Prophet. Tenskwatawa's insistence on moral reformation and rejection of white ways revitalized his culture and held out the promise of coordinated Indian action against the Americans; it also earned him the respect of Governor Harrison. The Prophet and Tecumseh he saw as worthy opponents because they valued their independence; they would not sell out. At the same time, of course, their manly courage made them extremely dangerous to American interests in the region.

Harrison learned this lesson the hard way. In the beginning, he thought of Tenskwatawa as simply another in a string of would-be prophets who had gained undue influence because of the British. He sent word to the Shawnee in August 1807 demanding that they observe the terms of the various treaties signed with the United States since 1795. The governor noted the importance of the annuities and the prevention of illegal white intrusion in Indian lands. Then he instructed the Shawnee to ignore the British, "the deceiver" whom Harrison held most responsible for "this business." He would "no longer suffer it. You have called in a number of men from the most distant tribes, to listen to a fool who speaks not the words of the Great Spirit but those of the devil, and of the British agents." When Harrison called the Shawnee "children," he meant it.

The Prophet's reply was short and to the point. He denied Harrison's charges of dealing with the British and creating a "disturbance": "I never had a word with the British and I never sent for any Indians. They came here themselves to listen and hear the words of the Great Spirit."

Harrison let this pass. But he remained suspicious and became overtly alarmed when he received news of Tenskwatawa's arrival on the Wabash in May 1808. The governor still had a hard time taking the Prophet seriously, even as he grew more formidable. He was an "imposter" who had "acquired such an ascendency" over the Indians because they were weak peoples who were easily deceived and intimidated. Whatever "religious duties" were performed at Prophetstown, moreover, "their prayers are always succeeded by or intermixed with warlike sports, shooting with the bow, throwing the tomahawk or wielding the war club." Harrison had no doubt of their intentions, and he wanted the president to authorize seizing Tenskwatawa and taking him further west.

In late June, Tenskwatawa sent Harrison word of his peaceful intentions along with a request for corn for the women and children at Prophetstown. He promised to visit Vincennes in the near future. Harrison accepted the Prophet's peaceful assurances, but he sternly warned him not to be "deceived" by the British. Follow the Americans and there would be peace and prosperity; follow the British and endure pain and misery. For Harrison, the choice was clear. The governor did not begin to understand the spiritual power of Tenskwatawa. He simply saw him as another easily manipulated Indian. When the Prophet visited Vincennes, Harrison told the secretary of war, he intended to use "the opportunity to endeavour to develop his character and intentions[.] nor do I think it at all impossible to make him an useful instrument in effecting a radical change and salutary change in the manners and habits of the Indians." After all, the man had already convinced his followers not to drink whiskey or to be ashamed of farming.

In August, the Prophet and some followers arrived for a stay of over two weeks in Vincennes. Harrison was impressed, to say the least. Tenskwatawa's sincerity persuaded him that he was a man "possessed of considerable talents" and a "really astonishing" power of speech. The governor would not give up the notion that the Prophet was "a tool of the British," but he now had serious doubts. Harrison heard Tenskwatawa say that he spoke for the Great Spirit; that he had "told all the red skins that the way they were in was not good, and that they ought to abandon it. That we ought to consider ourselves as one man, but we ought to live agreeable to our several customs, the red people after their mode and the white people after theirs"; and that the cause of most Indian problems lay in whiskey. The Prophet's success in promoting temperance, where American law and Christian suasion had failed, particularly affected Harrison. Tenskwatawa was a man worthy of the respect that Little Turtle had long since forfeited.

Precisely because Harrison's impression of the Prophet was so favorable, the governor kept a close eye on him. He was now too powerful personally to ignore. And Harrison was unable to shake the notion that Tenskwatawa's intentions toward the Americans who were flooding into the river valleys of southern Indiana were hostile. Harrison thought the disease and famine in Prophetstown during the winter of 1808 and 1809 would undermine the Prophet's influence, but reports from the village soon changed his mind. In April, the governor was briefly fearful enough to call out two companies of militia to protect Vincennes; he stationed them near the barracks and blockhouse that still bore the name of Fort Knox and hired a Frenchman to spy on the residents of Prophetstown. Somewhat calmer in May, Harrison announced his intention of negotiating another treaty to relieve the "much cramped" condition of white settlements. In July, the Prophet visited Vincennes again, assuring the governor that his intentions were peaceful. Harrison, ending his vacillation between trust and distrust of Tenskwatawa, turned his attention both to treaty making and to outlining ways in which the military position of the United States in the Great Lakes region could be strengthened.

The Treaty of Fort Wayne

The Prophet was only one of the factors leading the Indiana governor to assume a more martial stance. The wars of the French Revolution were once again impinging on the lives of the residents of the Wabash Valley. Tensions between the United States and Great Britain were growing in the wake of several naval incidents and Jefferson's imposition of an embargo in 1807. In the Old Northwest, the British government had maintained a relatively low profile since the Battle of Fallen Timbers; it was not willing to spend resources or men on the cause of the Great Lakes Indians. But British officials became somewhat more active after 1807. And, in any case, Americans were even more likely to suspect them, given the deteriorating state of relations between the two nations which would lead to declarations of war in 1812.

Ironically, as Harrison noted, many Indians hoped that the United States would go to war against France and lose. This was wishful thinking, of course. Still, the tribes around Vincennes could not help hoping that the French would once again gain control of the Wabash Valley. The Americans could do nothing to undermine that dream, Harrison wrote, for "the happiness they enjoyed from their intercourse with the French is their perpetual theme—it is their golden age. Those who are old enough to remember it, speak of it with rapture, and the young ones are taught to venerate it as the Ancients did." They could not understand why the Americans did not make them "happy as our Fathers the French did? They never took from us our lands, indeed they were in common with us—they planted where they pleased and they cut wood where they pleased and so did we—but now if a poor Indian attempts to take a little bark from a tree, to cover him from the rain, up comes a white man and threatens to shoot him, claiming the tree as his own." Harrison viewed this attitude as somewhat quaint and concentrated on the more pressing business of restoring Fort Knox to its former power.

At the end of the summer, the governor traveled to Fort Wayne. There he met with leaders of the Delaware, Miami, Eel River Miami, and Potawatomi, including Little Turtle. Harrison reminded the Indians of the importance of their annuities in the midst of the declining fur trade and urged them once again to take up raising domestic animals. On September 30, in return for a $250 to $500 increase in each tribe's annuities plus $5,200 in trade goods, the Indian leaders agreed, in the presence of close to 1,400 of their peoples, to cede their claim to over two and a half million acres in what is now southern Indiana and Illinois.

The Treaty of Fort Wayne was the climax of Harrison's seven years of negotiations with the Indians of the Wabash and Maumee valleys. From the American perspective, this moment of personal triumph for the governor meant that white settlers could now move farther north in their ongoing efforts to develop the territory into a model of domestic agriculture. But among the Indians, the treaty evoked a sharper definition of ideas about how to deal with the Americans. Tenskwatawa and Tecumseh angrily denounced the actions of accommodationists such as Little Turtle. Up to this point, the Prophet had talked of a rejection of white spiritual beliefs and cultural ways. Now, according to the reports Harrison and others received, he became more overtly hostile, not just toward the Americans but also toward the older chiefs who had signed away their land for permanent dependence on the goods and money of the whites. Both Tenskwatawa and Tecumseh redoubled their efforts to create a pan-Indian alliance to resist further American incursions.

News of the Prophet's anger and his activities made Governor Harrison jittery. In the spring of 1810, his letters to his superiors in Washington fluctuated wildly between fear of an impending attack on Vincennes by hundreds of warriors and a cocky confidence that Tenskwatawa was nothing more than a British tool who would not move unless the United States and Great Britain were at war. Despite his diplomatic victory the previous fall, Harrison was on the defensive. He warned Secretary of War William Eustis in late April that "hostile appearances" had driven away hundreds of settler families. The United States needed to build another fort on the Wabash or do something to drive "the rascally prophet . . . from his present position."

Harrison was smart enough to realize the real cause of the anger at Prophetstown. "The Indians of this county are in fact miserable," he told Eustis in June. Once "abundant" game was now "so scarce as barely to afford subsistance to the most active hunters"; European wars had reduced trade to a minimum. Consequently many Indians spent "half the year in a state of starvation." No wonder they were full of "hatred." The appeal of the Prophet was thus straightforward: he "has told them that the Great Spirit did not mean that the white and red people should live near each other, that the former poison'd the land and prevented it from producing the things necessary for their subsistance." And yet the perceptive governor still could not accept Indian anger as legitimate. It was all the fault of the "artful" deceivers, the British. Harrison, the son of Virginia gentry, husband, father, and slaveholder, simply could not take these dependent, malleable Indians seriously, except in an extremely paternalistic fashion.

1810

☙ 217

THE
WORLD
OF
TENSKWATAWA,
1795–1811

Neither Tenskwatawa nor Tecumseh was confused about purposes or about whom to blame. In June, the Prophet angrily refused to accept the salt annuity dispatched by Harrison. Not for him the path of Little Turtle. He continued his campaign against such accommodationist chiefs, holding them responsible for the general situation of the Indians symbolized by the trading of land for annuities at Fort Wayne. They had sold the land; they stood in the way of Indian unity; and they should die. Tenskwatawa's anger discredited more than it destroyed his enemies, but it was no less powerful for that. John Johnston told Harrison in June that he could still vouch for the acquiescence of most of the Miami, particularly Little Turtle. "I do not apprehend much difficulty with him," Johnston wrote of the decisive man who had played such a prominent role in the defeats of Harmar and St. Clair. "I have money to pay him. . . . The Turtle is contemptible, beyond description, in the eyes of the Indians." This was the fate of Little Turtle and other accommodationists: to lose the respect of both the Americans and the followers of the Prophet.

In July, with the tension as thick as the humidity in the Wabash Valley, Governor Harrison sent a kind of peace offering to Tenskwatawa. Trying to resolve the situation in a way that would reassure American settlers of their safety (and that of their animals, several of which were stolen or slaughtered by Indians), he informed the angry Prophet that it was still possible to repair the rift in Indian-white relations and to restore "the chain of friendship." Of course, Tenskwatawa should be well aware of the power of "the innumerable Warriors" of the United States: "Our blue coats are more numerous than you can count, and our hunting shirts are like the leaves of the forests or the grains of the sands on the Wabash." Bluster aside, the governor proposed sending Tenskwatawa to Washington, where he could explain his objections to the treaties that Harrison had negotiated. The Americans were willing to listen.

The Prophet did not take the governor up on his invitation, but his brother did—up to a point. Tecumseh informed Harrison that he would meet with him in Vincennes. On August 12, 1810, he arrived in the territorial capital, accompanied by upwards of 400 warriors in some eighty painted canoes. Harrison thought him arrogant and insolent, but a federal officer described him as "one of the finest men I ever saw—about six feet high, straight with large fine features and altogether a daring, bold-looking fellow." Tecumseh found Harrison reading on the porch of Grouseland. He refused the governor's invitation to stay in the house and took up temporary residence under an elm tree while territorial officials, supported by a recently arrived company of federal troops and two companies of militia, prepared a walnut grove between Grouseland and the Wabash for a council. Chairs were set up and a small enclosure constructed.

The council opened on August 15. Refusing a seat, Tecumseh reclined and sat on the ground in front of approximately 200 warriors. Harrison sat upright in a chair, surrounded by other officials and twelve regular soldiers. One hundred militia covered Grouseland, ready to protect the Harrison household if necessary. Anna Symmes Harrison and her children watched the proceedings from just outside the house.

Addressing Harrison as "Brother" rather than the more traditional and less egalitarian "Father," Tecumseh spoke at great length, summarizing concisely and angrily his perspective on Indian-European relations in the Wabash Valley over the past century. The French, he contended, "adopt[ed] us as their children and gave us presents without asking anything in return but our considering them as fathers." They only took "a small piece of country to live on which they were not to leave." Then the British arrived, promising similar treatment, but they sacrificed the Indians' good will by going to war against the Americans and treating the Indians badly. After the Treaty of Greenville, the victorious Americans made similar promises, which now seemed laughable in the face of murders, insults, and coerced land cessions. The point was simple: the Americans had surrendered their claims on Indian friendship. If Harrison thought the Indians dependent and malleable, Tecumseh saw the Americans as greedy liars. They could not be trusted: "[Y]ou have taken our lands from us and I do not see how we can remain at peace with you if you continue to do so." In the end, it was the Americans who were responsible for the troubles on the Wabash. They could have treated the Indians as the French did. Instead they "force[d] the red people to do some injury. It is you that is pushing them on to do mischief. . . . You are continually driving the red people when at last you will drive them into the great lake where they can't either stand or work." The American treatment of the Indians was "a very bad thing and we do not like it."

Given this situation, Tecumseh told Harrison, no one was going to Washington. Rather, the peoples of Prophetstown were trying "to level all distinctions[,] to destroy village chiefs by whom all mischief is done; it is they who sell our land to the Americans." Now the "object is to let all our affairs be transacted by Warriors." Harrison must understand that only a few Indians supported the treaties. Tecumseh was willing to demonstrate the breadth of opposition to land sales. Indeed, if Harrison did not restore the territory, he would be responsible for the deaths of the village chiefs who had agreed to the treaties. Tecumseh explained: "I tell you so because I am authorised by all the tribes to do so. I am at the head of them all. I am a Warrior. . . ." He was not about to be fooled, either. He would take presents from Harrison offered in friendship, but only if he was persuaded that it was not a trick by which they would be selling "another piece of land. . . . If we want anything we are able to buy it, from your traders."

Tecumseh finished with a warning and a sarcastic jibe: "If you will not give up the land and do cross the boundary of your present settlement it will be very hard and produce great troubles among us. How can we have confidence in the white people when Jesus Christ came upon the earth you kill'd and nail'd him on a cross, you thought he was dead but you were mistaken." The parallel with the resurrection of the Indians was clear enough. The people of Prophetstown were not about to be tricked again.

Harrison replied briefly with assurances that Americans had always dealt with the Indians with a "uniform regard to justice." In the middle of the translation, Tecumseh got up and, according to the governor, "with the most violent jesticulations and indications of anger began to contradict what I had said in the most indecent manner." The Shawnee was instructing the interpreter to tell Harrison that he was lying. Other Indians rose and brandished weapons. Territorial Secretary John Gibson ordered the twelve-man guard brought up. Harrison stood, sword drawn, and ordered Tecumseh back to his camp. The two men stared at each other in a tense silence. Then the Shawnee abruptly departed. A wary Harrison paraded his troops through the streets of Vincennes the next morning. Later Tecumseh sent an apology to Harrison and the council resumed in the afternoon. But all they did was continue an exchange of perspectives. Tecumseh finally left Vincennes to travel south of the Ohio River to rally Indians there to the cause of pan-Indian resistance. Before going, however, he told Harrison that when the governor spoke of annuities, "I look at the land, and pity the women and children." The American should remember not to cross the "present boundary line. . . . I assure you it will be productive of bad consequences."

The Battle of Tippecanoe

Despite Tecumseh's assertiveness, Harrison was optimistic that the crisis had passed. He was sure that the Prophet's influence was declining. He could not have been more wrong. Tenskwatawa was reaching out to other tribes while Tecumseh continued his journeying in search of Indian unity. The British strongly urged the Shawnee to be patient. But by the summer of 1811, it was clear that Tenskwatawa and Tecumseh expected a military confrontation imminently. Harrison had also changed his tune. Seeking reinforcements from Washington, he forbade the two Indian leaders from coming to Vincennes with large numbers of warriors and promised them a battle if they tried to descend the Wabash.

In July, Tecumseh sent word to Harrison that he would soon pay him a visit to discuss the situation face-to-face. Around 300 warriors accompanied him. Tecumseh traveled slowly, taking two weeks to float from Prophetstown to Vincennes, to prevent the Americans from becoming unduly alarmed. But they did anyway. Panic swept the Vincennes area; people were certain that the Indians were planning a surprise attack. Daniel Sullivan, who had been in the Vincennes area since the 1780s, wrote a series of resolutions demanding federal assistance in protecting property and persons and in seeking "a termination of the presumptious pretentions of this daring chief," the Prophet.

Harrison had about 800 militia available for "as great a display of force as possible" when Tecumseh arrived on July 27. The council began three days later. It accomplished little. Tecumseh soon left for a journey to the southern tribes. Harrison was hardly mollified, however. A rumor that Tecumseh was going to kill some chiefs and perhaps the governor himself if there was no repeal of the Treaty of Fort Wayne horrified him. He was certain that the Indians were simply looking to provoke a quarrel. Harrison urged the secretary of war that now was the time to act. The energetic Tecumseh was away. In his absence, the United States should destroy both the fabric and the foundations of his work. A military move would demonstrate both American power and American resolve and would sway the "timid" and the "wavering" away from the Prophet. With him removed or humiliated, American settlers could continue their transformation of the Indiana landscape.

While Harrison made plans for an expedition, Tenskwatawa got ready to receive him. The Prophet sent word to Vincennes that he wanted only peace, but he also asked the Kickapoo, Potawatomi, and Miami to send warriors and requested ammunition and supplies from British agents. Tenskwatawa would have preferred to postpone the confrontation until Tecumseh returned, but Harrison was moving too quickly. Sending out an advance group of Delaware to ascend the Wabash with the news that he meant no harm to peaceful Indians, the governor led his army from Vincennes on September 26, 1811. The 1,225 troops—345 men in the Fourth United States Regiment and several hundred militia—marched north along the east bank of the Wabash until they came to the site of what is now Terre Haute, where they began to build Fort Harrison.

Tenskwatawa had no alternative to resistance. He could not allow Harrison to cross the boundary without severely damaging his reputation and his power; he could not lose Prophetstown with its considerable stores of food and ammunition. Angry and defiant, he threatened the Delawares when they arrived at Prophetstown. In October, he confidently sent warriors to harass Harrison's men in the expectation that they would soon seek a final confrontation. At the end of the month, with Fort Harrison complete and one more peace delegation dispatched, Governor Harrison and his men proceeded north along the Wabash. He was under orders to "disperse" the Prophet and his followers with the promise "that in the future he shall not assemble or attempt to assemble any number of Indians, armed or in a hostile attitude. If he neglects or refuses to disperse he will be attacked and compelled to it by the force under your command."

While Tenskwatawa hoped to delay the inevitable battle until more warriors arrived, Harrison surprised him by crossing the Wabash to the northwestern side and marching 1,000 men directly toward the Indian village. By the middle of the afternoon on November 6, 1811, the Americans were about a mile from Prophetstown. Not wanting either a battle in the open fields around the town or a surrender of his village, Tenskwatawa sought a truce. Harrison, who was eager to avoid bloodshed, agreed to stop and meet with the Indians the next day.

That evening the American army camped on a small rise along Burnett's Creek about two miles below Prophetstown. Toward the town the hill descended about ten feet to a marshy prairie; on the other side, there was a sharp twenty-foot descent into a ravine created by the creek. The men took defensive positions amid the oak trees in what R. David Edmunds describes as "a hollow, unevenly shaped trapezoid, about 150 yards long and 50 to 75 yards in width." Harrison apparently did not expect an attack. To the contrary, he was planning a surprise assault on Prophetstown for the following evening after the expected failure of the negotiations.

After nightfall Tenskwatawa called his 600–700 warriors together and promised them victory in an attack on the Americans. According to Edmunds, he said he would send rain and hail to ruin the gunpowder and confuse Harrison's army. The warriors must attack at night. And they must kill Harrison; without him, the army would disintegrate and flee. One hundred warriors were assigned the task of finding the governor. It really did begin to rain; perhaps the Prophet was as powerful as he said? In any case, Tenskwatawa was clearly risking everything in the surprise attack. If his men failed to drive away the Americans, he would suffer a loss of face and influence from which it would be difficult to recover.

At about 4:30 in the morning, Harrison, who was already awake, heard a shot. A sentry had discovered the Indians sent to find the governor and fired at them. Other soldiers discharged their rifles. Suddenly the Indians appeared everywhere, shouting and screaming in the cold and wet darkness. The ensuing battle lasted about two hours. Harrison rode to the front on an aide's horse, narrowly escaping death when two Indians shot another officer by mistake. Tenskwatawa did not fight; he spent the early morning in ritually seeking the aid of the Master of Life. The Indians proved to be deadly marksmen, lining up targets, most frequently officers, in the light of campfires. The American lines buckled at times, but reinforcements kept them from breaking. At dawn the warriors started to pull back. Harrison ordered bayonet charges into the ranks of the remaining Indians. Shortly thereafter the firing on both sides ceased.

The Americans stayed on the field for the rest of a cold, damp November 7. They buried the dead and built temporary barricades; they also scalped and mutilated the bodies of dead Indians lying nearby. Mostly they waited for another attack. But it never came. The Prophet and his followers abandoned their town soon after leaving the field of battle. Angry warriors accosted Tenskwatawa and threatened to kill him for sending them on a foolhardy errand. He blamed the defeat on the fact that his wife, who had assisted in his rituals, was menstruating and had not told him. While Indians understood that a menstruating woman was unclean, they did not accept this explanation and barely let the Prophet escape with his life. Many sought revenge in raids on American farms and traveling parties.

Harrison sent spies into the Indian village on November 8. When they reported it empty, he dispatched a detachment of troops, who burned the place to the ground, saving only some corn. The following day the Americans broke camp and returned to Vincennes on November 18 after an excruciating journey for the wounded and their frightened comrades. The governor claimed a great victory, but the large numbers of wounded and dead were hardly reassuring to area residents. "I have seen the wounded arrive," John Badollet wrote to Albert Gallatin on November 19, "my God, what heart rending sight! what scene of woe!" Like others, Badollet was certain that had Harrison only built a fort beyond the treaty line, he would have accomplished enough. The price of victory was too high. Harrison's casualties amounted to one-fifth of his 1,000-man force—126 wounded and at least sixty-two killed.

William Henry Harrison became known as the Hero of Tippecanoe (the name came from the nearby Tippecanoe River) and the battle passed into popular history as an American victory. The criticisms that surrounded his actions in the immediate aftermath of his expedition were soon forgotten. What did Harrison accomplish at Tippecanoe? Not much. True, he asserted the power of the United States. But he did not put an end to either Indian raids or American fears. Settlers in the Indiana Territory remained profoundly anxious for many years. Even the governor admitted in April 1812 that "families, abandoning their homes and flying they know not whither and many of them without any means of support, are seen in every direction."

With the outbreak of formal war between the United States and Great Britain in June 1812 and the dismal failure of General William Hull's expedition against Canada later that year, matters got worse. An Indian raid at Pigeon Roost in what is now Scott County left twenty-four people dead on September 3. There were also assaults on Fort Harrison and Fort Wayne. In December, Harrison resigned as governor of the Indiana Territory; he had already assumed command of the northwestern American army and was pushing toward Detroit. In October 1813, Harrison's army defeated the British and their Indian allies at the Battle of Thames in Canada. Among the dead was Tecumseh. The Americans had accomplished what they had failed to achieve at Tippecanoe: they had removed the British as major obstacles to the development of the Old Northwest and had destroyed the last prospects for a pan-Indian alliance against them.

For Tenskwatawa, Tippecanoe was far more significant. While Harrison reported Indian casualties in the hundreds, the actual number killed was around fifty and the number wounded between seventy and eighty. The failure of the Prophet's power to protect his warriors or unravel the resolve of the Americans effectively destroyed his reputation. He and some of his followers returned to rebuild Prophetstown in July 1812, and from there they planned and launched attacks on Fort Harrison and Pigeon Roost. But American militia expeditions in the fall forced them away. Kentuckians again burned Prophetstown and confiscated the large stores of corn. Tenskwatawa left for Canada, where he subordinated himself to his brother and became ever more dependent on the British. He had a small band of followers even after the death of Tecumseh.

The failure of Prophetstown was the failure of the last great effort to build a strong, united resistance to American conquest of the Old Northwest. Tenskwatawa had engaged in a conflict as much with accommodationist chiefs as with Americans such as Harrison over the best way for the Indians to respond to what amounted to the disintegration not only of their territorial basis but of their customs and religion as well. Hundreds responded eagerly to the content of his visions, giving up alcohol and polygamy and rejecting white ways in an effort to restore their communal and individual dignity. Tenskwatawa enjoyed remarkable success for half-a-dozen years. Drawing on traditions of resistance and unity, he and his brother offered a vibrant and viable alternative to the path of accommodation chosen by Little Turtle. In the end, however, the nativist movement relied so heavily on the personal charisma of its leaders that it could not survive their loss of face.

As admirable as the refusal of Tenskwatawa, Tecumseh, and their followers to trade their autonomy for annuities and goods may appear to late twentieth-century Americans, Little Turtle had already learned the lesson they now learned. He had won victories and rallied people to fight the United States. But the sheer relentlessness of the Americans, the sheer scale of the environmental, economic, and demographic transformations they were bringing to the valley of the Wabash, made further resistance as quixotic as it was noble. Tenskwatawa was no tool of the British government, no crazy Indian medicine man. He had a vision and he tried to bring it to fruition. The fact that he lost everything doing so should not obscure his very real accomplishment in restoring a sense of moral pride to many Indians. The dissolute behavior the Moravians found on the White River became the defiant actions Harrison later encountered at Prophetstown.

Tenskwatawa, like many before him, had come to the Wabash Valley to implement an idiosyncratic notion of how the world should operate, how people should deal with each other and organize their lives. Like Vincennes, Memeskia, Clark, Hamtramck, and Little Turtle, his legacy was a mixed one. Things did not turn out as he would have wished. Still, at the very least he could go to his grave knowing that there had been something in his life worth risking everything for.

9.

THE WORLD OF JONATHAN JENNINGS, 1800–1816

It was always personal with Jonathan Jennings. No matter the specific issue, no matter whether he was leading the opposition to the regime of Governor William Henry Harrison or fighting for the cause of statehood as the territorial delegate to the United States Congress or serving as the first governor of the state of Indiana, politics was a struggle between one's friends and one's enemies. It was a full-time occupation, this business of meeting other men, shaking hands, playing cards, drinking, exposing the malevolence of deceitful opponents (especially the arch-fiend Harrison), encouraging men to start newspapers, writing letters to established editors, in a word, agitating, agitating, forever agitating. Which is not to say that Jennings had no consistent core of beliefs. He believed, in a vague but intense and impetuous fashion, in the rights of white men, the value of popular democracy, and the evils of slavery.

Indeed, it was Jennings's commitment to the essential equality of white men that made politics so personal. In a positive sense, he felt compelled to campaign, to mix and consult with his peers, his neighbors, who would choose him to represent them in Washington and Corydon. On the other hand, he felt obliged to assert himself against anyone who appeared to doubt or challenge his social status as a free-born American male. Like his allies and supporters, Jennings held no brief for pure democracy. Rather, he believed that

227

THE
WORLD
OF
JONATHAN
JENNINGS,
1800–1816

society should function so as to allow naturally talented men to stand out among their brothers. Anything that posed an obstacle to the rise of merit was despicable. More than that, it was a personal insult. Anyone who supported, or even refused to recognize, the inequity of such an obstacle was ipso facto an aristocrat trampling on the rights of his fellow Americans.

The Jonathan Jennings who arrived in Vincennes in 1807 to begin the practice of law was an ambitious and passionate young man. He was twenty-three years old, a native of either Hunterdon County, New Jersey, or Rockbridge County, Virginia, depending on which source you want to believe. In the early 1790s, Jacob and Mary Kennedy Jennings had moved Jonathan and his five older and two younger siblings to Dunlaps Creek, Pennsylvania. Apparently he acquired a decent education and some training in the law. John Badollet, the superintendent of the Public Land Office in Vincennes, for whom Jennings worked briefly as a clerk, described him in January 1808 as "a very estimable young man."

He was also very opinionated and hot-tempered. Jennings confided to his brother-in-law in June 1807 that Vincennes was tolerable (his "prospects" met his "expectations") but that it was "full of rascals." Prominent among the "rascals" was Henry Hurst, the clerk of the General Court of Indiana Territory since his appointment in January 1801. According to Jennings, Hurst was jealous of him, largely because of his position in the land office. In any case, the two young men did not like each other at all. At one point, Hurst must have said something that called Jennings's integrity into question. For Jennings told his brother-in-law quite matter-of-factly that "I fear I shall have to kill him before he will be at rest." He reported that he had challenged Hurst to a duel but that the other young man had "made concessions." Now Hurst was again "insinuating something, I know not what[,] to my disadvantage."

The Jennings-Hurst rivalry was hardly uncommon in the Indiana Territory. It is, after all, easy to forget how very young these men were. Even Governor Harrison was only in his thirties in the first decade of the nineteenth century. There were literally dozens of men like Jennings in the growing settlements along the Ohio, Wabash, and Whitewater rivers. Many of them were from Virginia via Kentucky and Pennsylvania. While, in general, they were less violent and less interested in demonstrating their mastery of the world than George Rogers Clark had been, not all of them were willing to follow the path of a gentry scion like William Henry Harrison and fulfill their ambitions by playing by the rules of a time-honored hierarchical game.

Creating a Politics of Patronage, 1800–1805

In the newly created world of the Indiana Territory, government offices were glittering prizes sought desperately by young men in a hurry. First and foremost, they provided a steady source of income, from either a salary or fees. No matter how small this source of income was, it was more predictable than reliance on the money one might make as a lawyer. Even clerks such as Hurst and Jennings had something to tide them over in a place that often seemed long on land and short on money and goods. Second, offices sealed one's admittance to the network of men who actually ran the territory; it was a way to make important acquaintances, to hone one's skills, and to learn how power was acquired and exercised. Impress your superior and he might well remember you when something more important and more profitable came along. Finally, government positions gave young men immediate social status in their society, as well as genuine power over others. Many of these jobs—clerkships, for example—sound trivial to us, accustomed as we are to the behemoth bureaucracies of the late twentieth century. But in the world of the Indiana Territory, where young, ambitious men who more often than not were little more than strangers to each other were jockeying for position, a title was more than a sinecure; it was a confirmation of one's importance.

In many ways, it is impossible to exaggerate the significance of the territorial government over which William Henry Harrison presided from 1800 to 1813. Usually, of course, historians do the reverse: exaggerate its insignificance. On the surface, that response is understandable. The government was really very tiny, particularly under the first stage delineated in the Northwest Ordinance of 1787.

Together Harrison and three judges governed the Indiana Territory until the governor proclaimed on December 5, 1804, that it had moved into the second stage of government under the Northwest

🏳 **229**

THE
WORLD
OF
JONATHAN
JENNINGS,
1800–1816

Ordinance and called for an election on January 3, 1805, to elect nine representatives to a General Assembly. In the four years preceding the proclamation, the governor and judges adopted only sixteen laws and passed only eleven resolutions. Governor Harrison created Clark County (from the eastern half of Knox) and Dearborn County and changed the boundaries of the counties in what are now Illinois and Michigan. In general, the government's officers seemed more preoccupied with land speculation and Indian negotiations than with exercising any serious influence over the development of the territory.

Still, the territorial government was easily the most important political and social institution in the region. Its offices may have been few, but they were highly coveted. It exercised its influence rarely, but powerfully. The governor and the legislature could make or break newspapers with patronage, direct the flow of people and trade with licenses for ferries and contracts for physical improvements, and invest certain men with enormous local influence by appointing them militia officers, sheriffs, or local judges with patronage to distribute themselves. They decided when to create new counties (and new jobs) and where their boundaries should lie.

Harrison's job as superintendent of Indian affairs reinforced the powers of the governorship. His decisions singled out certain men as promising; his decisions awarded military contracts to certain men; his decisions affected land sales and the location of towns. Men like Jonathan Jennings would characterize Harrison as dictatorial and tyrannical. These are familiar charges to students of American territorial governments. Whether or not Harrison, like Arthur St. Clair in the Northwest Territory, behaved in such a way was the subject of much controversy. But the fact that he had the legal power to do so is indisputable. Thanks to the provisions of the Northwest Ordinance, territorial governors were frontier potentates, legally responsible only to the president of the United States, who appointed them to office in the first place.

In practice, however, territorial governors could not govern without the cooperation of at least a few local men. This was the great lesson of St. Clair's tenure. Except in the Federalist town of Marietta, the governor had failed to use his patronage to build loyal followings of like-minded men. St. Clair's appointments in the

Scioto and Miami valleys had backfired, legitimizing and empowering Virginians and others who had serious cultural and ideological disagreements with him and who would eventually lead the movement to get rid of him.

Harrison was a much savvier politician than St. Clair. The Indiana governor was not about to waste his most valuable resource—his patronage. As important, if less prosaic, was the fact that Harrison was the son of a prominent Virginian. He had grown up on the James River, a world in which gentlemen had governed by forming alliances through patronage and by matching wits with royal governors over executive and legislative prerogatives. It was also a world in which county government mattered a lot; the colonial and then the state government invested men of economic and social standing with power by appointing them justices of peace. Through their local appointive powers and the workings of the county courts, these men functioned as the effective rulers of relatively discrete regions within the colony as a whole. In the last quarter of the eighteenth century, dozens of young gentlemen transferred this system of government—involving a direct correspondence between economic and political power and a reciprocal relationship between the state and local leaders, who legitimized each other, in effect—to Kentucky and beyond.

Governor Harrison apparently intended to govern the Indiana Territory in much the same way. Within a few years, he would go a long way toward creating a "court" party of men attached to his interest. He identified ambitious, talented young Virginians, groomed them, and helped them advance politically. But in the beginning, Harrison had to work with other men, often local notables in Vincennes or Kaskaskia, who saw him more as the first among equals than as a patron. In theory, he would recognize and confirm the standing of certain men by granting them offices; they, in return, would recognize and confirm his authority by enforcing the decisions of his government. Harrison could thus avoid the problems that had bedeviled and destroyed St. Clair. But matters did not develop exactly as the governor would have preferred.

Harrison had little influence over the selection of three judges with whom he would govern the territory until it had the population requisite for a territorial legislature. Of the initial appointees, two—

⮀ **231**

THE
WORLD
OF
JONATHAN
JENNINGS,
1800–1816

William Clarke, who died in 1802, and John Griffin, who transferred to the Michigan Territory in 1806—had little impact in Indiana. The other man was Henry Vander Burgh (1800–1812). Vander Burgh was a native New Yorker who had established himself as a trader of means and influence in Vincennes in the early 1790s. He was exactly the kind of prominent local person the territorial government needed on its side. Thomas Terry Davis, a former congressman from Kentucky (1797–1803), filled the spot opened by the death of Clarke. Davis's major claim to fame in the House of Representatives was pointing out in 1800 that Winthrop Sargent, the secretary of the Northwest Territory who had been appointed governor of the Mississippi Territory, "was hated and despised by the people of the Western country." Harrison worked smoothly with this group, but they were not his men.

Nor were the men the governor himself appointed. The choices of attorney-general and treasurer reflected the need to work with men already established in the territory. Harrison named John Rice Jones attorney-general, a post he held from January 29, 1801, until his resignation on August 4, 1804. Born in Wales in 1759, Jones reputedly studied law and medicine at Oxford University before migrating to Philadelphia in 1784. Two years later, he joined George Rogers Clark's futile 1786 campaign in the Wabash Valley. Jones distinguished himself as a commissary, securing supplies at Kaskaskia and winning a reputation as a skillful trader. He and his family lived in Kaskaskia in the 1790s; there he worked both as a lawyer and a licensed merchant. Jones was back in Vincennes in the early 1800s. Given his legal expertise and his standing in both the Wabash and Mississippi communities, he was a logical choice for attorney-general. At first Jones and Harrison were reasonably friendly. Jones was the secretary of the 1802 slavery convention, nominated for a territorial judgeship in the same year, and appointed to the Legislative Council in 1805. In 1808, when Jones and Harrison had fallen out, the governor expressed embarrassment at having been duped by a deceiver such as Jones. Still, Harrison admitted to President Jefferson that "his talents are unquestionable." Besides, he owned a lot of land and had moderated his Federalist principles. The governor therefore "could not with Justice" neglect him "in the arrangement of officers consequent upon the change of System" to the second stage of government. No doubt the same motives compelled Harrison to make him attorney-general in 1801. Jones was an able, important man; he could not be ignored.

Similarly, the man whom Harrison appointed treasurer on February 9, 1801, William McIntosh, was a long-time resident of Vincennes with considerable land holdings in the region. Scottish by birth and a former noncommissioned officer in the British army, McIntosh, like Jones, was a prominent local figure. He had a reputation as a man willing to cut corners to make a financial killing. But his local influence commanded the governor's attention. He served as treasurer until September 4, 1805.

Locally, Harrison also turned to men whose loyalties were clearly more to their community than to the territorial government. Several of the first judges of the Court of General Quarter Sessions for Knox County had familiar names in Vincennes: James Johnson, Pierre Gamelin, Luke Decker, Abel Westfall. The first two sheriffs were William Prince (1800–1804) and Daniel Sullivan (1804–1806). Initially, at least, the governor was at the mercy of men who had lived in the Indiana Territory for years. They were not necessarily willing to accommodate him in everything. And Harrison soon found himself at odds with Attorney-General Jones and Treasurer McIntosh. The governor later accused both of being unscrupulous land speculators and corrupt. They in turn accused him of executive tyranny, corruption, and favoritism.

The other major territorial-level appointment Harrison made was Henry Hurst as clerk of the General Court on January 14, 1801. This was the same Hurst who would later enrage Jonathan Jennings. In more ways than one, Hurst was typical of the kind of appointments Governor Harrison would make after his initial years on the Wabash. He was thirty-one in 1801, a native of what is now Jefferson County, Virginia, who had studied law in the office of Benjamin Sebastian of Louisville. Not only was Hurst younger than Jones and McIntosh; he was new to the territory, arriving nearly simultaneously with Harrison. The new clerk was a man without clear-cut local interests or ties, the kind of person more easily attached to the powerful governor than more established types such as McIntosh and Jones. No wonder, then, that Hurst became and remained a firm Harrison loyalist. Appropriately, he

233

THE
WORLD
OF
JONATHAN
JENNINGS,
1800–1816

rode next to the former governor at the latter's 1841 inauguration as president of the United States. Hurst's public life was a long clerkship. He held his territorial job until the dissolution of the territory in 1816; meanwhile, he was clerk of several sessions of the legislative council between 1805 and 1810. Later he was clerk of the United States District Court at Indianapolis. Hurst's only elected office was as a state representative from Clark County in 1837–1839. During the territorial period, Hurst was a virtual toady of Governor Harrison, serving as a stoolpigeon, spy, and mouthpiece.

Within a few years, Harrison had identified other young men, new to the territory but more talented than Hurst, who linked their careers with his. He strongly influenced the appointment of two new territorial judges in 1806 and 1808. The first, Waller Taylor, was a twenty-one-year-old native of Virginia at the time of his appointment; in 1812, he would unsuccessfully run against Jonathan Jennings for Congress and serve as one of Indiana's first United States senators. The second, Benjamin Parke, had moved from New Jersey to Kentucky when he was twenty and then to Vincennes in 1801 at age twenty-four; he had studied law in Lexington and had a long career as a judge in Indiana. Previous to his 1808 appointment, he had served as attorney-general (1804–1808) and territorial delegate to Congress. The governor had also named him a militia captain for Knox County in September 1805. When Harrison lobbied with President Jefferson for Parke's appointment in July 1806, the governor claimed that "my friend" Parke "would be more acceptable to the people of the Territory as a Judge than any other who could be appointed." And Jefferson listened.

To succeed Parke as attorney-general, Harrison appointed Thomas Randolph. Thirty-seven years old, Randolph was a graduate of William and Mary and a former member of the Virginia General Assembly. He arrived in Vincennes in May 1808 and won the attorney-generalship in June. He would serve in the job until his death at Tippecanoe in November 1811. Taylor, Parke, and Randolph were typical Harrison appointees—young men with Virginia or Kentucky in their background.

Slowly but surely, then, Governor Harrison overcame his initial reliance on men of local standing and created what amounted to a "court" party. He attached men to his standard, won their loyalty, through the judicious dispensation of his patronage. In so doing, Harrison was acting in the time-honored tradition of colonial governors and the provisions of the Northwest Ordinance. He employed his power to secure his own position and his government's position in a rapidly growing society of ambitious strangers. If the political structure of the Indiana Territory was thoroughly hierarchical in theory in 1800, it was so in fact by 1805. The president of the United States appointed the governor and the judges, who in turn appointed county officials. It was a straightforward, vertical chain of patronage in which men were personally dependent on each other for their positions, power, and prospects. They had to depend on each other, to trust each other, and they related to each other in ways that were as much personal as ideological.

Governor Harrison knew the game as well as anyone. After the election of Thomas Jefferson as president in 1801, he went out of his way to assure the new chief magistrate of his personal loyalty. In August 1802, he obsequiously informed the president that he had "taken the liberty" of naming the new seat of Clark County "Jeffersonville." It was Harrison's "ardent wish that it may become worthy of the name it bears." More to the point, the governor, already thinking about the possibility of reappointment in 1803, concluded by saying:

> If Sir it should again happen that in the wide Range which you suffer your thoughts to take for the benefit of Mankind—the Accomplishment of any of your wishes can in the smallest degree be aided by me—I beg you to believe that your Commands shall be executed to the utmost extent of my small talent.
>
> I have the Honour to be with sincere Attachment Sir your Most Humble Servant.

Harrison's wooing of Jefferson (and his successor, James Madison) paid off with the renewal of his commission as governor on February 8, 1803, December 17, 1806, and December 20, 1809. Despite his competence, Harrison was dependent solely on the favor of the president and he, like others in similar positions, engaged in a great deal of ego-stroking. Whether it was sincere or insincere is beside the point. It was necessary. It was the way politics worked. Later, in 1808, when Harrison demanded the removal of John Rice

235

THE
WORLD
OF
JONATHAN
JENNINGS,
1800–1816

Jones from the Legislative Council, he relied almost exclusively on the credibility of his relationship with the president. "I trust my dear Sir," he wrote, "that you entertain such an opinion of my Candor & attachment to you as to believe that I would not willingly be the means of inducing you to commit an improper act."

In return, Jefferson trusted the governor not only as a federal official but also as his eyes and ears in the territory. The president placed enormous confidence in Harrison, confidence that increased his power. By emphasizing his dependence on Jefferson, Harrison increased others' dependence on him. When the Indiana Territory entered the second stage of territorial government in early 1805, the Northwest Ordinance required the president to choose the five members of the Legislative Council from a list of ten names chosen by the General Assembly. But Jefferson returned the list to Harrison in April with a signed document and asked the governor to fill in appropriate names. Since the president knew nothing about the nominees, "it would be to substitute chance for choice were I to designate the five." Jefferson ordered Harrison to reject "dishonest men," "those called federalists" whose only purpose was "to embarrass & thwart" "public councils," and "land-jobbers." Harrison chose five men who suited him, and how was Jefferson ever to know whether he had followed his instructions to the letter? Similarly, Harrison granted his appointees a fair amount of leeway in handling their offices. But he expected that in return they would be as "attached" to him as he was to Jefferson.

The Issue Is Character

In this world, questions of character and trust were as important in politics as specific issues. The personal was political and vice versa. Since many of these men were strangers to each other, it took a long time before they fully trusted each other. And always they were on the lookout for some sign of deception, some indication that one of their "friends" was not reliable. Indeed, the charge that someone was not what he appeared to be was the most common allegation in public life. How could it be otherwise in a political culture of men who knew each other only slightly but who were utterly dependent on each other's good opinion?

When Benjamin Parke sought a job in the new federal land office in Vincennes in May 1804, he bristled at the rumor that he was "a federalist." Parke rushed to assure the president that he was not. In a most revealing passage, he asserted that

> with whatever hypocrisy I may have acted in the common ordinary concerns of life, with regard to the administration of our Government, I never acted with duplicity. It is a censure I never merited. And from the candour with which I have invariably expressed my sentiments, I suppose, I would sooner have been suspected for the commission of all the vices of the present profligate and depraved age, than for being a federalist.

Men such as Parke jealously guarded their reputation because they had to. If the charge of hypocrisy or deception stuck, their career was over. In a personal political culture, one's honor, the security that one's word was one's bond, was the most important currency of all.

In the Indiana Territory, the distance from the seat of federal power and between the various counties exacerbated distrust. Men who barely knew each other accused each other of reprehensible behavior. Do not believe him, they would tell Jefferson or Harrison; he cannot be trusted. Criticism of the governor was particularly strong in Kaskaskia and the surrounding Illinois Country. The creation of the Michigan Territory by Congress on January 11, 1805, and the Illinois Territory on February 3, 1809, removed this source of tension (and simultaneously reduced the Indiana Territory to the boundaries of the present-day state). In the meantime, however, charges flew back and forth between Kaskaskia and Vincennes about land fraud, favoritism, and neglect.

Each side (Harrison and his coterie and Jones and McIntosh and their friends) accused each other of the same thing: their opponents were unworthy of public trust. In August 1804, William McIntosh denounced the governor in a letter to the *Indiana Gazette* in Vincennes. He objected to the fact that Harrison was calling for an election to inaugurate the second stage of territorial government rather than responding to a call from the people and asserted that the governor was acting in defiance of popular wishes. Benjamin Parke immediately came to the defense of his patron. A bitter ex-

📖 **237**

THE
WORLD
OF
JONATHAN
JENNINGS,
1800–1816

change of letters ensued. McIntosh called Parke the governor's "knight-errant" as the delegate to Congress. Parke then advertised in the *Gazette*:

> Circumstances have recently occurred, which authorise me in pronouncing and publishing William McIntosh, an arrant knave: a profligate villain: a dastardly cheat: a perfidious radical: an impertinent puppy: an absolute liar: and a mean and cowardly poltroon.

These words amounted to a slap in the face. When McIntosh did not take the bait, Parke publicly challenged him. McIntosh avoided giving an answer. There was no duel, Parke's zealousness in trying to precipitate one notwithstanding.

Given the highly personal nature of territorial politics, duels were all but inevitable. They were not simply the products of "frontier" culture. Duels were common throughout the United States in the early republic. Some historians believe they resulted from a scrambling of social roles and cues in a period of intense growth and ideological confusion. Certainly dueling was a way for men to defend their honor, their reputation, from others. They also allowed men to demonstrate their character publicly, to show their courage and steadfastness in a crisis. No knave, no craven blackguard, would risk his life in a duel. Whether it was McIntosh and Parke or Hurst and Jennings, dueling was merely a potentially deadly extension of personal politics. It was also common enough that in 1807 the territorial legislature established fines of between $50 and $250 or three to twelve months in prison for challenging someone to a duel, of up to $100 or one to six months in jail for accepting a challenge, and $50 to $100 or one to six months in jail for serving as a second.

This action had little effect. Rice Jones, the son of John Rice Jones, died in an 1808 shooting in Kaskaskia which resulted from a conflict over Jones's behavior in an aborted duel. Five years later, Dr. Edward Scull killed the sheriff of Knox County, Parmenas Beckes, in a meeting on the so-called field of honor. Within a few months, in the fall of 1813, another fatal duel took place in Vincennes. The Knox County grand jury petitioned the territorial legislature for help and the representatives passed more stringent legislation to "more effectually" prevent dueling.

To some degree, the introduction of the second stage of territorial government in 1805 changed the character of political squabbling. It did so largely by focusing attention on the activities of an elected legislature. This had the effect of intensifying the level of political discourse; while remaining highly personal, debates became more clearly issue-oriented. Men began to take sides in ways that went beyond individual and geographical disputes.

The inauguration of the second stage was not much of an advance in representative democracy. To be sure, the "people" now elected a General Assembly. But this body was relatively small, one representative for every 500 free white males. The members of the assembly, moreover, had to own at least 200 acres within the territory. In addition, the "people" who did the electing were white men with at least fifty acres. The Legislative Council, or upper house, was even more restricted; the president of the United States chose its members from a list of nominees prepared by the assembly. All legislators served two-year terms. Ironically, the second stage strengthened the hand of the governor. Freed from having to work with appointed territorial judges, Harrison gained the authority to call and prorogue the legislature and to exercise an absolute veto over its actions. And since Jefferson granted him leeway in choosing members of the council, Harrison enjoyed a de facto power of patronage.

The manner in which county elections took place reveals the ambiguous nature of the more "democratic" second stage. The most important county official was the sheriff, appointed by the territorial governor. Sheriffs had tremendous local power. They, for example, appointed members of juries. The inauguration of elections for the territorial assembly in 1805 increased their influence. For voting took place orally, in the *viva voce* style employed extensively in eighteenth-century Virginia and other parts of Anglo-America. Moreover, there was only one polling place at a location determined by the sheriff. In other words, the voters, already a group made exclusive by property, age, gender, and race qualifications, had to make their choices publicly, more often than not in the presence of the sheriff and other important officials. While it would be difficult to prove that these powerful local men deliberately intimidated voters, only the foolhardy would have cast their ballots

🐚 **239**

THE
WORLD
OF
JONATHAN
JENNINGS,
1800–1816

without thinking carefully about the consequences of declaring their preference in such a small and highly personal political system.

Initially, Governor Harrison had opposed moving to the second stage, largely on financial grounds. The federal government was spending $5,500 per annum to cover the expenses of the Indiana Territory. Most of this money went for the salaries of the governor ($2,000), the secretary ($750), and the three territorial judges ($800 each). With the move to the second stage, there would be additional costs. Assembly members would get a dollar a day; there would have to be money to pay their staff and fuel bills; the attorney-general would receive $200; and the treasurer and auditor would divide $200. It was estimated that printing bills would run from $500 to $1,000 a year. Land speculators, such as Harrison, were understandably wary of these expenses, since taxes on land would undoubtedly be levied to cover them. In actuality, the total annual cost of the territorial government during the second stage averaged about $10,000, with the national government paying approximately two-thirds of the bill.

Despite these considerations, Harrison decided to support a move to the second stage in the summer of 1804. The growing population and interests of the territory made further postponement impossible. Responding to several petitions, on August 4 the governor called for an election on September 11 to determine the views of the citizens of the territory. Only a few men seemed to care. Of the 400 who voted, 175 resided in Knox County and another seventy-four in Dearborn and Clark counties. The measure passed by a margin of 138, supplied largely by the citizens of Knox. With this far-from-emphatic mandate, Harrison proclaimed the second stage on December 5 and announced the first election for the House of Representatives on January 3, 1805. There were to be nine members: two from Knox County, three from Wayne County, one from St. Clair, one from Randolph, one from Clark, and one from Dearborn. The creation of the Michigan Territory in early 1805 eliminated the need for elections in Wayne County; they were never held. A preliminary session of the territorial assembly also voided the results of the election in St. Clair County in response to charges of voting irregularities. When the General Assembly met in Vincennes from July 29 through August 26, 1805, then, there were a total of six members, Shadrach Bond and William Biggs from St. Clair County, Jesse B. Thomas from Dearborn, Davis Floyd from Clark, and Benjamin Parke and John Johnson from Knox.

The House of Representatives and the Legislative Council completed a sizable amount of work in their first meetings. They consolidated the county courts into one Court of Common Pleas (thereby increasing the power of judges), revised the militia law, provided for the preparation of a code of laws, regulated fees, and passed a black indenture law. But personal politics continued to overshadow the legislature. There were disputes over patronage, regional interests, and slavery. While there was little consistency in terms of sides, the debate increasingly circled the question of the nature of politics itself. More specifically, how should American males acquire and maintain power? How should they organize relationships among themselves?

Governor Harrison and his allies retained a commitment to politics as an essentially hierarchical business. He groomed men for appointed offices and expected them to win the assent of the legislature when necessary (as in Benjamin Parke's selection as the territorial delegate to Congress in 1805). They operated essentially as a personal faction, acquiring and exercising power through a vertical face-to-face system of patronage in which some men were more important than others. In many ways, their support of black slavery, or at least servitude, was fully in keeping with this position. Harrison and his Virginian friends were republicans; virtually anyone in eighteenth-century Europe or North America would have seen them as radical. But they were not ready to confront the full implications of popular sovereignty and social equality, even among white men. They still saw politics as the business of a small group of well-prepared, interconnected gentlemen.

The movement to the second stage of territorial government was the catalyst for the emergence of an alternative construction of political culture. It was born of mundane but significant issues— appointments, personal animosities, the relationship between Vincennes and other parts of the territory. And it evolved in a fashion familiar to students of colonial and territorial politics. Men who felt snubbed or rejected by Harrison began to accuse him of favoritism and corruption. McIntosh had sounded the charge in 1804. Then, in

241

THE
WORLD
OF
JONATHAN
JENNINGS,
1800–1816

1805, Isaac Darneille developed it more fully in an anonymous in-dictment of Harrison, published under the title *Letters of Decius*.

Darneille was apparently a native of Maryland who migrated to the Northwest Territory in the 1790s and ended up in Cahokia in 1794. He was an intelligent, well-educated man who earned a reputation as a lawyer and a seducer of women. The origins of Darneille's grievances clearly lay in the alienation of the western Illinois settlements from the government in Vincennes. Given the distance, it is hardly surprising that the citizens of Kaskaskia and Cahokia resented the fact that the seat of power was in Indiana or that many believed they had far more in common with the people in upper Louisiana.

Whether Darneille's charges against Harrison were true or false, his language reveals the nature of the ideological justification for disagreement with the governor. As early as January 1803, in a "Note on the Government of Indiana Territory," Darneille cited the effects of what he termed "despotism" on society. The corruption of courts, the neglect of education, the encouragement of vice—all were inevitable. In fact, "In all ranks of men a servile obedience, a want of candour assumes the ascendency over common sense and common honesty, insomuch, that from the governor to the petit justice of the peace, each hath his flock of sheep in subjection to him." Darneille explained that a century of obedience to "a *commandant*" predisposed the citizens of the Indiana Territory toward acceptance of such a system. Still, far from changing things, the "introduction" of American government had made them worse. Harrison's appointments and his refusal to listen to petitions were simply reinforcing tyranny. In September 1804, just before the election regarding the movement to the second stage of territorial government, Darneille wrote to the editor of the *Indiana Gazette* to repeat the argument. Like others in St. Clair and Randolph counties, he objected to the change because it seemed only to serve the interests of the executive. "The government of the United States," he said, "ought not to be understood to operate merely by the whim and caprice of the officers of administration."

Letters of Decius was the fullest statement of this perspective, a warning "against the undue influence of the executive." It was also about character and deception. Darneille wanted the members of the territorial legislature to guard against "the stratagem, finesse and fraud, used by some of the more artful members of the legislative assemblies." His real target was Harrison, a man interested in preserving the territorial status quo in order to preserve his power and salary. "Let not the graceful address, the affable manners and the artful, engaging and fascinating insinuations of the governor lead you from your duty. . . . Be assured that the *instrument* of the governor will never be a *friend* to the people." Supported by "sycophants and parasites," Harrison had governed through undue "art," "intrigue," and "influence."

Now the governor's friend Parke was off to Washington, for no other reason than "to keep the company of the members of Congress, & tell them & the several ministers of state, handsome stories about Mr. Harrison, and say how popular he is in the territory, in order that he may be assured of his commission." How else could Parke act? After all, to do otherwise "would be the height of ingratitude," for he owed his "political existence and consequence" to Harrison.

As for the governor, he was a duplicitous and overconfident man, oblivious of how much people truly detested him. "Men of honor and delicacy shudder at the baseness of the means you have employed to bring about your measures," Darneille wrote in a letter addressed to the governor. "The *premium mobile* of your conduct is your salary." He charged Harrison with "Notorious partiality" in granting land and appointments, unwarranted interference in the actions of courts, and a host of similar offenses. In sum, "The immense deserts of Indiana have not yet produced a Brutus to extirpate the monarch, and bring about a reformation; nor a Cato to oppose the tyranny of Sylla; nor has the illustrious example of Philip of Macedon taught *you to remember that you are a man.*"

At bottom, all of Darneille's charges, like McIntosh's, come down to questions of character and the mutability of human understanding. Even as he attacked Harrison as "artful," he worried that the people would not be alert enough or strong enough to resist Harrison's allurements. The governor was as a serpent in the garden. The untrustworthy man, the disguised deceiver who is not what he appears to be, was a common figure in the literature of the early American republic. So, too, in politics.

☙ **243**

THE
WORLD
OF
JONATHAN
JENNINGS,
1800–1816

Harrison, of course, lived in the same world. Informing the new assembly of irregularities in the elections in St. Clair County, he blamed them on "a Combination of factious & wicked men." In fact, many men in the Illinois Country were simply refusing to acquiesce in the second stage, preferring to separate from Indiana or join the upper Louisiana Territory. Harrison had told Thomas Worthington in the fall of 1803 that this was "a most ridiculous scheme." More generally, he warned the assembly in July 1805 to be wary of "local prejudices and local politics." The governor could also be quite personal. In July 1806, he informed Jefferson that Darneille had recanted, and he assured the president that he had "not extorted [it] by the dread of powder and ball or steel—Arguments which I have long declined the use of in private quarrels. . . ." Obviously, at the very least, the idea of a duel had crossed his mind.

According to John Badollet, whose opinion of Harrison soured with the years, Vincennes was little more than the scene of a multitude of violent, personal quarrels. In 1809, he told his friend Albert Gallatin that he had been the governor's "complete dupe." Harrison was simply a "moral cameleon he assumes a variety of appearances to answer his purposes." Thomas Randolph, ally of the governor, had now challenged Dr. Elias McNamee, Badollet's brother-in-law, for criticizing Harrison. He practiced shooting at marks while awaiting a reply. "And lately the same Gentleman attempted to cudgel in the streets a Mr. McIntosh for the same crime, but" received several stab wounds instead. "Such is the State of Society here, such the manner in which the governor watches over the peace and safety of the citizens!" Of course, Harrison thought Badollet "so little acquainted with the world that there is not a man on the earth more easily duped"; consequently, he was easily misled by evil men. But Badollet reported to Gallatin that Harrison was the evil genius whose power rested on his unlimited patronage. He laid out a litany of incidents proving the governor's devious nature.

> Blandishments and frowns are by him successfully employed and when you reflect that every office both civil and military is in his gift, you can easily guess without being an Oedippus, the effects such a conduct must necessarily produce in a limited community such as Indiana.

So ubiquitous were questions of character that when the trustees of Vincennes University, which was established in 1806, petitioned

Congress for taxes on salt and the Indian trade to support the insti-tution, they justified it in political terms. Indiana needed a univer-sity because "the only safeguard and secure shield, against the dark Cunning of individuals and of foreign governments, is the blaze of sciences which will reach the mind of the plowboy, as well as the most wealthy citizen." Indeed, without a university, "our excellent government . . . is liable to be assailed by the various arts of cunning and intrigue, of designing, ambitious, and desperate Individuals." The president of the trustees was William Henry Harrison and their clerk was Jonathan Jennings, the man who would soon make it his business to rid the Indiana Territory of both the governor and a po-litical system of vertical patronage.

Jennings and the Revolution of 1808–1810

When Jennings arrived in Vincennes in the spring of 1807, he was just one of a score of ambitious young men in the territorial capital. As we have seen, he immediately got himself in a scrape with the Harrison protégé Henry Hurst. More generally, Jennings found himself on the outs with the governor and his friends. As early as September 1807, he complained to his brother-in-law that "life is but a lottery, dueling and principles of honour are ever more re-garded the fa[r]ther you go to the Southard." Jennings believed that he could have had the position of clerk of the House of Representa-tives; he was already serving as an assistant clerk. But he was unwilling to play "a double part." Then, in the spring of 1808, the board of trustees of Vincennes University voted to investigate the conduct of their clerk, Jennings. It seems that the young man had certified a pamphlet by trustee General Washington Johnston detail-ing a fight over the continued use of the Commons by the French residents of Vincennes. Johnston and others had defeated a motion to curtail the practice, but the losers (who included board president William Henry Harrison) took their revenge on the hapless clerk. At the May meeting of the board, Jennings officially resigned.

Sometime later in 1808, Jennings left Vincennes altogether. He had never liked the place. The French in particular, with their "very ridiculous" customs, he found "grating to the feelings of an Ameri-can." More important, Vincennes had never matched his expec-

245

THE
WORLD
OF
JONATHAN
JENNINGS,
1800–1816

tations, either politically or economically. In addition to his inability to secure an office, he could not establish himself as a lawyer, merchant, or land speculator. In fact, he had to sell much of the land he purchased while in Vincennes at a loss because he was heavily in debt. No wonder Jennings complained of being seriously ill throughout 1808. In early December, he was so "embarrassed" financially that he asked his brother-in-law to get his father to send him money. "I am in want," Jennings wrote pathetically, "for I know not the time I may be pushed for the money, the name of which will be an injury to me in my profession; as I am settled where I may yet be called a stranger."

He was a stranger because he had moved to Clark County, settling first at Jeffersonville and then at Charlestown. Ultimately his decision to leave Vincennes for the southeastern region of the territory was a very smart one. But initially Jennings was very lonely. His life was not working out the way he had hoped it would. Trying to convince members of his family to join him in Indiana, he continually lamented his failure to find someone who would marry him. The confident, indeed cocky, young man who had come to Vincennes in 1807 was a rather dejected figure in Charlestown in late 1808. The nadir came in early December when his brother Ebenezer died of tuberculosis. Jonathan had been unable to visit him because of his poverty. All he could do was send "a long, a sad & last adieu for a Brother who holds him near his heart."

But matters turned around quickly. Within a year, Jonathan Jennings was well on his way to becoming a key figure in territorial politics. In no small part, his ascent was the result of his shift in residence. Clark County was in many ways an extension of Kentucky. Settled originally by veterans of the Clark campaigns, its economic and social ties were to Louisville rather than Vincennes. Indeed, the region's rapidly growing population had long resented the monopoly on territorial political structures by the residents of the capital. Thus Jenning's personal animosity found a legitimate outlet in regional animosity. Giving vent to his own frustrations with the territorial hierarchy, he became the leader of a geographically based opposition to Harrison and his protégés.

The citizens of Clark and Dearborn counties felt alienated from Vincennes for reasons that went beyond mere distance. Many of

them identified the governor's clique as a bunch of would-be aristocrats who wished to lord it over the majority of the territorial citizens
through a closed system of patronage. Opposition to slavery was
very strong in Clark County. This had little to do with feelings of
compassion or justice for blacks. Rather, many men were concerned
that the influx of slaves would degrade their labor and enhance the
power of Harrison and his crowd. Several men in Dearborn County
sent anti-slavery petitions to Congress in 1805 and 1807; in the latter,
they asked to be annexed by the free state of Ohio. In October 1807,
a meeting of citizens of Clark County, presided over by James Begg
with Davis Floyd acting as secretary, drafted a memorial to Congress objecting to the efforts of the territorial legislature to get the
national government to allow slavery in the Indiana Territory. According to the petition, "The toleration of slavery is either right or
wrong"; the writers hoped that Congress would agree with them that
it was, in fact, wrong.

The growing tension between the eastern counties and Knox
County also appeared in the territorial legislature. In October 1808,
that body elected Jesse B. Thomas of Dearborn County as the territorial delegate to Congress. Thomas had served as speaker of the
legislature since his election in 1805 and was a very popular figure.
But Harrison opposed him and he won with a bare majority of six
out of ten votes. The key to Thomas's election was an alliance between representatives from the Illinois counties, who wanted their
own territory, and those from the eastern counties. Thomas pledged
himself to work for the creation of an Illinois Territory. Meanwhile
the lower house adopted anti-slavery resolutions and repealed the
black-indenture law. None of this became law because of the opposition of the council and the governor. Significantly, the house also
petitioned Congress to disallow Harrison the power of veto over
their acts and to call and dismiss legislative sessions.

These machinations were primarily the work of men from outside Vincennes, although a handful of characters in the capital,
most notably General Washington Johnston, were also involved.
While the origins of the partisanship lay in the regional differences
and resentments that always bedeviled American territories (and
states, for that matter), it increasingly took on an ideological cast.
After all, the opponents of the governor had to ground their actions

📖 **247**

THE
WORLD
OF
JONATHAN
JENNINGS,
1800–1816

in something more than spite and selfishness. What better way was there to handle things?

Clues can be found in Johnston's anti-slavery resolution. He objected to slavery as a moral abomination in a land of liberty and a serious obstacle to economic development. But at the core of his polemic was an indictment of the character of slaveholders, that is, Harrison and his pro-slavery friends. Where there was no slavery, not only would industry be "honorable and honored," but "the man of an independent spirit" would find that "no proud nabob can cast on him a look of contempt." In other words, owning slaves made certain men haughty and passionate. "[W]hen men are invested with an uncontrouled power" over human beings, how could anyone expect them to behave with compassion and reason in their lives? More directly, continued Johnston,

> it may be worthy of enquiry how long the Political Institutions of a People admitting slavery may be expected to remain uninjured, how propper a school for the aquirement of Republican Virtues, is a state of things wherein usurpation is sanctioned by law, wherein the commands of Justice are trampled under feet . . . the habit of unlimited domination in the slave holder will beget in him a spirit of haughtyness and pride productive of a proportionabl habit of servility and dispondence in those who possess no negroes . . . the Lord of three or four hundred negroes will not easily forgive and the mechanic and labouring man will seldom venture a vote contrary to the will of such an influential being.

Johnston should have known, since he had once owned slaves himself. The larger point, however, is that the opponents of Harrison were developing a rhetoric of resentment against the governor. They were portraying him and his pro-slavery allies as aristocrats; their support of slavery revealed their tendencies toward oligarchy as well as anything. Increasingly Harrison's critics began to think of themselves as more *democratic* than the governor. This was as much a question of style as anything else. The white men of the territory should gain and exercise power not through a system of vertical patronage but in fraternal contests among peers. To be against slavery was, in effect, to be against aristocracy. It was to be for independence rather than dependence.

The United States Congress responded to various petitions from the Indiana Territory in the spring of 1809 in ways that undercut

1809

the position of Governor Harrison. It divided the territory in half with a line following the course of the Wabash River north from its mouth to Vincennes and then due north from that point. The creation of the Illinois Territory on February 3, 1809, reduced the political conflict in Indiana to a struggle between Knox County and the eastern regions of the territory. More important from the perspective of Indiana residents, Congress declared that the territorial delegate and the members of the legislative council would hereafter be elected by the people rather than the house of representatives. In addition, the legislature was to decide how to apportion seats in the lower house. These measures, combined with a reduction in the property qualifications for voting the previous year, amounted to a significant opening of the political system in the Indiana Territory. Governor Harrison's power to direct politics through patronage was severely reduced.

The clearest demonstration of the shifting political structures in the territory was the race for territorial delegate to Congress in 1809. There were three candidates: long-time Knox County resident John Johnson, who was in favor of slavery but not Harrison; the governor's recent protégé, territorial Attorney-General Thomas Randolph; and Jonathan Jennings of Clark County. According to rumor, Jennings proposed himself as a candidate while on a visit to Vincennes in the spring of 1809. Such boldness was hardly unprecedented; but it also reflected Jennings's rejection of politics as usual. In any case, he quickly brought a new style and spirit to Indiana politics.

For Jonathan Jennings campaigned for office. This seems such an unremarkable thing to late twentieth-century Americans who seem to live in the midst of perpetual campaigns. But it was novel in 1809. Jennings traveled throughout Clark, Dearborn, and Harrison counties directly courting voters. Legend has it that he did not simply harangue men; he joined in their work and their games, winning their friendship. In fact, treating men like friends was the crux of the matter for Jennings. He wanted nothing to do with patronage and slavery. Instead he stood for unfettered competition in which men offered themselves to voters for approval or disapproval. While Johnson and Randolph stayed in Vincennes, Jennings went about the business of cultivating his constituents.

249

THE
WORLD
OF
JONATHAN
JENNINGS,
1800–1816

All in all, he appeared to enjoy himself. By this time, a man in his late twenties, Jennings had perfected the skills of a gregarious kibitzer far more than those of a lawyer or a businessman. By nature passionate, he was something of a tease. He liked to be with people. He hated to be alone. Testimony to this lies in a letter to John Graham, who had left Jeffersonville for St. Louis, albeit temporarily. Jennings reacted strongly to the news of Graham's departure. "Much was my disappointment," he wrote,

> when I returned to this place and found you gone—gone for four years—gone without even leaving me one line to remind me of the past—the past which promised me (I thought) a lasting friendship—a friendship which I prised as being founded on the firmest basis—a basis which alone is capable of supporting real friendship, I mean the basis of an honest heart—a free and generous mind guarded by the strongest barriers of well settled principles of morality & rectitude. Graham, to you could I have deposited the greatest secrets of my heart & in your friendship I anticipated much.—I hope you will not forget me, we may see each other I fondly hope it.

In the end, they did, for Graham returned to Jeffersonville within the year. But the letter reveals Jennings as a strong and insecure man, desperate to hold on to a friend with a charming, even disarming, eloquence.

Jennings's behavior was similar when he married Ann Gilmore Hay, a nineteen-year-old native of Harrodsburg, Kentucky, on August 8, 1811. For years he had been trying to find a wife, without success. Now, he told his sister, he had "a little black eyed wife." Soon Jennings was dismissing the prospect that his wife might, as he assumed frequently happened, become a scold. "Some good wives say, for excuse, that they *mean no harm by it* and *perhaps* they are candid in such declarations. Ha ha ha !!!!" he wrote to his sister. "For my part, I am determined, that my wife shall never act *such* a part. . . ."

These exclamations of assertive exuberance alternated with periods of despondency, however. In fact, Jennings seems to have been quite moody. Certainly he was never satisfied with his position in the world. He made friends easily but was unable to trust relationships. He was such a successful campaigner because he was so eager to be loved. Yet he was an indifferent statesman and governor, perhaps because he was more interested in the winning of public adulation than in the exercising of authority. Adept at playing games and glad-handing, he was not very good at laying out an agenda and achieving its implementation. Ultimately Jennings was a popular but rather weak character. As time went on, indeed, the casual drinking that marked his easy camaraderie gave way to a severe case of alcoholism. By the 1820s, Jennings was a well-known sot, a convivial drunk.

In his early campaigns, however, his courting of voters and his lambasting of the aristocratic tendencies of Governor Harrison made him extremely popular outside Knox County. He won the 1809 race for delegate with 428 votes to Randolph's 402 and Johnson's 81. Jennings achieved his plurality by doing exceedingly well in Dearborn and Clark counties. In fact, he did so well that Randolph demanded an investigation, charging voting irregularities. Both men went to Washington in November to claim the seat. A committee reported that the election had been illegal, but Congress overruled this report and certified Jennings as delegate.

The defeat of Randolph was also a repudiation of Governor Harrison and the politics of patronage. Delighted when the House voted to seat him, Jennings exclaimed that he had "exposed the conduct of my great enemy the Govenor, & have also been able to retain my seat in spite of all the sanguin expectations of my rivals & Enemies." Jennings then unsuccessfully opposed Harrison's December 1809 reappointment. This was fully in keeping with the wishes of his constituents, many of whom petitioned Congress against Harrison on the grounds that he had been in office too long and was in favor of slavery. According to a group of Clark County citizens, Harrison's "principles" were simply "repugnant to the Spirit of *Republicanism*." In December 1809, Jennings wrote to William Duane, editor of the *Aurora and General Advertiser* in Philadelphia, "as a foe to all speculating and intriguing men in office" to raise questions about Harrison's probity. Several of his charges had to do with the governor's support of Randolph in the race for delegate and his distrust of Jennings. As always, politics was basically personal.

While Jennings and his allies could not stop the reappointment of the governor, they did succeed in convincing Congress to weaken his authority. In response to lobbying by the territorial delegate and

☙ **251**

THE
WORLD
OF
JONATHAN
JENNINGS,
1800–1816

petitions from both citizens and legislature, Congress in 1810 gave the vote to all white men over twenty-one who had lived in the territory for a year and paid a county or territorial tax. Congress also made it impossible for any appointee of the governor to serve in the territorial assembly, although exceptions were made for justices of the peace and militia officers. These reforms, coupled with those of the previous year making the delegate and the council elected officials, effectively undid the politics of patronage in the Indiana Territory. By the fall of 1810, a majority of the assembly was clearly hostile to Harrison, voting to repeal the 1805 act regarding indentured servants and to move the seat of government away from Vincennes. They also formed three new counties, apportioned representation in the legislature, and set the date for the election of territorial delegate. Harrison, bowing to the obvious, made no effort to veto any of this.

Jennings, reelected delegate in 1811 (defeating Randolph), 1812 (defeating Waller Taylor), and 1814 (defeating Elijah Sparks), advocated further changes; they included the direct election of sheriffs and the right of appeal from territorial courts to the federal government. Congress did nothing. But in its 1811 session, the territorial legislature reiterated the call for the election of sheriffs and made voting easier by creating a poll tax of fifty cents. Above all, the representatives changed the ways in which elections took place. Previously the county sheriffs conducted them in one place in each county. Now the handling of elections became the responsibility of judges of the Court of Common Pleas. They were to open polls in each township and to make the voting by ballot.

Politically, the tide had shifted in the Indiana Territory. When Harrison resigned at the end of 1812, the move was relatively anticlimactic. Only a few months earlier, the legislature had sealed the repudiation of his world by voting to move the territorial capital to Corydon and by resolving that no one who was pro-slavery should become governor. What amounted to a revolution in government had taken place in the space of three years, transforming a centralized, vertical system of politics into a decentralized, local system. Historians often refer to this process as the "democratization" of territorial politics. In a general sense, they are right. But the change was less an embracing of democracy than a rejecting of the status quo. For Jonathan Jennings and his friends had not rushed to the standard of liberty as much as they had overthrown a government that seemed to exclude them. Politics in territorial Indiana was regional and ideological, but at bottom it was personal, an argument among gentlemen or would-be gentlemen about the best way to acquire and hold power. Whatever the advantages of vertical patronage, it was far too constrictive for the ambitious young men of Indiana. In the long run, more of them preferred to risk everything on the whims of their peers rather than the whims of one man.

Organizing the Nineteenth State

By 1815, with the conclusion of the War of 1812 and a population in excess of 63,000, Indiana had become an obvious candidate for admission to the United States as an equal member. Accordingly the territorial legislature petitioned Congress to call an election for delegates to a convention to determine whether statehood was "expedient or inexpedient." If the former, they were to devise a "frame of Government." Jonathan Jennings brought the petition before Congress in December 1815. Within a month, he was offering a bill enabling Indiana to become a state. Passed on April 11, 1816, this act provided for an election on May 13. A month after that, forty-three men met in Corydon and voted to form a state government.

This decision was not quite as straightforward as it sounds. There was opposition to statehood, largely on financial grounds; some men thought the whole business too expensive, preferring to rely on the largess of the United States government. The leader of the opposition was Governor Thomas Posey, whom President James Madison had appointed to succeed Harrison on March 3, 1813. Like his predecessor, Posey was a Virginian by birth. He had lived in Kentucky and in Louisiana, where he was appointed to the United States Senate in 1812. But Posey was never the dominant figure in Indiana politics Harrison had been. While this was partly a matter of temperament and talent, it was also a reflection of the much weaker position of the governor after the revolution of 1808 and 1809. Posey simply could not accumulate the kind of power Harrison had acquired through near-total control of government patronage.

📖 **253**

THE
WORLD
OF
JONATHAN
JENNINGS,
1800–1816

The members of the constitutional convention were a fair cross-section of the territory's European-American male population. Of the forty-three members, thirty-four had lived somewhere in the South (twenty-seven in Kentucky) before coming to Indiana. Eleven or twelve were natives of Virginia, six of Kentucky, five of Maryland, and one each of North and South Carolina. Only two were from the Northeast (Connecticut), while seven were from Pennsylvania, two from New Jersey, and one from Delaware. Six were born in Europe, four in Ireland, one in Switzerland, and one in Germany. The delegates ranged in age from twenty-eight to fifty-eight, with the vast majority in their thirties or forties. Over half of them had some sort of legal experience, and at least half had served as justices of the peace.

Together these men drafted a constitution that was a variation on the documents already in place in Kentucky and Ohio. Like them, it placed power firmly in the hands of a democratic oligarchy of white males. The Indiana Constitution of 1816 was not the fulfillment of a dream of frontier democracy but a relatively common reaction to the vertical structure of government established by the Northwest Ordinance of 1787. Indiana's government would amount to a power-sharing arrangement among men like Jonathan Jennings, men whose political obligations lay in their relationships with their peers rather than their ties with superior officials.

Meeting on June 10, 1816, the members of the convention first chose Jennings to preside over their sessions. They then selected William Hendricks, a thirty-four-year-old native of Westmoreland County, Pennsylvania, as their secretary. Although not a delegate, Hendricks was an ally of Jennings who had served as clerk of the territorial house during the Fourth and Fifth Assemblies; he had represented Jefferson County and been elected speaker of the house in the first session of the Fifth Assembly. Hendricks was also briefly the territorial printer in 1813. Given this experience and his correct relationship with Jennings, he was a natural choice for secretary.

In general, according to John Barnhart, the convention's closest historian, Jennings and his friends dominated the group's actions. The opposition to them was diffuse; most of it came from the delegates from Knox and Gibson counties, Harrison protégés such as Benjamin Parke, two territorial judges, and a son-in-law of Arthur

St. Clair. Only one-third of the men who supported the same positions as Jennings had been appointed to an office by William Henry Harrison. Jennings's supporters were particularly strong in the southern and eastern parts of the territory, where opposition to slavery was widespread. As president, Jennings appointed the twelve committees charged with drafting portions of the constitution. Occasionally he turned to potential opponents, perhaps because he had a sizable majority on his side. The delegates repeatedly turned back efforts to delay their work, as when they defeated a proposal to make two-thirds of the delegates constitute a quorum. Instead, a simple majority of the convention could act on its business. The decisive moment came on June 11, when the delegates voted thirty-four to eight "to proceed to form a Constitution and State Government."

In the end, the convention adopted a form of government which, while dividing power among three branches, concentrated it most clearly in the hands of the legislators and county officials. The preamble announced that they were acting as "the Representatives of the people of the Territory of Indiana . . . in order to establish Justice, promote the welfare, and secure the blessings of liberty to ourselves and our posterity." Of course, they defined "people" rather narrowly, excluding women, African Americans, and Native Americans. The constitution was, to be sure, a triumph for a certain kind of people. In the long run, the implications of the ideas it contained would, like those of the federal constitution, lead to a revision of the definition of "the people." But, for the moment, they were talking about securing the blessings of liberty for the white, adult males with one year's residence in Indiana who were the only people eligible to vote.

Still, our knowledge of the limitations of the rhetoric should not blind us to its enormous power. What may seem trite to many Americans in the late twentieth century was powerful, heady stuff in the aftermath of winning independence and conquering the Ohio Valley. According to the first article of the Indiana Constitution, "the general, great and essential principles of liberty and free Government" were "that all men are born equally free and independent, and have certain natural, inherent, and unalienable rights; among which are the enjoying and defending life and liberty, and of acquiring, possessing, and protecting property, and pursuing and obtaining happiness and safety." More specifically, it declared "that

📜 **255**

THE
WORLD
OF
JONATHAN
JENNINGS,
1800–1816

all power is inherent in the people." These paraphrases of Thomas Jefferson's elegant sentences in the Declaration of Independence were particularly striking in the political culture of Indiana Territory. For, however petty and trivial their quarrels may seem in retrospect, many contemporaries believed that they involved fundamental principles of social and political organization. In rejecting government by the territorial hierarchy, they were rejecting far more than a temporary form of government. Thus the members of the convention moved first to affirm freedom of religion, "free" elections, trial by jury, and other familiar American rights. Given the history of territorial politics, however, it is hardly surprising that they also granted the legislature the sole power to suspend "the operation of the laws" and guaranteed freedom of the press to anyone who wanted to examine the operations of the government.

Article II established three "departments" of government, which were to be strictly separate; no person could serve in more than one capacity, thereby eliminating a common practice under the territorial government that tended to encourage patronage. Article III created a General Assembly consisting of a Senate and a House of Representatives. The assembly, not the governor, had the right to apportion its seats among the citizens of the state as it saw fit. To serve, senators had to be at least twenty-five and have been in Indiana for two years, representatives twenty-one with one-year residence in their county. Voters were to elect all members of the house every year and one-third of the senators, who would have three-year terms.

The constitution gave the General Assembly almost complete authority over its own affairs. The two houses chose their own officers, determined the qualifications of their members, policed themselves, and adjourned themselves. Section 20 of Article III made all those with appointments from the president of the United States ineligible for election. Section 24 extended the right of impeachment and trial of executive officers to the assembly. It was no coincidence that the laws of Indiana were to carry the words "Be it enacted by the General assembly of the State of Indiana," for that is where power lay.

Had Indiana become a state while Harrison was still governor, the constitution might have made the executive weaker. As it was, the state governor, while more powerful than his counterpart in

Ohio, was still largely a creature of the legislature. The document provided that the man with the most votes would assume the office. But the ballots were to be opened and counted publicly in the General Assembly, which was the final arbiter of all election disputes.

The governor, who had to be at least thirty, was to have a three-year term, but he could serve for only six out of every nine years. While he was to nominate state officers, he could do so only "by and with the advice and consent of the senate." The governor could call the assembly into session only on "extraordinary occasions." He did have the power to pardon criminals and remit fines. Still, his primary responsibility was neither to initiate legislation nor pursue an agenda of his own but "from time to time, give to the General Assembly information" about the state "and recommend to their consideration, such measures as he shall deem expedient." The governor could veto legislation if he chose to do so, but the assembly could override his action with a simple majority in both houses; moreover, he had only five days to register an objection before legislative acts became law.

Other executive officers included a lieutenant-governor, who was to be elected in the same manner as the governor. In addition, the assembly was to choose a secretary of state to serve for four years and a treasurer and auditor for three years. The constitution also provided for the election of two county officers—a sheriff and a coroner—every two years.

The final branch of the state government was the judiciary. The constitution established a Supreme Court (with three judges) and three circuit courts (with a president and two associates, each of which could hold court without the other) and provided for the creation of other inferior courts at the discretion of the General Assembly. The terms of all state judges were seven years. Their selection was a mixture of methods. The governor, with the "advice and consent of the senate," appointed the Supreme Court judges. The circuit court presidents were to be elected by the assembly and the associates by the voters "in the respective Counties." The white men of each township were to choose "a competent number of Justices of the peace" to serve for five years.

Article VI regulated elections. In addition to prescribing the qualifications for voting as being male, white, and twenty-one or

☙ **257**

THE
WORLD
OF
JONATHAN
JENNINGS,
1800–1816

older, it determined that all elections would be held "by ballot." Interestingly, this was a controversial provision. The constitution said that, after 1821, the assembly could change the method to *viva voce*. But if they did so, "it shall remain unalterable." Secret ballots apparently were being employed on a trial basis. Sentiment seemed to lie on the side of ballots, but some members preferred *viva voce*, a method that would clearly favor the interests of a county's wealthier and more influential citizens. Perhaps not coincidentally, Section 5 of Article XI made it impossible for anyone to hold statewide office who had "been convicted of having given, or offered, any bribe, treat, or reward to procure his election." The legislature later imposed a penalty of up to $500 in fines and a two-year ban on holding office on anyone who engaged in "treating," that is, trying to influence voters with drinks and food, a common practice in eighteenth-century elections. Election officials convicted of fraud or corruption while performing their duties were to be fined up to $500.

These provisions notwithstanding, prominent local figures remained very powerful when it came to election days. Under the provisions of a law passed by the first General Assembly of the state of Indiana, county commissioners appointed an inspector of elections to supervise proceedings in each township; the inspectors then chose two voters to assist him. Together the three men then appointed two clerks. The sheriffs distributed poll books and ballots at least ten days in advance of the election. On the appointed morning, sometime between 9:00 and 11:00, the three judges were to announce that the polls were open. The inspector then proclaimed the name of each prospective voter, who marked his choices on a blank piece of paper and placed it in a box in front of the judges. When the polls closed, usually by 4:00 in the afternoon, the judges counted the votes publicly, announced the result, and one of them delivered the ballots to the county clerk.

The hitch was that men could object to the qualifications of voters after their names were called and before they voted. Judging from Kenneth Winkle's study of voting in neighboring Ohio, this probably occurred frequently, with objections being raised with regard to the length of residency. Since the inspector and his two appointees were the judges of the validity of such challenges, they had enormous power over who voted. In this way, however open elections may have seemed, the influential local men who served as sheriffs, commissioners, judges, and clerks exerted a great deal of power.

In Article VIII, the constitution allowed voters to decide every twelve years whether another constitutional convention should be held. The new body could "revise, amend, or change" as it saw fit, with one exception. Because "holding any part of the human Creation in slavery, or involuntary servitude, can only originate in usurpation and tyranny," no future convention could change the state constitution "so as to introduce slavery or involuntary servitude" into Indiana, except as punishment for a crime. Other provisions of the constitution regarding education and banks will be discussed in the next chapter.

Since the constitution was not submitted to voters for their approval or disapproval, it went into effect on June 29, 1816. On that day, the convention adjourned and President Jennings officially notified sheriffs to hold elections on the first Monday in August. They did so on August 5. The first General Assembly met on November 4, 1816, and Governor Jonathan Jennings took the oath of his office on November 7.

Jennings had come a long way since his early days in Vincennes. In essence he had replaced Harrison as chief executive of Indiana only a decade after arriving in the territory. His final hurdle was the defeat of territorial Governor Thomas Posey, who ran against him. About two-thirds of the eligible voters went to the polls in early August. Jennings received 5,211 ballots to Posey's 3,934. The returns for most of the counties have been lost. Judging from Jennings's showing in 1819, when he won reelection, and from Posey's vote in an 1817 bid for Congress, Jennings's strength continued to lie in the eastern and southern parts of the state. Posey did well in Knox and Posey counties, where support for slavery remained strong and where the territorial government had been most influential. William Hendricks won the race for Indiana's sole representative in Congress, an achievement he repeated in 1817, 1818, and 1820; then Jennings won the seat by a margin of 13,211 to 5,926.

In many ways, the new elections simply cemented the positions of the men who had emerged as important figures in the last half of

☙ **259**

THE
WORLD
OF
JONATHAN
JENNINGS,
1800–1816

the territorial period. Jennings, Hendricks, and United States Senators James Noble and Waller Taylor (chosen by the legislature in November) were well-known figures. One-third of the thirty-nine members of the first General Assembly had been delegates to the constitutional convention; eleven of them were veterans of the territorial legislature. In the counties, the voters elected sheriffs who already held that position under the territorial government. Indeed, within a few years, Jennings, Hendricks, and Noble would be the targets of the same kind of charges of aristocracy which they had leveled at Harrison and Posey. Many citizens of the new state seemed to believe by the 1820s that they had merely exchanged one oligarchy for another.

There was some truth to this observation. Jennings and his allies had intended to create a system that would keep men like them in power. But there was more than a paper change involved in the transition from the territorial aristocracy to the state aristocracy. The shifts from government by patronage to government by election and from the governor to the legislature as the center of political power were not inconsiderable. They reflected a revolution in the style and procedures of politics. To some extent, at least, would-be officeholders had to appeal to their neighbors to secure offices; officially, the source of their authority was not the president of the United States or the Northwest Ordinance or the governor of the Indiana Territory but the narrowly defined conception of "the people." Debates over the meaning of that term would be at the core of Indiana politics for the next several generations.

Historians will argue that these changes were not really so momentous, that they were made all but inevitable by the provisions of the Northwest Ordinance and the democratization of politics in the United States as a whole in the early republic. In retrospect, they are right. But it is important to remember that the people of the Indiana Territory did not see themselves or the events in their world in retrospect. What seems inevitable to us hardly seemed so to them. Rather, to Jennings and his colleagues the more open electoral system embodied in the Constitution of 1816 was the result of years of labor in both legislative bodies and on the stump. When, on December 11, 1816, President James Madison signed a resolution of the Congress of the United States proclaiming Indiana to be "on an equal footing with the original States in all respects whatever," he marked more than an institutional transition. He ritually affirmed the end of one political era and the beginning of a new one for the peoples who inhabited the banks of the Wabash River and its many tributaries.

IO.

THE END OF THE FRONTIER, 1816–1850

The second decade of the nineteenth century was a watershed in the history of Indiana. It was not that society changed a great deal in its essentials but that an atmosphere of solidity about the white American presence in the upper Ohio and Wabash valley started to emerge. With the defeat of the Shawnee, Miami, and their Indian and British allies in the War of 1812 and the admission of Indiana as a full-fledged, equal member of the American Union in 1816, a sense of inevitability about the future of the region set in. Of course, Virginians and other Americans had long exuded a cocky confidence about their ability to "settle" and "improve" the Old Northwest. And neither military victory nor statehood brought to an end contests over land and power. Still, if the Miami, Delaware, and Potawatomi remained an important segment of the population in the northern half of the state, there was no longer any real doubt about who would control the future and very little doubt about what shape it would take. For half a century, the Wabash had been at the center of violent conflict about such questions. Now it was moving toward the periphery, clearly within a white American sphere of influence, as the main stage of the centuries-old drama of Indian-white encounters drifted to the west and north like a hazy collection of storm clouds.

The end of the frontier did not mean the end of history. Rather, as white Americans transformed the economic and political structures and remade the landscape of Indiana, they increasingly found themselves at odds with each other over how and to what extent they would take this process. Eighteenth-century issues gave way to nineteenth-century ones, the latter produced by the resolution of the former. Victory over British, French, and Indians sharpened awareness of the fact that the victors were not all the same. While white Americans generally embraced market capitalism, social egalitarianism, and Protestantism, they often disagreed strongly over the implementation and implications of their beliefs.

The Final Conquest

The Shawnee, Miami, and Delaware had surrendered their claims to southern Indiana to William Henry Harrison in the first decade of the nineteenth century. In the two decades following the War of 1812, the Miami, the Delaware, and the Potawatomi gave up the northern half as well. This they did partly in response to pressure from agents of the United States government. More important, however, was the complete disruption of their way of life. The declining importance of the fur trade in the lower Great Lakes made the Native Americans ever more dependent on annuities. The advancing line of European encroachment soon forced a cruel choice: either become more like the white Americans, accept their economic and social structures, or migrate farther west and north. Disagreements over how to proceed exacerbated factionalism, which only made resistance even more difficult.

Some chose the path of acculturation, at least to the extent that it served their purposes. Christian missionaries, such as the Kentucky Baptist Isaac McCoy, who had twenty students in a mission school in Fort Wayne in 1820, met with some success in converting Native Americans to their customs as well as their religion. But the well-regulated and heavily didactic operations of missions alienated far more than they persuaded. Generally the Potawatomi and the Miami were willing to accept the obvious benefits of European-American civilization. They highly prized superior cloth, blankets, hats, combs, ribbons, and cookware. By and large, however, they re-

🕮 **263**

THE
END
OF
THE
FRONTIER,
1816–1850

mained adamantly against becoming a society of sedentary farm families. If they modeled themselves on any European, as David Edmunds has suggested, it was still the French fur trader.

Historians believe that most of the Indians who chose at least some degree of acculturation were people of mixed-blood heritage. Among the most prominent in northern Indiana was Jean-Baptiste Richardville, the descendant of French men and Indian women who had lived in the middle of the eighteenth century. Richardville was the nephew of the Miami chief Pacan and a disciple of Little Turtle. After their deaths (in 1816 and 1812), he was the acknowledged chief of the Miami until his death on August 12, 1841. As he got older, the well-educated Richardville, who spoke both French and English, chose to dress and speak as a Miami. A controversial figure, the chief was an adept bargainer and managed to secure a great deal of land for himself and his friends during treaty negotiations. Many saw Richardville as selfish and duplicitous. If true, such characterizations would only reveal how thoroughly acculturated he had become—and how little Americans understood the Indians. A more charitable explanation is that Richardville, understanding the importance of private property to the white Americans, secured unassailable titles to land that he expected his kin to live on. The supposed rapacity of Richardville, whose eighty years marked the complete arc of the American conquest of Indiana, meant that when he died he left $200,000 in cash and that at least half of the Miami were not subject to removal to the West because they lived on privately owned land. In other words, the chief acculturated to the degree that he was able to outmaneuver both settlers and their governments. In 1960, at least 200 Miami still resided within the borders of the state of Indiana.

While hundreds of Miami and Potawatomi hung on in northern Indiana after the War of 1812, the relentless signing of treaties with the United States paved the way for more legal incursion by white settlers from the south. Governor Jonathan Jennings and his old nemesis Benjamin Parke traveled to St. Marys, Ohio, in 1818 to accept the surrender by the Potawatomi, Wea, Miami, and Delaware of what the Americans called the New Purchase. This tract included everything north from the 1809 treaty line to the Wabash River; in addition, the Americans gained two parcels of land, one south of the

Vermilion River and the other north of the Wabash and between the Vermilion and Tippecanoe rivers. In return, the Miami received individual grants of land, $15,000, a salt annuity of 160 bushels, a grist mill, and a sawmill. The Delaware, however, simply gave up all claims and agreed to move west of the Mississippi River. The next year, the Kickapoo on the Vermilion also promised to leave the area. Later, in 1826 and 1828, the Potawatomi ceded most of northeastern Indiana to the white Americans. By the mid-1830s, the United States had acquired virtually all of the land in the state. Meanwhile, Secretary of War John Calhoun had informed Congress in 1825 that there were only 11,579 Indians left in Indiana and Illinois (2,350 in Ohio). Soon the federal government would force many of them to relocate on the other side of the Mississippi River.

The apparent resolution of the Indian question initially meant a decline in the presence of federal authority in Indiana. The United States Army had long since abandoned Fort Knox, north of Vincennes, and, in the aftermath of the War of 1812, it did the same with Fort Harrison (Terre Haute) and Fort Wayne. The last outpost, first constructed by Hamtramck and his men in 1796, was rebuilt in 1817 and 1818. It no longer made sense to keep troops in Indiana who were now needed in the region west of the Great Lakes. And so in April 1819, not quite three decades after the great Indian victory over Harmar and his men, the army left the fortification and moved on.

In the wake of the troops came an equally powerful agent of national authority—the land agent. Before statehood, settlers could purchase land from the United States at offices in Vincennes (1804) and Jeffersonville (1807). The flurry of Indian cessions, however, created a need for more and the national government established offices in rapid succession at Terre Haute (1819), Brookville (1819), Fort Wayne (1822), Crawfordsville (1823), and La Porte (1833). Under the provisions of the Land Act of 1800, the United States maintained two officers at each office, a register who kept track of applications and land entries, and a receiver who handled financial matters, including receiving payment and issuing receipts. Most important, the law established a credit system for buying federal land. While applicants had to pay at least two dollars for every acre, they had forty days to pay one-fourth of the total price, two years to pay another quarter, three years for a third, and four years to extinguish

265

THE
END
OF
THE
FRONTIER,
1816–1850

the debt completely. They had to pay 6 percent interest on what they owed, but they could earn an 8 percent discount by paying an installment off early. Congress later set the minimum purchase at 160 acres (1804), then eighty acres (1817) and forty acres (1832). In the meantime, it also passed legislation for the relief of those who found themselves unable to pay off their debts within the official time limits.

As the historian Malcolm J. Rohrbough has demonstrated, the land office was as important as the military post in making the United States government a visible presence on American frontiers. In the end, individuals and corporations would own most of the land in Indiana; private property, after all, was one of the central tenets of American society. But it is important to remember that land passed from Indians to white settlers through the agency of the federal government. There were, of course, squatters and speculators who often tried and occasionally succeeded in circumventing the operations of the land office. More significant, however, is the fact that federal agents—surveyors, registers, and receivers—directed and supervised the disposal of the so-called national domain. Men such as John Badollet and Nathaniel Ewing, the register and receiver at the Vincennes land office, were not only significant figures in Indiana politics and society; they were also at the center of a small federal bureaucracy: they hired clerks, deputy surveyors, chain carriers, axmen, cooks, and hunters and gave irregular employment to sheriffs and printers.

If the land offices at Vincennes and Jeffersonville were busy from the beginning, they were overwhelmed after the War of 1812. According to the Swiss-born Badollet, the amount of land sold at public sales in 1816 was "extraordinary." Sales were up by 30 percent at Jeffersonville and 425 percent at Vincennes. In 1817, "the applications were so numerous that it was impossible to record them as rapidly as they came on." Indeed, the Vincennes office led the United States in total sales in 1817 with the dispersal of 286,558.36 acres for $570,923.52. Jeffersonville was not far behind, collecting $512,701.78 in return for 256,350.92 acres. By 1820, the United States had sold 2,490,736 acres in Indiana and earned $5,137,350.

Meanwhile, people were illegally squatting on lands north of the Ohio River, prompting a December 1815 proclamation from President James Madison threatening intruders on the public lands with removal by the military if they persisted in their illegal actions. Congressional delegate Jonathan Jennings rose to the defense of squatters, arguing that blame lay with the federal government for taking so long to get the lands on the market. Too many people, according to Badollet, were under "the delusive hope of obtaining pre-emption rights." Many proceeded to ask Congress for relief. One petition, received in January 1816, suggested that settlers had earned the land by confronting "the danger of the ruthless savage with Intagerty & success. . . . We Still have hopes that surely the Guardians of our Liberties & rights will not suffer the farmes we have Made at such greate inconveniancyes & riskes To bee Expose,d to publick Sail & the profits thereoff Redownd to A welthy Republick." This and other arguments persuaded Congress to enact legislation allowing squatters to remain on the land before they purchased it.

A more difficult problem faced the federal government with the collapse of the credit system in the wake of the national financial panic of 1819. The postwar boom in land sales had left purchasers in debt to the United States for $9,868,295. When the Bank of the United States suspended specie payments in the summer of 1818, the contraction of the money supply and the concomitant fall in prices and demand made it impossible for purchasers to fulfill their obligations. In the midst of a serious financial depression, Congress abolished the credit system in the Land Act of 1820. No longer would Americans be able to buy federal land on a foundation of dreams of prosperity. Now they had to pay in advance. To avoid the complete destruction of the land office business, Congress lowered the minimum price to $1.25 per acre.

By the early 1820s, the citizens of the Old Northwest were recovering from the economic crises and turning their attention to the lands recently ceded by the Miami, Potawatomi, and Delaware in northern Indiana. As bad as the crises provoked by squatters and the Panic of 1819 seemed in the short run, a longer perspective shows that the agents of the United States government acquired and sold millions of acres—the preponderance of Indiana—in the space of a few decades. In the 1820s, the Indiana land offices sold 1,963,947 acres and collected $2,500,000. Between 1830 and 1837, what Rohrbough calls "the height" of the business, the Indianapo-

📖 267

THE
END
OF
THE
FRONTIER,
1816–1850

lis, Crawfordsville, and Fort Wayne offices sold approximately 1.5, 1.68, and 2.37 million acres respectively. At Fort Wayne, purchasers exchanged $1,620,617.34 for 1,294,357 acres (the equivalent, Rohrbough points out, of 8,090 160-acre farms) in the single year of 1836. Whatever one thinks of the European conquest of North America, this transfer of land from one group of people to another through the intermediary of a government was an altogether remarkable occurrence, unmatched anywhere else in the history of the world. Indiana's amount of improved land (that is, usable for grazing, grass, tillage, or lying fallow) rose from 125,530 in 1810 to 1,751,409 in 1830 to 8,161,717 in 1860.

Migration and Settlement

With Indian treaties and land offices in place, white and black settlers went about the business of developing Indiana from what they thought of as a wilderness into their vision of a commercial, agricultural paradise. Prior to 1816, most migration to the region had occurred along the rivers; the vast majority of the population was located along the Ohio River and the two streams that flow along Indiana's eastern and western borders—the Whitewater and the Wabash—as far north as what are now Richmond and Terre Haute. But in the second half of the 1810s, settlers began to flood the interior, initially in the hilly southern region called the Knobs and then into the White River valley and the prairies north of Indianapolis.

The process of settling this world took about four decades. Nothing demonstrates its essential trajectory as well as population figures. In 1800, there were 5,641 people in the territory (including Michigan and Illinois). By 1810, that number had risen to 24,520; by 1820, 147,178; by 1830, 343,031; by 1840, 685,866; and by 1850, 988,416. These are unquestionably huge increases. What sustained them was largely natural reproduction. The vast majority of the migrants to Indiana arrived in the decades between the late 1810s and the late 1830s. Only 9,080 immigrants settled in the state in the 1840s. And by the 1850s, Indiana actually had more white emigrants than immigrants. Just over 40,000 people left Indiana in the 1850s. Fifty-seven percent of the population in 1860 had been born within the boundaries of the state. Within a few decades, Indiana had become home to many people, a point of embarkation rather than a point of destination.

Yet whether people were coming or going, according to all kinds of witnesses, Indiana was a place of strangers. Traveler David Thomas protested strongly against "the fashion amongst the middle or lower classes to salute us by the name of 'stranger.'" But why shouldn't they have? Indiana was a crossroads, a place in demographic flux. Still, the white settlers of Indiana were not quite as heterogeneous as those in the other states of the Old Northwest. As we have seen, most of its first residents were upland southerners, women and men from Kentucky, Virginia, western Pennsylvania, and the Carolinas. Important exceptions existed, of course, including the Swiss in the region around Vevay, the Germans in Harmony, and the French in Vincennes and its environs. Not all Southerners, moreover, were alike; they disagreed over slavery, religion, and a host of other issues. The Quakers from North Carolina who dominated the Whitewater Valley were not the same as the Virginia gentry in Knox County. But it is easy to exaggerate the isolation and segregation of Indiana's southern settlers, especially the degree to which they were really strangers. The experiences of the Van Arsdale household of Mercer County, Kentucky, demonstrates clearly the critical role played by kinship networks in the settlement of Indiana.

Peter Van Arsdale's father died in 1802, and the fifteen-year-old was then bound out as a blacksmith's apprentice. After a stormy relationship with his "derangd" employer, Peter made a living as a builder and blacksmith. He got married in the fall of 1809; his wife came with a dowry of two cows and some "houshold furniture." Indeed, Peter could not have survived without the assistance of a large network of relatives and friends who provided food, clothing, and books on regular occasions.

Around 1814, Peter "became very much dissatisfied" with life in Mercer County, perhaps because he and his wife had lost two of their four children, and "began to look about for a State of Society where I would like to rais my children." His household then moved to a 197-acre farm near New Providence, Kentucky, but he continued to look farther afield. With several friends, he traveled to Missouri in 1816. While Peter concluded that Missouri land was better, he decided not to move. His reason: he "could not think of moving out with my family to a new and unsettled region where they would not for a long time be any prospect of good Society." In other words, as his autobiography makes clear, his wife's desire to be near people overruled his preference for new land.

Over the next few years, several relatives and friends of the Van Arsdales moved across the Ohio to Indiana. Peter and his wife visited her brother's family in Switzerland County in the fall of 1819. Two years later, still coveting land and increasingly disgusted by slavery, Peter accompanied "a number" of friends and relatives to an advertised sale at Indianapolis. Disappointed there, he and a half-dozen others explored the Wabash Valley. On the way home, they stayed "a few days" with "some Relatives and acquaintenances" in Dubois County. The Van Arsdales did not move in 1821. They came much closer to doing so in 1823. In that year, Peter's brother-in-law, Isaac Smock, proposed to relocate his household in central Indiana. The Van Arsdales, who had hesitated before because of their fear of social isolation, decided to go with them. Peter explained that their motivation had more to do with relationships than with money. "As we had been raisd together, and had been long very intimate, and he had Married my wifes younger sister and as our wives were very much attatched to each other, we all found that it would be very hard to separate." In May, Peter, Isaac, and his son John went to the Brookville land office, got "a plat of the Country," investigated and chose some land for adjoining farms, and returned to Brookville "to make the entries." The whole business took only three or four weeks.

The sudden death of another brother-in-law prevented the Van Arsdales from moving when the Smocks did; Peter had to act as guardian of his son and administrator of his estate. Still, they visited their relatives in Indiana in 1824 and the Smocks came to see them in 1825. The following year, Peter, his father-in-law, and several other men traveled through southern Indiana visiting people. The Van Arsdales had decided against moving across the river, in large part because of reports from relatives of sickness and the difficulty of farming heavily timbered, hilly soil. In 1829, Mrs. Van Arsdale visited the Smocks on her own. Again they contemplated migration and again decided against it. As before, Peter seemed much more eager than his wife. Despite his role as head of the household, however, he allowed her veto power over any move. He "had determined not to move to any place where she would be dissatisfied."

When the Van Arsdales finally did leave Kentucky, it was for a new home in Illinois. The immediate cause of their migration was neither economic conditions nor slavery. Rather, it was the absence of the people who had made it difficult for them to move in the first place. By 1832, most of their friends and relatives were gone, thus "greatly weaning or loosing our attatchments to the neighbourhood." They finally departed in 1836. From the perspective provided by Peter Van Arsdale's autobiography, migration seems a much more ambiguous, murky business than it does at the level of statistics. A variety of factors, ranging from marital negotiations to family ties to religious beliefs, influenced the decision. The Van Arsdales' move followed two decades of debate.

The African Americans who came to Indiana from Kentucky and other slave states were less conflicted about the move but faced far greater obstacles than the quality of the soil and the loss of friends. Despite the prohibition of slavery in the 1816 constitution, the government of Indiana made it difficult for free blacks to settle in the state. An 1831 statute required them to register with county officials and to post a bond. The 1851 constitution simply excluded them altogether. Still, the lure of a free state and land was strong. Between 1820 and 1860, the African American population rose from 1,420 to 11,428, or about 1 percent of the total in both cases.

Thanks to Emma Lou Thornbrough's remarkable work, *The Negro in Indiana*, we know a great deal about these black pioneers. In many ways, they were typical settlers. Of the 2,150 men listed in the 1850 census, 976 were farmers; in addition, Thornbrough believes that many of the 720 who were listed as laborers worked on farms. The first black purchaser of land, according to Thornbrough, was named Spencer; he bought a quarter section in Wayne County in July 1813. Members of the Alexander family acquired nearly 2,000 acres in Randolph County in the 1830s and 1840s, and two men named Benson purchased 200 acres. In Hamilton County, the Roberts family owned land; in Gibson, the Lyles; in Grant, the Weavers. According to the English traveler E. S. Abdy, approximately eleven black families were living near Madison in the early

271

THE
END
OF
THE
FRONTIER,
1816–1850

1830s. The men had cleared land and owned animals. One farmer explained to Abdy that he had secured his freedom by paying his master $100 a year for seven years. He then worked his farm until he had made enough money to buy the freedom of his wife and children. Abdy reported his eighty-acre farm was now worth $700. Thornbrough's study of census records suggests that these were far from atypical cases. While only a few black men owned farms, many others worked as tenant farmers. Including town lots as well as farms, the 1850 census records revealed that 671 African Americans owned real estate valued at $421,755. Given a total population of over 11,000, this is a small percentage. Although Thornbrough hardly minimizes the significance of this figure, she reminds us that when women and children are accounted for, approximately one-quarter of black households had property of some kind.

As important as the attraction of property was, social and family considerations affected black immigrants as much or more than whites. African Americans tended to settle in areas that they knew were more congenial than others. Whereas Knox County had had the greatest number of blacks in the Indiana Territory (because of the existence of de facto slavery), Wayne, Randolph, and Rush counties had large black populations, largely because of the presence of Quakers. Work prospects and proximity to Kentucky also attracted African American settlers to counties along the Ohio River between Madison and Louisville. Yet, wherever they lived, blacks, like whites, remained intensely committed to the preservation of their households. Stories of men working to free other members of their family were common. So, too, was the tendency to settle with or near relatives and friends. So important was the Kersey family, consisting of fugitive slaves from Georgia, in Vernon Township in Jennings County that some people began to refer to the area as "Africa."

Whether black or white, the dominance of southern households in Indiana was hardly unique among the states north of the Ohio River. Still, Indiana was far more southern than its neighbors. Over the course of the first half of the nineteenth century, Ohio and Illinois attracted more immigrants from the Northeast and Europe than did Indiana. This divergence may have occurred because swamps and sand dunes, not to mention Michigan, limited access to

Indiana from the Great Lakes, or because of the lack of a great urban center like Cincinnati. In any case, there was far less north-to-south migration than the reverse. When twentieth-century wags suggested that "Kentucky had taken Indiana without firing a shot," they were essentially speaking the truth. In 1850, Indiana had the smallest percentage of Yankee-born settlers (that is, persons from New England and the middle Atlantic states) of the five states of the Old Northwest. They constituted only 8.8 percent of the total population, compared with 17.4 percent in Illinois, 45.2 percent in Michigan, 18.9 percent in Ohio, and 35.0 percent in Wisconsin. The average for the Old Northwest as a whole was 19.8 percent.

The preference of many southern households for life in the Knobs and away from water confounded travelers. For people interested in commercial development, it made no sense to live so far from the only reasonable mode of transportation. Apparently, however, many people were less interested in access to markets than they were in familiar territory. Farms in the Knobs allowed for some continuity with life in the areas from which many people had come, that is, Kentucky and the western parts of Pennsylvania, Virginia, and the Carolinas. Forests provided excellent opportunities for hunting and tracking fresh meat and a ready source of timber for cabins, fences, and fuel. The traveler David Thomas noted while riding along the Wabash in the summer of 1816 that it was easy to underestimate the population of the region because wood "is an object of such importance to the farmer, that none is yet found willing to forego that convenience, and to seat himself out in the prairie."

Hilly country also satisfied requirements that may seem peculiar to late twentieth-century Americans who would prize the bottom-lands along rivers, not to mention urban lots, much more highly. The highlands offered a multitude of freshwater springs, superb drainage, and little in the way of fevers and diseases that people quite rightly associated with life in the muggy, well-traveled, and relatively crowded wetlands along the rivers. Lacking the technology of the modern world, settlers tended to avoid marshy land as dangerous and unproductive. Travelers regularly denounced these early settlers as simple, dirty, careless, and lazy. No doubt their characterizations were sometimes on the mark. But it also seems true that many people simply were comfortable with their lives. In

273

THE
END
OF
THE
FRONTIER,
1816–1850

time-honored tradition, men and women kept their households together by growing corn and beans, raising hogs, and having as many children as possible. So great was the number of migrants and travelers in the 1810s and 1820s that many households had no farther to look for a market than their own front door.

These settlers were hardly isolated and self-sufficient, but they were less involved in a web of market relationships than people in the scores of little towns that appeared along the rivers and creeks of Indiana. By the 1820s, important older urban centers such as Vincennes and Jeffersonville had been joined by Brookville, Centerville, and Richmond in the Whitewater Valley; Madison, Vevay, New Albany, and Evansville along the Ohio; Terre Haute on the Wabash; and Corydon, Bloomington, and Indianapolis in the interior. The last, of course, was the new state capital, authorized by the legislature in order to locate the seat of government at the exact center of Indiana and, more important, to end the constant rivalry for the right to welcome the General Assembly every year.

According to Timothy Flint, perhaps the most knowledgeable and authoritative writer on the Ohio and Mississippi valleys in the early nineteenth century, no state had shown "a greater propensity for town making" than Indiana. "In no part of the world," wrote Flint in 1826, "has the art of trumpeting, and lauding the advantages, conveniences and future prospects, of the town to be sold, been carried to greater perfection. To mention, in detail, all the villages, that have really attained some degree of consequence, would only furnish a barren catalogue of names."

The founders of all these places had incredibly high hopes for their futures. Americans were sensitive to the point of irritation about urban prospects. There was simply too much money to be made from the sale of lots and the development of commerce to have any doubts. Boosterism was rampant. The thoughtful David Thomas recorded that when his traveling companion asked a delegate to the constitutional convention how long the *"little town"* of Madison "had been laid out," the man, "assuming all the majesty of republican greatness, . . . exclaimed 'I hope you don't call this a *little town.'*" Thomas drolly remarked in his diary that in fact his "friend had seen some cities, if not characters rather greater." Nonetheless, he thought Madison "a thriving place" with a promising future.

Other towns also did well. In the 1817 *Western Gazetteer*, Samuel R. Brown quoted extensively from B. F. Morris, the editor of *The Plain Dealer*, to puff his hometown of Brookville on the Whitewater. Laid out in 1811, the place was apparently prospering in the aftermath of war. Morris reported it had close to eighty mostly frame buildings, not including "shops, stables, and out houses." More specifically, there were "one grist mill and two saw mills, two fulling mills, three carding machines, one printing office, one silversmith, two saddlers, two cabinet makers, one hatter, two taylors, four boot and shoemakers, two tanners and curriers, one chairmaker, one cooper, five taverns and seven stores." But there was more, including "a jail, a market house, and a handsome brick court house nearly finished."

Farther north lay Centerville and Richmond, the two giants of Wayne County, vying for preeminence in the second quarter of the nineteenth century. Centerville had the early advantage; it was the seat of county government. By the 1840s, the place had close to 1,000 residents and manufacturing investments totaling some $87,000. Richmond, however, was more than double that size (2,070 people), in large part because it was on the river. As early as 1824, the Richmond *Public Leger* had informed the world that the town had "453 inhabitants, principally mechanics." It, too, had a list of business concerns: eight dry goods stores, three taverns, a post office, a printing office, seven blacksmiths, four hatters, four cabinetmakers, six shoemakers, three tailors, three coopers, three potters, one gunsmith, one saddler, one pumpmaker, one bakeshop, a steam distillery, and hordes of carpenters, brick and stone masons, plasterers, etc. Finally, saving the best for last, the breathless editor proudly announced that "of professional men there are but two—physicians; of lawyers we have NOT ONE, although every other town in the state abounds with them." That, of course, had less to do with the state of society than the fact that the courthouse was in Centerville. After a week's respite, the industrious editor returned with enthusiasm to his calling, listing occupations—a silversmith, a painter—and businesses—three tanning yards, a brewery—as if they were the contents of a treasure box.

🏳 275

The
End
of
The
Frontier,
1816–1850

These descriptions of Brookville and Richmond were similar to those of every place with an editor or enterprising entrepreneur. In all cases, they were little more than advertisements, designed to attract paying customers in the form of new settlers. In fact, what is striking is how thoroughly they described marketplaces, how eagerly they coveted commerce. Unlike the people who settled in the Knobs and away from major waterways, the residents of these fledgling (I will not use "little") towns were interested in specialization, exchange, and communication with distant places. They did not want to be lost in the woods. They wanted to be noticed. They wanted people to come to them. They wanted to be linked together with the rest of the United States.

The advantages were clear—prosperity, refinement, stimulation; more affluent townspeople would live in frame or brick houses, hire servants, eat off china, read newspapers, travel to Cincinnati, New Orleans, even Philadelphia, hang portraits of themselves and their children in well-appointed parlors. But so too were the disadvantages—diseases that came from mosquitoes and travelers (thus the cholera outbreaks of the early 1830s), increasing distance between working- and middle-class peoples, and the dirt and grime that accompanied trade.

Depending on one's perspective, the tragedy or glory of nineteenth-century Indiana was that none of these little towns ever became a big city. In 1840, only Madison, New Albany, and Indianapolis qualified as urban centers with populations in excess of 2,500. By 1850, Fort Wayne, Lafayette, Terre Haute, Evansville, and Lawrenceburg had joined them. Still, the largest towns had just over 8,000 citizens. True, they acquired a local economic and cultural hegemony; their hinterland was their county; they dominated a small area. But the big cities of Indiana were not in Indiana. For the Whitewater Valley and southeastern parts of the state, the urban center was Cincinnati, Ohio, a metropolis with tens of thousands of people by the 1830s. For the south, even the lower Wabash Valley, the center was Louisville, Kentucky (and, to some extent, New Orleans). Later, Chicago, Illinois, would dominate the northern regions of the state. Whatever the reason—geography, timing, politics, the lack of a central major north-south river—Indiana became and

1850
Fort Wayne
2,500+

remained largely a state of farms and small towns until the second half of the twentieth century.

The Culture of Capitalism

Despite the lack of a major urban center, Indiana was integrated into national and international economic structures by the middle of the nineteenth century. Residents of the Wabash Valley had been involved in market transactions with the rest of the world since the early eighteenth century. But nineteenth-century integration was far more encompassing. Indians and traders had been consumers and producers at the end of a fragile chain of commerce; the world of the marketplace affected but did not completely dominate their lives. Their relationship was ambivalent and ambiguous. By the early nineteenth century, this was no longer the case for many citizens. Men were now falling all over themselves to do more than forge links with distant markets; they wanted to turn Indiana into a marketplace. Customers were not in New Orleans or Paris; they were traveling down rivers or across roads or living somewhere nearby.

Historians John Lauritz Larson and David G. Vanderstel have detailed this transformation in their study of the life of William Conner, an Indian trader who became a local businessman. Conner and his brother, John, arrived in the White River valley (near Noblesville) at the beginning of the nineteenth century. Both married Delaware women. They made their living as middlemen, exchanging iron goods, blankets, jewelry, whiskey, and gunpowder for Indian furs and pelts and then trading the latter for more finished goods. Operating between Indian and American society, William Conner became an indispensable figure in treaty negotiations. When, in keeping with the provisions of the 1818 Treaty of St. Marys, the Delaware left the White River valley in the early 1820s, Conner chose not to accompany his wife and children. Rather, he quickly adjusted to a changing environment. Three months after his first wife's departure in 1820, he married seventeen-year-old Elizabeth Chapman. He secured title to ample amounts of prime soil, began to grow wheat, rye, and corn, and started a store to sell imported goods to travelers and new settlers. He opened a distillery in 1825 and ran a mill his brother had established in 1824. More than

🐚 **277**

THE
END
OF
THE
FRONTIER,
1816–1850

a farmer or a merchant, William Conner was also a produce vendor, import-export jobber, retailer, wholesaler, credit agent, and money-lender. As the most important economic resource in the region, he was also immensely powerful in political and social matters. According to Larson and Vanderstel, Conner's "life was governed most of all by the free pursuit of private gain." As significant, his economic success made him a patriarch until his death in 1855. William Conner's career exemplified the transformation of the Indiana economy in the early nineteenth century.

To some extent, this new world of commerce grew along the lines established in the 1700s. The principal port for the crops and products of Indiana farmers remained New Orleans and the principal transportation routes the Wabash and Ohio rivers. But there were also differences. Whereas eighteenth-century exports had consisted largely of furs and skins, nineteenth-century exports were mostly agricultural products. Most important was corn, a ubiquitous crop. Farmers and merchants shipped corn as corn; they also sent it as meal, as hogs, and as whiskey. Indianans also produced wheat (usually in the form of flour), cattle, and a variety of other grains and animals for the market.

According to the historian Logan Esarey, the *Western Sun* reported that "152 flatboats passed Vincennes bound for New Orleans" in the spring of 1826; they contained 250,000 bushels of corn, 100,000 barrels of pork, 10,000 hams, 2,500 live cattle, 10,000 pounds of beeswax, plus quantities of venison, oats, meal, and chicken. Three years later, Indiana Canal commissioners "estimated the annual trade of the Wabash at 7,000 barrels of salt, 3,000 barrels of whisky, at Terre Haute alone; 3,000 barrels of pork from Terre Haute, 10,000 barrels from the whole valley, and 450 tons of dry goods."

The difficulties (and costs) of transporting these products, combined with time constraints imposed by fears of spoilage, put a premium on processing them into more manageable forms. In particular, farmers wanted mills (to grind corn and wheat) and slaughterhouses (to pack pork and beef). They also required a great many ancillary services of the kind provided by blacksmiths, tanners, and general merchants. In other words, the nature of the primary products of the Old Northwest demanded some degree of economic specialization and encouraged the growth of small towns where specialists could congregate. Places that were at the intersection of a sizable hinterland, a variety of processors and services, and easy access to navigable water tended to thrive. At least, the price of their lots rose temporarily.

The most obvious example of a town that bloomed as a transporting and processing center is Cincinnati. Less important but nonetheless revealing of the dynamics of urban and commercial growth is Madison. Founded in December 1810, the town was little more than a collection of a few houses on the north bank of the Ohio River for the first decade of its existence. In the late teens, with a population of around 150 people, it had no public landing; trees continued to obscure the town from the potential customers who were coming down the Ohio. Still, Madison was a commercial center of sorts. The three taverns and two general stores it had in the summer of 1811 demonstrate the degree to which its trade focused on the river. Its target customers were travelers and migrants. The village also offered the services of two blacksmiths, a brickmaker, and a stonemason for those with more permanent interests, but one doubts that they were as busy as the tavern keepers.

By 1825, Madison's population had swelled to a thousand people. It had over a dozen brick buildings. The fourteen dry goods stores, ten groceries, market house, and two taverns no doubt still found most of their customers among river travelers. Now, however, Madison had other businesses designed to attract trade from residents of the surrounding countryside. They included two cotton spinning factories, a wool-carding establishment, two oil mills, a rope factory, a grist mill, a steam mill, and a printing office (home of the *Indiana Republican*). Other symbols of permanence were the two churches and an academy. Madison no longer seemed quite so transitory. Indeed, its economic history shows the shift in Indiana's economic structures as the town became more involved in specialized businesses and trade.

By the 1830s, as the historian Donald T. Zimmer has explained, Madison was a lively commercial center. Farmers brought corn, wheat, and pork to the town and shipped them out from one of its several wharves to New Orleans and beyond. In 1832, two entrepreneurs opened a five-story stone and wooden mill; inside were four

📣 **279**

THE
END
OF
THE
FRONTIER,
1816–1850

pairs of steam-operated mill stones. With the addition of two similar mills, Madison was able to grind around 1,800 bushels of wheat per day by the 1840s. The town had been able to offer the services of some kind of slaughterhouse as early as the late teens. A decade later, both slaughtering and packing were available. In 1836, 15,000 hogs were killed and packed; in 1846, 64,000; and in the early 1850s, 120,000. Other industries also prospered, including breweries, lard renderers, candle and soap makers, bristle and curled brush makers, cooperage and tanning factories, steamboat construction, furniture factories, lumber mills, and an iron foundry.

Madison's commerce involved imports as well as exports. Its early merchants had traveled to Baltimore and Pittsburgh for goods to sell, bringing back cloth, glass, china, books, buttons, hats, spices, and other hard-to-acquire items. By the 1830s, steamboats brought such things directly to the wharves of the town from New Orleans as well as Pittsburgh. The *Indiana Gazetteer* claimed that in March and April 1833 alone, around $120,000 worth of merchandise arrived in Madison. Much of this was dispersed to farmers in the surrounding area, but a considerable amount was sold to the families of merchants and professionals who lived in brick and Greek Revival mansions built on a foundation of commercial prosperity. And some went to the laboring people of Madison, the women and men who worked in the mills and along the wharves. In places like Madison and Indianapolis, black people were an important part of the population; they not only worked as laborers but also as skilled artisans, barbers, seamstresses, and domestic servants.

Madison, with a population of 8,000 in the early 1850s, was not simply linked to the world of market capitalism; it was the embodiment of a market town. Within a few years, the coming of the railroad would reduce the commercial importance of the Ohio River and bring Madison's growth to a halt. But in the first half of the nineteenth century, Madison had all the elements necessary for success in a world of commercial capitalism.

Of these elements, none was more central than banks. There were three of them in Madison in the 1850s, plus several insurance companies. Banks were the engine of commerce. They provided credit for men interested in buying land or building mills; their notes served to make commercial exchange easier and safer. In an era in which the United States had no official currency, bank notes were the most reliable means of transferring value from one person to another. They served to increase the amount of capital available to finance economic development and generally support entrepreneurship.

There had been two official banks in the Indiana Territory. The legislature had chartered the Vincennes Bank and the Farmer's and Mechanic's Bank of Madison in 1814. They were to run for two decades, limit interest on loans to 6 percent, pay specie on all notes, and loan money to the territorial government. An act passed the next year allowed private individuals to issue notes, if the names of the bankers appeared on the scrip. Two such private banks were operating in 1816—one in Brookville and one in Vincennes. The General Assembly affirmed their right to act as banks in 1818. More important, it transformed the Vincennes Bank into the State Bank in January 1817. The charter of this institution ran for twenty-one years. It was to be capitalized at $1,500,000. Fourteen branches were planned, but only three opened—in Brookville, Corydon, and Vincennes. The Farmer's and Mechanic's Bank in Madison simply refused to participate.

As important as these banks were to the land business and economic development of Indiana, they all suffered greatly as a result of the Panic of 1819. The contraction of the money supply led by the Second Bank of the United States meant hard times for the commercial people of Indiana. Banks in Madison and Vincennes were forced to suspend the issuing of its notes. Some of the problems were the result of ignorance, some of fraud. But mostly the ambitious entrepreneurs and developers who were likely to support banks had been wildly overconfident about them. The suspension of payments along with the federal government's refusal to deposit land office receipts after 1820 ruined the reputation of the State Bank in Vincennes. After months of controversy, the institution went out of business. As significant was the foundation of a widespread sense of distrust in banks; with good reason, many people saw them as "monsters" that caught them in a tangle of dependence and largely benefited the wealthy and powerful.

The absence of state-chartered banks meant that the citizens of Indiana remained heavily dependent on the branches of the Bank of

📯 281

THE
END
OF
THE
FRONTIER,
1816–1850

the United States in Cincinnati and Louisville. Despite the persistence of widespread suspicions, resentment over out-of-state influence and good economic times in the early 1830s gave birth to a campaign for another state bank. The General Assembly created the second State Bank of Indiana in 1834, and it enjoyed a monopoly on banking in the state until 1852. Better managed than the first, the second bank gave considerable independence to the officers of the initial ten branches (Lawrenceburg, Madison, New Albany, Evansville, Vincennes, Bedford, Terre Haute, Indianapolis, Richmond, and Lafayette), most of whom were local notables. With minor modifications, the bank lasted until the expiration of its charter in 1857. At that time, it had a surplus of over a million dollars and was paying annual dividends of 11 to 22 percent.

Like banks in all the other states of the Old Northwest in the second quarter of the nineteenth century, banks in Indiana were at the center of political controversy. Members of the Whig party, which emerged in the 1830s, tended to support the idea of a state-regulated banking system, while the views of Jacksonian Democrats ranged from toleration of a state bank to antipathy to banks altogether. The problem was that what some people saw as beneficial means to prosperity and development, others viewed as tyrannical impediments to the liberty of a free people. Banks were stark evidence of Indiana's integration into a national, indeed international, banking system. Men who were interested in entrepreneurial enterprise, urban development, and the place of Indiana in the larger world—merchants and professionals—largely welcomed this development. But men who were interested in the preservation of the status quo, the protection of local prerogatives, and farming generally worried about it. For good or ill, however, the coming of banks meant the triumph of a capitalist economy. The yelps of Indianans at the fluctuations of the market only testified to how much it had come to dominate their lives.

The Politics of Improvement

Indiana's economic structures did not evolve simply in the uncoordinated actions of thousands of people. While the vast majority of the women and men concentrated on feeding themselves and their households, some men actively sought to direct the development of the region. Their fundamental motives were to make money and boost the interests of their friends. To achieve their goals they had to persuade frequently reluctant people to delay immediate gratification in order to invest in the unrealized potential of the future. In other words, they had to convince them to pay taxes for canals and schools whose material and social benefits seemed distant and vague.

This question of improvements—whether and, if so, how and where and by what means, government should direct the construction of roads, canals, and public schools—dominated political discourse at all levels. Hamlets contended for county courthouses, towns fought to have roads or canals pass by or through them, state legislators wrangled over whose region would benefit from government spending and worked to make Indiana competitive with Ohio and Illinois, and national representatives lobbied to ensure that Indiana got its fair share of federal dollars. Virtually every leading politician in Indiana in the second quarter of the nineteenth century called for internal improvements. Pleas for roads, canals, and public education took up considerable space in governors' inaugural addresses and congressmen's letters to their constituents. The most popular schemes were for a canal linking Lake Erie and the Ohio River (growing out of a simpler plan to negotiate the portage between the Wabash and the Maumee), another canal in the Whitewater valley, the National Road running across the middle of the state, and a north-south road.

William Hendricks, who began his career as a Jonathan Jennings associate and then served as Indiana's only congressman from 1816 to 1822, governor from 1822 to 1825, and United States senator from 1825 to 1837, devoted most of his public life to government-sponsored improvements. While in the Senate, Hendricks was the chairman of the Committee on Roads and Canals. Willing to support improvements in transportation elsewhere in the United States, Hendricks expected other politicians to return the favor when it was Indiana's turn.

The supporters of internal improvements used the language of economic development and social progress when advocating their construction. According to Governor Jennings's December 1818 message to the legislature,

☙ 283

THE
END
OF
THE
FRONTIER,
1816–1850

Roads and canals are calculated to afford facilities to the commercial transactions connected with the exports and imports of the country. . . . They enhance the value of the soil by affording to the agriculturalist the means of deriving greater grain from its cultivation with an equal proportion of labor, thereby presenting stronger inducements to industry and enterprize, and at the same time by various excitements invite to a more general intercourse between the citizens. . . .

In a larger sense, Jennings and Hendricks believed in what the latter called "the fostering hand of government" in his 1822 inaugural address. That is, they endorsed the idea of a relatively activist government, one that would take the lead in removing physical obstacles to the navigation of rivers, establishing and supporting state libraries and educational systems, and regulating the activities of banks. To achieve prosperity, wrote Hendricks to the legislature in 1825,

it only remains for us to improve the means within our power, our roads and the great highways to the markets as they are. It is our business to increase facilities of intercourse with each other, and with the neighbouring states; to make our internal and municipal regulations as perfect as possible; to encourage industry; and above all to economise our expenditures and lessen as much as possible at all times, the public burdens upon the people.

As always in American politics, it was the last point that was the rub. People had few objections to an activist state or federal government as long as they did not have to pay much to support it and as long as they perceived its actions as equitable. Hendricks could dream of a canal that would unite Lake Erie and the Ohio River, thus completing "the great northern avenue of commerce to the ocean and the lakes," uniting New York and New Orleans. But how to pay for it? How to win the support of Indianans who would not be directly affected by it? The answer in the 1820s largely lay with the national government.

When Indiana became a state, Governor Jennings had hoped to raise money for a canal around the Falls of the Ohio and to build some roads from the 3 percent of net proceeds from public land sales granted to Indiana upon its admission to the Union. In the first seven years of statehood, however, this fund amounted to just $71,950.08, hardly enough to support a great scheme of internal improvements, which would cost hundreds of thousands of dollars.

Despite the rhetoric of improvement, the representatives of the people of Indiana were unwilling to assess the necessary taxes, particularly in the midst of the economic depression created by the Panic of 1819. In December 1821, the General Assembly called for the construction of over twenty-four roads within the state, but little was done about it. When a canal finally bypassed the Falls of the Ohio in the late 1820s, it did so on the Kentucky side of the river.

The taxes levied on Indianans were small and were collected irregularly. They included three levels of taxation on the three classes of land; on first-class land, the rate fluctuated from $1.00 for every hundred acres in 1817 to $1.50 in 1821 to 80 cents in 1831. There was also a poll tax; 50 cents in 1822, it fell to 37.5 cents by 1827. These and other levies raised $14,717 in 1817. Expenses, however, totaled $19,247, including $17,000 for salaries. In 1827, Indiana took in approximately $33,000 in taxes and spent $33,208. It owed $18,700. According to the *Western Sun*, even these low amounts were difficult to collect. The fact that forty-four of forty-eight counties were behind in their payments in 1823 was not considered extraordinary.

In this environment, indefatigable Indiana developers had no choice but to lobby the national Congress for land grants that would make the construction of canals and roads more economically feasible. In 1824, Congress granted 621 acres between the Maumee and the Wabash. Two years later, it authorized surveys to determine whether it was realistic to construct Indiana canals. Meanwhile, Governor James Brown Ray, a colorful and volatile figure who succeeded William Hendricks as chief executive in 1825 and was a strong advocate of railroads, reaffirmed the commitment to an economical plan of internal improvements. Ray's language demonstrated the degree to which the world of the Wabash had changed in a century. For decades, rivers had dictated much of people's lives; now Indianans looked to control and even to ignore them. According to Ray, "The rough appearances of nature must be overcome, and made to yield to human enterprize. Our waters must be imprisoned in new channels, and made to subserve the essential purposes of commerce." There could be no more emphatic or succinct statement of American purposes in transforming Indiana.

In March 1827, Congress laid the foundation for a north-south canal with a donation of a strip of 527,271.24 acres, five miles wide

⯅ 285

THE
END
OF
THE
FRONTIER,
1816–1850

and 160 miles long from the mouth of the Auglaize on the Maumee to the mouth of the Tippecanoe on the Wabash. The following January, the anxious legislature, desiring to exploit a gift estimated to be worth $1,250,000, accepted the cession and authorized a canal to link the waters of the Maumee and the Wabash. But there were still further delays. And it was not until the more prosperous years of the 1830s that work actually began. Ground was broken at Fort Wayne on February 22, 1832, and a canal opened as far as Huntington by July 4, 1835. Amidst an outpouring of enthusiasm for canals, their supporters were easily elected to the legislature, and in the 1835–1836 session they enacted a "Mammoth" Internal Improvement Bill.

In addition to providing for roads and railroads, this bill created an extensive canal system for Indiana. It called for extending the Wabash and Erie to Terre Haute. As important, there were to be two new canals. The first, in the southeast, would realize a decades-old dream of a Whitewater Canal, running from Cambridge City to Lawrenceburg through Brookville. The second, called the Central Canal, was to go from the Wabash and Erie at a place to be determined near Peru to Evansville via Indianapolis. Only the Whitewater and the Wabash and Erie came to fruition. The latter was open to Lafayette in 1843, Terre Haute in 1848, and Evansville in 1853; the former was completed by a private company in the 1840s. A few miles of the Central were completed, primarily in Marion County.

The reasons for this unfinished business were many and have preoccupied several historians. Almost as suddenly as it had appeared, the general canal system collapsed under the weight of fraud, mismanagement, and an international economic crisis in the late 1830s. The state had borrowed heavily to fund the new system, and it could not pay off its debts on time. In 1841, Indiana owed $9,000,000 as a result of its internal improvements extravaganza and another $4,000,000 for other things. Not surprisingly, the 1851 state constitution prohibited future governments from going into debt except "to meet casual deficits in the revenue; to pay the interest on the State debt; to repel invasion, suppress insurrection, or, if hostilities be threatened, provide for the public defense."

Canals were the most expensive and controversial of internal improvements. Perhaps more important was the establishment of roads. They were largely financed by the 3 percent fund (which had raised $224,464 by 1835) and local assessments. In 1836, a major north-south road from South Bend to Logansport and on to Greensburg and Madison opened after several years of construction and expenditures of over $200,000. One hundred feet wide and 265 miles long, the partially graded highway was passable about eight months of the year. Other roads had already been laid out, including one from Indianapolis to Fort Wayne, another from Vincennes to Indianapolis, and yet another from New Albany to Bloomington with legs to Wabash and Indianapolis.

Unquestionably the most important highway was the National Road. Authorized by Congress in 1806, it was to run from Cumberland, Maryland, to Wheeling, Virginia, then across central Ohio, Indiana, and Illinois. Constitutional scruples, lack of money, and political objections slowed down the process, and surveyors did not reach Indiana until 1826. As late as 1832, the road was open only to Columbus, Ohio. But eventually the coming of what people later called "the old pike" created great excitement along its route from Richmond to Terre Haute via Indianapolis.

In the first stages, the removal of stumps and the erection of bridges across the White and Wabash rivers meant at least temporary work for some men. Meanwhile, eager entrepreneurs started the towns of Cambridge City, Greenfield, Knightstown, Plainfield, Belleville, Stilesville, Putnamville, and Harmony to take advantage of the highway's commercial possibilities. The price of lots in Centerville and Richmond skyrocketed. Once the National Road was open, tavern keepers and businessmen rushed to offer services and goods to people traveling in their own coaches or by one of the dozen stage lines, to the wagoners who carried the heavy volume of freight, and to the men delivering the mail. By the 1840s, many towns had several taverns and at least one wagon house. The growth of these establishments was such that in 1832 the legislature required those who wished to sell liquor to maintain certain minimum standards: posted rates, good stabling, and at least one spare room with two beds.

Contemporaries thought the road a marvel. It seemed to them to be perpetually in use. Memories of fine horses, painted coaches, and elegant travelers lingered for a long time in the minds of resi-

287

THE
END
OF
THE
FRONTIER,
1816–1850

dents of central Indiana. Benjamin S. Parker recalled the National Road in a romantic haze: "We could hear the driver playing his bugle as he approached the little town that lay just beyond us, and it all seemed too grand fine to be other than a dream." The historian Logan Esarey, while prosaically noting that the highway demonstrated the value of the national government, was also swept up in the spirit. "For months at a time," he wrote, "there was no moment in the daytime when a family wagon was not in sight. At night the road appeared like the picket line of an army."

Historians like to dwell on the dramatic failure of the canal and the road-building schemes. And with good reason. The easily caricatured fiascoes of the 1830s left in their wake a profound resistance to direct government intervention in economic development. Private companies finished much of the National Road, and corporations, rather than the state, would build the railroads in Indiana. Still, when the railroads came, they simply put into place the relatively inexpensive and efficient system of transportation and communication which developers had been seeking for years.

In the end, despite years of internal improvement schemes, Indiana remained more rural and less economically developed than most of the other states north of the Ohio River. The improvements in transportation reduced but did not overcome its reputation as a relatively inaccessible and provincial place.

Whose Millennium?

Ironically, as enthusiasm for state-supported internal improvements waned, support for a public school system grew. In 1846, Wabash College professor Caleb Mills addressed an open (but anonymous) letter to the Indiana General Assembly demanding the adoption of a tax-based system of free common schools. Mills was a Presbyterian minister and a native of New England who had come to Indiana in 1833 as a missionary for the American Sunday School Union. Failing to get a satisfactory response, Mills sent another letter in 1847. The legislature, bowing to pressure from Mills and other activists, weaseled out of a decision by agreeing to submit the question to voters in an 1848 referendum. The question passed by a margin of 78,523 to 61,887; 56 percent of voters endorsed a free school system supported by public taxes. A reluctant legislature responded with a vague law in 1849. It took another referendum and three more years of lobbying before the legislature created a system of free schools. Two years later, in 1854, the Indiana Supreme Court declared that it was unconstitutional to levy a property tax for the support of common schools—a decision not reversed until 1867.

Why was there such strong opposition from those in power? When traveling across northern Indiana in 1845, the Presbyterian minister Henry Ward Beecher offered an answer while complaining about the poor quality of the roads.

> Churches, Schoolhouses and *good roads*, are three infallible marks of *public* spirit. The common excuse, that in a new country there is no time to make roads, will be admissible when less time is wasted in towns, in political soldiering, in lounging and resting at home. We think that there is in the State rather a want of *public spirit*, than of men or time to make good roads.

According to Beecher and others like him, the issue was not simply a question of money. It was also a question of character. By the 1830s, some people were beginning to refer to the citizens of Indiana as "Hoosiers." The clear implication of the term was that they were largely unrefined country folk, lacking both genteel manners and progressive temperament.

Since historians have largely pieced together the history of Indiana from the writings of people such as Caleb Mills, it has proved difficult to avoid mimicking their prejudices. Almost without thinking about it, we accept the idea that the opponents of a tax-supported public school system or canals or banks were backward people. In so doing, however, we accept the assumptions of developers and reformers. We agree with their definition of progress, their sense of what was best for Indiana and its citizens. To be fair to all people, we might try seeing the struggles over schools and reform not as a contest between civilization and barbarism, enlightened educators and backwoods hicks, but as evidence of legitimate disagreement over what kind of society people wanted to nurture in Indiana.

Professionals, urban dwellers, settlers from the northeastern region of the United States, free blacks, Quakers, and Presbyterians

☛ 289

THE
END
OF
THE
FRONTIER,
1816–1850

tended to be the strongest supporters of internal improvements and public education. Beecher and Mills both fit the profile. Whigs in politics, they believed in the importance of government stepping forward to improve social as well as economic structures. Presbyterian ministers by training, they endorsed the idea that certain people had to step forward to lead unwilling people to a more perfect world. The challenge was to help deeply flawed human beings overcome their natural inclination to sin and weakness and become useful citizens. The solution was to structure society so as to channel and direct popular interests in productive ways.

Supporters of improvements tended to have a low opinion of human nature. They regularly denounced drinking alcohol, swearing, devoting more time to recreation than work, fighting, and gambling. Sloth and egoism were the parents of poor individual character. In other words, the reformers sounded very much like British officers writing about the French in the 1760s and the Federalists complaining about settlers in the 1790s. There were a lot of similarities. But there were also critical differences. Persons like Beecher believed that human beings must choose to be good people and that the choice had to be internal rather than external. In other words, they did not dismiss other people as irredeemable nor put their faith in coercion by governments or armies. Quite the contrary. Reform would only take place—a secular millennium occur—if large numbers of Americans experienced a genuine and personal conversion. They had to decide themselves to become useful citizens. Certainly government and the better sort of people had the responsibility to create an environment that would encourage them to make the right choice, thus the need for public schools, public libraries, public lectures, and churches. Both secular and spiritual education were the foundation of an enlightened civilization.

More practically, a more specialized, integrated economy required certain skills of its workers. It needed people who could read and write, who could add and subtract, who had some knowledge of the world beyond their home, who knew history, to work as bankers, lawyers, teachers, doctors, clerks, insurance agents, and the like. An expanding world of strangers also required the inculcation of etiquette, rules by which people who barely knew each other could transact business at long distances. It was precisely this kind of information which was found in popular textbooks, most notably the famous McGuffey readers. Schools taught economic and social skills as much, if not more, than intellectual curiosity. They taught children how to behave in a particular kind of society, a society committed to commerce, gentility, industry, and integration with the rest of the world. It is hardly surprising that people such as free blacks who wanted to be fully accepted in Indiana society were strong supporters of education.

In essence, reformers such as Mills were telling Indianans that they had to adjust to a new world. Canals and banks not only served to link them more tightly to other regions of the United States; they also symbolized the growing interdependence of American society. Schools not only offered practical skills; they also were civic laboratories in which children would learn the social discipline that would make them better citizens as adults. The frontier was over. The time of conflict over the structures of Indiana was over. The place was now a state in the American Union, an integral part of an international capitalist marketplace, and its people had to behave accordingly. If the demands of this new world included taxes, then so be it. Paying taxes to support schools and canals was recognizing interdependence and honoring mutual obligations.

In many ways, Indiana did not measure up to these lofty goals in the mid-nineteenth century, especially in comparison with its neighbors. In 1840, an estimated one-seventh of Indianans could not read; in 1850, the proportion had reached one-fifth. In some southern counties—Jackson, Martin, Clay, and Dubois—barely 50 percent of the population was literate. Only one-third of children in the state attended school. Indianapolis did not have a free public school at all until 1853. As a result, Indiana ranked at the bottom of the free states in terms of literacy and means of popular education. Not coincidentally, it offered the lowest number of periodicals and newspapers of the states of the Old Northwest.

Meanwhile, Indianans did appear to spend a great deal of time drinking and playing. Samuel B. Judah, an 1827 visitor, observed that "whiskey is drunk like water." Although he had "seen fewer drunkards than" he had expected, "Men drink it by the quart & even the wealthy prefer it to any of the foreign liqours." If they did, they were hardly unusual in the United States. According to the

☙ 291

THE
END
OF
THE
FRONTIER,
1816–1850

historian William J. Rorabaugh, Americans were consuming alcohol at the highest rate in their history. Per capita consumption peaked at close to four gallons in 1830. But most of the imbibers were adult men. The American Temperance Society concluded that in the late 1820s the average male was drinking about half a pint of distilled spirits per day. About half the adult male population was supposedly drinking six ounces or more, thus consuming two-thirds of a national total of 72,000,000 gallons per year.

In his study of court records in Marion County, David J. Bodenhamer found plenty of anecdotal evidence to support the conclusion that Indianans did not always demonstrate the kind of character Beecher admired. Typical was the 1845 complaint of the *Indiana State Sentinel* in Indianapolis that "the moral influence of a dozen churches is not enough to check the vicious propensities of our population." Analysis of criminal statistics, on the other hand, suggested that matters were not really so bad. There were few serious or violent crimes, and prosecutions as a percentage of population did not increase between the 1820s and the 1850s. Bodenhamer's point is that the frontier was not really as lawless as American popular culture has suggested.

His evidence, however, suggests a couple of other significant conclusions. Bodenhamer shows that the "most frequently prosecuted" crimes were "two moral-order misdemeanors—gambling and violations of liquor laws." In addition, "prosecutions for immorality account for the bulge in crime after the mid-thirties." Indeed, "Moral-order offenses constituted over half of all criminal cases in the circuit court during the thirties and forties and almost half the criminal prosecutions in circuit and justice of the peace courts." Bodenhamer quite correctly ascribes this to a shift in values. The appearance of temperance societies in the 1830s reflected a growing interest in restraining drinking. So it was hardly surprising that an 1830 grand jury report condemned laws licensing taverns as "abettors of crime and immorality. They are nuisances. They rob the poor and break up families. . . . [And they are] one of the greatest evils that mars the peace and prosperity of our county."

In part, as Bodenhamer suggests, the emphasis on temperance was a reaction to the growing numbers of Irish and Germans in Marion County. But objections to drinking, gambling, and fighting were hardly limited to those against European immigrants. For years they had been the most common refrain of newspaper editors, ministers, and travelers. The behavior of the citizens of Madison during an 1831 mustering of the militia appalled Ludwig David von Schweinitz, a Moravian bishop. Political candidates "made speeches to the people and great excesses were committed. Although no drinks at all were served in respectable inns, I have rarely seen so many people drunk and nowhere so many brawls and rows, for the populace of Indiana develops a fearful rudeness on such occasions." Von Schweinitz was not alone. The historian R. Carlyle Buley quoted the editor of the Richmond *Public Leger* as complaining in 1825 that "intemperance has been called the national vice of Americans, and one is almost ready to acknowledge the correctness of the charge, from observing on election, muster and other public days, so many persons in a state of beastly intoxication." Intemperance was simply "the most brutalizing vice of which a man can be guilty."

Presbyterian ministers were particularly upset by the damage they believed alcoholism visited upon families. Occasionally, congregations publicly rejected drunken men. Others—such as the Salem and LaPorte churches in 1832—formally excluded those who would not take a pledge of abstinence. Despite the firm belief in the superior power of the father, Presbyterians were willing to allow women some redress from violent husbands. In 1846, the Sugar Creek church suspended Katherine Hadden for seeking a divorce on the grounds of abuse. The Indianapolis presbytery affirmed the subordinate position of a wife but also allowed the divorce if Mrs. Hadden never remarried.

> No crime, except the crime of adultery, relieves a woman from the relation of a wife to her husband. But when her personal safety, or the maintenance of herself and her children demand it, she may take advantage of a divorce, so far as these objects are secured; but she is still to consider herself by the law of God, as truly a wife to her husband as ever, (although she is not permitted to live with him as such.) and is no more at liberty to think of marrying another, than she would had they lived in happiness together.

It was this kind of concern that made Presbyterian ministers, professionals, and other middle-class townspeople supporters of

293

THE
END
OF
THE
FRONTIER,
1816–1850

temperance societies, Sunday schools, strict observing of the Sabbath, and free public schools. Unless these means encouraged large numbers of people to see the light and get control of themselves, then the very foundations of society would be at risk. Progress for men such as Beecher and Mills meant schools and churches as much as roads and canals.

Still, despite all the rhetoric and activity, many Hoosiers resisted the kinds of reforms they proposed. It was not that they objected to schools. Nor was it as simple as a reluctance to pay taxes. The problem was that the changes suggested by Presbyterian ministers and others threatened ways of life with which many people were comfortable, if not happy. Not everyone danced with delight at the appearance of the National Road. A state school superintendent was as much a symbol of a loss of local control and personal independence as a bank. Many people in Indiana simply preferred to do the business of building character themselves. Until the adoption of a new constitution in 1852, three trustees handled the hiring and supervising of local school districts. A superintendent and state-directed reforms meant centralized, standardized control.

In particular, many people were interested in preserving the integrity of the patriarchal household. Frequent migration, the availability of land, and the growth of the market economy were doing serious damage to that institution anyway. But the public school and temperance movements could also be interpreted as evidence that some people had decided that outside organizations and institutions could do a better job of raising and protecting children than the traditional family. One basic function of the household had always been to produce children, nurture them, and help to socialize them. Southern, rural, and nonprofessional people often had a hard time accepting the notion that some could do a better job at these tasks than others. Resistance to taxes and state schools was allegiance to time-honored household roles.

Drinking, gambling, and fighting were also, as the historian Elliott J. Gorn has argued, something more than the evidence of moral breakdown that reformers saw. From the perspective of rural and working people, they were critical components of a traditional masculine culture that valued competition and personal honor. Imbibing alcohol, betting on sporting events, and having a good time were long-standing customs for southern rural males. It was hardly a coincidence that observers found the worst examples of such behavior at militia musters or on election days when large numbers of men gathered together. This culture was decidedly patriarchal, and it could foster the abuse of women and children. But we do not need to romanticize it to say that it was important, or to say that one person's notion of improvement is another's idea of tyranny.

Because Indiana remained far more southern and rural than its counterparts north of the Ohio River, opponents of moral and educational reform had much greater success there. Indiana was still debating the necessity of public schools long after Ohio and Illinois had committed themselves to them. Not surprisingly, most Presbyterian ministers and missionaries were not happy in the state and many prospective servants of the Lord actively avoided it. Their religion, which elsewhere in the United States appealed strongly to middle-class, urban professionals and merchants, had great difficulty taking hold. In 1816, Indiana had only four Presbyterian churches with approximately thirty members. By 1850, that number had grown to 282 churches and 105,582 members in a total population of 988,416. No wonder the Presbyterian minister John M. Dickey moaned in 1836 that "for several years those who were laboring in Indiana, seemed almost to labor in vain. Frequently I was ready to conclude that I was a curse instead of a blessing to the people among whom I labored."

Indiana, however, was not without religion. In 1850, there were 266,372 Methodists in 779 churches and 138,783 Baptists in 403 churches. The presence of Presbyterians, Quakers (eighty-nine congregations, the fourth highest in the United States), Roman Catholics, Lutherans, and Episcopalians notwithstanding, evangelical Protestantism dominated the state. It was in many ways a folk religion. Methodists and Baptists were hardly primitive and ignorant peoples; they counted well-known and educated men and women among their numbers. But in general they tended to stress the democratic character of their theology and liturgy more than Presbyterians. Evangelicals were less interested in the education of their preachers than in their persuasiveness and sincerity; they were far more likely to value emotion over intellect; they emphasized the power of human beings to choose salvation as well as the

295

THE
END
OF
THE
FRONTIER,
1816–1850

omnipotence of God. And while evidence is scanty, Methodists and Baptists seemed less interested in creating a secular millennium than in fostering communities of people, as concerned with increasing affection as in restraining sin. Evangelical camp meetings were rowdy, emotional affairs where people mingled with each other and had a good time; they permitted at least a measure of immediate gratification and dramatized the love that people might share with each other.

Some historians have suggested that southern evangelicals were more willing to tolerate the foibles of their kin than Presbyterians. According to L. C. Rudolph, the latter tended

> to appeal to people who sometimes had little in common but their economic status and their education while evangelicals overlapped households and congregations. In terms of religion, Indiana remained very much a southern state, certainly far more than Ohio or Illinois, and thus the symbiotic relationship that developed between economic change and Protestantism that historians have found in western New York and northeastern Ohio never really took root. If the capitalist transformation of Indiana was less thorough than elsewhere in the north, it is also true that the acceptance of a middle-class Protestantism was less widespread.

In the end, the women and men who wanted to reform Indiana society had to limit their activities largely to voluntary activities in urban areas. If the immediate impact of Presbyterian reforms was small, they did leave a cultural and institutional legacy. The Indianapolis Sabbath School, started in 1823, for example, was largely a Presbyterian institution. Presbyterians were responsible for many of the first private high schools and male and female academies. Perhaps their most lasting impact was in higher education. Presbyterian elder David H. Maxwell of Bloomington was influential in getting the state seminary located in his town. Presbyterians founded Hanover College (chartered in 1829) and helped to found Wabash College (1834).

Of course, there were plenty of Methodists, Baptists, Quakers, and Catholics who were interested in education and other kinds of improvement. The Methodists established Indiana Asbury, later called DePauw, in Greencastle in 1837. For Baptists, there was Franklin College (1834), while Catholics had the University of Notre

Dame (1842) and Quakers had Earlham College (1847). The point is not that Presbyterians had a monopoly on good works. Rather, they tended to be more eager to reform social behavior and individual character to the emerging capitalist culture of Indiana while southern evangelicals concentrated on improving existing social relationships.

Whose Freedom?

As critical as attitudes toward banks, canals, and public schools were in polarizing the people of Indiana, the issue that most agitated them was the question of race. After adoption of the 1816 constitution, there was never any serious call for the reintroduction of slavery. But there was also only scattered support for allowing African Americans the full rights of citizens of Indiana. On the contrary, the General Assembly systematically denied them the most basic rights. The racism that had been evident for years was codified into law with the abolition of slavery.

At the same 1816 convention that drafted an eloquent article against slavery, delegates rejected the idea that blacks should be allowed to vote by a margin of 122 to one. One member shouted that whenever anyone began "to talk about making Negroes equal with white men, I begin to think about leaving the country." In accordance with this view, the constitution specifically denied "negro and mulatto . . . the right of suffrage." Two years later, the General Assembly declared blacks and mulattoes incompetent to serve as witnesses in a trial, except in cases involving only black people. (In 1853, the law was expanded to cover anyone who was one-eighth black.)

The same General Assembly also outlawed interracial marriage. According to Emma Lou Thornbrough, this was rarely an issue until 1840. In that year, a crowd attacked the house of a white woman who, with her mother's permission, was planning to marry a white-skinned man with some black blood. The angry mob warned the man to get out of town and rode the woman around on a rail. The law against "the amalgamation of whites and blacks" outlawed marriages among people who had a black great-grandparent on penalty of $1,000 to $5,000 and ten to twenty years in jail; a minis-

🐚 **297**

THE
END
OF
THE
FRONTIER,
1816–1850

ter who married such a couple could be fined up to $10,000 and a clerk who issued a license, $500. Although the penalties were briefly repealed, they were later reenacted.

Indiana law also forbade African American children from attending public schools. In 1837, the General Assembly declared that "the white inhabitants of each congressional township" were to handle school business. An 1841 statute excluded the property of blacks from assessment for education. When Indiana finally adopted a system of free common schools in 1852, the legislation expressly excluded blacks. The General Assembly in 1855 generously compensated for this provision by also excusing blacks from paying taxes to support public education.

As important, the 1851 constitution of Indiana made the state off-limits to further black migration. Indiana was to be a democracy of white males. Hoosiers explained this restriction in economic and social terms. They did not want what Governor Ray called in 1829 "*known paupers*." Many whites believed that blacks would be little more than a drain on their pocketbooks. Others stressed the cultural consequences of black migration. In the words of an 1830 correspondent of the *Indiana Journal* in Indianapolis, "The dregs of offscourings of the slave states are most likely to change residence, and they are too incurably affected with that horrible gangrene of morals which slavery engenders, to be welcomed among a virtuous and intelligent people." Protesting the failure to enforce an 1831 law requiring blacks to post a bond, the editor of the Richmond *Jeffersonian* observed in 1842:

> We presume there is not a nigger in this town that has given his bond, and any white man that employs them is daily exposing himself to an indictment and heavy fine. By enforcing this law, we should rid ourselves of a worse than useless population, drive away a gang of pilferers, make an opening for white laborers to fill the places of the blacks, and relieve our town of the odium now resting on it.

Whatever the origins, racial hostility was commonplace in Indiana. The Committee on Education of the state Senate explained the situation in an 1842 report on a petition "to prevent Negro and mulatto children from being forced into the district schools contrary to the will of the people concerned." It stated that blacks are here, unfortunately for us and them, and we have duties to perform in reference to their well-being. It is our duty to elevate them and happify [sic] their condition so far as we can; but it is not our duty to do so by adopting any means calculated in its nature to degrade our own race. God in his wisdom has caused us to differ; this difference, too, consists in more than the color of the skin. . . . That the *blacks* should be educated by some means, your committee do not doubt; but at this time they are not called upon to indicate the means. The opposition of the large majority of our people to any thing like a close intimacy with the African, is too well known to need comment. The only question for the committee is, whether it is expedient to have our public schools disquieted, and in many instances broken up, by having the negro thrust into them, contrary to the wishes of those concerned.

The answer, quite obviously, was no.

The antipathy "of the large majority of our people to any thing like a close intimacy with the African" produced violence as well as legislation. The most notorious examples involved the kidnapping of both fugitive slaves and free blacks. Jonathan Jennings spoke out against this practice as governor, and the General Assembly established a fine of $500 to $1,000 for committing the crime of "manstealing." Of course, Indiana would not object to the return of human property, whether it be male or female. If procedures were followed, including obtaining a warrant and holding a trial, slaves could be returned. In any case, people evaded the law. Apparently kidnapping was big business along the Ohio River. Blacks armed themselves and carried freedom certificates while Quakers worked hard to return people once captured. But kidnappings continued, sometimes with the more than tacit approval of local officials.

Even when white neighbors helped, the results were still frequently heartrending. One former slave, Martha, the wife of a tenant farmer named Charley Rouse, was living peacefully with her husband in Washington County in 1851. They had been together for several years. One evening when Charley was away, a group of men suddenly burst into their home and abducted Martha. Some white men chased the group to Jeffersonville and offered $600 for Martha's freedom. The kidnappers agreed but insisted that the contract had to be signed in Kentucky. Once across the river, they refused to sell Martha and took her away. There is no record of Charley or anyone else in Washington County ever seeing her again.

The discriminatory legislation, the acts of violence, and the general racism of many Indianans raised the ire of many black and white citizens. African Americans protested through conventions and petitions. But their strongest response was to organize institutions and networks that would protect them. Of these, the most important was the African Methodist Episcopal Church. In the early 1800s, most blacks were either Methodists or Baptists. (Very few became Quakers, despite that denomination's efforts on their behalf.) By the 1840s, blacks were increasingly worshipping in their own churches. In 1854, one-fifth of all Indiana blacks belonged to the African Methodist Episcopal Church. Black Baptists in Indianapolis and elsewhere had formed their own congregations.

In a world in which they were not full citizens, blacks built their own institutions. But these institutions were remarkable in the extent to which they paralleled the interests of their white counterparts. Many blacks, for example, particularly those in urban areas, were concerned with education and temperance. They talked about the importance of industry. William Paul Quinn, born to Hindu parents in Calcutta, was a tireless worker in the cause of black middle-class institutions. An African Methodist Episcopal missionary in the Old Northwest since 1832 and elected a bishop in 1844, Quinn had a hand in the founding of forty-seven churches with 2,000 members (including congregations at Richmond in 1836, Indianapolis in 1836, and Terre Haute in 1839), fifty Sunday schools, and forty temperance societies.

Not all whites were hostile to these efforts. By the 1840s, many were ready to work with blacks to bring an end to slavery and some aspects of racial discrimination. Whites with southern backgrounds were involved in some of these measures, to be sure, but by and large anti-slavery agitation won more support among urban, professional northeasterners than it did among southern farm families. Indiana, again probably because it was more southern and rural than its neighbors, experienced far less anti-slavery agitation than did Ohio or Illinois. The hard work of Quakers and some Presbyterians notwithstanding, on the question of race, the vast majority of Hoosiers were determined to limit, if they could not eliminate, all forms of "intimacy" with African Americans.

By 1850, in sum, the frontier had given way to a society that, while far from consensual, was pretty clearly defined. On their farms or in their small towns, Indianans operated within the parameters of a world defined by the pervasiveness of commercial capitalism (particularly private enterprise), the importance of national economic networks, a preference for local rather than state or national control over cultural questions, the supremacy of heads of households, and the exclusion or restriction of people not formally dependent on them (that is, Native Americans and African Americans). The history of frontier Indiana had been the history of a struggle for the power to control the development of the region. By 1850, the victors were clear: they were white male southerners, the social descendants of the Virginians who had accompanied George Rogers Clark in the late 1770s. To the extent that any power remained to contend with theirs, it lay in the authority of the government of the United States of America. The legacy of Josiah Harmar, John Hamtramck, and William Henry Harrison was the existence of a federal authority that would eventually legislate the reform of this new world and force white men to confront the prospect of sharing their hard-won power with women, blacks, and other people, who, like they, found the status of dependent incompatible with the rights of an American citizen.

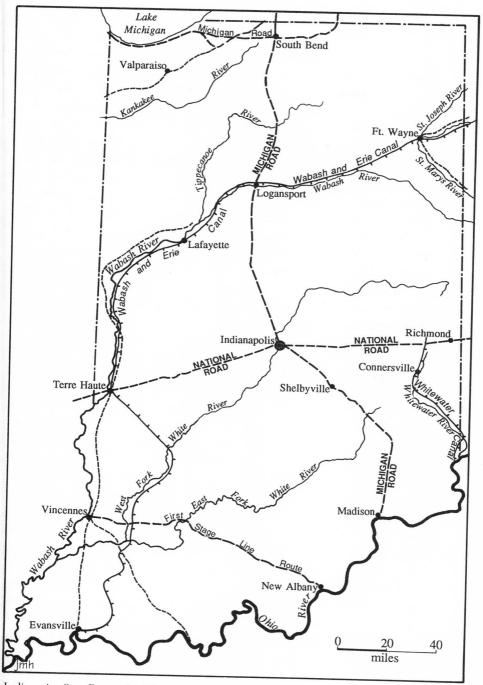

Indiana in 1850. Drawn by John Hollingsworth.

EPILOGUE:
"THIS COUNTRY OF LIBERTY"

The Fletchers of Indianapolis

On January 1, 1839, Calvin Fletcher greeted the new year with one of his regular exercises in self-reflection. He began less gloomily than usual, noting that it had been a "Pleasant day." Several families had "dined" with the Fletchers and enjoyed "a roast Turkey" in their home on the south side of East Ohio Street between Alabama and New Jersey in Indianapolis. At the age of forty, Calvin appeared to be a happy man. And with good reason. A prosperous lawyer, banker, and landowner, Fletcher was one of the most prominent citizens of the capital of Indiana. More important, he and his wife, thirty-eight-year-old Sarah Hill Fletcher, had shared seventeen and a half years as an affectionate and well-matched couple. They had eight healthy children (seven boys and one girl) and would have three more. Since Calvin was originally from Vermont and Sarah's family had migrated to Ohio from Virginia (via Kentucky), the Fletcher household was located at the intersection of white American cultures in the Old Northwest. In their home on Ohio Street, New England and Virginia were uniting to produce Indiana.

Calvin began his review of 1838 by concluding that the year had "been as happy & cheerful as I could reasonably expect." He had "met with no serious misfortune"; his family had survived sicknesses. "God has wonderfully blessed us & I have tried to feel thankful." Fletcher's debts concerned him, as one would expect in the middle of the national depression occurring in the wake of the Panic of 1837. Yet Calvin took responsibility for this "affliction." He "deserve[d] it somewhat." Certainly he alone could make things better, and he resolved "to get out of these imbarrassments by patience & industry." Debt was something to despise: "so long as I remain in debt I shall feel that I am the slave of my creditors." Fletcher finished his entry by assuring himself that he had tried to "read & improve my mind & especially my temper over which I have I trust a better controle. I have learned too late in life that I have lost much comfort & happiness for want of a proper control of my temper."

In his obsession with self-control and improvement, as in so many ways, Calvin Fletcher was the very model of the middle-class citizen. While acknowledging the power of omnipotent God, he was constantly striving to make himself and the world around him better. Publicly and privately, Fletcher devoted much of his time to the work of improvement. A Whig in politics, Calvin Fletcher strongly supported the development of canals and roads. A member of the Methodist Church since January 1829, he had encouraged the development of the Marion County Seminary, joined the Indiana Total Abstinence Temperance Society in June 1838, and would soon take up regular duties as a Methodist Sunday school teacher. An invitation to give a speech at a ceremony marking the laying of the cornerstone of Indiana Asbury University in June 1837 was evidence of the respect of his fellow citizens, as were his elections to the state Senate from 1826 to 1833 and as a director of the State Bank. In 1865, tax records listed him as the man with the highest income in Indianapolis.

As important as material success and public approbation were to Calvin Fletcher, personal character was more important. Because he was certain that each individual was accountable for himself, he could not expect to improve his neighbors without first improving himself. The temper that had gotten him charged with assault on another lawyer soon after his arrival in Indianapolis in the early 1820s had to be controlled. The respect of others—his honor or public reputation—meant little unless he respected himself.

Good son of Vermont that he was, Calvin highly valued intro-
spection and self-recrimination. When his oldest son, Cooley, wrote
from Phillips Exeter Academy in Massachusetts in the spring of
1842 to say that his "defects of character" made him doubt whether
he should go to college—perhaps he should be a simple farmer?—
Fletcher could barely conceal his paternal pride. This "awakening"
in Cooley was "one of the best symptoms of his talents." After all,
"true 'Knowledge was to Know how little could be known / To see
all others faults & feel our own.'" A few weeks later, Cooley had
reverted to bad habits, particularly "his disposition to be greater
than he is. He has a terrible *pensient* for show off. I hope he will get
over that." But the son was simply a reproduction of the father.
Both possessed that curious mixture of confidence and self-doubt,
of ambition and diffidence, of passion and self-control, which
would characterize the Midwestern middle class.

Sarah Hill Fletcher was not so introspective. Her diary entries
were highly irregular and almost always limited to terse comments
on the weather or the activities of the day. She was extremely busy.
Beyond bearing and caring for children, she also supervised the
business of the household. One day she was acting as a midwife or
nursing the sick; another she was supervising butchering or corn
planting; yet another she was making sugar or preserving fruits.
Sarah was an eminently practical and energetic woman.

Calvin, of course, had considered these matters when he was
contemplating marrying her in early 1821. Love and ambition were
in conflict as he struggled to reconcile his personal desires with his
quest for respectability. Sarah was "poor and without Education."
Still, she was "amiable notwithstanding" such "defects." What to
do? Calvin answered the question by reassuring himself that he
would be serving God and society by marrying and devoting himself to improving Sarah. "I have thus far been successful in this life,
and could I repay that maker and preserver of my existence in a
more ample way than in doing good to all my fellow creatures and
for instance where virtue is invelloped with life's common misfortune poverty and ignorance, would it not be amiable in me to
rescue the victim from these two mal[a]di[e]s? I think it would."
This calm reasoning contrasts with the haste of his decision. Indeed,
rumor had it that Calvin had impregnated another young woman

and wanted to be free of her. He himself called it a "precipitate marriage." In any case, it seems clear that ardor, if not lust, led him to seek Sarah's hand. Yet Calvin recorded it as a logical move. "[O]n the 2d day of February I mounted my horse and without much excitement I rode with carless steps and slow across the river thro' mud to be the herald of my own intentions."

Fortunately for him, Sarah accepted his proposal, her parents agreed, and they were married. Later that year they moved to Indianapolis. What a pair they were! Calvin was an ambitious young man in a hurry, struggling to maintain control of his passions, forever chewing over his prospects and character. "I find that I have much to do to attain any emenance in my profession," he wrote in March 1821. "And to droop in the grades of mediocrity is painful to me. I moan that my feelings of honors are not more acute—that my resentment and pleasure are not more extreme. I am sensible that if I ever wish to attain any worthy honors in my profession they must come thro' the medium of application integrity and virtue. Let me pursue. Let me reach forward."

Sarah, on the other hand, was a patient and direct young woman, blessed with a constitution capable of dealing with a temperamental husband as well as bearing eleven children. She was the kind of woman who could begin a letter to Calvin's younger sister by writing, "Pardon me for this abrupt introduction to you as your sister by marriage." Or record on the first page of her diary (a habit no doubt encouraged by her husband): "Sunday August the 19 1821. I this day commenced reading the life of George Washington, commander in chief of the Armies of the United States of America, throughout the war which established their independence and the first president of the United States, by David Ramsay, M.D. Author of the history of the American Revolution." Two months later, her entries were even more spare. "Tuesday October 23, 1821. I commensed Arithmetic. Fryday Oct. 26. I commited the multiplication table. Saturday. I red a few pages in the elements of Gesture &c. &c. and wrote a verse which was the last of essay on Man."

Whatever the influence of his wife, Calvin Fletcher never lost his conviction that the ills of this world were somehow connected with personal character. If things went bad, the first place to look was inside one's self. To make things better, the place to start was inside one's self. Thus the importance of education and temperance. Indiana would progress to a higher state of civilization if its citizens would progress as individuals. Calvin could not see the world as the product of anything but individual character. And this blinded him, as it did so many people just like him, to the costs of the great economic progress of the state of Indiana in the first half of the nineteenth century.

Nine years and one week before January 1, 1839—Christmas Day, 1829, to be exact—Calvin Fletcher arose from his bed to celebrate the fact that "Temperance & Sabbath School societies have at this time in our place produced almost a calm." He was delighted that he neither heard the usual firing of gun nor saw the usual parade. Instead, he went to the Senate, then to the courthouse. There he assisted his partners in representing "a yellow womman & 3 childrin who are claimed by her master a Virginian by name of Suel." The court was crowded with people; each side had vocal supporters. In the midst of this excitement, Fletcher matter-of-factly "spoke in behalf of the woman & read law." The next day he ate breakfast, went to the Senate, but did not go to court to hear the judge's decision, which was to rule against the Virginian because "the moment that his slaves & himself reached a free state they were free." Calvin expected an uproar over the judgment. He wondered, "What violence what outrages may yet be committed on poor negroes." But he did nothing else. For he had "discharged my duty towards them & in accordence with my own sober convictions."

While Fletcher was opposed to slavery and sympathetic to the plight of blacks, he saw his connection to them as solely a matter of personal responsibility. He had done his duty. That was all that he owed to them or anyone else. Much as he devoted his life to the cause of improvement and reform, the world of Calvin Fletcher was actually a very narrow one. Self-absorbed and egocentric, he understood the rest of the world only in terms of how he had behaved toward it. The question of his life was not "What can we do to improve our world?" but "What can I do to make myself a better person?" He acted from the inside out, making sense of the world through the lens of his own behavior. Dutiful he was. Sensible, too. But sympathy and empathy were beyond him. Fletcher was so obsessed with examining himself that he could not understand himself in relation to the larger society in which he lived. He lacked self-irony, or at least a sense of perspective on himself.

For all the Fletchers, the world of the Indians and the French was a world of legends and memories. It had little direct impact on their lives. The frontier was over for them not because of population statistics or economic development or statehood or military defeat. It was over because they saw Indiana as their home. They were comfortable there. The Fletchers did not make history in the dramatic fashion of Vincennes and Little Turtle, or even Jennings and Harrison. The crises of their lives were less about life and death than about whether drinking was good or bad and whether one had enough money to retire from the law and take up farming. Indiana was settled.

Indiana Is a Memory

A little over a week before the end of 1838, Calvin Fletcher "Spent the day at DeHaven's tavern" in Covington, Indiana. There, on that Sunday, the twenty-third day of December, he "Saw old Judge Polk on his return from the Indian country where he had been with the last Potwatimes." It was one of the rare times that Indians appear in Fletcher's diary and correspondence. Just over a century after the establishment of Vincennes, no Miami or Shawnee or Piankashaw played a direct role in the life of one of the most important figures in Indiana. Indeed, Fletcher was far more worried about the growing importance of European banks and creditors than he was about the remnants of Indian tribes.

The Potawatomi whose removal William Polke supervised as an agent of the United States government left us no detailed diaries. They had no time to reflect on the difficulties of living up to high moral standards. Eighteen thirty-eight had been an eventful year for them, too. But by Fletcher's standards, God did not appear to be on their side. They had not recovered from sickness, and they had every reason to lose their tempers, not control them. In the 1832 Tippecanoe treaties and in the 1833 Treaty of Chicago, they had surrendered virtually all of their lands east of the Mississippi. By 1835, the government of the United States was escorting Potawatomi from northern Illinois across the Mississippi into Iowa and Missouri. The hundreds of Potawatomi still living along the Wabash, the Tippecanoe, and the Eel did not want to go west. Led by the chief Menominee, they resisted efforts to remove them by petitioning the federal government and trying to seek legal redress.

They could not, however, stop the American settlers or the government. Menominee protested in August 1838 that

> the President does not know the truth. He, like me, has been imposed upon. . . . He does not know that you made my young chiefs drunk and got their consent and pretended to get mine. . . . He would not by force drive me from my home, the graves of my tribe, and my children who have gone to the Great Spirit, nor allow you to tell me that your braves will take me, tied like a dog, if he knew the truth. . . . when he knows the truth he will leave me to my own. I have not sold my lands. I will not sell them. I have not signed any treaty, and will not sign any. I am not going to leave my lands, and I don't want to hear anything more about it.

This was language that had echoed along the Wabash for a century, the language of fathers and children, the appeal to a benevolent patriarch to act as a mediator, to find common ground. But President Andrew Jackson and most other Americans had no use for such words. They did not need to create a middle way. They had won and they demanded the spoils of victory. They wanted the land.

In August 1838, white squatters tried to seize some of the land on the reservation; the Potawatomi burned a hut and the Americans responded by burning a dozen Indian cabins. Indiana Governor David Wallace ordered Senator John Tipton to recruit one hundred men and forcibly remove the Potawatomis. On August 29, Tipton's men seized Menominee and surrounded his village. Other Potawatomi in the area were rounded up and gathered together. With Indians arriving from Michigan and all over northern and central Indiana, there were more than 859 present when the entire group set out for Kansas on September 4, 1838. Menominee went, too, but he and other chiefs traveled in what amounted to a cage. After their departure, only about 150 Potawatomi remained within the borders of Indiana, most of them living on land they owned privately.

General Tipton and his volunteers escorted the Indians to Danville, Illinois, where William Polke took over and led them west to Quincy, across the Mississippi, through Missouri to Independence, and across the Missouri River into Kansas. As they proceeded across the plains of northern Illinois, the Indians and their escorts made quite an impression. They were like a parade, symbolizing the victory of the authority of the United States and the subjection of the Potawatomi, who were no longer welcome within the borders of the republic. At the head of the party were a dragoon, bearing the flag of the United States, and an officer. Behind them were the baggage and the carriage that confined Menominee and other chiefs. Then came a file of 250 to 300 horses carrying men, women, and children away from their homes, from the lakes and streams of northern Indiana, from the graves of their ancestors and the memories of their youth. On either side of the Indians were armed soldiers and volunteers. According to Father Benjamin Marie Petit, who accompanied the Potawatomi, the guards enforced the line of march "often with severe gestures and bitter words." Finally there was a file of forty wagons carrying both possessions and people. The latter were the sick and the infirm. For them, the journey was sheer torture. They were "rudely jolted, under a canvass which, far from protecting them from the dust and heat, only deprived them of air, for they were as if buried under this burning canopy."

Of the 859 Potawatomi who left Indiana, forty-three were dead before they reached their final destination—the Osage River Subagency—on November 4, 1838. Day after day, a similar sentence reappeared in the journal kept by Tipton and Polke: "A child died this morning. . . . A child three years old died and was buried. . . . A child died since dark. . . . A child died since we came into camp. . . . Two small children died along the road. . . . A child of six or eight years old died this Evening." The causes of death were clear. In addition to poor food (mainly beef and flour) and exhaustion, typhoid fever was the major culprit. It was rampant in eastern Illinois, affecting white settlers as well as Indians. Making matters worse for the migrating Potawatomi was the lack of a regular supply of fresh water until they reached the Mississippi Valley. The general health of the party improved once they were out of Illinois, but the disease that killed over forty people left hundreds of others weak and despondent.

Neither the journey nor illness destroyed the spirit of the Indians, however. Children were also born during the two-month trek. Potawatomi men demanded and were eventually allowed to hunt for food; it was they who brought in the venison and other game that sustained the migrants and their escorts during the latter half of their journey. The Indians also demanded that Father Petit be permitted to say mass. Polke agreed, and on several occasions he delayed the start of the march by an hour to accommodate the services. Toward the end of the ordeal, the Indians sought the removal of the doctor assigned to care for them. Polke tried to placate and then to put them off. He did not fire the doctor, but neither did the Indians give up. They "retired," according to Polke, but "not, without . . . first requesting leave to renew the subject again." And, even when they reached their final destination, "a considerable number of the Indians" came together on November 5 and "expressed a desire to be heard in a speech." In Polke's words, a chief said

> that they had now arrived at their journey's end—that the government must now be satisfied. They had been taken from homes affording them plenty and brought to a desert—a wilderness—and were now to be scattered and left as the husbandman scatters his seed.

Defiant to the end. Polke, a native of Kentucky who had once been held prisoner with his mother and two siblings by Indians, was sympathetic. But he left anyway.

Back in central Illinois, the migrating Indians had attracted a great deal of attention. When they went by or through towns such as Springfield and Jacksonville, Polke encouraged them to wear their finest clothes and display themselves as well as they could under the circumstances. Apparently the Potawatomi were pleased to do so, taking pride in their appearance as they marched through the growing settlements. Occasionally the appearance of this large group made whites anxious. More often than not, however, they viewed the Indians in the role of what Polke called "spectators." Outside of Jacksonville on October 1, people came out to the camp in the evening to satisfy their curiosity. While a local band played, they stared at the Indians like they were a side-show amusement. Which, in fact, was what they appeared to be. As Polke noted, "the sight of an emigration or body of Indians is as great a rarity [for the citizens of Jacksonville] as a travelling Caravan of wild animals."

The Potawatomi had become curiosities in the minds of most whites. But they were not freaks. They were migrants, human beings unwillingly moving from one place to another while trying to hold on to their customs and their self-respect. When they reached Kansas, they became settlers. The Potawatomi had done it before. And they would do it again, even in a "desert." For them, the Wabash and its tributaries were sources of nostalgia, the water nurturing the land of their ancestors. Indiana had become a memory.

The Short, Happy Life of Benjamin Marie Petit

Notwithstanding the fact that they had not had a Catholic priest among them for decades, the Potawatomi were still using the rituals and customs of Jesuit fathers in the 1820s. "An American minister wished to draw us to his religion," a chief told a priest in 1830, "but neither I nor any of my village wished to send our children to his school, nor go to his meetings; we have preserved the way of prayer taught our ancestors by the black robe who used to be at St. Joseph."

That year, a Jesuit, Father Stephen Theodore Badin, began to minister to the Indians near Niles, Michigan, and in northern Indiana. In the early 1830s, Badin established a mission at St. Mary's Lake. The Potawatomi welcomed Badin and his associate, Father Louis Deseille, who arrived in 1833, like long-lost relatives. In fact, what amounted to a revival of French Catholicism took place among the Potawatomi in Indiana. In the spring of 1835, Indians on the Tippecanoe turned out in their best clothes "to see the chief of the Black-robes [Simon William Gabriel Brute de Remur, first Bishop of Vincennes], of whom their fathers had spoken so much, whose departure several had regretted until their last breath and died bidding their children to listen to them, if the great Lord of Life sent them again." When Deseille died at his mission in September 1837, the Lord sent one last priest. His name was Benjamin Marie Petit.

Born in April 1811 in Rennes, France, Petit had renounced a promising career as an attorney in order to become a priest. Bishop Brute recruited him while on a trip to France in 1836. Brushing aside the opposition of his mother and brothers, the twenty-five-year-old seminarian eagerly accepted the challenge of missionary service. Petit was as enthusiastic as Calvin Fletcher was gloomy.

Although he was following in the footsteps of seventeenth-century Jesuits, Petit's itinerary reflected how much North America had changed in two centuries. The young man did not go to Canada; he never set foot in Quebec or saw the St. Lawrence River. Instead he arrived in New York City on July 21 with several other recruits and proceeded to Vincennes by way of Pittsburgh, Cincinnati, and Louisville.

Vincennes was more than a century old and in relative decline. While still one of the more important urban centers in Indiana, it lacked the resources and the location to compete with Madison, Richmond, Terre Haute, or Indianapolis. Indeed, the only thing that Vincennes was still at the center of was Catholicism, evidenced by its position as the see of a diocese in the midst of a sea of Protestantism. In the church on the eastern bank of the Wabash, Benjamin Marie Petit received minor orders and became a subdeacon in December 1836. During 1837, he traveled throughout northern Indiana. Returning to Vincennes, he became a deacon in September. On October 14, Bishop Brute ordained him a priest.

Petit was beside himself with joy. He wrote to his mother the next day with boundless enthusiasm. He was so ecstatic, he was almost breathless. "I am now a priest, and the hand which is writing to you bore Jesus Christ this morning!" he began. "How my lips trembled this morning at my first Mass when, at the *Memento*, I commended you all to God! And shall I again tomorrow, and the day after, and every day of my life until the last!" Certain that he was nothing, Petit was equally certain that God had great plans for him. In two days, he would leave Vincennes to take Deseille's place at the St. Mary's mission. There was none of the angst of Calvin Fletcher, none of the matter-of-factness of Sarah Fletcher, none of the defiance of Menominee, simply endearing optimism. "I shall conclude this glorious day by telling you that the dominant feeling in me is a profound joy under the burden of newly contracted obligations. I know not whether I should have some inquietude, but I feel so light at heart, so happy, so content, that I am wholly overwhelmed by it. To go from Mass to Mass to heaven! the sweet rapture of God's will, who Himself ordains and executes through His grace. Ah, with what delight I put my trust in Him! Pray much for me; now is the time." Petit considered himself a "lucky" man because he had the opportunity to serve others, to feel obligations to others. "I have always longed for a mission among the savages; we have only one in Indiana; and it is I whom the Potawatomi will call their 'Father Black-Robe.'"

Nothing could dampen Petit's enthusiasm. He enjoyed his work and relished the role of father. The Potawatomi he considered his children. They told him they were orphans and welcomed his help. Petit performed the sacraments with abandon. He baptized dozens, heard innumerable confessions, and married several couples. Traveling through deep snow, he laughed when he and his companion were overturned into drifts. For Benjamin Petit, missionary and priest, life was full of adventure and meaning because he was sharing the joy of his religion with other human beings. He claimed to care little about his old companions in France. "[L]et them marry, run about, dance, die . . . I scarcely bother myself about it any longer, now that I am old and an Indian," he wrote to a friend in March 1838.

Over this idyllic life, of course, grew the shadow of removal. Petit fretted about the impending disaster. More important, he tried to do something about it. He offered legal advice, lobbied federal officials, and urged his superiors to do what they could. Over the summer, he determined to accompany them if they were forced to leave. The thought of "these Christian souls" dying "without the aid of the sacraments of which they partook with such love, and languish[ing] under a strange sky" was more than "their father" could bear. By July, Petit's passion was running high. Removal was simply not fair. In a portion of a letter to John Tipton which he later deleted, he gave full voice to his anger.

> You had right perhaps, if duly authorised, to take possession of the land, but to make from free men slaves, no man can take upon himself to do so in this free country. Those who wish to move must be *moved*, those who want to remain must be left to themselves.

How could Tipton "act in such a dictatorial manner[?]" "[I]t is impossible for me, and for many to conceive how such events may take place in this country of liberty." Petit had "consecrated" his "whole life, [his] whole powers to the good of [his] neighbours." And he simply could not understand. What was going on?

In September, Petit received permission from Bishop Brute to travel with the Potawatomi. The Americans were happy about this, for men such as Tipton and Polke saw the priest as an obstacle to their plans. With his resignation to their fate, surely the Potawatomi would be more docile. The departure wounded Petit deeply. It was a pitiful occasion. He told his family:

> I said Mass. Then my dear church was stripped of all its ornaments, and at the moment of my departure I called all my children together. I spoke to them one more time; I wept; my listeners sobbed. It was heartrending. We, the dying mission, prayed for the success of other missions, and we sang with one accord:
>
>> In thy protection do we trust,
>> O Virgin, meek and mild.
>
> The voice which intoned was stifled by sobs, and only a few were able to finish. I left.

Petit did go west with the Indians. He, too, suffered from the poor food and the fever during the journey. More important, he suffered from the shattering of his optimism, of his faith in the goodness of human beings. Broken in spirit as well as in body, he went to St. Louis in early January. There his illness grew worse. By February 6, the priests who were caring for him had given up hope for his recovery. On the evening of the 10th, unable to talk, Petit twice kissed a crucifix and received absolution. Disillusionment and depression had not destroyed his faith. After a few more hours of agony, the twenty-eight-year-old man asked for water, then stopped breathing. It was twenty minutes until midnight. Buried in St. Louis, Petit's body was disinterred in 1856 and transported to St. Mary's Lake, where the priest had spent the happiest days of his life. By then, his mission was long gone. In its place was the University of Notre Dame.

Petit never sent John Tipton his question about how removal could take place in "this country of liberty." Who knows what the senator's response, if any, would have been. Our answer can be no less elusive. With rare exceptions, the peoples who had lived together and struggled against each other for more than a century on the banks of the Ohio and the Wabash, the White and the Maumee, were not malevolent. They often treated each other horribly, to be sure. But the tragedy of their acts lies less in their violence than in the fact that virtually all of them were motivated by a desire to protect what they held most dear: their families, their friends, their ways of life. Nearly everyone in frontier Indiana had been frightened, not simply of each other but also of their inability to understand themselves, other peoples, and the world around them. In their own fashions, they had tried to make sense of all of this and protect their illusions from anything and anyone who threatened them. The history of frontier Indiana is more than a story of one group of human beings gaining the power to remake the world and call it progress while demonizing and destroying the worlds of others. It is a tale of how the strivings of flawed human beings to survive and comprehend life so often led them to misperceive, misunderstand, and mistrust each other, and ultimately to behave in unforgivably brutal ways. Of all the people who came to Indiana, Benjamin Marie Petit was almost unique in his joyful innocence and simple faith. In the end, it is the great value of history to offer not answers to the kind of question he asked, but simply to perpetuate his question, to keep asking "Why?"

"Happy at Home"

In the largest sense, the Potawatomi had gone to make room for the Fletchers. By Christmas 1842, Calvin and Sarah had had another son and another daughter, bringing the total number of their children to ten. They had moved their expanding household into a new and larger home. Calvin was even more worried about being trapped in a tangle of debt. Sarah continued to run the house and care for the children she had borne. Cooley had finally entered Brown and was doing well. His brother Elijah had gone to New England to get ready for college.

Ever dutiful, Calvin wrote to Elijah on Christmas Day to let him know how his brothers and sisters had celebrated the occasion. Cousins and friends had arrived on the 24th. The Fletchers spent the bulk of Christmas Eve cooking and debating what to do with some chickens given them as presents. The merriment continued on Christmas Day. "St. Nicholas came down chimny of course & filled every pocket." Sixteen-year-old Calvin, Jr., who had taught himself the art of making fireworks, put together one hundred small rockets. After supper, he exploded them. His father reported to his brother that "the sky rockets were the best I ever saw of the kind." Family and friends then made candy. "It was," Calvin Fletcher wrote, "a joyful time." One of his friends inspected the candy and "was much pleased. He said your mother & I did right in making our children happy at home."

Happiness would come and go, of course. But the Fletchers were indeed at home. In Indiana.

Acknowledgments

Because the books in the History of the Trans-Appalachian Frontier series are being published without footnotes, it is difficult to convey adequately my dependence on the work of other scholars. I referred to historians by name in the text when I borrowed directly from their work, and I discuss both primary and secondary sources on early Indiana in the Essay on Sources. Still, I want to acknowledge the extent to which the synthetic narrative presented in *Frontier Indiana* rests on an evidentiary foundation constructed by such dedicated scholars of early Indiana as Caroline and Jacob Dunn, Frances Krauskopf, Emma Lou Thornbrough, Gayle Thornbrough, John Barnhart, Dorothy Riker, and Donald Carmony. Without their work—particularly in compiling and editing the extensive holdings of the Indiana Historical Society—I could not have written this book. I am profoundly in their debt.

I thank Walter Nugent and Malcolm Rohrbough for asking me to write *Frontier Indiana* and offering wisdom and support as I worked on it. John Lauritz Larson generously shared his knowledge of early Indiana with me when I was beginning the project, and James Madison offered great encouragement when he read the penultimate draft. John Gallman, the Director of Indiana University Press, had faith in the manuscript at a crucial moment and gave me a very helpful critical reading of it. I owe Fred Anderson more than I can say for wonderful conversations about questions of evidence, narrative, and meaning.

As always, my greatest obligation is to Mary Kupiec Cayton, not for reading *Frontier Indiana*, or even for talking about it, but simply for loving me as I obsessively fretted my way through the process of researching and writing it. And by insisting that history should be about people ("Even if they're dead, Daddy"), Elizabeth and Hannah Cayton remind me of why I became interested in it in the first place.

Essay on Sources

Abbreviations

IHB *Indiana History Bulletin*
IHBu Indiana Historical Bureau
IHC Indiana Historical Commission
Ind Indianapolis
IHS Indiana Historical Society
ISHS Illinois State Historical Society
IMH *Indiana Magazine of History*
IUP Indiana University Press, Bloomington
OAHQ *Ohio Archaeological and Historical Society Quarterly*
WMQ *William and Mary Quarterly*, 3d. Series
WSHS Wisconsin State Historical Society

General

The most recent surveys of the state's history are James H. Madison, *The Indiana Way: A State History* (IUP and Ind: IHS, 1986), and Peter T. Harstad, "Indiana and the Art of Adjustment," in *Heartland: Comparative Histories of the Midwestern States*, ed. James H. Madison (IUP, 1990), 158–85. Older works include John B. Dillon, *A History of Indiana* (Ind: Bingham and Doughty, 1859); Jacob P. Dunn, *Indiana: A Redemption from Slavery*, rev. ed. (Boston: Houghton, Mifflin, 1904); and Logan Esarey, *History of Indiana*, 2 vols., 3d ed. (Fort Wayne: Hoosier Press, 1924–1925). The definitive study of the period covered in this book is John D. Barnhart and Dorothy L. Riker, *Indiana to 1816: The Colonial Period* (Ind: IHBu and IHS, 1971).

One of the major ways in which my interpretation differs from the interpretations of many previous scholars of early Indiana is in the treatment of Native Americans. Here I have relied heavily on Richard White, *The Middle Ground: Indians, Empires, and Republics in the Great Lakes Region, 1650–1815* (Cambridge: Cambridge University Press, 1991); Gregory Evans Dowd, *A Spirited Resistance: The North American Indian Struggle for Unity, 1745–1815* (Baltimore: Johns Hopkins University Press, 1992); R. David Edmunds, *The Potawatomis: Keepers of the Fire* (Norman: University of Oklahoma Press, 1978), *The Shawnee Prophet* (Lincoln: University of Nebraska Press, 1983), and *Tecumseh and the Quest for Indian Leadership* (Boston: Little, Brown, 1984); Bert Anson, *The Miami Indians* (Norman: University of Oklahoma Press, 1970); and Harvey Lewis Carter, *The Life and Times of Little Turtle: First Sagamore of the Wabash* (Urbana: University of Illinois Press, 1987).

Studies of Anglo-American intrusion into the Old Northwest include John D. Barnhart, *Valley of Democracy: The Frontier versus the Plantation in the Ohio Valley, 1775–1818* (IUP, 1953); R. Carlyle Buley, *The Old Northwest: Pioneer Period, 1815–1840*, 2 vols. (IUP, 1950); Andrew R. L. Cayton, *The Frontier Republic: Ideology and Politics in the Ohio Country, 1780–1825* (Kent: Kent State University Press, 1986); Cayton and Peter S. Onuf, *The Midwest and the Nation: Rethinking the History of an American Region* (IUP, 1990); William Cronon, *Nature's Metropolis: Chicago and the Great West* (New York: Norton, 1991); John Mack Faragher, *Daniel Boone: The Life and Legend of an American Pioneer* (New York: Henry Holt, 1992), and *Sugar Creek: Life on the Illinois Prairie* (New Haven: Yale University Press, 1986); Onuf, *Statehood and Union: A History of the Northwest Ordinance* (IUP, 1987); Richard L. Power, *Planting Corn Belt Culture: The Impress of the Upland Southerner and Yankee in the Old Northwest* (Ind: IHS, 1953); *Always a River: The Ohio River and the American Experience*, ed. Robert L. Reid (IUP, 1991); and Malcolm J. Rohrbough, *The Trans-Appalachian Frontier: People, Societies, and Institutions, 1775–1850* (New York: Oxford University Press, 1978).

1. The World of the Miami, 1700–1754

Essential in writing this chapter were W. J. Eccles, "Iroquois, French, British: Imperial Rivalry in the Ohio Valley," in *Pathways to the Old Northwest*, (Ind: IHS, 1988), 19–32, and *The Canadian Frontier, 1754–1760*, rev. ed. (Albuquerque: University of New Mexico Press, 1983); Edmunds, *Potawatomis*, 3–74; Carol M. Judd and Arthur J. Ray, eds., *Old Trails and New Directions: Papers of the Third North American Fur Trade Conference* (Toronto: University of Toronto Press, 1980); Michael N. McConnell, *A Country Between: The Upper Ohio Valley and Its Peoples, 1724–1774* (Lincoln: University of Nebraska Press, 1992); Thomas Elliot Norton, *The Fur Trade in Colonial New York, 1686–1776* (Madison: University of Wisconsin Press, 1974); George A. Rawlyk, "The 'Rising French Empire' in the Ohio Valley and Old Northwest: The 'Dreaded Juncture of the French Settlements in Canada with those of Louisiana,'" in *Contest for Empire, 1500–1775: Proceedings of an Indiana American Revolution Bicentennial Symposium*, ed. John B. Elliott (Ind: IHS, 1975); *Beyond the Covenant Chain: The Iroquois and Their Neighbors in Indian North America, 1600–1800*, ed. Daniel K. Richter and James H. Merrell (Syracuse: Syracuse University Press, 1987); Richter, *Ordeal of the Longhouse: The Peoples of the Iroquois League in the Era of European Colonization* (Chapel Hill: University of North Carolina Press for the Institute of Early American History and Culture, 1992); Daniel Usner, *Indians, Settlers, and Slaves in a Frontier Exchange Economy: The Lower Mississippi Valley before 1783* (Chapel Hill: University of North Carolina Press for the Institute of Early American History and Culture, 1992); and White, *Middle Ground*, 1–185.

The basic sources on the Vincennes are Pierre-Georges Roy, *Sieur de Vincennes Identified* (Ind: C. E. Pauley, [1919]), and Jacob P. Dunn, *Mission to the Ouabache* (Ind: Bowen-Merrill, 1902). See also *Ouiatanon Documents*, ed. Frances Krauskopf (Ind: IHS, 1955), and Shirley S. McCord, comp., *Travel Accounts of Indiana, 1679–1961* (Ind: IHBu, 1970), 1–29. On the events surrounding the death of François-Marie Bissot, see *Indiana's First War*, trans. Caroline and Eleanor Dunn (Ind: William B. Burford, 1924), 73–143. Scattered letters are in *The French Regime in Wisconsin, 1634–1727*, ed. Reuben G. Thwaites, 3 vols. (Madison: WSHS, 1902–1908). An excellent recent collection of primary sources is *Letters from New France: The Upper Country, 1686–1783*, ed. Joseph L. Peyser (Urbana: University of Illinois Press, 1992).

Oscar J. Craig, *Ouiatanon: A Study in Indiana History* (Ind: Bowen-Merrill, 1893), 317–48; James H. Kellar and Glenn A. Black, "The Search for Ouiatanon," *IHB* 47 (1970), 123–33; and Paul G. Phillips, "Vincennes in Its Relation to French Colonial Policy," *IMH* 17 (1921): 311–37, are valuable studies of early French-Indian settlements in the Wabash Valley.

The basic source on the Miami is C. C. Trowbridge, *Meearmeear Traditions*, ed. Vernon Kinietz (Ann Arbor: University of Michigan Press, 1938). See also George Croghan, "A Selection of Letters and Journals Relating to Tours into the Western Country," in *Early Western Travels*, ed. Reuben Gold Thwaites (Cleveland: A. H. Clark, 1904–1907), vol. 1, 47–176; Krauskopf, *Ouiatanon Documents*; Dorothy Libby, "An Anthropological Report on the Piankashaw Indians," in *Piankashaw and Kaskaskia Indians* (New York: Garland, 1974), 27–342; McCord, comp., *Travel Accounts*, 1–29; and Peyser, *Letters from New France*. The essential secondary works besides those of Dowd, Edmunds, and White, cited above, are Anson, *Miami Indians*; C. S. Weslager, *The Delaware Indians: A History* (New Brunswick: Rutgers University Press, 1972); and James A. Brown, "The Impact of the European Presence on Indian Culture," in Elliott, *Contest for Empire*, 6–24. See also *Handbook of North American Indians*, vol. 17, ed. William Sturtevant (Washington: Smithsonian Institution, 1978), 588–601, 622–35, 681–89, 725–42.

The account of Memeskia and Pickawillany follows Carter, *Little Turtle*, 20–51; R. David Edmunds, "Pickawillany: French Military Power versus English Economics," *Pennsylvania Historical Magazine* 58 (1975): 169–84; and White, *Middle Ground*, 215–40. I also used Alfred T. Goodman, ed., *Journal of Captain William Trent from Logstown to Pickawillany* (Cincinnati: W. Dodge, 1871), 83–105, and A. A. Lambing, ed., "Journals of Celoron de Blainville and Father Joseph Pierre de Bonnecamps," *OAHQ* 29 (1920): 335–423.

2. The World of George Croghan, 1750–1777

On Pontiac, see Howard H. Peckham, *Pontiac and the Indian Uprising* (Princeton: Princeton University Press, 1947). More valuable are Edmunds, *Potawatomis*, 39–95, and White, *Middle Ground*, 269–314.

Croghan's journal of his journey up the Wabash is in Thwaites, *Early Western Travels*, vol. 1, 124–69. See also Nicholas B. Wainwright, *George Croghan, Wilderness Diplomat* (Chapel Hill: University of North Carolina Press for the Institute of Early American History and Culture, 1959).

On land speculators and British imperial policy, see Thomas Perkins Abernethy, *Western Lands and the American Revolution* (New York: Russell and Russell, 1959); Marc Egnal, *A Mighty Empire: The Origins of the American Revolution* (Ithaca: Cornell University Press, 1988); McConnell, *A Country Between*; Francis Jennings, *Empire of Fortune: Crowns, Colonies, and Tribes in the Seven Years War in America* (New York: Norton, 1988); Jack M. Sosin, "Britain and the Ohio Valley, 1760–1775: The Search for Alternatives in a Revolutionary Era," in *Contest for Empire*, 60–76, and *Whitehall and the Wilderness: The Middle West in British Colonial Policy, 1760–1775* (Lincoln: University of Nebraska Press, 1961); and White, *Middle Ground*, 223–365.

Primary sources include *Papers of Sir William Johnson*, ed. James Sullivan et al. (Albany: State University of New York Press, 1921-1960), vols. 5, 6, 9, and 13; *Correspondence of General Thomas Gage*, ed. Clarence E. Carter, 2 vols. (New Haven: Yale University Press, 1931–1933); and *Documents Relating to the Constitutional History of Canada, 1750–1791*, ed. Adam Shortt and Arthur Doughty (Ottawa: J. de L. Tache, 1907–1918), vol. 2.

My account of Abbott follows Paul L. Stevens, "'To Keep the Indians of the Wabache in His Majesty's Interest': The Indian Diplomacy of Edward Abbott, British Lieutenant Governor of Vincennes, 1776–1778," *IMH* 83 (1987): 141–72.

3. The Village of Vincennes, 1765–1777

For information on eighteenth-century Vincennes, see Christopher B. Coleman, ed., "Letters from Eighteenth-Century Indiana Merchants," *IMH* 5 (1909): 137–59; "George Croghan's Journals"; *Documents Relating to the French Settlements on the Wabash*, ed. Jacob P. Dunn (Ind: Bowen-Merrill, 1894); McCord, comp., *Travel Accounts*, 1–26 (the letter from Gibault quoted at the beginning of the chapter is on pages 24–25); Janet P. Shaw, ed., "Francis Bosseron" and "Account Book of Francis Bosseron," *IMH* 25 (1929): 204–11, 212–41; Constantin François Chasseboenf Volney, *A View of the Soil and Climate of the United States of America, 1804*, in *Indiana as Seen by Early Travelers: A Collection of Reprints from Books of Travel, Letters and Diaries Prior to 1830*, ed. Harold Lindley (Ind: IHC, 1916), 17–25; and Florence G. Watts, ed., "Some Vincennes Documents of 1772," *IMH* 34 (1938): 199–212. The petitions regarding land are in *Territorial Papers of the United States*, ed. Clarence E. Carter (Washington: United States Government Printing Office, 1934–1962), vol. 2.

Scattered documents are in Clarence W. Alvord and Clarence E. Carter, eds., *The Critical Period, 1763–1765* (Springfield: ISHS, 1915), *The New Regime, 1765–1767* (Springfield: ISHS, 1916), and *Trade and Politics, 1767–1769* (Springfield: ISHS, 1921); *The French in the Mississippi Valley*, ed. John Francis McDermott (Urbana: University of Illinois Press, 1965); and Peyser, *Letters from New France*. See also Paul L. Stevens, "'One of the Most Beautiful Regions of the World': Paul Des Ruisseaux's Memoire of the Wabash-Illinois Country in 1777," *IMH* 83 (1987): 360–79.

The information on the enslaved Africans in Vincennes is in Emma Lou Thornbrough, *The Negro in Indiana: A Study of a Minority* (Ind: IHBu, 1957), 1–4. The history of the Richervilles is Donald Chaput, "The Family of Drouet de Richerville: Merchants, Soldiers, and Chiefs of Indiana," *IMH* 74 (1978): 103–16. See also Dorothy Riker, "Francis Vigo," *IMH* 26 (1930): 12–24.

Important works on the French settlements are Joseph P. Donnelly, *Pierre Gibault, Missionary, 1737–1802* (Chicago: Loyola University Press, 1971); Gilbert J. Carraghan, "Vincennes: A Chapter in the Ecclesiastical History of the West," *Mid-America* 13 (1931): 324–40; Frances Krauskopf, "The French in Indiana, 1700–1760" (Ph.D. diss., Indiana University, 1953); Charles B. Lasselle, "The Old Indian Traders of Indiana," *IMH* 2 (1906): 1–13; John Francis McDermott, "French Settlers and Settlements in the Illinois Country in the Eighteenth Century," *The French, the Indians, and George Rogers Clark in the Illinois Country* (Ind: IHS, 1977), 3–33, and "The Enlightenment on the Mississippi Frontier, 1763–1804," *Studies on Voltaire and the Eighteenth Century* 26 (1963): 1129–42.

Lee Burns, *Life in Old Vincennes* (Ind: IHS, 1929), is informative; August Derleth, *Vincennes: Portal to the West* (Englewood Cliffs: Prentice-Hall, 1968), is lively but superficial. More useful were Morris S. Arnold, *Colonial Arkansas: A Social and Cultural History* (Fayetteville: University of Arkansas Press, 1991); Susan C. Boyle, "Did She Generally Decide? Women in Ste. Genevieve, 1750–1805," *WMQ* 44 (1987): 775–89; and Winstanley Briggs, "Le Pays des Illinois," *WMQ* 47 (1990): 30–56, "Slavery in French Colonial Illinois," *Chicago History* 18 (Winter 1989–1990): 66–81, and "The Enhanced Status of Women in French Colonial Illinois," in Clarence A. Glasrud, ed., *The Quiet Heritage/Le Heritage Tranquil: Proceedings from a Conference on the Contributions of the French to the Upper Midwest, November 9, 1985* (Moorhead, Minn.: Concordia College, 1987).

4. The World of George Rogers Clark, 1778–1787

Basic secondary accounts are George C. Chalou, "George Rogers Clark and Indian America, 1778–1780," *The French, Indians, and George Rogers Clark*, 34–46; Randolph C. Downes, *Council Fires on the Upper Ohio: A Narrative of Indian Affairs in the Upper Ohio Valley until 1795* (Pittsburgh: University of Pittsburgh Press, 1940); Reginald Horsman, "The Collapse of the Ohio River Barrier: Conflict and Negotiation in the Old Northwest, 1763–1787," *Pathways to the Old Northwest*, 33–46; Charles G. Talbert, "A Roof for Kentucky," *Filson Club Quarterly* 29 (1955): 145–65; and George M. Waller, "Target Detroit: Overview of the American Revolution West of the Appalachians," *French, Indians, and George Rogers Clark*, 47–66, and "George Rogers Clark and the American Revolution in the West," *IMH* 72 (1976): 1–20. See also Jack M. Sosin, *The Revolutionary Frontier, 1763–1783* (New York: Holt, Rinehart, and Winston, 1974).

John Bakeless, *Background to Glory: The Life of George Rogers Clark* (Philadelphia: Lippincott, 1957), and James A. James, *Life of George Rogers Clark* (Chicago: University of Chicago Press, 1928), are standard biographies. More insightful are Bernard W. Sheehan, "'The Famous Hair Buyer General': Henry Hamilton, George Rogers Clark, and the American Indian," *IMH* 79 (1983): 1–28, and White, *Middle Ground*, 368–78.

I also consulted *Kaskaskia Records, 1778–1790*, ed. Clarence W. Alvord (Springfield: Illinois State Historical Library, 1909); *Henry Hamilton and George Rogers Clark in the American Revolution with the Unpublished Journal of Lieut. Gov. Henry Hamilton*, ed. John D. Barnhart (Crawfordsville: R. E. Banta, 1951); *Letters from Canadian Archives*, ed. H. W. Beckwith (Springfield: Illinois State Historical Library, 1903); *Detroit to Fort Sackville, 1778–1779: The Journal of Norman MacLeod*, ed. William A. Evans and Elizabeth S. Sklar (Detroit: Wayne State University Press, 1978); *Frederick Haldimand Papers* (East Lansing: Michigan Pioneer and Historical Society, 1888–1908); Margaret Margery Harding, comp., *George Rogers Clark and His Men: Military Records, 1778–1784* (Frankfort: Kentucky Historical Society, 1981); and especially *George Rogers Clark Papers, 1771–1784*, ed. James Alton James, 2 vols. (Springfield: ISHS, 1912–1926). See also *The Revolution on the Upper Ohio, 1775–1777*, ed. Reuben Gold Thwaites and Louise Phelps Kellogg (WSHS, 1905); Thwaites and Kellogg, eds., *Frontier Defense on the Upper Ohio, 1777–1778* (WSHS, 1912); Kellogg, ed., *Frontier Advance on the Upper Ohio, 1778–1779* (WSHS, 1916); Kellogg, ed., *Frontier Retreat on the Upper Ohio, 1779–1781* (WSHS, 1917).

On Indian-white relationships in the 1780s, see Dowd, *Spirited Resistance*, 47–115, and White, *Middle Ground*, 366–453 (esp. 421–33). The basic primary sources on Vincennes are Beverley W. Bond, Jr., "Two Westward Journeys of John Filson, 1785," *Mississippi Valley Historical Review* 9 (1923): 320–30; Clarence W. Alvord, ed., "Father Gibault and Vincennes," *American Historical Review* 14 (1909): 544–57; and L. C. Helderman, "Danger on Wabash: Vincennes Letters of 1786," *IMH* 34 (1938): 455–67, and "The Narrative of John Filson's Defeat on the Wabash," *Filson Club Quarterly* 12 (1938): 187–99. See also Helderman, "The Northwest Expedition of George Rogers Clark, 1786–1787," *Mississippi Valley Historical Review* 25 (1938): 317–34.

5. The World of Josiah Harmar and John Francis Hamtramck, 1787–1790

On the origins and development of United States policy toward the Old Northwest, see Onuf, *Statehood and Union*, 1–66; Cayton, *Frontier Republic*, 1–50; Cayton and Onuf, *Midwest and the Nation*, 1–24; and Cayton, "'Separate Interests' and the Nation-State: The Washington Administration and the Origins of Regionalism in the Trans-Appalachian West," *Journal of American History* 79 (1992): 39–67. Reginald Horsman, *The Frontier in the Formative Years, 1783–1815* (New York: Holt, Rinehart, and Winston, 1970), is an excellent overview.

Primary sources include *Outpost on the Wabash, 1787–1791: Letters of Brigadier General Josiah Harmar and Major John Francis Hamtramck*, ed. Gayle Thornbrough (Ind: IHS, 1957); Carter, ed., *Territorial Papers*, vols. 2 and 3; *Military Journal of Major Ebenezer Denny*, ed. William H. Denny (Philadelphia: Lippincott, 1860); John Heckewelder, "To the Falls of the Ohio and Vincennes: 1792," *Travels of John Heckewelder in Frontier America*, ed. Paul A. W. Wallace (Pittsburgh: University of Pittsburgh Press, 1958), 258–93; William Henry Smith, *The St. Clair Papers: The Life and Public Services of Arthur St. Clair*, 2 vols. (Cincinnati: Robert Clarke, 1882). See also John Parker Huber, "General Josiah Harmar's Command: Military Policy in the Old Northwest, 1784–1791" (Ph.D. diss., University of Michigan, 1968), and F. Clever Bald, "Colonel Francis Hamtramck," *IMH* 44 (1948): 335–54.

6. The World of Little Turtle, 1790–1795

Excellent studies of attitudes toward Indians are Reginald Horsman, *Expansion and American Indian Policy, 1783–1812* (East Lansing: Michigan State University Press, 1967); Dorothy V. Jones, *License for Empire: Colonialism by Treaty in Early America* (Chicago: University of Chicago Press, 1982); Francis Paul Prucha, *The Great Father: The United States Government and the American Indians*, 2 vols. (Lincoln: University of Nebraska Press, 1984); and Bernard W. Sheehan, *Seeds of Extinction: Jeffersonian Philanthropy and the American Indian* (Chapel Hill: University of North Carolina Press for the Institute of Early American History and Culture, 1973). For the British perspective, see Colin G. Calloway, *Crown and Calumet: British-Indian Relations, 1783–1815* (Norman: University of Oklahoma Press, 1987), and Reginald Horsman, *Matthew Elliott: British Indian Agent* (Detroit: Wayne State University Press, 1964). See also Joyce G. Williams and Jill E. Farelly, *Diplomacy on the Indiana-Ohio Frontier, 1783–1789* (IUP, 1976).

The Gamelin journal is in Smith, *St. Clair Papers*, vol. 2, 155–60. On Miamitown, see Paul Woehrmann, *At the Headwaters of the Maumee: A History of the Forts of Fort Wayne* (Ind: IHS, 1971), 1–58, and White, *Middle Ground*, 448–54. The key primary source is Henry Hay's journal, published in M. M. Quaife, *Fort Wayne in 1790* (Greenfield: William Mitchell, 1921). My account of Little Turtle largely follows Carter, *Little Turtle*. Especially useful are Robert B. Whitsett, Jr., "Snake-Fish Town, the Eighteenth Century Metropolis of Little Turtle's Eel River Miami," *IHB* 15 (1938): 72–82, and Helen Hornbeck Tanner, "The Glaize in 1792: A Composite Indian Community," *Ethnohistory* 25 (1978): 15–39.

My narrative of the military conflicts and treaty negotiations derives largely from *American State Papers, Indian Affairs*, 2 vols. (Washington: Gales and Seaton, 1832–1834), and *American State Papers, Military Affairs*, 7 vols. (Washington: Gales and Seaton, 1832–1861); *Memoirs of Rufus Putnam*, ed. Rowena Buell (Boston: Houghton Mifflin, 1903); Carter, ed., *Territorial Papers*, vols. 1 and 2; *Anthony Wayne, a Name in Arms: The Wayne-Knox-Pickering-McHenry Correspondence*, ed. Richard C. Knopf (Pittsburgh: University of Pittsburgh Press, 1960); Smith, *St. Clair Papers*; and *A Surgeon's Mate at Fort Defiance: The Journal of Joseph Gardner Andrews for the Years 1795*, ed. Knopf (Columbus: Ohio Historical Society, 1957). See also Denny, ed., *Military Journal of Major Ebenezer Denny*; "Winthrop Sargent's Diary while with General Arthur St. Clair's Expedition against the Indians," *OAHQ* 33 (1924): 237–73; Dresden W. H. Howard, ed., "The Battle of Fallen Timbers, as Told by Chief Kin-Jo-I-No," *Northwest Ohio Quarterly* 20 (1948): 37–49; R. C. McGrane, ed., "William Clark's Journal of General Wayne's Campaign," *Mississippi Valley Historical Review* 1 (1914): 418–44; and Basil Meek, "General Harmar's Expedition," *OAHQ* 20 (1911): 74–108.

On the Harmar campaign, see Michael S. Warner, "General Josiah Harmar's Campaign Reconsidered: How the Americans Lost the Battle of Kekionga," *IMH* 83 (1987): 43–64. See also "Josiah Harmar and His Indian Expedition," *OAHQ* 55 (1946): 227–41, and Dwight L. Smith, "Wayne's Peace with the Indians of the Old Northwest, 1795," *OAHQ* 49 (1950): 239–55.

For the American perspective, see Wiley Sword, *President Washington's Indian War: The Struggle for the Old Northwest, 1790–1795* (Norman: University of Oklahoma Press, 1985); Paul David Nelson, *Anthony Wayne, Soldier of the Early Republic* (IUP, 1985); and Francis Paul Prucha, *The Sword of the Republic: The United States Army on the Frontier, 1783–1846* (IUP, 1969). For the British perspective, see Horsman, *Matthew Elliott*, and "The British Indian Department and the Resistance to General Anthony Wayne, 1793–1795," *Mississippi Valley Historical Review* 49 (1962): 269–90. For the Indian perspective, see Carter, *Little Turtle*, 52–155; Paul A. Hutton, "William Wells: Frontier Scout and Indian Agent," *IMH* 74 (1978): 183–222; and White, *Middle Ground*.

7. The World of Anna Tuthill Symmes Harrison, 1795–1810

There is no biography of Anna Harrison. See *Intimate Letters of John Cleves Symmes and His Family*, ed. Beverley W. Bond, Jr. (Cincinnati: Historical and Philosophical Society of Ohio, 1956); Bond, Jr., *Correspondence of John Cleves Symmes, Founder of the Miami Purchase* (New York: Macmillan, 1926); John D. Barnhart, ed., "Letters of William Henry Harrison to Thomas Worthington," *IMH* 47 (1951): 53–84; Carter, ed., *Territorial Papers*, vols. 7 and 8; and *WHH*, ed. Logan Esarey, 2 vols. (IHC, 1922). Freeman Cleaves, *Old Tippecanoe: William Henry Harrison and His Time* (New York: Charles Scribner's Sons, 1939), and Dorothy Burne Goebel, *William Henry Harrison: A Political Biography* (Ind: IHBu, 1926), are useful but dated.

Demographic information is in John Modell, "Family and Fertility on the Indiana Frontier, 1820," *American Quarterly* 23 (1971): 615–34; Gregory Steven Rose, "Hoosier Origins: The Nativity of Indiana's United States–Born Population in 1850," *IMH* 81 (1985): 201–32; Elfreida Lang, "Southern Migration to Northern Indiana before 1850," *IMH* 50 (1954): 349–56; James M. Berquist, "Tracing the Origins of a Midwestern Culture: The Case of Central Indiana," *IMH* 77 (1981): 1–31; Robert W. Bastian, "Indiana Folk Architecture: A Lower Midwestern Index," *Pioneer America* 9 (1977): 115–36; and Thomas J. Schlereth, "The New England Presence on the Midwest Landscape," *Old Northwest* 9 (1983): 125–42.

For interpretive arguments about migration and households, see Rowland Berthoff, "A Country Open for Neighborhood," *IMH* 84 (1988): 25–46; Cayton and Onuf, *Midwest and the Nation*, 25–52; Faragher, *Sugar Creek*; Malcolm J. Rohrbough, "'A Freehold Estate Therein': The Ordinance of 1787 and the Public Domain," *IMH* 84 (1988): 46–59; Rohrbough, "Diversity and Unity in the Old Northwest, 1790–1850: Several Peoples Fashion a Single Region," *Pathways to the Old Northwest*, 71–87; and Robert P. Swierenga, "Settlement of the Old Northwest: Ethnic Pluralism in a Featureless Plain," *Journal of the Early Republic* 9 (1989): 73–106.

On the origins and development of the federal land system, see Malcolm J. Rohrbough, *The Land Office Business: The Settlement and Administration of American Public Lands, 1789–1837* (New York: Oxford University Press, 1968), 5–42. See also Hildegard Binder Johnson, "Perceptions and Illustrations of the

American Landscapes in the Ohio Valley and the Midwest," *This Land of Ours: The Acquisition and Disposition of the Public Domain* (Ind: IHS, 1978), 1–38.

The description of the settlement of the Whitewater Valley is in Lawrence Henry Gipson, ed., *The Moravian Indian Mission on the White River: Diaries and Letters, May 5, 1799, to November 12, 1806* (Ind: IHBu, 1938). See also Chelsea L. Lawlis, "Settlement of the Whitewater Valley, 1790–1810," *IMH* 43 (1947): 23–40. On the road from New Albany to Vincennes, see George R. Wilson and Gayle Thornbrough, *The Buffalo Trace* (Ind: IHBu, 1946).

Slavery Petitions and Papers, ed. Jacob Piatt Dunn (Ind: Bowen-Merrill, 1894), is an important compilation of primary documents. See also Carter, ed., *Territorial Papers*, vols. 7 and 8. The best accounts of the slavery controversy are Paul Finkelman, "Slavery and the Northwest Ordinance: A Study in Ambiguity," *Journal of the Early Republic* 6 (1986): 343–70, and "Evading the Ordinance: The Persistence of Bondage in Indiana and Illinois," *Journal of the Early Republic* 9 (1989): 21–51; and Onuf, *Statehood and Union*, 109–32.

8. The World of Tenskwatawa, 1795–1811

The primary source for my account of the Moravian missionaries is Gipson, ed., *Moravian Indian Mission on the White River*. See also the biographical information in Earl P. Olmstead, *Blackcoats among the Delaware: David Zeisberger on the Ohio Frontier* (Kent: Kent State University Press, 1991).

My interpretation of Tenskwatawa closely follows Edmunds, *Shawnee Prophet*, and Dowd, *Spirited Resistance*, 123–47. See also Carter, *Little Turtle*, 156–221.

On John Johnston and the Fort Wayne agency, see Woehrmann, *At the Headwaters of the Maumee*, 83–218, and *Fort Wayne, Gateway of the West, 1802–1813: Garrison Orderly Books, Indian Agency Account Books*, ed. Bert J. Griswold (Ind: IHBu, 1927).

On the battle of Tippecanoe, I have followed Edmunds, *Shawnee Prophet*, 94–116. I also used Harrison's letters to the secretary of war in Esarey, ed., *Messages and Papers of William Henry Harrison*, vol. 1, 518–685, and *American State Papers: Indian Affairs*, vol. 1, 776–78; Wesley Whickar, ed., "Shabonee's Account of Tippecanoe," *IMH* 18 (1921): 366–59; Florence G. Watts, ed., "Lieutenant Charles Larrabee's Account of the Battle of Tippecanoe, 1811," *IMH* 57 (1961): 225–47; *Indiana Gazette* (Vincennes), August 7, 1804-April 12, 1806; *Western Sun* (Vincennes), July 11, 1807; *John Tipton Papers*, ed. Nellie A. Robertson and Dorothy Riker (Ind: IHBu, 1942), vol. 1, 57–118; and *Correspondence of John Badollet and Albert Gallatin, 1804–1836*, ed. Gayle Thornbrough (Ind: IHS, 1963), 194–226. See also Marshall Smelser, "Tecumseh, Harrison, and the War of 1812," *IMH* 65 (1969): 25–44.

9. The World of Jonathan Jennings, 1800–1816

"Unedited Letters of Jonathan Jennings," ed. Dorothy Riker (Ind: IHS, 1932), 149–278, and Riker, ed., "Some Additional Jennings Letters," *IMH* 39 (1943): 279–95, are the foundation of my understanding of Jennings. Other important sources on territorial politics are Barnhart, ed., "Letters of William Henry Harrison to Thomas Worthington"; Esarey, ed., *WHH*, vols. 1 and 2; Carter, ed., *Territorial Papers*, vols. 7 and 8; Thornbrough, ed., *Correspondence of Badollet and Gallatin*; and *Indiana Gazette* (1804–1806) and *Western Sun* (1807–1816) (Vincennes).

John D. Barnhart has collected the letters of Decius in *IMH* 43 (1947): 263–96. The slavery issue can be followed in Dunn, ed., *Slavery Petitions and Papers*, 521–27; Carter, ed., *Territorial Papers*; and Thornbrough, ed., *Correspondence of Badollet and Gallatin*. See also *The Laws of the Indiana Territory, 1809–1816*, ed. Louis B. Ewbank and Dorothy L. Riker (Ind: IHBu, 1934); *The Laws of Indiana Territory, 1801–1809*, ed. Francis S. Philbrick (Springfield: Illinois State Historical Library, 1930); and *Journals of the General Assembly of Indiana Territory, 1805–1815*, ed. Gayle Thornbrough and Dorothy Riker (Ind: IHBu, 1950).

Dorothy Riker provides a sympathetic narrative in "Jonathan Jennings," *IMH* 28 (1932): 223–39. See also Logan Esarey, *Messages and Papers of Jonathan Jennings, Ratliff Boon, and William Hendricks* (Ind: IHC, 1924), 27–28, and George R. Wilson, "General Washington Johnson," *IMH* 20 (1924): 123–54. Philbrick, *Laws of the Indiana Territory*, ccxxvii–cclxxxii, and Thornbrough and Riker, eds., *Journals*, 953–1018, include brief biographies of dozens of important figures. See also William Wesley Woollen, *Biographical and Historical Sketches of Early Indiana* (New York: Arno, 1975 [1883]).

The most important secondary source is Barnhart, *Valley of Democracy*, esp. 161–91. For political culture in the neighboring state of Ohio, see Cayton, *Frontier Republic*, esp. 51–80, and "Land, Power, and Reputation: The Cultural Dimension of Politics in the Ohio Country," *WMQ* 47 (1990): 266–86; Kenneth J. Winkle, *The Politics of Community: Migration and Politics in Antebellum Ohio* (Cambridge: Cambridge University Press, 1988); and Jeffrey P. Brown and Andrew R. L. Cayton, eds., *The Pursuit of Public Power: Political Culture in Ohio, 1787–1861* (Kent: Kent State University Press, 1994). On the Old Northwest as a whole, see Cayton and Onuf, *Midwest and the Nation*, 65–83, and Onuf, *Statehood and Union*, 67–87. See also Donald F. Carmony, "Indiana Territorial Expenditures, 1800–1816," *IMH* 39 (1943): 237–62, and "Fiscal Objection to Statehood in Indiana," *IMH* 42 (1946): 311–21; and Daniel Wait Howe, *The Laws and Courts of Northwest and Indiana Territories* (Ind: Bowen-Merrill, 1886).

My discussion of the 1816 constitution and the subsequent elections is based on information in *Constitution Making in Indiana: A Source Book of Constitutional Documents with Historical Introduction and Critical Notes*, ed. Charles Kettleborough (Ind: IHC, 1916-1930), vol. 1, and Dorothy Riker and Gayle Thornbrough, comps., *Indiana Election Returns, 1816–1851* (Ind: IHBu, 1960), which contains a valuable introduction on election procedures (ix–xxv) as well as returns.

10. The End of the Frontier, 1816–1850

The overall interpretation of this chapter follows Cayton and Onuf, *Midwest and the Nation*, 25–83.

On the Indians after 1815, see Chaput, "The Family of Drouet de Richerville," 114–16. On the fate of the Fort Wayne post, see Woehrmann, *At the Headwaters of the Maumee*, 257–73. On federal land sales, see Rohrbough, *Land Office Business*, 73–144, 177–214 [1830s], and "The Land Office Business in Indiana," in *This Land Is Ours*, 39–59; and Buley, *Old Northwest*, vol. 1, 94–137.

Population statistics are in Richard K. Vedder and Lowell E. Gallaway, "Migration and the Old Northwest," *Essays in Nineteenth-Century Economic History: The Old Northwest*, ed. David C. Klingaman and Richard K. Vedder (Athens: Ohio University Press, 1975), 159–76. See also "The Autobiography of Peter Van Arsdale," in *Religion on the American Frontier*, ed. William Warren Sweet (New York: Henry Holt, 1931–1946), vol. 2, 797–811; Donald J. Carmony, ed., "From Lycoming County, Pennsylvania, to Parke County, Indiana: Recollections of Andrew TenBrook, 1786–1823," *IMH* 61 (1965): 1–30; and Margaret Story Jean and Aline Jean Treanor, "The First Families of White Oak Springs, 1810–1817," *IMH* 36 (1940): 231–70.

On economic behavior and attitudes, see Faragher, *Sugar Creek*, and John Lauritz Larson and David G. Vanderstel, "Agent of Empire: William Conner on the Indiana Frontier, 1800–1855," *IMH* 80 (1984): 311–28. Economic development is discussed in Gary M. Walton, "River Transportation and the Old Northwest Territory," in *Essays on the Economy of the Old Northwest*, ed. David C. Klingaman and Richard K. Vedder (Athens: Ohio University Press, 1987), 225–42; Erik F. Haites, James Mak, and Gary M. Walton, *Western River Transportation: The Era of Early Internal Development, 1810–1860* (Baltimore: Johns Hopkins University Press, 1975); and Buley, *Old Northwest*, vol. 1, 395–564.

Primary sources include *Solon Robinson, Pioneer and Agriculturist: Selected Writings*, ed. Herbert Anthony Kellar, 2 vols. (Ind: IHBu, 1936); Robertson and Riker, eds., *John Tipton Papers*; and *Diary of Calvin Fletcher*, ed. Gayle Thornbrough and Paula Corpuz, 9 vols. (Ind: IHS, 1972–1983); McCord, comp., *Travel Accounts*; and Lindley, ed., *Indiana as Seen by Early Travelers*. See also Pamela J. Bennett and Shirley S. McCord, comps., *Progress after Statehood: A Book of Readings* (Ind: IHBu, 1974).

The rivalry between Richmond and Centerville is discussed in Bernhard Knollenberg, *Pioneer Sketches of the Upper Whitewater Valley: Quaker Stronghold of the West* (Ind: IHS, 1945), 47–53. On Madison's development, see Donald T. Zimmer, "The Ohio River: Pathway to Settlement," in *Transportation and the Early Nation: Papers Presented at an Indiana American Revolution Bicentennial Symposium* (Ind: IHS, 1982), 61–88. See also Timothy R. Mahoney, *River Towns in the Great West: The Structure of Provincial Urbanization in the American Midwest, 1820–1870* (Cambridge: Cambridge University Press, 1990), and Don Harrison Doyle, *The Social Order of a Frontier Community: Jacksonville, Illinois, 1825–1870* (Urbana: University of Illinois Press, 1983). For working-class culture, see Steven J. Ross, *Workers on the Edge: Work, Leisure, and Politics in Industrializing Cincinnati, 1788–1890* (New York: Columbia University Press, 1985), and Michael Allen, *Western Rivermen, 1763–1861: Ohio and Mississippi Boatmen and the Myth of the Alligator Horse* (Baton Rouge: Louisiana State University Press, 1990).

On banks, see Logan Esarey, *State Banking in Indiana, 1814–1837* (IUP, 1912); Buley, *Old Northwest*, vol. 1, 565–632 (esp. 594–97, 612–20); Donald R. Adams, "The Role of Banks in the Economic Development of the Old Northwest," in Klingaman and Vedder, eds., *Essays in Nineteenth-Century Economic History*, 208–45; James H. Madison, "Business and Politics in Indianapolis: The Branch Bank and the Junto, 1837–1846," *IMH* 71 (1975): 1–20; and William Gerald Shade, *Banks or No Banks: The Money Issue in Western Politics, 1832–1865* (Detroit: Wayne State University Press, 1972).

On internal improvements, see Harry N. Scheiber, *Ohio Canal Era: A Case Study of Government and the Economy, 1820–1861* (Athens: Ohio University Press, 1969); Ronald E. Shaw, "The Canal Era in the Old Northwest," *Transportation and the Early Nation*, 89–112; Logan Esarey, *Internal Improvements in Early Indiana* (Ind: Edward J. Hecker, 1912); and Roger L. Ransom, "Public Canal Investment and the Opening of the Old North-West," in Klingaman and Vedder, eds., *Essays in Nineteenth-Century Economic History*, 246–68.

My account of the Mammoth Internal Improvements Bill and the construction of canals in Indiana follows Ralph D. Gray, "The Canal Era in Indiana," *Transportation and the Early Nation*, 113–34, and John Lauritz Larson, "To Try to Make a State of It: Indiana's Mammoth Internal Improvements Bill," *Indiana Academy of the Social Sciences Proceedings*, 3d ser., 22 (1987): 77–84. Paul Fatout, *Indiana Canals* (West Lafayette: Purdue University Studies, 1972), is the most detailed study. See also Esarey, ed., *Messages and Papers of Jennings, Boon, and Hendricks*; Buley, *Old Northwest*, vol. 1, 612–20, and vol. 2, 280–87; Frederick D. Hill, "William Hendricks: Popular Nonpartisan," *Their Infinite Variety: Essays on Indiana Politicians* (Ind: IHBu, 1981); Charles R. Poinsatte, *Fort Wayne during the Canal Era, 1828–1855: A Study of a Western Community in the Middle Period of American History* (Ind: IHBu, 1969); *Messages and Papers Relating to the Administration of James Brown Ray, Governor of Indiana, 1825–1831*, ed. Dorothy Riker and Gayle Thornbrough (Ind: IHBu, 1954); and *Messages and Papers Relating to the Administration of Noah Noble, Governor of Indiana, 1831–1837*, ed. Riker and Thornbrough (Ind: IHBu, 1958). Most of the information on the National Road can be found in Lee Burns, *The National Road in Indiana* (Ind: C. E. Pauley, 1919).

My interpretation of educational reform in Indiana follows Carl F. Kaestle, "Public Education in the Old Northwest: 'Necessary to Good Government and the Happiness of Mankind,'" *IMH* 84 (1988): 60–74, and "The Development of Common School Systems in the States of the Old Northwest," in "*. . . Schools and the Means of Education Shall Forever Be Encouraged.*": A History of Education in the Old Northwest, 1787–1860, ed. Paul H. Mattingly and Edward W. Stevens, Jr. (Athens: Ohio University Libraries, 1987): 45–56; and Edward W. Stevens, Jr., "Structural and Ideological Dimensions of Literacy and Education in the Old Northwest," in Klingaman and Vedder, eds., *Essays on the Economy of the Old Northwest*, 157–86. See also Buley, *Old Northwest*, vol. 2, 326–417. On Caleb Mills, see Charles W. Moores, *Caleb Mills and the Indiana School System* (Ind: Wood-Weaver, 1905), and Val Nolan, Jr., "Caleb Mills and the Indiana Free School Law," *IMH* 49 (1953): 81–90. Edward Eggleston, *The Hoosier School-Master: A Novel* (New York: Grosset & Dunlap, 1899; orig. pub., 1871), remains engrossing reading.

On drinking, see W. J. Rorabaugh, *The Alcoholic Republic: An American Tradition* (New York: Oxford University Press, 1979). See also Buley, *Old Northwest*, vol. 1, 313–94. The Elliott J. Gorn article is "'Gouge and Bite, Pull Hair and Scratch': The Social Significance of Fighting in the Southern Backcountry," *American Historical Review* 90 (1985): 18–43. David J. Bodenhamer's piece is "Law and Disorder on the Early Frontier: Marion County, Indiana, 1823–1850," *Western Historical Quarterly* 10 (1979): 323–36.

I have relied heavily on the superb book by L. C. Rudolph, *Hoosier Zion: The Presbyterians in Early Indiana* (New Haven: Yale University Press, 1963). Less helpful is Elizabeth K. Nottingham, *Methodism and the Frontier: Indiana Proving Ground* (New York: Columbia University Press, 1941); readers should consult her primary source, Allen Wiley, "Methodism in Southeastern Indiana," *IMH* 23 (1927): 3–62, 130–216, 239–332, 339–466 (reprinted from *Western Christian Advocate*, 1845–1846). See also *Autobiography of Peter Cartwright, the Backwoods Preacher*, ed. W. P. Strickland (New York: Carlton and Porter, 1857); Edward Eggleston, *The Circuit Rider: A Tale of the Heroic Age*, ed. William Randel (New Haven, Conn.: College and University Press, 1966). B. R. Hall, *The New Purchase: or, Seven and a Half Years in the Far West*, by Robert Carlton, esq. (pseud.), ed. James A. Woodburn (Princeton: Princeton University Press, 1916), is a fictionalized memoir of a Presbyterian minister and teacher. As always, Buley, *Old Northwest*, vol. 2, 417–88, is a compendium of information. See also Grover L. Hartman, "The Hoosier Sunday School: A Potent Religious/Cultural Force," *IMH* 78 (1982): 215–41, and Timothy L. Smith, "Uncommon Schools: Christian Colleges and Social Idealism in Midwestern America, 1820–1950" (Ind: IHS, 1978), 3–36.

The section on slavery and blacks follows Thornbrough, *Negro in Indiana*, 31–182. See also Knollenberg, *Pioneer Sketches of the Upper Whitewater Valley*; and Juliet E. K. Walker, *Free Frank: A Black Pioneer on the Antebellum Frontier* (Lexington: University Press of Kentucky, 1983). On the politics of slavery, see Kenneth M. Stampp, *Indiana Politics during the Civil War* (Ind: IHBu, 1949); Eric Foner, *Free Soil, Free Labor, Free Men: The Ideology of the Republican Party before the Civil War* (New York: Oxford University Press, 1970), and William E. Gienapp, *The Origins of the Republican Party, 1852–1856* (New York: Oxford University Press, 1987).

Epilogue: "This Country of Liberty"

The source for the sections on the Fletchers is Thornbrough and Corpuz, eds., *Diary of Calvin Fletcher*, vols. 1 and 2. For the removal of the Potawatomi, see "Journal of an Emigrating Party of Pottawattomie Indians, 1838," *IMH* 21 (1925): 315–36; Irving McKee, *The Trail of Death: Letters of Benjamin Marie Petit* (Ind: IHS, 1941); and Edmunds, *Potawatomis*, 240–72.

Index

[handwritten annotation:] & see Kekionga

ANDREW R. L. CAYTON,

Professor of History at Miami University in Oxford, Ohio, is the author of *The Frontier Republic: Ideology and Politics in the Ohio Country, 1780–1825* and, with Peter S. Onuf, *The Midwest and the Nation: Rethinking the History of an American Region.*

1820
pop 147,78

1850 pop 988,416

Fort Wayne
aka Kekionga
Miamitown
(Indians)

Miami
Shawnee
Delaware

Sulenda Fritz
Arthritis
Potosin